THE TREATY

DEBATING AND ESTABLISHING
THE IRISH STATE

Liam Weeks is a lecturer in the Department of Government & Politics, University College Cork, and is author of *All Politics is Local: A Guide to Local Elections in Ireland* (with Aodh Quinlivan, 2009), *Radical or Redundant? Minor Parties in Irish Political Life* (co-edited with Alastair Clark, 2012) and *Independents in Irish Party Democracy* (2017).

Mícheál Ó Fathartaigh is a lecturer in the Department of Humanities & Social Science, Dublin Business School, a research officer with Teagasc and a member of the Social Sciences Research Centre at the National University of Ireland Galway. He is author of *Irish Agriculture Nationalised: The Dairy Disposal Company and the Making of the Modern Irish Dairy Industry* (2014) and *Developing Rural Ireland: A History of the Irish Agricultural Advisory Services* (forthcoming, 2019).

THE TREATY

DEBATING AND ESTABLISHING THE IRISH STATE

EDITED BY

LIAM WEEKS AND MÍCHEÁL Ó FATHARTAIGH

IRISH ACADEMIC PRESS

First published in 2018 by
Irish Academic Press
10 George's Street
Newbridge
Co. Kildare
Ireland
www.iap.ie

9781788550413 (Paper)
9781788550406 (Cloth)
9781788550420 (Kindle)
9781788550437 (Epub)
9781788550444 (PDF)

British Library Cataloguing in Publication Data
An entry can be found on request

Library of Congress Cataloging in Publication Data
An entry can be found on request

Interior design by www.jminfotechindia.com
Typeset in Minion Pro 11/14 pt

Cover/jacket design by Colin Moore
Cover/jacket front: Éamon de Valera at a rally, c.1920 (Alamy); Michael Collins
addressing an election meeting, c.1922 (National Library of Ireland).
Cover/jacket back: Michael Collins arriving at Earlsfort Terrace, Dublin,
December 1921 (National Library of Ireland).
Printed by TJ International Ltd, Padstow, Cornwall

Contents

Acknowledgements

This book has its origins in a workshop on the Treaty debates held in the National University of Ireland in November 2016. This was part of a wider project that was funded by the Irish Research Council New Foundations Scheme, the support of which is gratefully acknowledged.

We are extremely grateful to Irish Academic Press for the opportunity to publish the material emanating from this workshop. In particular, we would like to thank Conor Graham for his enthusiasm for our initial proposal and Fiona Dunne for her work in the production process.

We are especially grateful to the efforts of the contributors to this volume. They put up with our many demands, responding with patience and efficiency.

Different drafts of various chapters have been presented at academic conferences, and we are all grateful for the feedback received. In particular, we would like to thank the Political Studies Association of Ireland for awarding our paper, with Slava Mikhaylov and Alex Herzog, the annual prize at its 2017 conference for best paper presented at the 2016 annual conference in Belfast.

We acknowledge gratefully the grant support that this publication received from the National University of Ireland and from the College of Arts, Celtic Studies and Social Sciences at University College Cork.

We also record a special acknowledgement to Director John McDonough of the National Archives of Ireland for his permission to reproduce the foundation document for our book, and the foundation document for independent Ireland, the Anglo-Irish Treaty of 1921.

Finally, we thank the support, as always, of our loved ones. They know who they are.

Foreword

As we approach the one hundredth anniversary of the Anglo-Irish Treaty signed in December 1921, there is an ironic coincidence that Ireland is in the throes of concluding yet another treaty of sorts as the United Kingdom removes itself from the European Union. Our current political leaders are facing the challenge of separating, and in some cases severing, very close links we have shared in political, economic and social spheres with our closest neighbour but particularly with our neighbours in Northern Ireland. Yet they must ensure we can still have a good working relationship with the United Kingdom, which is home to many Irish people and to where we export a wide range of goods.

A re-reading of some of Michael Collins's words around the time of the Treaty would be useful to our leaders now as they confront the changes and challenges Ireland will face in the new manifestation of the European Union. Fortunately, the words of Collins after he had signed the Treaty, where he professed his worry that he may have 'signed his own death warrant', will not be words our Taoiseach, or our minister for foreign affairs and trade, will have to declare when a new deal with our European Union partners is eventually completed in 2020.[1] However, our leaders should reflect on just how appropriate Collins's words are to today's challenges:

> We have to build up a new civilisation on the foundations of the old. And it is not the leaders of the Irish people who can do it for the people. They can but point the way. They can but do their best to establish a reign of justice and of law and order which will enable the people to do it for themselves … The strength of the nation will be the strength of the spirit of the whole people. We need a political, economic, and social system in accordance with our national character.[2]

What the Irish people had wanted for so long was to be found in the Treaty concluded by Michael Collins, Arthur Griffith and the other signatories with the British between October and December 1921: full self-government; the end of centuries-long rule by London via Dublin Castle, the withdrawal of the British army and police, and democratic power in their own country. The Treaty gave independence in all matters of practical government, complete control of most of the territory and its resources, an independent parliament with an executive responsible to it – in short, the opportunity for Ireland to take its place among the nations of the earth of which Robert Emmet and so many others before and after him had dreamed. Arthur Griffith defended the agreement without pretence; it was not an ideal thing, it could be better, but it had no more finality than that they were the final generation on the face of the earth.[3] Collins put it even more cogently: 'it gives us the freedom, not the ultimate freedom that all nations desire and develop to, but the freedom to achieve it'.[4]

The essays in this publication will be a reminder of the different and at times the deadly reactions of the Irish people to the signing of the Treaty. We are the current protectors of our hard-won democracy and we owe our gratitude to the leaders who won our independence to ensure we hand on a sound, successful country in which every man, woman and child can flourish – a society in which everyone belongs.

Nora Owen, former TD, Minister for Justice and grand-niece of Michael Collins

Notes

1   Michael Collins to John O'Kane, 6 Dec. 1921, cited in Deirdre McMahon, 'Michael Collins – his biographers Piaras Béaslaí and Rex Taylor' in Gabriel Doherty and Dermot Keogh (eds), *Michael Collins and the making of the Irish state* (Cork, 1998), p. 134.
2   Michael Collins, *The path to freedom* (Dublin and London, 1922), pp. 103–4.
3   *Dáil Éireann deb.*, T, no. 15, 337–8 (7 Jan. 1922).
4   Ibid., no. 6, 32 (19 Dec. 1921).

Introduction

Liam Weeks and Mícheál Ó Fathartaigh

The Irish state was established under the Anglo-Irish Treaty of 6 December 1921. For such an important founding document, remarkably, it has not been the subject of a great deal of scrutiny. More attention has been focused on the 1916 Easter Rising, or on the proclamation of independence issued by its combatants, as the key contributions that spawned, and underpin, the state. For many, this is because of the failure of the Treaty to achieve the nationalist ideal of a sovereign republic for the whole island, and because it was seen by some as a betrayal of the aspirations of the 1916 proclamation. However, for better or worse, 'the Treaty' is the founding point of the Irish state. One hundred and twenty years since the Irish parliament was dissolved under the Act of Union, 270 years since the Cromwellian conquest, 852 years since the invasion of the Normans, the Articles of Agreement for a Treaty Between Great Britain and Ireland, to give the Treaty its proper title, was the moment when Irish sovereignty was restored. At a time when the centenaries of other historical events from the revolutionary period are being commemorated, this book is a starting point from which to mark the anniversary of a document that proved the culmination of all these other events.

The Treaty was signed on 6 December 1921 by British and Irish negotiating teams, coming into force a year later. This settlement came about following almost a decade of political turmoil, during which time a series of significant events brought Ireland to a state where the British government was prepared to negotiate over the island's future. These events include the Home Rule Bill of 1912, the separate gun runnings at Larne and Howth two years later, the foundation of two diametrically opposed private armies (the Ulster Volunteer Force and the Irish Volunteers), the Easter Rising of 1916 and the War of Independence (1919–21). While in hindsight the path these events took might appear to have been inevitable and to have developed in a natural way, it would be naïve to think the course of events followed a predictable outcome. In particular, it could all have been very different had the Treaty of 1921 been rejected by the Irish parliament, Dáil Éireann. David Lloyd George, the British prime minister, is reputed to have threatened 'terrible and immediate war' if the negotiated terms were not accepted, and it is difficult to fathom what future path the island would have followed had this happened. Apparently down to the bare bones of its resources, the revolutionary nationalist movement might have been wiped out by a full-scale British onslaught. A rejection of the Treaty might also have resulted in a different type of civil war on the island, not between pro- and anti-Treatyites, but a more sectarian conflict, between nationalist and unionist, Catholic and Protestant forces. Of course, this is idle speculation, as the Treaty was narrowly accepted by the Dáil in January 1922, and the Irish Free State was established on 6 December 1922. It survived an ensuing civil conflict, and the basic structure of what the Treaty outlined for the political future of the island remains in place 100 years later.

The Treaty was a critical moment in modern Irish history, and it is somewhat surprising then that the debates in the Dáil on its ratification over the Christmas period of 1921–2 have not been the subject of greater scholarly focus. Only two books to date have been dedicated to the Treaty and to the debates surrounding it. Furthermore, both Frank Pakenham's *Peace by ordeal*, which was first published in 1935, and Jason Knirck's *Imagining Ireland's independence: the debates over the Anglo-Irish Treaty of 1921*, published in 2006, are overviews, rather than analyses of the Treaty and the debates. What is lacking is a forensic examination of the contents of the debates and its participants. Some myths persist about the reasons for the Dáil division, including whether it had a class or economic basis, and in this volume, we unravel the truth. We draw together the work of fifteen diverse scholars to re-examine the dynamics of this critical period in Irish political history. A range of perspectives is provided, with the ultimate aim of understanding what caused the split over the Treaty, what it actually represented, and its legacy.

The Revolutionary Period

There had been rebellions against British rule in previous centuries, but none achieved their aims, and few had any lasting political legacy. These included the Nine Years War (1593–1603) led by the O'Neills of Tyrone and the O'Donnells of Donegal against Elizabethan rule at the end of the sixteenth century; the Irish rebellion of 1641 led by the Catholic gentry; and the Irish Confederate wars that followed. Following separate suppressions by both Oliver Cromwell and William of Orange in the seventeenth century, insurgency dissipated until the 1798 Rebellion by Wolfe Tone and the United Irishmen. This was quickly followed five years later by another uprising, led by Robert Emmet. The Young Irelander rebellion of 1848 and the Fenian rising of 1867 were relatively small events but remained the last uprisings against British rule until the Easter Rising of 1916. It was initially thought that the latter event was yet another in the series of sporadic rebellions against British rule. After all, it was primarily Dublin-based, was quelled within five days, and was widely condemned by various Irish quarters, including popular sentiment. However, the events of Easter week 1916 ultimately proved somewhat different to the insurgencies which went before, and in hindsight, came to be seen as representing one episode in a series of events that decade that culminated in Irish independence.

It is difficult to pinpoint the exact origins of the revolutionary decade, but certainly the tempo upped with the foundation of the movement for Irish 'home rule' in 1870 by Isaac Butt. He sought to succeed where Daniel O'Connell had failed in the 1830s and 1840s, namely to repeal the 1800 Act of Union, which had dissolved the Irish parliament. The British Liberal prime minister, William Gladstone, introduced separate home rule bills in 1886 and 1893, the first of which was defeated in the House of Commons, and the second in the House of Lords. These both proposed the creation of a devolved Irish assembly, which would preside over domestic affairs, while Ireland remained part of the United Kingdom. A third home rule bill was introduced by another Liberal prime minister, Herbert Asquith, in 1912. Following the Parliament Act of 1911, under which the House of Lords lost its permanent veto, it seemed as if Ireland was set to have devolved government restored in 1914. However, the First World War (1914–18) interrupted this process, and it was during this time that unionist opposition to home rule became particularly apparent. By the end of the war in November 1918, it seemed doubtful that home rule for the whole island would be granted. This was confirmed by the Government of Ireland Act of

1920, which restored parliamentary government to Ireland, but to two different jurisdictions, Northern and Southern Ireland. In the meantime, the nationalist community, now mobilised in the form of the Sinn Féin party, had upped the ante. Having soundly beaten the Home Rule Party in the elections to the House of Commons in December 1918 (a victory magnified by the first-past-the-post voting system), the Sinn Féin MPs assembled in the Mansion House in Dublin a month later, and sat as the First Dáil, when it concurrently issued a declaration of independence. On the same day in January 1919, what are generally seen as the first shots of the War of Independence were fired, when two officers of the Royal Irish Constabulary, escorting a consignment of explosives, were killed in an ambush in County Tipperary. This conflict continued for two years until a truce was declared in July 1921, following which peace talks took place in London between a British delegation and representatives of the Irish cabinet (known as the 'plenipotentiaries'). These talks concluded with the signing of the Treaty. Its ratification was discussed by the Dáil over several weeks in December 1921 and January 1922, and these debates are the focus of this volume.

The Second Dáil

The Dáil that decided the fate of the Treaty is known as the Second Dáil; it comprised TDs elected under the 1921 elections to the newly established houses of commons in Northern Ireland and Southern Ireland. No polling took place for the latter body as all 128 candidates were returned unopposed. Candidates comprised 124 from Sinn Féin and four independent unionists from the University of Dublin (Trinity College), with the latter meeting in June 1921 as the House of Commons of Southern Ireland. The Sinn Féin MPs, refusing to recognise the latter body and the partition of the island as confirmed by the 1920 Government of Ireland Act, convened as the Second Dáil, along with the six members of Sinn Féin elected to the House of Commons of Northern Ireland. The total membership of this Dáil was 125, as five of its TDs (Michael Collins, Éamon de Valera, Arthur Griffith, Seán Milroy and Eoin MacNeill) had been elected to both houses of commons, north and south of the putative border.[1] The unelected nature of the Dáil is perhaps its most striking feature; it was a product both of intimidation by Sinn Féin and of the Labour Party's decision not to contest the 1921 election. Both the latter policy and the lack of opposition to Sinn Féin ensured the election of a Dáil that may not have been as representative of the Irish population as one that could have resulted from competitive elections, with many of the candidates being picked by Michael Collins and Harry Boland.[2] For example, in the June 1922 Dáil election, 78 per cent of first preferences were cast for pro-Treaty candidates, whereas only 53 per cent of the Dáil of 1921–2 was pro-Treaty. It also resulted in the election of a number of untried and untested politicians at a critical stage in Irish history, many of whom may not have been equipped to deal with the tasks before them.

The Second Dáil was elected in the middle of a guerrilla war of independence against British rule, with many of its members directly involved in the warfare. Consequently, it did not meet until 16 August, following the negotiation of the truce the previous month. The newly elected Dáil met eight times in August, and once more in September to ratify the five plenipotentiaries (Arthur Griffith, Michael Collins, Robert Barton, Erskine Childers and George Gavan Duffy; all members of the Dáil, with the first three also members of the cabinet) who travelled to London to negotiate a settlement with the British government. The British delegation comprised experienced politicians, including Prime Minister David Lloyd George, Austen Chamberlain (Lord Privy Seal and leader of the House of Commons), Max Aitken, Lord Birkenhead (Lord Chancellor), Winston Churchill, Sir Laming Worthington-Evans, Sir Gordon Hewart and Sir Hamar Greenwood, all members of the cabinet, with Hewart being the serving Attorney General. The experience of the Irish delegation paled in significance to this formidable line-up and may have been one reason why the president of the Dáil, Éamon de Valera, did not attend the talks. His absence could be used as an excuse by the Irish side for not being coerced into signing a settlement; this would explain why de Valera wanted all decisions first deferred to him and the cabinet in Dublin. Indeed, de Valera had given secret instructions to the delegates that they were not to sign any document without first sending it back to him for consideration, which calls into question their full plenipotentiary status. De Valera was later to state that 'it would be ridiculous to think that we could send five men to complete a treaty without the right of ratification by this assembly. That is the only thing that matters. Therefore it is agreed that this treaty is simply an agreement and that it is not binding until the Dáil ratifies it. That is what we are concerned with.[3] The ambiguity of the Irish delegation's position created difficulties for it when negotiating with the British. For example, near the end of the discussions, Lloyd George said that he and his team were prepared to put their neck on the line by signing the Treaty, and that the Irish side should be prepared to do likewise. Griffith, in particular, resented the interference by de Valera, and in correspondence with the latter in late October 1921, the Irish delegation wrote: 'We could not continue any longer in the Conference and should return to Dublin immediately if the powers were withdrawn. We strongly resent, in the position in which we are placed, the interference with our powers. The responsibility, if this interference breaks the very slight possibility there is of settlement, will not and must not rest on the plenipotentiaries.'[4] The following day, de Valera assured Griffith: 'There is obviously a misunderstanding. There can be no question of tying the hands of the Plenipotentiaries beyond the extent to which they are tied by their original instruction.'[5] The Irish delegation ignored de Valera's secret instructions and signed the Treaty in the early hours of 6 December 1921. When it returned to Dublin with the signed agreement, de Valera was furious and wanted to reject the Treaty immediately. He was overruled by his cabinet, with William T. Cosgrave backing the three cabinet members who had attended the London talks (Griffith, Collins and Barton), and favouring the idea of the Dáil deciding the fate of the Treaty.

The Treaty

The Treaty itself is not that long; at 1,800 words it is about the length of the average undergraduate essay at university. In its opening words, it declares that 'Ireland shall have the same constitutional status in the Community of Nations known as the British Empire as the Dominion of Canada, the Commonwealth of Australia, the Dominion of New Zealand, and the Union of South Africa'. It also establishes the name of the new jurisdiction as the Irish Free State. In 1998, the *Documents on Irish foreign policy* series published the correspondence between the Irish delegation and representatives in Dublin, and it is a rich source on the nature of discussions between the British and Irish teams.[6] It is also quite revelatory in terms of the compromise that makes up the final draft of the the text. For example, perhaps the trickiest topic throughout the talks was how to resolve the 'Ulster' issue. Even though Griffith was willing for the talks to collapse on this issue, the Irish delegation ultimately agreed to the de facto partition as under the Government of Ireland Act, but it was (perhaps naively) optimistic that a boundary commission would restore Fermanagh, Tyrone and parts of Armagh to the Free State, leaving Northern Ireland an unviable jurisdiction. This issue was dealt with in Article 12, with the ambiguous phrase that the border would be decided on 'in accordance with the wishes of the inhabitants, so far as may be compatible with economic and geographic conditions'.

Perhaps the most controversial aspect of the Treaty was Article 4, which outlined an oath of fidelity to the British monarch to be taken by members of the Dáil. This crossed a line for many nationalists and was one of the issues on which Sinn Féin was to split. Nationalists who wanted to assert Irish sovereignty in foreign policy matters were also dismayed by an additional annex, which specified the required naval facilities that were to 'remain in charge of British care and maintenance parties'. These were the dockyard ports at Berehaven, Queenstown (Cobh), Belfast Lough and Lough Swilly. The British had insisted on retention of these naval facilities to prevent Ireland from becoming a harbour for enemy forces.

Article 5 stated that 'The Irish Free State shall assume liability for the service of the Public Debt of the United Kingdom', although the exact amount was to be determined by international arbitration. Ultimately, another agreement between the two countries in December 1925 saw the British government write off most of Ireland's liabilities arising from the Treaty. Article 16 prohibited religious discrimination in either jurisdiction, but beyond this, for a document that was supposedly to resolve the two countries' troubled relationship, the Treaty said very little. It was to come into law if ratified by the British parliament and the House of Commons of Southern Ireland. In 1924, it was registered with the League of Nations.

The Debates

The Dáil met on 14 December to discuss the Treaty, and what followed were fifteen days of debate, with a break for the Christmas period. There were twelve public sessions of parliament, as well as three private sessions on 15–17 December, and the morning of 6 January. These private debates were not released to the public until the 1970s, and this privacy was decided upon both to shield the Dáil's disharmony and to encourage free and frank debate. Jason Knirck describes the proceedings as 'rancorous, rambling, and confused', and suggests that they only served to heighten the divisions between the factions.[7] Overall, he is quite critical of the quality of the debates, noting how standing orders were ignored, speakers interrupted, and that: 'speeches – with few notable exceptions – meandered through bouts of self-justification, necromancy, martial machismo and republican histrionics'.[8]

The Dáil broke for the Christmas period, and it is argued that this was decisive in swinging momentum towards an acceptance of the Treaty. Dorothy Macardle claims that, had the vote been taken on 22 December, the settlement would most likely have been rejected by the Dáil.[9] However, over the Christmas period, the churches spoke out vehemently in favour of the Treaty, and there were media headlines such as 'Ratification or Ruin', 'Rejection or Chaos', which swung public opinion very much in favour of an acceptance.[10] While de Valera later claimed this sentiment motivated the Dáil to vote for the Treaty, Michael Laffan argues that the reverse could also be implied.[11] In the absence of a great deal of information about the Treaty and the political process, public opinion was strongly influenced by leaders, and had the Dáil been against the Treaty, this would have swung some opinion in that direction.

Many of the TDs were inexperienced politicians, with few being accustomed to parliamentary debate. These debates were, therefore, the first opportunity to see the capabilities of the future generation of political leaders in the new state, with Jason Knirck calling it their 'first real public trial'.[12] Many of the backbenchers were not capable of stepping up to the challenge, with some such as Liam de Róiste complaining that they were treated as sheep, being expected to go along with the wishes of the party elite. There was also some sentiment that, with most TDs having been nominated rather than elected and with the Dáil having primarily been ignored during the War of Independence, it was not appropriate to defer such an important political decision to them at that point.[13] For this reason, much of the debate tended to centre on personalities, rather than issues, with Joe Lee observing: 'The debate exposed not only the intensity of the passions, and the occasional nobility of purpose, but the viciousness of personal animosities, and the mediocrity of mind of many deputies'.[14] Laffan claims that 'some of the speakers were lucid and passionate, while others were hypocritical and self-righteous. Rarely were the debates enlivened by humour … there were frequent lapses into bathos'.[15]

Over 250,000 words were spoken in total over the fifteen days of debates. Much was made of the powers of the plenipotentiaries to sign the Treaty, and of the role of the king in the new state. However, there was little reference to Ulster, which Joseph Curran suggests 'can be ascribed to support of them [the clauses on Ulster], inability to devise a better alternative, or simply the belief that there was no solution to partition'.[16] Knirck claims that it is impossible to separate the Treaty debates from the personalities discussing it.[17] De Valera and Cathal Brugha tended to lead the arguments against the Treaty, with Collins and Griffith being its primary defenders. The pro-Treaty side tried to move the debate away from symbols, as it had lost out in negotiations on key issues such as the status of the monarch and the oath of fidelity. It wanted to focus on the practical gains made from the Treaty, while the anti-Treatyites, on the other hand, focused on symbolic matters that could generate passions and tug at the heartstrings of the ardent nationalists.

Despite the animosity of the split, few have been able to determine from the debates what divided the deputies. Laffan observes that all TDs who worked in the Dáil land settlement commission supported the Treaty, that the young were more radical than elders, that the irreconcilables were more likely to include gentry (either foreign-born/reared or of foreign descent), and that all six female TDs voted no.[18] Warner Moss uses the latter two characteristics to hypothesise about a social-psychological explanation motivating the anti-Treatyites.[19] He claims that their being outsiders made them more militant and more attracted to the romance and emotion of nationalism. Tom Garvin found that 'a detectable if not strong relationship existed between social background and political militancy', although this analysis was confined to the sixty-nine TDs elected to both the First and Second Dáils, thus excluding almost half of those involved in the Treaty debates.[20] It may have been that little divided the deputies because neither side differed radically in its interpretation of the Treaty. Both sides lamented the loss of the North and would have desired a republic for the whole island, while both would have preferred a full, clean break from the United Kingdom. However, there were many pragmatists within the Dáil who also recognised what could be achieved realistically as set against what they would prefer idealistically. The narrow gap between the two sides was noticeably evident in the alternative settlement produced by de Valera on the first day of the private debates. Known as 'Document No. 2', in many respects this version differed little from the Treaty, apart from the concept of 'external association' and the removal of the oath of fidelity. If this was all that divided the two sides, many questioned the *raison d'être* of the split.

Ultimately, the vote on the Treaty took place on 7 January, with sixty-four TDs in favour of the Treaty, fifty-seven against, and with the ceann comhairle (chair) Eoin MacNeill and three others not voting. These were Frank Drohan from Waterford-Tipperary East, who resigned his seat on 5 January, because he was anti-Treaty while his local Sinn Féin branch was pro-Treaty and had instructed him to vote in favour; Laurence Ginnell (anti-Treaty) was absent as he was the Irish government's representative in Argentina and South America generally; and Thomas Kelly (pro-Treaty), who was was ill. Frank Gallagher in *The Anglo-Irish Treaty* describes a long silence after the vote, following which de Valera spoke before he put his head in his hands and cried, as did most TDs.[21] The Dáil met for a further two days following the decisive vote, when de Valera failed to be re-elected as president of the Republic and Arthur Griffith was elected in his stead. This further cemented the division within Sinn Féin, and marked the beginning of an irrevocable split that provoked a civil conflict later that year.

These debates proved to be a critical moment in modern Irish history and shaped the path of future political competition in the state. Knirck ascribes great importance to them because of their revelatory nature: 'The debates reveal many disagreements and tensions lurking underneath and behind the seemingly unified wartime façade of Irish nationalism. The Treaty certainly did not create these differences, but it magnified them and, more importantly, publicised them, allowing the Irish people the chance to weigh in on these important issues.'[22] He outlines five other reasons for the significance of the Treaty debates: (1) they provide a 'window' into important issues in European and Irish history as this was an example of nation-building; (2) they represent a rehearsal for the process of decolonisation within the British Empire; (3) they outline 'the

lingering psychological and economic effects of the colonial experience'
on the new state; (4) they highlight the differences between the strains
of Irish nationalism; and (5) they shaped gender assumptions in Irish
political culture, as the manner in which the six female TDs all spoke
vehemently against the Treaty resulted in a feminisation of republicanism,
which led many leaders in the new state to cast women out of the body
politic.[23]

Some of these issues, and more, are dealt with by the fifteen
contributors to this volume. Mel Farrell considers the stance of the pro-
Treatyites. He argues that while it is often assumed that the ideologues
in the Dáil voted against the Treaty, values, and not just pragmatism,
prompted many TDs to vote for the Treaty as well. Following on from
this, Martin O'Donoghue considers the relevance of the home rule
movement, which has largely been forgotten, given the Home Rule
Party's eradication in 1918. Having been the main proponent of Irish
nationalism for half a century, it had an undoubted influence in shaping
the political agenda. John Dorney considers the other side, namely
the anti-Treaty republicans, who are often portrayed as adhering to an
unrealistic, narrow, doctrinaire philosophy. Eunan O'Halpin and Mary
Staines consider one such anti-Treatyite, P.J. Moloney, and compare his
position with that of a pro-Treaty TD, Michael Staines. Sinéad McCoole
examines the six female TDs, all of whom were opposed to the Treaty,
and asks what caused this gender-based consensus. Her discussion is
complemented by Mary McAuliffe, who profiles the neglected pro-Treaty
female perspective outside the Dáil.

The socio-economic dimension is explored by both Brian Hanley
and Tony Varley. Hanley notes that class was not an issue much discussed
at the Treaty debates, although he finds that the middle class was
overrepresented amongst the TDs, compared to the population at large.
Both O'Halpin and Staines's, and Hanley's chapters provide fascinating
details about the background of the TDs, comparing both sides of the
split, and the Dáil, to the population at large. Their findings challenge
many preconceptions about the basis of the division, as well as previous
studies in this area. Varley examines one particular socio-economic
group, and the largest vocation of the time, the farming sector. Land and
nationalism were intertwined since the mid-nineteenth century in Irish
politics, and Varley traces how this relationship evolved in the Treaty

debates. Weeks *et al.* take a different approach to the parliamentary proceedings, and examine them from a political science perspective, using a novel statistical technique. Finally, considering that the Treaty is, fundamentally, a legal text, legal experts Laura Cahillane and Paul Murray provide an annotation of the Treaty document itself.

In many ways, the events surrounding Ireland's withdrawal from the United Kingdom can be compared to the process of Britain withdrawing from the European Union following the 'Brexit' referendum in 2016. Granted, there were some key differences, with the British leave vote in part inspired by both a paradoxical desire for a return to splendid isolation and to be top dog once more; in contrast, the Irish motivation to leave the United Kingdom was fuelled by a desire no longer to be the underdog and also to be part of a community of independent nations. In spite of these divergences, however, and the supporters of the two fractures might not like to hear it, the similarities between the two events are nevertheless quite considerable. Brexiteers were motivated by a combination of nationalist sentiment and a desire to restore national sovereignty and parliamentary democracy. One hundred years earlier, Ireland likewise chose to leave the largest trading bloc in the world for both nationalist reasons and a desire for sovereign power. A mutual desire to leave a union provoked similar sentiment within the ruling elites of the separate unions, with some happy to be rid of a meddlesome constituent but others fearful of the ramifications for their respective union in the years to come. It is also quite remarkable that the border on the island of Ireland remains just as much a difficult issue to resolve in the Brexit negotiations as it did the in the debates over Ireland's independence. So, although it is difficult to fathom Irish nationalists and British Brexiteers as likely bedfellows, and granted, they would be unlikely to share a matrimonial bed for too long were they forced into an unholy alliance, the two sides surprisingly have plenty in common. What we propose to examine in this book is what motivated the 'Eirexiteers' of 1921–2, and what caused them to split. Brexit will be a significant event for the British political system, but the 'Eirexit' of 1922 was of far greater significance in Irish political history. In spite of this, it has received less attention in the 100 years since than Brexit has warranted in the two years since the referendum of 2016. This volume aims to rectify that lacuna.

Notes

1   Seán O'Mahony from the Fermanagh and Tyrone constituency was the sole
     member of the Second Dáil who was elected only to the Parliament of Northern
     Ireland. The five TDs with a dual mandate had just one vote in the Dáil, with one
     of them (Eoin MacNeill) elected ceann comhairle, thus only having a casting vote
     in the event of a tie.

2   Joseph Curran, *The birth of the Irish Free State* (Tuscaloosa, AL, 1989), cited in
     Jason Knirck, *Imagining Ireland's independence: the debates over the Anglo-Irish
     Treaty of 1921* (Lanham, MD, 2006), p. 122.

3   *Dáil Éireann deb.*, T, no. 2, 12 (14 Dec. 1921).

4   Letter from combined Irish delegation to Éamon de Valera, 26 Oct. 1921, in Ronan
     Fanning, Michael Kennedy, Dermot Keogh and Eunan O'Halpin (eds), *Documents
     on Irish foreign policy, 1919–1922* (10 vols, Dublin, 1998), i, p. 293.

5   Memorandum from Éamon de Valera to Arthur Griffith, 27 Oct. 1921, in ibid., p.
     294.

6   Ibid.

7   Knirck, *Imagining Ireland's independence*, p. 184.

8   Ibid., p. 40.

9   Dorothy Macardle, *The Irish Republic* (New York, 1965), p. 568.

10   Ibid., p. 569.

11   Michael Laffan, *The resurrection of Ireland: the Sinn Féin party, 1916–1923*
     (Cambridge, 1999), p. 357.

12   Knirck, *Imagining Ireland's independence*, p. 186.

13   Laffan, *Resurrection of Ireland*, p. 360.

14   J.J. Lee, *Ireland 1912–1985: politics and society* (Cambridge, 1989), p. 54.

15   Laffan, *Resurrection of Ireland*, p. 355.

16   Curran, *Irish Free State*, p. 135.

17   Knirck, *Imagining Ireland's independence*, pp. 124–5.

18   Laffan, *Resurrection of Ireland*, p. 360.

19   Warner Moss, *Political parties in the Irish Free State* (London, 1933), pp. 19–21.

20   Tom Garvin, 'Nationalist elites, Irish voters and Irish political development: a
     comparative perspective' in *Economic and Social Review*, viii, no. 3 (1977), pp.
     161–86.

21   Frank Gallagher, *The Anglo-Irish Treaty* (London, 1965), p. xx.

22   Knirck, *Imagining Ireland's independence*, p. 184.

23   Ibid., pp. 2, 184.

CHAPTER 1

'Stepping Stones to Freedom': Pro-Treaty Rhetoric and Strategy During the Dáil Treaty Debates

Mel Farrell

In the early hours of 6 December 1921, *realpolitik* collided with the aspirations of revolutionary Sinn Féin. For four years, the party had stood for Ireland's full independence as a 32-county republic. Since its breakthrough in the December 1918 general election, the party defied British authority by abstaining from Westminster, issuing a declaration of independence, and establishing an underground counter-state. Sinn Féin had also ignored the British government's first attempt at a peace settlement, the Government of Ireland Act of 1920, which partitioned the island into 'Northern' and 'Southern' Ireland with limited 'home rule' parliaments established in Belfast and Dublin. However, at the negotiating table in 1921, a Sinn Féin delegation felt compelled to conclude a peace treaty that gave those twenty-six counties of 'Southern Ireland' self-government as an Irish free state with dominion status and that recognised the right of 'Northern Ireland' to 'opt out', with a boundary commission to determine the border between the two jurisdictions. Moreover, the Treaty stipulated that members of the Free State parliament would have to swear an oath of fidelity to the British monarch. While these terms were repugnant to most Sinn Féiners, the leaders of the Irish delegation, Arthur Griffith and Michael Collins, emphasised the document's potential. For Collins, in particular, the Treaty offered Ireland its first real step on the road to full independence. By mid-December, he and Griffith had to go before the Dáil to convince Sinn Féin's elected representatives that they had made the correct decision.

While the broader pro-Treaty case has been examined by numerous scholars of the Irish Revolution, this chapter will examine the rhetoric and strategies deployed by pro-Treaty Sinn Féiners during the acrimonious Dáil debates on the settlement.[1] While attitudes to the Treaty remained in flux in the aftermath of 6 December, two distinct factions began to crystallise around leading members of the Dáil. Griffith and Collins each had their loyalists and this chapter will focus on pro-Treaty contributors representing both moderate (Kevin O'Higgins, Patrick Hogan and W.T. Cosgrave) and more hard-line, militarist-republican opinion (Seán Mac Eoin, Eoin O'Duffy and Seán Hales) within the Dáil. As John Regan observed, these moderates and hard-liners joined together to support Collins and Griffith 'on the promise that one day they would advance together toward the republic'.[2]

When the debate commenced, a pro-Treaty majority was by no means a foregone conclusion. Sitting in judgement were the elected representatives of one party – Sinn Féin. The party was a broad church representing a wide range of Irish nationalist opinion. Launched by Griffith in 1905 as a 'dual-monarchist' party, Sinn Féin was reconstituted in October 1917 in order to accommodate republicans. Some of the more militant newcomers bore a deep distrust of the moderate tendencies of the party's founders.[3] Leading up to the debates, the party's leader, and symbolic head of the Irish Republic, Éamon de Valera, had already landed a heavy blow by denouncing the Treaty out of hand and voting against it in cabinet. However, de Valera's opposition to the Treaty was somewhat compromised by his own refusal to join the delegation in London.[4] Moreover, much of the Dáil's new intake of TDs, elected to the Second Dáil in May 1921, were intimately acquainted with the Easter Rising and the Anglo-Irish War, either as participants or as relatives of prominent republican figures. Therefore, the Second Dáil was representative of a more hard-line, republican position than the First Dáil. December 1918 had coincided with the 'Wilsonian Moment' and there were hopes that Ireland's case would be heard at the Paris Peace Conference. By May 1921, however, the context had changed. The principle of 'self-determination' was applied in central and eastern Europe, not Ireland, while close to thirty months of guerrilla warfare and British reprisals had hardened attitudes on both sides. With 128 seats available in the May 1921 elections to the proposed 'Southern' Ireland parliament, Sinn Féin needed candidates and turned to individuals who were prominent in the revolutionary war. As such, the new Dáil was strongly representative of the militarist-republican wing of the movement with a number of TDs representing brigades and divisions as much as their constituents.[5] Therefore, in order to win the Dáil vote, Collins, Griffith and their lieutenants effectively had to challenge de Valera's authority, counter republican accusations that their bargain was a betrayal of those who had fought and died for full independence, and demonstrate that beneath the Treaty's repugnant trappings of British imperialism, lay a document of some potential. In succeeding, they built a pro-Treaty coalition – including moderate Sinn Féiners and militarist republicans – held together by Collins's 'stepping stones to freedom' interpretation of the settlement. During the Free State's formative years, Cumann na nGaedheal would struggle to hold that coalition together.

Free State or Republic?

Given their role in determining revolutionary Sinn Féin's position on the Anglo-Irish settlement of 1921, the Dáil Treaty debates are of singular importance in the emergence of modern Irish democracy. Veteran Home Rule Party politician Tim Healy was rather captivated by the Treaty debates, remarking that it was 'more interesting to me than thousands of debates I have heard in the House of Commons' and declaring that the 'ability displayed on both sides' gave him 'great hope and encouragement as to the future'.[6] While an ex-constitutionalist like Healy could regard the Treaty settlement as a 'happy solution' to the Anglo-Irish conflict, it was clear in December 1921 that a large number of Dáil deputies – and quite possibly a majority – were of a different opinion.[7] Although the Dáil vote on 7 January 1922 revealed a pro-Treaty majority of seven, it was widely believed that the Treaty would have been narrowly defeated had the vote been taken before Christmas.[8] This serves to underline both the effectiveness of the pro-Treaty party's strategy and the impact of public opinion.

As it set out to secure Dáil endorsement for the 'Articles of Agreement', the emerging pro-Treaty party faced a number of serious obstacles.

In order to secure Dáil backing for the Treaty, these would have to be overcome. These difficulties centred on the make-up of the Dáil itself, the stark divisions that had emerged in the Sinn Féin leadership, and the reality that some elements of the Treaty settlement were objectionable to most Sinn Féiners, whether moderate or republican. Many advocates of the Treaty were themselves uncomfortable with its imperial trappings. Since the cabinet had split narrowly in favour of the Treaty (by four votes to three), it was widely acknowledged that the Dáil vote was in the balance.[9] Collins and Griffith needed to demonstrate that the Treaty, despite its trappings of British imperialism, could in fact be congruent with the aspirations of the revolutionary period: full independence, Irish unity and the Republic. In that context, the Treaty's insistence on a boundary commission and dominion status were undoubtedly vexed issues for Sinn Féin. However, the most divisive issue of all proved to be the stipulation that Free State parliamentarians swear an oath before taking their seats. The wording of the oath, which was finally agreed on the morning of 5 December, called for 'faith and allegiance to the Constitution of the Irish Free State', and that members of the Dáil be 'faithful to His Majesty King George V, his Heirs and Successors' as head of the British Commonwealth.[10] In an irony that would not have been lost on its supporters in the Dáil, when the terms of the Anglo-Irish settlement were debated in the House of Commons on 14 December – a debate covered extensively in the Irish press – the ambiguous wording of the oath proved one of its more contentious issues.[11] Tory die-hards preferred an unambiguous expression of allegiance to the Crown, while there were concerns that the formation of an Irish Free State would weaken Britain's hold on the empire. Unionist leader Sir Edward Carson wondered why the new Irish state needed an army 'unless it is to invade us?' and went so far as to describe the Treaty as 'an abject humiliation' for Britain.[12] Other Tory die-hards talked of the betrayal of southern unionists and 'the surrender of the rights of the crown in Ireland'.[13]

For anti-Treatyites in Sinn Féin, the oath was both a recognition of the British Crown in Ireland and a contravention of their own oath to the Republic. They argued, therefore, that the Treaty was a surrender to British imperialism. Those hostile to the settlement also claimed that it was signed under duress and a threat of immediate and terrible war; they questioned whether or not the delegation had the authority to conclude a treaty without referring to the cabinet for approval. Before Sinn Féin had even entered into negotiations it was clear that a settlement could only be made to endure if there was a consensus behind it from within the Sinn Féin leadership. However, as was clear from the cabinet vote, the Sinn Féin leadership was bitterly divided. De Valera's stern opposition also called into question the delegation's action in signing the Treaty without conferring with the ministers who had remained in Dublin.

These challenges notwithstanding, the pro-Treatyites enjoyed some important advantages. It helped that the accomplished, and widely respected, Sinn Féin organiser Dan McCarthy (then president of the Gaelic Athletic Association (GAA)) was a supporter of the Treaty. McCarthy put his skills to good use acting as a whip of the embryonic pro-Treaty party, and he was later employed as its director of elections. Griffith's old Sinn Féin committee men – Seán Milroy, W.T. Cosgrave and Paddy O'Keeffe – had rowed in behind the Treaty, creating a link to the party's foundation in 1905. More significantly, Collins drew on his Irish Republican Brotherhood (IRB) network to bring key Irish Republican Army (IRA) figures into the pro-Treaty fold. More importantly, as Peter Hart observed, the pro-Treaty ranks contained Sinn Féin's better debaters, 'savvy journalists and propagandists, lawyers, war heroes and the majority of the cabinet'.[14] Together, they would use rhetoric, logic, legal expertise and their reputations to justify Dáil acceptance of the Treaty.

Before the debates commenced on 14 December, deputies were furnished with a comprehensive report on the progress of the talks in London. This set out the details of full plenary sessions of the peace conference, and also the controversial sub-conferences involving Griffith and Collins only.[15] On the very day that the debates commenced there was a bitter argument about whether it was in the public interest to discuss the delegation's credentials and instructions. During their tense opening salvo, Collins and de Valera clashed over whether the Dáil should discuss these matters in private session. De Valera had intimated that the delegation had exceeded its authority and indicated that this could be addressed more freely in a private Dáil sitting. Unsurprisingly, Collins and Griffith took exception to de Valera on this point. Collins forcibly defended the actions of the delegation and expressed his opposition to a Dáil private session:

The thing has already taken an unfair aspect and I am against a private session. I have no particular feeling about it. I suggest that a vital matter for the representatives of the nation, and the nation itself, is that the final document which was agreed on by a united Cabinet, should be put side by side with the final document which the Delegation of Plenipotentiaries did not sign as a treaty, but did sign on the understanding that each signatory would recommend it to the Dáil for acceptance.[16]

Other pro-Treaty deputies expressed similar opposition to the idea of a private session, with Cork Borough representative J.J. Walsh stating there was 'nothing which I am entitled to hear at this meeting which every member of the Irish nation has not an equal right to hear'.[17] However, the question of a private session did not break evenly along pro-Treaty/anti-Treaty lines. Cathal Brugha, a staunch anti-Treatyite, supported having the debates in public, while Richard Mulcahy in the pro-Treaty camp backed up de Valera's desire for private debate, at least to discuss the genesis of the Treaty. As Jason Knirck has argued, for figures in both camps, it made sense to conceal the 'cabinet's dirty laundry' from the public and 'the true state of the IRA from British ears'.[18] In the event, a compromise was agreed whereby the Dáil would go into private session to discuss the genesis of the Treaty before debating its ratification in public. During the private session, Collins reiterated his preference for public debate.[19]

Deploying 'Fighting Men'

In order to refute republican accusations that the Treaty was a betrayal of those who had died fighting for a republic, Collins sent out his military lieutenants – individuals who could be found in each arm of the revolutionary movement – to shore up his military support and the republican flank in the early stages of the debates. Of course, the very fact that Collins – whom Griffith described as the 'man who won the war' during the debates – was arguing for acceptance was also referenced by several advocates of the Treaty.[20] In the private sessions, Kevin O'Higgins, then a rising star within the party and assistant minister for local government, summed this attitude up by declaring: 'What was good enough for Arthur Griffith and Michael Collins is good enough for us.'[21] O'Higgins repeated this line of argument on the resumption of the public sessions on 19 December. He agreed that the delegation may have fallen short of what Sinn Féin desired but was prepared to trust their judgment.

Whereas O'Higgins spoke as a politician, Collins's military contacts – Seán Mac Eoin, Seán Hales, Richard Mulcahy and Eoin O'Duffy – spoke to the Dáil as plain soldiers.[22] These men were particularly useful to Collins in that they could offer a realistic assessment of the military situation.[23] Mac Eoin was an influential guerrilla commander from County Longford with close connections to the IRA leadership at general headquarters (GHQ). Mac Eoin was respected for the exploits of his North Longford Flying Column, particularly in engagements at Ballinalee and Clonfin.[24] He was also close to Collins on account of his membership of the IRB and the Cork man's associations with north Longford. While the IRB's Supreme Council had voted in favour of the Treaty, and had played a covert role in drafting an acceptably worded oath for Collins during the negotiations, the brotherhood allowed its members who were Dáil deputies to vote according to their consciences. O'Duffy, by December 1921, was a member of the revolutionary movement's inner circle and was seen as a protégé of Collins. Like Collins and Mulcahy, O'Duffy was known for his administrative efficiency and he became one of Collins's successors as GHQ director of organisation. Locally, in County Monaghan, there was a murkier side to O'Duffy's revolutionary record, and he emerged from the Anglo-Irish conflict with a reputation as a hardliner who had dealt ruthlessly with suspected informers.[25] As a representative of a constituency on the border between the proposed Free State and Northern Ireland, he was a respected voice on the North and this was useful to Griffith, and Collins in particular, during the Treaty debates. In August 1921, while touring County Armagh with Collins, O'Duffy made an incendiary speech in which he advocated Irish unity by use of force. According to his biographer, this helped reassure Northern nationalists during the autumn and winter of 1921 while serving to strengthen the Irish delegation's hand during the negotiations in London.[26] Seán Hales was also a respected IRA man with an impressive *resumé* as commandant of the Cork No. 3 Brigade. These men had the authority to warn the Dáil about the weakness of the military position, and their words carried weight with wavering deputies.[27]

During the debates, Collins's military lieutenants were carefully prepared with the best pro-Treaty lines, indicative of the considerable degree of back-room co-ordination in the embryonic parliamentary party. On message, they rattled off the consistent argument – the Treaty was merely a 'stepping stone', or in a variation used by Hales:

> If I thought this Treaty which has been signed was to bar our right to freedom, if it was to be the finality, I wouldn't touch it but I took it that it is to be a jumping off point to attain our alternative ends, because if it is one year or in ten years, Ireland will regain that freedom which is her destiny and no man can bar it. The only thing is that at the present moment if there was anything like a split it would be more dangerous than anything else … Posterity will judge us all yet. There is no getting away from that. When the time comes there is one thing certain. Speaking from the column which I was always with through the battlefields and willing and ready to carry on the fight but still I look upon that Treaty as the best rock from which to jump off for the final accomplishment of the Irish freedom.[28]

While objecting to some aspects of the settlement, Mac Eoin claimed that he made up his mind to support the Treaty while returning to Longford from a meeting in Monaghan. According to Mac Eoin's handwritten notes before the Treaty debates, he felt that the settlement, despite reservations about its symbols, offered the substance of what he had fought for. It provided for the evacuation of Britain's armed forces and the possibility of the 'development of Ireland as it should be for all creeds and classes without distinction'.[29] Each of these was, for Mac Eoin, 'enough guarantee of safety to our interests'.[30] As respected guerrilla commanders, O'Duffy and Mac Eoin also had the authority to speak convincingly of the weakness of the IRA's position in December 1921. In private session on 17 December, Mac Eoin and O'Duffy each made impactful contributions that left deputies in no doubt about their perception of the IRA's position in December 1921. Responding to Cathal Brugha's assertion that the Dáil was prepared for war if it became a necessity, and pointing to his own record, Mac Eoin stated that he wished for the Dáil to 'understand me as a plain soldier who realises what it is to be at war … and I want everybody to realise … I am prepared to go into it now just the same as I went in before. I want everyone to realise what we are going in for, because I hold we have a duty to the civil population'.[31] Mac Eoin strongly refuted Brugha's suggestion that the IRA was stronger than it had been in July. While 'training is a bit stronger', he had one rifle for every fifty men at his disposal and enough ammunition to 'last them about fifty minutes for that one rifle'.[32] Pointedly, he said that those who were talking lightly about going to war 'do not know a damn thing about it'.[33]

In his 'skilful' contribution, O'Duffy declared that he supported the Treaty for two reasons.[34] Like Mac Eoin, he was satisfied that Britain's armed forces would be evacuating and that the formation of an Irish army was a guarantee of independence. Whereas de Valera and the republicans had claimed that the Free State's army would be 'the army of His Majesty', O'Duffy saw things differently:

> I want to be as brief as possible and to state the position from my knowledge of the country. I should say at the very outset that I take full responsibility for saying unreservedly that I am in favour of the ratification of this Treaty. I may be called a coward for making that statement but I do not mind whether I am or not so long as I have not been called coward for the last 2 or 3 years. I did not study the Treaty very carefully but I see two points in it that commend themselves to me. The first is that it achieves what we have been talking and striving for since the fight began and that is that the British soldier and British Peeler will never again be seen in Ireland. The second point that struck me was that we would have an army of our own fully armed and equipped.[35]

Pointing to 'Document No. 2', de Valera's alternative to the Treaty that was produced in the private debates, O'Duffy reminded deputies that they were not being asked to choose between the Treaty and the Irish Republic. Claiming that the opening days of the debates had brought the Dáil into a 'muddle', O'Duffy asked deputies to remember that they had an opportunity to either support a Treaty agreed by representatives of both Britain and Ireland or risk everything for a 'second treaty' that differed only slightly from that signed by the Irish delegation.[36] This line of argument was a strong one given how close de Valera's Document No. 2 came to the Treaty settlement without being acceptable to the British.[37]

Kevin O'Higgins and Fionán Lynch (Kerry-Limerick West), also used this line of argument in their contributions. Lynch declared that his party was 'not afraid to show the Irish people that it is not a difference between this Treaty and the Republic. It is as between this Treaty and a compromise which is less than the Republic'.[38] O'Higgins queried how doctrinaire republicans could stand with de Valera in the debates given that his Document No. 2 did not provide recognition of the Republic. For O'Higgins, the shades of difference between these two positions were not worth risking a new war. In public session, O'Higgins was clear on this point in a speech that outlined the limitations of the Treaty, and also the future direction of the British Commonwealth:

> It is true that by the provisions of the Treaty, Ireland is included in the system known as the British Empire, and the most objectionable aspect of the Treaty is that the threat of force has been used to influence Ireland to a decision to enter this miniature league of nations. It has been called a league of free nations. I admit in practice it is so; but it is unwise and unstatesmanlike to attempt to bind any such league by any ties other than pure voluntary ties. I believe the evolution of this group must be towards a condition, not merely of individual freedom but also of equality of status. I quite admit in the case of Ireland the tie is not voluntary, and in the case of Ireland the status is not equal. Herein lie the defects of the Treaty. But face the facts that they are defects which the English representatives insisted upon with threats of war, terrible and immediate. Let us face also the facts that they are not defects which press so grievously on our citizens that we are entitled to invite war because of them. I trust that when we come to cast our votes for or against the ratification of this Treaty, each member will do so with full advertence to the consequences for the nation. I trust each member will vote as if with him or her lay the sole responsibility for this grave choice.[39]

While the delegation had, like the army, 'fallen somewhat short', they had brought back a settlement, 'something that can be honourably accepted'.[40]

O'Duffy also dismissed republican concerns about the oath, arguing that it was an oath of allegiance to the new Irish state's constitution. Here the Treatyites could rely on the legal expertise of figures like solicitor Patrick Hogan, the Galway TD who went on to become minister for agriculture in the Free State. In a convincing speech, Hogan asserted that the wording of the oath meant that Dáil deputies would be endeavouring, merely, to be faithful to the king as head of the Commonwealth and this was 'the only relation which we have ... with King George V'.[41] Hogan argued that this oath would regulate relations between Great Britain and Ireland. Under Hogan's interpretation, 'Ireland is an equal under the letter of that Treaty with England, and if England is a Sovereign State so is Ireland under the letter of that Treaty; I believe that to be good constitutional law'.[42] Hogan saw the Treaty as 'a bargain between two sovereign states, and our delegates in making that Treaty made the first Treaty that was ever made by Ireland with England and went further to get recognition of Ireland's sovereign status than all that has been done in all our history ... I ask are we going to throw that away, and for what?'[43] While O'Duffy lacked Hogan's command of constitutional law, he was prepared to recognise the potential that was contained within the Treaty. He accepted that the oath's wording emphasised that members were required to swear allegiance to the new constitution, and that this 'neutralises' the clause referring to fidelity to the king. Using this logic, O'Duffy claimed, in private and public session, that his support for the Treaty was consistent with his long-held republican beliefs. The Treaty was, he said, 'a stepping stone only, I regard it as not being final, otherwise I would be false to my oath and my country'.[44] Intriguingly, W.T. Cosgrave seemed to suggest that there had been much too great an emphasis on alternative legal interpretations of the 'relative distinctions as between faithfulness and allegiance'.[45] A 'Doctor of Divinity in explaining this matter to me in connection with the oath points out that one can be faithful to an equal. And it is in that sense that I interpret this oath, and I believe I gave expression in the cabinet to the opinion that this oath could be interpreted whatever way you looked at it'. [46]

Public Session

On the resumption of public debate, on 19 December, one report noted that the tone was 'animated and solemn' in turn.[47] During the private session, speeches seemed crafted in order to persuade deputies. During the public sessions, speeches on all sides took much greater cognisance of public opinion. Moreover, the longer the debates dragged on, the bulk of contributions 'were made with at least one eye on posterity and future elections' given that most deputies had declared one way or another.[48] By the first week of January, most deputies were simply speaking 'for the record'.[49] As the debates progressed, it became clear that the Treaty had the broad acceptance of the general public. This allowed the embryonic pro-Treaty party to present its case as representing the will of the people.[50]

On Monday 19 December the public sessions resumed with Arthur Griffith rising to propose the motion that the Dáil approve of the articles of agreement. Unbeknownst to the public, both the military situation and de Valera's Document No. 2 alternative to the Treaty had been debated at length by deputies in private session. This, Jason Knirck argues, considerably 'changed the timbre of the debate'.[51] Griffith began with a cogent, succinct defence of the conduct of negotiations. He argued, forcefully, that the agreement signed on 6 December was the best deal that could be obtained in the circumstances and claimed that it safeguarded Ireland's national interests. As a nod to nationalist aspirations, Griffith highlighted the potential of the Treaty. While it was a compromise, the Treaty offered an opportunity to rebuild the 'Gaelic civilisation' that had been 'broken down at the battle of Kinsale'.[52] Now, in public session, the pro-Treatyites again deployed the 'fighting men' to good effect. For tactical reasons, Mac Eoin was chosen to second Griffith's motion in the public session. It was hoped that Mac Eoin could counter the impression that senior IRA figures opposed the Treaty. In his speech seconding Griffith's motion, Mac Eoin assured the Dáil that the agreement brought back from London represented what he and his comrades had fought for:

> I take this course because I know I am doing it in the interests of my country, which I love. To me symbols, recognitions, shadows, have very little meaning. What I want, what the people of Ireland want, is not shadows but substances, and I hold that this Treaty between the two nations gives us not shadows but real substances, and for that reason I am ready to support it. Furthermore, this Treaty gives Ireland the chance for the first time in 700 years to develop her

own life in her own way, to develop Ireland for all, every man and woman, without distinction of creed or class or politics. To me this Treaty gives me what I and my comrades fought for; it gives us for the first time in 700 years the evacuation of Britain's armed forces out of Ireland. It also gives me my hope and dream, our own Army, not half-equipped, but fully equipped, to defend our interests. If the Treaty were much worse in words than it is alleged to be, once it gave me these two things, I would take it and say as long as the armed forces of Britain are gone and the armed forces of Ireland remain, we can develop our own nation in our own way.[53]

This contribution was seized on by Mary MacSwiney who accused the pro-Treatyites of betraying all those who had died for the Republic:

Commandant Sean MacKeon [*sic*] seconded that abominable document, I am sorry to say. I know that he would fight to the death for the Republic of Ireland still, but he does not realise what he is giving away. I am glad that he is here alive to-day to fight for the Republic again, but if he were my brother, I would rather he were with Kevin Barry.[54]

Dan Breen, one of the leaders of the Tipperary IRA, also took exception to Mac Eoin's remarks. In a letter to Mac Eoin, Breen stated that:

I wish to point out to you that you are reported to have stated in the Dáil today that this Treaty brings the freedom that is necessary & for which we all are ready to die. You are also reported to have stated previously that this Treaty gives you what you & your comrades have fought for. As one of your comrades I say that I would never have handled a gun, nor fired a shot, nor would I have asked any of my comrades living or <u>dead</u> [original emphasis] to raise a hand to obtain this Treaty.

Let me remind you that today is the second anniversary of Martin Savage's death. Do you suppose that he sacrificed his life in attempting to kill one British Governor General in order to make room for another British Governor General?[55]

Breen concluded his letter by stating that 'I take no party's side but I still stand by our old principle of complete separation'.[56] Copies of this letter were circulated to the press.[57]

In a similar vein, much was made of Collins's own record. During the debates, pro-Treaty speakers responded to republican jibes that the Treaty had been signed under duress by pointing to Collins's war record. George Gavan Duffy and Robert Barton, reluctant signatories of the Treaty, had revealed the intimidating atmosphere in which the Treaty was signed. Kevin O'Higgins appeared to accept the argument that the Treaty had been signed under a threat of war and believed this was the most objectionable aspect of the agreement. However, the stance of another pro-Treaty TD, Fionán Lynch, was more typical: 'One argument that has been made against this Treaty by the other side … is that this thing was signed under duress. It is an insult to the men who signed to say so, and it is an insult to your intelligence to try to make you believe it, and the people of Ireland are not going to believe it'.[58] A number of pro-Treaty speakers objected to those republican deputies who had co-opted the voices of the dead. Pro-Treatyites rejected such emotive language and pointed to those within their own ranks who had risked their lives to defend the Republic. According to Piaras Béaslaí:

We have no right to say how any man who is dead would have voted. It is a mere accident that Commdt. McKeon has not inscribed his name on the tomb of Irish martyrology. It is fortunate he is here to-day to speak for himself and not to be quoted by other people when he could not speak for himself. It is a mere series of accidents, and I know intimately all the facts, that the Minister of Finance is here today, and it is the merest accident that all of us are here to-day, not to have our names as arguments against what we think the best thing to do for Ireland now.[59]

More 'middle-ground' pro-Treaty contributors used similar arguments to those put forward by Mac Eoin, O'Duffy and Hales. Éamonn Duggan, one of the signatories of the Treaty, asserted confidently that the Treaty would deliver full Irish independence. If the country did not work the Treaty to 'achieve their freedom, it is the fault of the Irish people and not of the Treaty. I have more faith in Ireland than the people who put forward the other point of view'.[60] On the same day, Cosgrave laid emphasis on the potential of the Treaty while, as late as 4 January, Desmond FitzGerald stressed the temporary nature of the settlement. The Treaty would be adhered to, he claimed, so long as it suited each side.[61]

Collins and Griffith

As the leading signatories of the Treaty, Collins and Griffith accepted a major share of the responsibility for 'selling' the Treaty during the Dáil debates.[62] During the debates, de Valera's refusal to join them was skilfully exploited by Collins and Griffith. Who was de Valera to criticise the Treaty when he had refused to travel with the delegation on 3 December?[63] In the early stages of the debates, Collins challenged republican assertions that the delegation had not been given the authority to conclude a treaty, arguing, convincingly, that the delegation had been given authority, by the Dáil, to negotiate and conclude a settlement.[64] Collins and Griffith pointed to the official letters of appointment exchanged between de Valera and David Lloyd George. These letters were explicit that the delegation had been appointed as 'Envoys Plenipotentiary from the elected Government of the Republic of Ireland to negotiate and conclude on behalf of Ireland with the representatives of his Britannic Majesty, George V, a Treaty or Treaties of Settlement, Association and Accommodation between Ireland and the community of nations known as the British Commonwealth'.[65] When republicans alleged that the atmosphere in London had got to the Sinn Féin delegation and that the Treaty had been signed under duress, Collins and Griffith both stated, in public and private session, that they would still have signed the Treaty if the negotiations had taken place in Dublin.[66]

Collins withheld his most convincing arguments for the Treaty until the resumption of the public sessions. He had asserted repeatedly that these should not be heard in private. As a result, his 19 December speech was impactful and forced the anti-Treatyites on the defensive.[67] Whereas Griffith's speech had focused on the potential of the Treaty, Collins combined the aspirational with the tangible. His speech emphasised that, in his view, Britain's connection to Ireland had been maintained by the military presence of its armed forces. Echoing Mac Eoin and O'Duffy, Collins suggested that the promised withdrawal of British military forces from Ireland was proof of the Free State's independence. He claimed that a rejection of the Treaty would be tantamount to a declaration of war by Ireland. Like Mac Eoin, O'Duffy and Mulcahy, Collins had the credentials to speak with authority about the military position. Rejection of the Treaty by the Dáil would, Collins argued, have been the first occasion in which Ireland declared war. He claimed that, prior to the Treaty, Ireland had been defending itself against a foreign aggressor. Now the Treaty would guarantee that the country would be 'rid' of the occupying force. Collins also used logic to refute de Valera's charge that a better result would have been achieved through more skilful handling by pointing out that any fault with the make-up of the delegation rested with the Dáil – and by implication de Valera – for not selecting a better negotiation team. Collins also suggested that Sinn Féin's acceptance of peace talks on the basis of Lloyd George's 29 September letter was the moment when the Republic had been compromised. On the question of the Commonwealth, Collins again spoke with conviction, arguing that 'We have got rid of the word "Empire".'[68] Commonwealth membership would, in fact, guarantee and protect the Irish Free State's independence. Canada and the other dominions would become, in effect, 'guarantors of our freedom' in a way that would not be possible if Ireland was isolated in the world.[69]

Collins concluded his speech to the public session strongly. He asked the Dáil to focus on the living rather than the dead and urged deputies, as the people's representatives, to accept responsibility themselves for the important decision before them and the country:

Deputies have spoken about whether dead men would approve of it, and they have spoken of whether children yet unborn will approve of it, but few of them have spoken as to whether the living approve of it. In my own small way I tried to have before my mind what the whole lot of them would think of it. And the proper way for us to look at it is in that way. There is no man here who has more regard for the dead men than I have (hear, hear). I don't think it is fair to be quoting them against us. I think the decision ought to be a clear decision on the documents as they are before us — on the Treaty as it is before us. On that we shall be judged, as to whether we have done the right thing in our own conscience or not. Don't let us put the responsibility, the individual responsibility, upon anybody. Let us take that responsibility ourselves and let us in God's name abide by the decision.[70]

It was, in the words of one of his many biographers, the speech of Collins's life and 'one of the great statements of political rationality in Irish history'.[71] In private, Collins is likely to have gone further in reassuring wavering deputies about his future intentions once the Treaty was ratified. Numerous pro-Treaty people made it clear that they had accepted the settlement in the belief that it would lead to the achievement of the Republic at some point in the future. Alec McCabe described the Treaty as 'goods delivered and not promised to us goods that we all know were never offered or, indeed, seriously asked for before'.[72] He declared that he was voting for the Treaty 'as a Republican and will continue to pursue the ideals of the Republic as long as I am in public life'.[73] The argument that the revolutionary aspirations of the Republic, the Gaelic state and Irish unity were achievable via the Treaty's stepping stones was seductive and was to prove of vital importance in ensuring there would be a Dáil majority in its favour. It allowed middle-ground deputies and militarist republicans such as O'Duffy, Mac Eoin, Hales and Mulcahy to reconcile their aspirations for a republic and united Ireland with the Treaty settlement.[74]

Christmas Conversions

With so many members of the Dáil determined to speak, it was not possible to conclude the debates before Christmas. Instead, the debates adjourned until January, giving oscillating deputies ample time to reflect, not just on the views of the Sinn Féin leaders, but also those of their constituents. Outside the Dáil, public opinion seemed to be aligned with the pro-Treaty position. The evidence would suggest that a cross-spectrum of views seemed to recognise that the Treaty offered a greater degree of independence than anybody could have imagined prior to the First World War.[75] It was also apparent that the meticulous detail in which the 'memorable' debates were reported in the Irish newspapers ensured that the arguments and rhetoric deployed inside the Dáil were having an impact on public opinion.[76] As the sole political representatives in the debates, Sinn Féin deputies found themselves responsible for determining Ireland's future. This was a considerable responsibility given that the voices of hundreds of thousands of voters who had never voted for Sinn Féin were unrepresented. Displaying considerable maturity, a number of Sinn Féin deputies took these voices into account when casting their vote. On 19 December, O'Higgins reminded deputies that they represented the whole country 'not merely … a particular political party within the nation'.[77] In the weeks that followed, the various public declarations, and favourable press coverage, served to underline his point. Over Christmas, it was clear that there was a strong desire for peace and that public opinion was siding with what was later described by the bishop of Kerry as the 'less romantic' interpretation of the Treaty.[78] In Longford, the county council and other public bodies agreed with the sentiments Mac Eoin had expressed in the Dáil and voted to give their support to the Treaty.[79] In like manner, Sinn Féin's Cavan West TD Peter Paul Galligan was made aware of the pro-Treaty sentiment evident across the county. On 28 December, Cavan Urban District Council passed the following resolution:

That this Meeting of the Cavan Urban District Council specially Convened desired to place on record its high appreciation of the terms of the Treaty entered into by our Nation's Plenipotentiaries and whilst recognising the great services rendered by the members of An Dail [sic] who are in opposition we unanimously request them for the sake of our dear Country to bury their differences and stand with Arthur Griffith and Sean McKeon for the ratification of the Treaty.[80]

By the time the Dáil voted on the Treaty on 7 January, some 328 public bodies had voted to support the Treaty with just five declaring against. This must have weighed heavily on deputies participating in one of the most important debates in Irish history. Although much of the national and provincial press acknowledged the country was 'overwhelmingly in favour of ratification', the outcome of the Dáil's deliberations remained in the balance.[81] Sinn Féin, at national and local level, was split. Within Sinn Féin's organisation it was clear that activists were bitterly divided on the terms of the Treaty. All over the country, Sinn Féin units voted on whether to endorse the Treaty or reject it as a basis of settlement. While there tended to be a majority of branches in favour of the Treaty, the minority against the settlement was a sizeable one.

When the Naas branch in County Kildare met in early January, just two hands were raised in opposition to the Treaty out of an attendance of over 200.[82] The north Leitrim and north Roscommon Sinn Féin organisations went so far as to call on the elected deputies from these constituencies to vote for the Treaty when the debates resumed.[83] The Sinn Féin organisations in O'Duffy's Monaghan constituency and Mac Eoin's Longford-Westmeath constituency also backed the Treaty. Yet, in each case, there was a strong anti-Treaty minority as the split percolated through the revolutionary movement. Even within Mac Eoin's specific north Longford heartland, some of his erstwhile comrades took exception to his words in support of the Treaty. One member of the Sinn Féin executive, moving that the local organisation delay taking a vote until the Dáil debates had concluded, challenged the local deputy's statement that the settlement was 'what he and his comrades had fought for'.[88] The amendment was carried by nine votes to eleven.[89] Michael Laffan suggests that de Valera's open hostility to the terms of the Treaty, and that of such republicans as Liam Lynch and Tom Barry, is likely to have stimulated a certain degree of grassroots opposition.[84] After all, de Valera still commanded respect within the pro-Treaty parliamentary party. Pro-Treaty contributor J.J. Walsh (Cork Borough), strongly rebuffing an inaccurate statement in the *Cork Examiner*, defended de Valera in the Dáil and spoke of his 'very great regard for the honour and integrity and ability of the President and his great patriotism and sacrifice for his country'.[85] As Maryann Gialanella Valiulis has demonstrated, prominent pro-Treaty figures like Richard Mulcahy maintained that de Valera's opposition to the settlement ensured that the split came in the centre of the revolutionary movement rather than at its margins. De Valera, like much of the pro-Treaty leadership, was a moderate who was prepared to compromise. In a post-Civil War context, pro-Treaty veterans argued that his opposition to the exact terms of the settlement, and the nature in which it was signed, had given political cover to hard-line opinion in Sinn Féin and the IRA. One Cork city pro-Treatyite, Liam de Róiste, would later claim that de Valera and the anti-Treatyites regarded as traitors anybody who did not share their point of view.[86] For these reasons de Valera was the man the pro-Treatyites would never forgive.[87]

On the resumption of the public debates in early January, numerous deputies made reference to the impact public opinion had had on them. De Valera acknowledged that the public supported the settlement yet there was still a risk that the Dáil would reject it.[90] There was an obvious desire for peace and acceptance of the settlement, and this gave confidence to those deputies who had declared for the Treaty prior to the Dáil recess. In Monaghan, O'Duffy was the darling of the Sinn Féin organisation on account of Seán MacEntee's resolve to vote against the Treaty despite the express wishes of his constituents. Both of Sinn Féin's Monaghan executives had called on MacEntee to resign his Dáil seat.[91] O'Duffy's speech on 4 January drew attention to this fact. Unlike many republicans, MacEntee had based his opposition to the settlement on the Treaty's provision that Northern Ireland could 'opt out' of the Free State. Whereas much anti-Treaty sentiment rested on opposition to the oath of fidelity, loyalty to individual leaders or the precise form that the new state's dominion status would take, MacEntee appears to have been motivated by partition and he was one of the few deputies, on either side, to draw attention to it during the debates. In the period between the Dáil vote on the Treaty and the outbreak of the Civil War, MacEntee continued to express concern for Northern nationalists and highlighted the extent of sectarian violence in Belfast.[92]

Like his anti-Treaty constituency rival, O'Duffy, in a speech laced with intemperate language, also drew attention to partition. However, much like his republicanism, O'Duffy felt that his desire for a united Ireland was compatible with support for the Treaty. Claiming to know 'Ulster better than any man or woman in this Dáil' (having 'faced Ulster's lead on more than one occasion with lead, and in those places where I was able to do it, I silenced them with lead'), O'Duffy said that unionists would be attracted into a united Ireland if the Free State proved its economic viability.[93] In essence, this would remain the pro-Treaty strategy for a united Ireland under Cumann na nGaedheal during the 1920s. O'Duffy's flamboyant style made use of evocative sporting analogies to persuade opinion that the Treaty was a major milestone for Irish nationalism and that full independence would soon be achieved if they could all unite around the settlement. Borrowing GAA terminology, he said that, with the Treaty, nationalists had taken the ball 'inside the fourteen yard line' with the goal of an independent and united Ireland in sight.[94]

However, the striking impact that the Christmas recess had on deputies is underlined by the speeches made in the final days of the debates. On 6 January, Vincent White (Waterford) declared that he was 'not in ecstacies [*sic*] over this Treaty', but felt it should be ratified by the Dáil and confirmed he would 'support this Treaty because there is some finality in it; and I support it because, when I went to my constituents in Waterford during Christmas, they suggested to me that it deserved ratification'.[95] The impact of public opinion is underlined by the deeply personal remarks made by Mayo South-Roscommon South deputy Daniel O'Rourke. He can be categorised as a middle-ground deputy whose conversion to the Treatyite side was critical to its ratification. O'Rourke asserted that his vote had been influenced by the public's clear support for the Treaty. O'Rourke confirmed that he was, in fact, opposed to the Treaty and would have voted against its ratification if the Dáil vote had occurred before the Dáil adjourned for Christmas. However, O'Rourke had:

> returned to my constituency at Christmas and I went there to the people – not the resolution passers – to the people who had been with me in the fight, the people whose opinion I valued, the people who are, I believe, Die-Hards [*sic*]; and I consulted them about this question and I must say that unanimously they said to me that there was no alternative but to accept the Treaty. Everything that is personal in me is against the Treaty; I yield to no man in my hatred for British oppression, and in my opposition to any symbol of British rule in Ireland; but I say I would be acting an impertinent part by putting my own views and opinions against the views of my best friends, the men who are the best fighters with me ... I say this for myself: that while I would vote for the Treaty I am just as well pleased if the Treaty is thrown out.[96]

O'Rourke's contribution demonstrates the magnitude of the choice facing the Dáil and underlines the difficulty in applying neat binaries to the Treaty split. O'Rourke would have voted against the Treaty but for the impact of public opinion. With the Treaty being passed narrowly (64 to 57) in the Dáil every vote counted, and the conversion of O'Rourke and others was highly significant. Relaying the results of the vote, the *Irish Independent* claimed that, while the majority was narrow, 'it proved larger than was generally expected in the closing stages of the fateful debate'.[97] O'Rourke later joined Fianna Fáil and also served as president of the GAA, 1946–9. He was first elected to the Dáil for Fianna Fáil in the 1932 election and went on to have a mostly successful political career until losing his Dáil seat in 1951.

Conclusion: Pro-Treaty Coalition?

In order to win Dáil support for the Treaty and overcome nationalist abhorrence of the more objectionable aspects of the settlement, the pro-Treaty leadership walked a delicate tightrope. Collins and Griffith had appealed to moderates and hardliners within the Dáil. Their Treaty could mean different things to different people. For some Sinn Féin veterans, the agreement conceded much of what the old, pre-1916, Sinn Féin had demanded and could therefore be accepted with honour.[98] However, given the make-up of the Second Dáil it had also been necessary to win over deputies who were more strident in their politics. To achieve this, the Treaty had to be presented as something capable of delivering on the aims of the revolutionary movement. With considerable skill, Collins and Griffith used various rhetorical devices to bring a slender majority of the Dáil with them. As Daniel O'Rourke's contribution to the debates shows, Dáil acceptance of the 'Articles of Agreement' and the subsequent establishment of the Irish Free State itself, rested on the strength of the pro- and anti-Treaty speakers' arguments in the debates and the willingness of deputies – who were unaccustomed to the rigours of parliamentary democracy – to consider the wider views of the non-Sinn Féin electorate.

In essence, Collins and Griffith had built a fragile pro-Treaty coalition in order to secure Dáil ratification of the Treaty. Moderates, republicans, guerrilla commanders and reluctant deputies, feeling the pressure of their constituents, had joined together to secure the Treaty's safe passage with a majority of seven votes. Collins and Griffith had just about secured enough concessions from the British to enable them to secure a slim majority of Sinn Féin deputies, though the wing of the party they were left with would itself come to resemble a coalition of diverse elements and interpretations of what the Treaty could achieve. Following the vote in favour of the Treaty, the standpoint of some deputies remained in flux. When de Valera resigned as president (after an abortive attempt to retain his services at the head of the Dáil in the event of a pro-Treaty majority), and immediately stood for re-election, he lost this vote by an even more slender margin, fifty-eight votes to sixty.[99] On the following day, as deputies looked set to elect Arthur Griffith as their new president, de Valera led his followers out of the Dáil to Collins's anguished cry 'Deserters all! We will now call on the Irish people to rally to us. Deserters all!'[100] The Dáil record shows that sixty-one deputies remained in the chamber to formally vote for Griffith as de Valera's replacement.

With Dáil ratification secured, the focus shifted to the Sinn Féin grassroots and the wider electorate. In appealing to the country, in the spring of 1922, the pro-Treaty party utilised much of the rhetoric deployed to good effect in the Dáil debate. As this handwritten note from Eoin MacNeill to Desmond FitzGerald shows, the pro-Treatyites wished to use the time following the Dáil vote to build unassailable momentum behind the agreement:

> The main thing is for the supporters of the Treaty to act on the offensive and show up the weakness of their opponents. They should make full use of the Press, Dublin and local, and of public bodies, for this purpose. Deputies who are against the will of their constituents should be called on to resign – publicly, insistently, repeatedly.[101]

While the political evolution of the state's two main parties is often linked to the Treaty debates, the subsequent Civil War significantly altered the context. After the Treaty debates, it was clear that Sinn Féin was in a downward spiral of disintegration from which it would not recover. In February 1922, de Valera suggested that anti-Treatyites should organise independently of the Sinn Féin standing committee given its pro-Treaty majority. That month, Cumann na Poblachta ('League of the Republic') was launched as an anti-Treaty organisation.[102] In March, the pro-Treatyites established their own, separate election committees though it would be 29 August before a serious effort was made to form a distinct pro-Treaty political party.[103] By that stage, the two architects of the Treaty, Collins and Griffith, were both dead and Irish nationalists were engaged in the bitter Civil War over the Treaty. In the latter stages of the Civil War, the pro-Treatyites adopted 'Cumann na nGaedheal' as the name for their new party.[104]

Although the evolutionary potential of the Treaty was emphasised as it meandered its way through the Dáil in December 1921 and January 1922, the Civil War hardened pro-Treaty attitudes. While the embryonic pro-Treaty party had offered conditional support for the settlement in the winter of 1921/2, now that people had fought and died for the Treaty, Collins's and Griffith's successors in Cumann na nGaedheal could not so easily dismiss their settlement as a means to an end. During the 1920s, Cumann na nGaedheal did use the Treaty to push the parameters of the Free State's independence. Cosgrave proved that the settlement offered the substance of independence by registering the Treaty as an international agreement with the League of Nations – against Britain's wishes – and his government was also instrumental in asserting the independence of the dominions as confirmed by the 1931 Statute of Westminster.[105] As Jason Knirck observes, there remained a distinct 'anti-colonial dimension' to Cumann na nGaedheal policy throughout the 1920s.[106] However, Cosgrave was reluctant to significantly alter the terms of the Treaty and thus handed the initiative for more radical change to de Valera's new Fianna Fáil party. As Fianna Fáil emerged as the dominant party in the early 1930s, Cumann na nGaedheal continued to defend the Treaty as an article of faith that could not be breached by the Free State. Arguably, its rigid commitment to the Treaty curtailed Cumann na nGaedheal's political development in the turbulent 1930s, forcing it to accept the merger, as an equal partner, with the National Centre Party and the 'Blueshirts' in the new Fine Gael party in September 1933.[107]

Notes

1   See, for example: John M. Regan, *The Irish counter-revolution: Treatyite politics and settlement, 1921–36* (Dublin, 2001); Peter Hart, *Mick: the real Michael Collins* (London, 2005); Jason Knirck, *Imagining Ireland's independence: the debates over the Anglo-Irish Treaty of 1921* (Plymouth, 2006); Michael Hopkinson, *Green against green: the Irish Civil War* (Dublin, 2004); Frank Pakenham, *Peace by ordeal: an account, from first hand sources, of the negotiation and signature of the Anglo-Irish Treaty* (London, 1935); Michael Laffan, *The resurrection of Ireland: the Sinn Féin party, 1916–1923* (Cambridge, 1999); Thomas Jones, *Whitehall diary, iii: Ireland, 1918–1925*, ed. Keith Middlemas (Oxford, 1971); Joseph M. Curran, *The birth of the Irish Free State* (Tuscaloosa, AL, 1980); and it is also covered in Mel Farrell, *Party politics in a new democracy: the Irish Free State, 1922–37* (London, 2017).

2 Regan, *Counter-revolution*, p. 49.
3 Richard English, *Irish freedom: the history of nationalism in Ireland* (London, 2006), p. 284.
4 Thomas Bartlett, *Ireland: a history* (Cambridge, 2010), p. 409.
5 Knirck, *Imagining Ireland's independence*, p. 112; Hart, *Mick*, pp. 327–8.
6 *Irish Independent*, 9 Jan. 1922.
7 Ibid.
8 Ibid.
9 Knirck, *Imagining Ireland's independence*, p. 111.
10 Copy of memorandum of an interview between Michael Collins and David Lloyd George, 5 Dec. 1921, in Ronan Fanning, Michael Kennedy, Dermot Keogh and Eunan O'Halpin (eds), *Documents on Irish foreign policy, 1919–1922* (10 vols, Dublin, 1998), i, pp. 350-1; Jones, *Whitehall diary*, p. 144; *Cork Examiner*, 16, 23 Dec. 1921.
11 *Irish Independent*, 15–17 Dec. 1921; *Cork Examiner*, 15 Dec. 1921.
12 *Irish Independent*, 17 Dec. 1921; Philippa Levine, *The British Empire: sunrise to sunset* (2nd ed., London, 2013), p. 192; Laffan, *Resurrection*, p. 354.
13 *Irish Independent*, 17 Dec. 1921; Philippa Levine, *The British Empire*, p. 192; Laffan, *Resurrection*, p. 354. The House of Commons approved the Treaty by a margin of four-to-one on 16 December 1921 (Knirck, *Imagining Ireland's independence*, p. 111).
14 Hart, *Mick*, p. 327.
15 'Report to Dail Eireann [*sic*] from the Irish Delegation of Plenipotentiaries', 14 Dec. 1921 (University College Dublin Archives (UCDA), Seán MacEoin Papers, P151/76).
16 *Dáil Éireann deb.*, T, no. 2, 9 (14 Dec. 1921).
17 Ibid.
18 Knirck, *Imagining Ireland's independence*, p. 115.
19 *Dáil Éireann deb.*, T, no. 5, 255 (17 Dec. 1921).
20 Ibid., no. 6, 20 (19 Dec. 1921).
21 Ibid., no. 3, 148 (15 Dec. 1921).
22 Hart, *Mick*, p. 329.
23 Michael Hayes, 'Dáil Éireann and the Irish Civil War' in *Studies*, lviii, no. 229 (spring 1969), p. 4.
24 Charles Townshend, *The British campaign in Ireland, 1919–1921: the development of political and military policies* (Oxford, 1975), p. 152; Marie Coleman, *County Longford and the Irish Revolution, 1910–1923* (Dublin and Portland, OR, 2003), pp. 144, 167.
25 Fearghal McGarry, *Eoin O'Duffy: a self-made hero* (Oxford, 2005), pp. 73–5.
26 Ibid., pp. 80–1.
27 John M. Regan, 'The politics of reaction: the dynamics of Treatyite government and policy, 1922-33' in *Irish Historical Studies*, xxx, no. 120 (1997), pp. 547–8.
28 *Dáil Éireann deb.*, T, no. 5, 263 (17 Dec. 1921).

29 'Notes' for speech in Dáil seconding Griffith's motion, 19 Dec. 1921 (UCDA, Seán MacEoin Papers, P151/80/1-2).

30 Ibid.

31 *Dáil Éireann deb.*, T, no. 5, 225 (17 Dec. 1921).

32 Ibid.

33 Ibid., 225–6.

34 McGarry, *Eoin O'Duffy*, p. 91.

35 *Dáil Éireann deb.*, T, no. 5, 240 (17 Dec. 1921).

36 Ibid.

37 Hayes, 'Dáil Éireann and the Irish Civil War', p. 4.

38 *Dáil Éireann deb.*, T, no. 7, 58 (20 Dec. 1921).

39 Ibid., no. 6, 45–8 (19 Dec. 1921).

40 Ibid.; John P. McCarthy, *Kevin O'Higgins: builder of the Irish state* (Dublin, 2006), pp. 38–40.

41 *Dáil Éireann deb.*, T, no. 7, 62 (20 Dec. 1921).

42 Ibid.

43 Ibid., 63.

44 Ibid., no. 5, 242 (17 Dec. 1921); ibid., no. 7, 62 (20 Dec. 1921).

45 Ibid., no. 8, 102 (21 Dec. 1921).

46 Ibid.

47 *Westmeath Examiner*, 24 Dec. 1921.

48 Knirck, *Imagining Ireland's independence*, pp. 112, 127.

49 Ibid.

50 Ibid.

51 Ibid., p. 125.

52 *Dáil Éireann deb.*, T, no. 6, 23 (19 Dec. 1921).

53 Ibid., 23–4.

54 Ibid., no. 8, 122 (21 Dec. 1921). De Valera said: 'I am afraid we will have to sit to-morrow night. We wish to try to have the debate ended before Christmas', with Griffith adding: 'The whole business was held up this evening by one Member who spoke for two hours and forty minutes' (ibid., 127).

55 Dan Breen to Seán Mac Eoin, 19 Dec. 1921 (UCDA, Seán MacEoin Papers, P151/79/2).

56 Ibid.

57 Ibid.

58 Michael Laffan, *Judging W.T. Cosgrave* (Dublin, 2014), p. 106.

59 *Dáil Éireann deb.*, T, no. 5, 231 (17 Dec. 1921). Subsequently pro-Treaty campaign leaflets would ask voters to question whether republicans would use Collins's name against the Treaty if he had died in any of the conflicts between 1916 and 1921.

60 *Dáil Éireann deb.*, T, no. 8, 98 (21 Dec. 1921).

61 Ibid., no. 11, 235 (4 Jan. 1922).

62 Hart, *Mick*, p. 323.

63   J.J. Lee has concluded that de Valera's presence would not have made a significant difference to the terms agreed (J.J. Lee, *Ireland 1912–1985: politics and society* (Cambridge, 1989), pp. 51–3; Hart, *Mick*, p. 312).

64   See *Anglo-Celt*, 17 Dec. 1921.

65   Official letters of appointment, Éamon de Valera to the British delegation, 7 Oct. 1921 (UCDA, Hugh Kennedy Papers, P4/196).

66   See, for example, *Dáil Éireann deb.*, T, no. 5, 228 (17 Dec. 1921).

67   *Westmeath Examiner*, 24 Dec. 1921; Hart, *Mick*, p. 329.

68   *Dáil Éireann deb.*, T, no. 6, 34 (19 Dec. 1921).

69   See also Hart, *Mick*, pp. 333–5.

70   *Dáil Éireann deb.*, T, no. 6, 36 (19 Dec. 1921).

71   Hart, *Mick*, p. 337.

72   *Dáil Éireann deb.*, T, no. 11, 214 (4 Jan. 1922).

73   Ibid.

74   See Regan, *Counter-revolution*, pp. 44–5.

75   Laffan, *Judging W.T. Cosgrave*, p. 107; Bartlett, *Ireland*, p. 408.

76   *Irish Independent*, 9 Jan. 1922.

77   *Dáil Éireann deb.*, T, no. 6, 46 (19 Dec. 1921).

78   Charles O'Sullivan, bishop of Kerry, to Dr Brian MacMahon, president of the Tralee Cumann na nGaedheal branch, 19 July 1923 (UCDA, Desmond and Mabel FitzGerald Papers, P80/1099).

79   John Kiernan, clerk of Granard Rural District Council, to Seán Mac Eoin, 31 Dec. 1921 (UCDA, Seán MacEoin Papers, P151/81).

80   Cavan Urban District Council, resolution, 28 Dec. 1921 (UCDA, Peter Paul Galligan Papers, P25/68).

81   *Westmeath Examiner*, 7 Jan. 1922. See also, Hayes, 'Dáil Éireann and the Irish Civil War', pp. 4–5 on this point.

82   Laffan, *Resurrection*, p. 361; *Kildare Observer*, 7 Jan. 1922.

83   North Leitrim and north Roscommon endorsement of Treaty (UCDA, Desmond and Mabel FitzGerald Papers, P80/256/14).

84   Laffan, *Resurrection*, p. 356.

85   *Dáil Éireann deb.*, T, no. 8, 88 (21 Dec. 1921).

86   Liam de Róiste diary entry, 2 Mar. 1923 (Cork City and County Archives, Liam de Róiste Papers, U271A/Book 48).

87   Maryann Gialanella Valiulis, '"The man they could never forgive" – the view of the opposition: Éamon de Valera and the Civil War' in J.P. Carroll and J.A. Murphy (eds), *De Valera and his times* (Cork, 1983), pp. 92–100.

88   *Longford Leader*, 7 Jan. 1922.

89   Ibid.; *Freeman's Journal*, 3 Jan. 1922; *Irish Independent*, 4 Jan. 1922.

90   Laffan, *Resurrection*, p. 356.

91   Ibid., pp. 356–7.

92   Dáil Éireann, questions, 6 Mar. 1922 (UCDA, Seán MacEoin Papers, P151/94/1).

93   *Dáil Éireann deb.*, T, no. 11, 226 (4 Jan. 1922).

94 Ibid., 224.

95 Ibid., no. 14, 287–8 (6 Jan. 1922).

96 Ibid., no. 15, 315–16 (7 Jan. 1922).

97 *Irish Independent*, 9 Jan. 1922.

98 Laffan, *Resurrection*, p. 351.

99 Hayes, 'Dáil Éireann and the Irish Civil War', pp. 5–6.

100 *Dáil Éireann deb.*, T, no. 17, 410 (10 Jan. 1922).

101 Eoin MacNeill to Desmond FitzGerald, 13 Jan. 1922 (UCDA, Desmond and Mabel FitzGerald Papers, P80/258).

102 Ann Mathews, *Renegades: Irish republican women, 1900–1922* (Cork, 2010), p. 311.

103 General and election committee, minutes of meeting, 29 Aug. 1922 (UCDA, Cumann na nGaedheal Papers, P39/min/1).

104 Preliminary conference of Cumann na nGaedheal, minutes of meeting, 7 Dec. 1922 (ibid.).

105 Donal Lowry, 'The captive dominion: imperial realities behind Irish diplomacy, 1922–49' in *Irish Historical Studies*, xxxvi, no. 142 (Nov. 2008), pp. 202–6.

106 Jason Knirck, *Afterimage of the Revolution: Cumann na nGaedheal and Irish politics, 1922–1932* (Madison, WI, 2014), pp. 19, 45; see also Ciara Meehan, *The Cosgrave party: a history of Cumann na nGaedheal, 1923–33* (Dublin, 2010).

107 See Farrell, *Party politics*, pp. 252, 263–7.

CHAPTER 2

'We Should for the Present Stand Absolutely Aloof': Home Rule Perspectives on the Treaty Debates

Martin O'Donoghue

When one movement is succeeded by a rival it often happens that the achievements of the first are overshadowed and minimised. There was this tendency when some thirty years ago the Volunteer and Sinn Féin movements won the support of the people from the Irish Parliamentary Party. But without the Land League, without the destruction of the powers of the landlords, without the political education given by, and the enthusiasm engendered in the early days of the Parnellite Movement, the success achieved by the Volunteers and by Sinn Féin and its successors would have been much more difficult.

> Éamon de Valera at Michael Davitt centenary,
> Straide, County Mayo,
> 9 June 1946[1]

In 1946, on the centenaries of the birth of Charles Stewart Parnell and Michael Davitt, Taoiseach and 1916 veteran Éamon de Valera paid generous, if careful, tribute to the Irish Parliamentary Party (IPP). De Valera's remarks might suggest an easy transition from the party which dominated Irish politics up to the Easter Rising and its successors in Sinn Féin and later parties. However, the events of the intervening years show that this was not always the case. De Valera noted the importance of the Irish Party and the Land War period in a struggle which was later taken on by the movements in which de Valera himself played such a leading part, yet he did not refer explicitly to the latter-day Irish Party led by John Redmond. The Irish Party had acted as the voice of Irish nationalism for almost fifty years with a constitutional campaign for self-government – various legislative versions of 'home rule' may have appeared limited in retrospect, but the Irish Party enjoyed widespread support and was largely unopposed in nationalist constituencies for decades.

However, the party suffered effective political annihilation in the 1918 general election. It was reduced to just six Westminster MPs for the island of Ireland (five of whom were in Ulster) as its rival Sinn Féin won seventy-three seats. While the party bequeathed a legacy to later parties, in the immediate aftermath of the post-war election, the remnant of the old Irish Party was a small, beleaguered presence in the British parliament.[2] Sinn Féin's MPs abstained from Westminster and established Dáil Éireann in January 1919. From this point on, the Dáil became the de facto Irish parliament. In December 1921, it was this chamber which would begin to debate the proposed Anglo-Irish Treaty. The dispute which followed was very much a Sinn Féin dispute. The 'Civil War parties' which emerged from the confrontation over the Treaty claimed derivation from Sinn Féin, not the IPP. The older party was thus very much peripheral to the Treaty debates held in 1921 and 1922 and few academic or popular discussions of the subject refer to the party which had been so swiftly sidelined after its electoral meltdown only three years previously.

Yet, considering the central role played by the Home Rule movement in Irish life and the fact that the IPP still retained the backing of approximately 220,000 voters in 1918, it remains important to place the debates on Irish sovereignty in 1921 and 1922 in a wider historical context and also to ask how former Irish Party leaders and supporters responded to the settlement with Britain.[3] This chapter seeks to complete both tasks by examining the text of the Treaty debates, but also by assessing how nationalists outside the Sinn Féin school perceived the events of December and January 1921–2. It analyses the Irish Party's demand for self-government and scrutinises how public debates evolved from home

rule to republic and, ultimately, acceptance of the Treaty. It investigates the
reactions of those who remained loyal to the Irish Party and references to
the Irish Party and its leaders in the Treaty debates before examining the
diffusion of home rule influences in the First and Second Dáils. Finally,
this chapter concludes with reflection on the longer-term consequences
of the fact that many supporters of the Treaty settlement in 1922 had
been individuals with Irish Party heritage who had not taken part in the
Revolution and the effect this had on politics in the 1920s and beyond.

Home Rule for Ireland

The history of the Irish Parliamentary Party up to 1918 has benefitted
from a wealth of scholarship in recent years which has illuminated much
of the party's work both at Westminster and at constituency level in
Ireland.[4] Nevertheless, as the term 'home rule' was actually applied and
used by both sides during the Treaty debates, it is instructive to analyse
what was meant by its invocation through the period of the Irish Party's
political ascendancy. The Home Rule League, founded in 1873 by Isaac
Butt, soon became the largest political movement in the country. Butt's
creation was a conservative organisation, focused on land reform and
providing an alternative to Fenianism.[5] 'Home rule' was very much
seen within the context of the empire and was a modest demand.[6] The
movement, however, developed a far more strident edge under Charles
Stewart Parnell, leader from 1880, and party rhetoric could sometimes
run the gamut from limited powers to the talk of full sovereignty. A
bill granting Ireland 'home rule' or limited self-government within
the United Kingdom was defeated in the House of Commons in 1886.
Under this measure, the Crown was to be represented in Ireland by the
lord lieutenant who would have power to 'appoint ministers; summon,
prorogue or dissolve' the parliament. Money bills would also have to have
the lord lieutenant's recommendation.[7] Another home rule bill passed the
House of Commons in 1893 only to suffer defeat in the House of Lords
before the issue was raised for the third time in 1912. This legislation
(the Home Rule Act was subsequently placed on the statute book in 1914
but never enacted) introduced by the Liberal government was broadly
on the same lines as before – as in 1893, it provided for two chambers
and a number of powers were still reserved for the UK government.[8]

The Westminster parliament thus remained supreme with powers over the Crown, peace and war, military force and foreign policy. The Irish parliament's powers to alter taxes, customs and excises would also be restricted.[9] The Irish parliament would not be given immediate power for administering land acts and it would only gain power over policing after six years. The Dublin legislature would also be debarred from endowing any religion.[10] Irish representation at Westminster was to remain, but in reduced form, with just forty-two MPs.

While the IPP and its supporters in Ireland could encompass a broad church of various ideas, by 1912, this measure was strongly defended as a settlement to the Irish question by party leader John Redmond and his followers throughout the country.[11] The political crisis, which lasted from 1912 up to the outbreak of war in Europe in 1914, turned, therefore, on unionist opposition to the measure and the prospect of some form of partition. By the time home rule was placed on the statute book, but suspended for the duration of the First World War on 18 September 1914, provision for the exclusion of Ulster counties was built into British legislative thinking.[12] Fresh home rule negotiations beginning in the aftermath of the Rising in 1916 took largely the same powers as a starting point. The home rule administration was still not to have any power over military affairs, the making of peace and war, the post office or the Dublin Metropolitan Police in time of war and the lord lieutenant would retain certain existing powers until the conflict in Europe ended.[13] On the question of partition, Redmond and his Belfast colleague Joe Devlin fought to persuade supporters to agree to temporary exclusion for six Ulster counties for a period to be decided by imperial conference. However, even this proposed solution was to prove a chimera as, in the British cabinet, Lord Lansdowne and Walter Long undermined any prospect of the settlement becoming reality.[14]

After this failure, David Lloyd George, then prime minister of a wartime coalition government, proposed an Irish convention constituted of representatives of all shades of Irish nationalism and unionism in 1917. This body met in private and Redmond put his faith in the British government implementing the settlement if the convention could come to agreement. However, northern unionist delegates arrived at the convention without the authority from the Ulster Unionist Council to agree to any tangible compromise.[15] Redmond's deputy John Dillon refused to be a part of the convention chaired by Sir Horace Plunkett, while Sinn Féin shunned the conference, in addition to William O'Brien, who had led the breakaway constitutional nationalist All-for-Ireland League.[16] Although it looked like Redmond had come to terms with southern unionists at the convention, the loss of customs and therefore 'fiscal autonomy' was deemed too much of an imposition on Irish claims to freedom for two traditional Redmond allies: Devlin and Bishop Patrick O'Donnell of Raphoe. When they indicated their refusal to support Redmond's proposal, no complete settlement on any substantive issue proved possible. Eventually, southern unionists and moderate nationalists led by Galway MP Stephen Gwynn agreed to Lloyd George's scheme of self-government without control of customs and a proviso that a commission would rule on the matter after the war.[17] However, this scheme was never implemented.

By 1917, even members of the Irish Party were looking beyond the Home Rule Act. Although Cork West MP Daniel O'Leary, only elected the previous November, retained Irish Party loyalties for years after the party's fall, in 1917 he harboured deep misgivings about the direction of Redmond's party.[18] Writing to fellow MP Matthew Keating, he enclosed a letter for Redmond in which he declared that some within the party were 'striking out for a new programme'.[19] Confident that the plans would succeed as the only chance to 'save' the party, this plan conceived that all of Ireland would gain self-government 'based on the models of South Africa and Australia'.[20] O'Leary further added that if the convention failed to come to a conclusive report, or if it decided on a 'constitution on the colonial model' and the British refused to give it effect, the party should unite all Irish nationalists in an appeal to the United States, Russia and France, and finally to the post-war international peace conference.[21] Prior to the 1918 general election, the rhetoric of US President Woodrow Wilson and appeals to the Paris Peace Conference were utilised by Sinn Féin, but also by the Irish Party.[22] In another sign of party opinion moving beyond the 1912 proposal, prominent Cork IPP activist J.J. Horgan called for a joint conference of the Irish Party and Sinn Féin to present a united front to the Paris Peace Conference. However, Dillon, who succeeded Redmond as IPP leader after the latter's passing in March 1918, was not favourable towards the idea and doubted that Sinn Féin would grant the IPP such respect.[23]

But how did O'Leary's idea differ from the legislation Redmond had proudly defended between 1912 and 1914? O'Leary's letter envisaged a settlement for Irish self-government along the lines of the other major British settlements such as South Africa, Australia and New Zealand. The term 'dominion home rule' was ill-defined but, notwithstanding some earlier comparisons between home rule and dominion status, this new term represented a vague shift from the previous demand.[24] Sinn Féin's Arthur Griffith had previously propounded a dual-monarchy model as a settlement to the Irish question and, in 1918, the party also used the term 'dominion home rule' in its newspaper, *Nationality*, which noted that it was 'very close to real independence'.[25]

Despite its use by Lloyd George in the House of Commons and in subsequent scholarship, the phrase 'dominion home rule' had little actual basis in law.[26] As Thomas Mohr has explained, 'the Irish Parliamentary Party were happy to make analogies between Ireland and the dominions when making fiery speeches before their own electorate but they recognised, once they were in quieter surroundings, that Irish home rule would stop well short of dominion status in key areas such as trade, taxation, defence and autonomy from the parliament at Westminster'.[27] In fact, Mohr has argued that home rule was in some ways 'a child of dominion status', as the British used the dominion model as a basis for further settlements, and allusions to countries like Canada were made during debate.[28] It was this relationship between the two concepts that led to the 'hybrid term' dominion home rule. By 1918, dominion status was quite different from its conception in the pre-war era. While it may not have provided a clear path to greater autonomy in 1912, after the Imperial War Conference of 1917, dominions were now to be recognised as 'autonomous nations of an Imperial Commonwealth'.[29] Nevertheless, home rule was never coterminous with dominion status as Ireland was always to remain part of the UK while dominion status would represent autonomy within the empire.

The political landscape in Ireland changed dramatically in any case with the post-war general election. Sinn Féin swept the Irish Party aside, having declared that it would eschew attendance at the Westminster parliament and instead appeal to the Paris Peace Conference.[30] Although Sinn Féin received no hearing at the conference, it continued to dominate the political scene. As violence broke out in the country, the old Irish

Party and its activists were increasingly marginalised. The party's branch organisation, the United Irish League (UIL) and its Catholic fraternal support body, the Ancient Order of Hibernians (AOH), were both beleaguered by apathy and defections.

Although some retained loyalty to the old home rule message, they remained mostly silent observers as the War of Independence (1919–21) unfolded. IPP leader John Dillon, who had lost his parliamentary seat in 1918, offered little encouragement to grassroots workers who sought to maintain organisation. 'Old Nationalists' maintained a presence at the local elections in 1920 as urban areas returned 238 'Nationalist' councillors among the 1,806 elected nationwide in contests fought on an older, more restrictive franchise rather than that used in 1918, while the advent of proportional representation also favoured minority candidates.[31] Such an outcome highlighted an extant constituency of Irish Party opinion; yet, it was an opinion without a party by this point. In county council elections in June, Sinn Féin candidates were returned unanimously in many areas and even made inroads into Ulster where 'old Nationalist' support was sustained by the AOH.[32]

Instead, some former Irish Party members pursued other constitutional options. Stephen Gwynn had moved towards acceptance that integrating unwilling northern unionists into any home rule settlement was impossible.[33] He formed the Centre Party in January 1919; this advocated federal self-government with a parliament for national affairs and four assemblies, one for each of the provinces – designed to smooth over the 'Ulster problem' by taking away unionist fears of southern or Catholic domination. Members included former IPP MP Thomas Grattan Esmonde, but also Sir Hubert Gough, who had been at the heart of the 'Curragh Incident'.[34] Gwynn's party merged with Horace Plunkett's Irish Dominion League (IDL), launched in June. This advocated dominion status for Ireland and also included former Parnellite MP Henry Harrison. However, these movements failed to win popular support in an era of increasing violence.[35]

Their ideas also held little attraction for the last Irish Party leader John Dillon or other former Home Rulers who remained either aloof from politics or loyal to the older, if then inactive, party.[36] The 1920 Government of Ireland Act, partitioning the country, provided for separate parliaments in Belfast and Dublin and gave largely the same autonomy as the 1914 Home Rule Act. In addition to reserved powers over agriculture, education, pensions and health insurance for one year, neither parliament was granted much autonomy over taxation or customs and excise.[37] Only in the event of unity could both parliaments combine to attain full control of customs and excise. As Alvin Jackson has observed, in that case the only legal obstacles to dominion status would be defence.[38]

At this point, Plunkett and Harrison, and many other moderates in the IDL, rejected the Government of Ireland Act on the grounds of partition.[39] Nonetheless, Plunkett's efforts to try to get a dominion bill through the House of Commons were regarded as practically impossible by Dillon and suffered from an obvious lack of Sinn Féin support and British reluctance to attach too much significance to an initiative which did not command serious support in Ireland.[40] Elections were held in May 1921 under the Government of Ireland Act, but while Nationalists of the Irish Party school contested the Northern elections, Irish Party figures withdrew from any contest for the southern parliament.[41] Sinn Féin was therefore unopposed in all constituencies bar one in southern Ireland; Sinn Féin candidates returned in these elections made up the Second Dáil, which would later debate the Treaty.

Announcing that the Irish Party would not contest the election in the south, John Dillon had characterised the difference between the Irish Party and the newer party thus:

> We, the Nationalists, believe that the age-long quarrel between the British Government and the Irish Nation can best be settled on terms of compromise, without the establishment of an Irish Republic, and by peaceful means. The republicans hold that it can only be settled by war between the two nations, by driving the British forces forcibly out of Ireland, and by the setting up of an Irish Republic totally separated from Great Britain.[42]

Of course, the terms of the invitation to negotiate what would become the Anglo-Irish Treaty later that year aimed at 'ascertaining how the association of Ireland with the community of nations known as the British Empire may be best reconciled with Irish national aspirations'.[43] By Dillon's description, such negotiations could never meet Sinn Féin's demands. However, by the same measure, the Treaty settlement as a compromise between the Irish and British without the establishment of a republic would seem to have constituted a settlement which would satisfy what Dillon interpreted as the old nationalist stance, even if it had taken violence to achieve it.

'Home Rule' and the Treaty Debates

It has been argued that, in contrast to 1912 or 1914, dominion status was 'an ideal compromise' in the Irish case in 1921 because dominion status had evolved significantly in the intervening time – encompassing some form of international presence 'with the possibility of a pathway to greater sovereignty'.[44] Nonetheless, the evolutions in imperial law which took place over the previous decade did not prevent ambiguity, debate and insult about both home rule and the nature of settlement offered by the Treaty in December 1921. As outlined in Table 3.1, the term 'home rule' appears fifty-seven times in the debates – certainly fewer than the occurrences of terms such as 'republic' and 'treaty' referred to elsewhere in this collection (though more than the thirty-five references to 'unionists'). In the debates, the pro-Treaty side remained insistent that the Treaty was not simply another measure of home rule, pointing out correctly that it exceeded the powers granted in any previous home rule legislation.

Table 3.1. References to Home Rule in the Treaty Debates

Term	Appearances in Treaty debates
Home Rule	57
Redmond	23
Parnell	23
Irish Parliamentary Party	5
Irish Party	2
Devlin	3

Source: *Oireachtas debates*. Terms were searched for using the oireachtas.ie search function for the period 14 December 1921–7 January 1922. Search function available at: http://oireachtasdebates.oireachtas.ie/debates%20authoring/debateswebpack.nsf/combinedsearch?readform

Opponents of the Treaty, by contrast, sought to associate the proposed settlement with the very notion which had been washed out with the Irish Party in 1918 – home rule. Philosophically, it was clear that for some anti-Treatyites, the Treaty was equivalent to the ambiguous notion of 'dominion home rule'. Neither side differentiated between the terms with any explicit reference to evolution in imperial law; pro-Treatyites claimed the settlement exceeded any home rule measure because the Irish had negotiated with the British on equal terms and signed a treaty rather than accept an act of parliament. As has been pointed out, some opponents recognised the practical rather than theoretical nature of dominion rights and felt the Treaty did not equate to full dominion status because Ireland, unlike, for example, Canada, was so close geographically to Britain.[45] However, for many speakers on the opposing side, the Treaty was equivalent to home rule or similar legislation simply because it did not provide for a republic – it was a compromise and, as Liam Mellows argued, it was consequently a betrayal of the proclamation of Easter week.[46]

References to 'home rule' in the debates were thus generally negative, whether the allusions were to the 1912 Home Rule Bill, 'colonial home rule' or 'dominion home rule'. For obvious reasons, no one debating the Treaty was going to propose dominion home rule or declare themselves in favour of anything approaching that description. As Jason Knirck has observed, 'neither pro-Treatyites nor anti-Treatyites dared stray too far from the Sinn Féin political legacy and the credibility it bestowed.'[47] In line with the tendency of the debates to focus on constitutional status rather than the issue of partition, 'home rule' appeared far more frequently than 'Devlin' or allusions to the Irish Party's previous attempts to secure self-government with unity.[48] During the private session on 16 December, the ceann comhairle (speaker), Eoin MacNeill, declared: 'I am an Irish Republican now and I am going to remain one. So are we all. Isn't that so? (applause). Yes, and there are no Dominion Home Rulers here, not one, and there is not going to be one (No), no matter what any person reads out of it. Isn't that unanimous? (applause). Very well then, aren't we wasting our time with a lot of nonsense?'[49]

The following day, Liam Mellows reminded MacNeill of his words: 'the Speaker of the House addressing us yesterday asked us were not we all republicans, and everybody said yes. I just wish to show what a great deal of harm may be done in thinking. He then asked were any of us Dominion Home Rulers, and everybody said no.'[50] Piaras Béaslaí supported MacNeill at this point, finding fault in the debate as being 'in the spirit of a discussion at the Home Rule Bill. For God's sake will we get a grip of realities? This is a Treaty now at the cannons' mouth in guerrilla warfare from a power against whom we could never expect a military decision in our favour.'[51]

De Valera himself, explaining his concept of external association (which proposed an Irish republic associated with the empire for external purposes such as defence while remaining essentially independent on internal affairs; the British monarch would be head of the 'associated states' including Ireland), argued that the British entered the Treaty negotiations with the goal of granting dominion home rule.[52] Other anti-Treaty speakers openly described the Treaty in terms of dominion home rule, including Joseph MacDonagh, Séamus Robinson, Dr Ada English and Mary MacSwiney – 'the biggest Home Rule Bill we have ever been offered' in the words of Kathleen Clarke.[53] For Constance Markievicz, the settlement was a 'home rule bill covered over with the sugar of a Treaty'.[54] Seán Etchingham lamented any suggestion that those who had given their lives since 1916 had died for 'colonial home rule'.[55] Margaret Pearse took umbrage at the suggestion that her son would have endorsed the Treaty: 'Now another thing has been said about Pádraig Pearse: that he would accept a Home Rule Bill such as this. Well he would not.'[56] Pearse then related an encounter with her son after coming off a tram in Dublin in 1915 or 1916 to support her point. Patrick Pearse had, however, given cautious support to the third home rule bill at a rally in Dublin on 31 March 1912, though he famously threatened 'red war' in Ireland if the British government did not honour its commitment.[57]

These arguments remained anathema to those on the pro-Treaty side, who pointed to the strength of the Treaty over and above the measures broadly known as 'home rule'. In the words of Michael Hayes, the Treaty was 'not a Home Rule Bill, but an international instrument, not granting us rights but acknowledging rights that have long been questioned and are now admitted in face of the world by England'.[58] Others like W.T. Cosgrave insisted that the Treaty offered more than Parnell or Redmond ever attained. MacNeill argued that the Treaty needed to be interpreted as setting up a constitution – in his words, 'if you regard either of those documents [referring to previous home rule measures] as a document creating a constitution for Ireland the sooner we all go on a pilgrimage to John Redmond's grave the better, because why he and his followers fell was because they admitted the right of the British Government to fix a constitution in this country, or the right of the British Government conjointly with Irishmen to devise and create a constitution for this country.'[59]

Irish Party Politicians and the Treaty Debates

De Valera's studied attempt in 1946 to emphasise praise for the Home Rule movement in the era of Parnell and Davitt over the latter-day Irish Party led by John Redmond echoed the rhetoric of Sinn Féin during the 1918 general election campaign which had maintained esteem for Parnell while lambasting the party which had, it argued, strayed from his message.[60] Accordingly, in the Treaty debates, references to Parnell, mentioned in Table 3.1, were generally more positive than allusions to Redmond, Devlin or the Irish Party. Kevin O'Higgins defended the oath of fidelity to the Crown by pointing to oaths taken by Gaelic chieftains and to Parnell who still maintained that no man had 'a right to set bounds to the march of a nation'. To applause, O'Higgins declared that 'we who stand for this Treaty stand for it in the full truth of Parnell's dictum'.[61] However, while former Home Rule leaders were, of course, not the only historical figures quoted for rhetorical or tactical reasons in the debates, on 19 December de Valera used Parnell to criticise the Treaty, arguing that its endorsement was indeed setting that boundary to the progress of the nation.[62] Erskine Childers took up the same point when opposing the Treaty, declaring that 'Parnell was right'.[63] However, the divisive schism which followed Parnell's downfall also held currency. J.J. Walsh, Seán T. O'Kelly and others wanted to ensure the country did not go back to the Parnellite split. Addressing support for the Treaty as a matter of expediency, Seán MacEntee reminded the Dáil that Parnell was overthrown as a matter of expediency and it was similarly on the grounds of expediency that people supported Redmond and his war strategy.

The occurrences of the term 'Irish Party' in the Treaty debates are passing references.[64] For Liam Mellows, who was utterly opposed to the Treaty, which he called a 'surrender', those supporting it were like the IPP and other compromising parties which may do good work for a time, but ultimately fall away. According to Mellows, every argument used for the Treaty had been made previously for the IPP.[65] Joseph MacDonagh cast doubt on the value of the Treaty on the grounds of practicality, contrasting the perceptions of Redmond as a practical man and Pearse as a visionary. Referencing Redmond, he lamented the return of ideas 'to give way, compromise, climb down, abandon principle'.[66] The same deputy scoffed at the assurances of Griffith and Seán Milroy on partition, likening them to those previously offered by Joe Devlin.[67]

As seen in Table 3.2 below, some TDs did have some form of home rule lineage. However, many of these links were tenuous or came with a significant health warning. Laurence Ginnell had been a Nationalist MP for many years, but he had always remained a maverick MP with a long history of agrarian radicalism and was far from the Redmondite line.[68] Ginnell opposed the Treaty but missed the debates due to his absence in South America. The only other TD with any vague home rule link to oppose the Treaty was George Noble, Count Plunkett, but his connection went back to the Parnellite faction of the IPP in the 1890s and Plunkett was, of course, the father of a 1916 leader and the conqueror of the Irish

Table 3.2. TDs in the Second Dáil with Home Rule Links

James Dolan	Brother of former Nationalist MP who defected and stood for Sinn Féin in 1908	Pro-Treaty
Laurence Ginnell	Former Nationalist MP	Anti-Treaty
Peter Hughes	Former Nationalist councillor who defected to Sinn Féin	Pro-Treaty
Joseph McGuinness	Veteran of Easter week 1916. His brother had been an election agent for a Nationalist MP before defecting to Sinn Féin in 1917	Pro-Treaty
Kevin O'Higgins	Nephew-in-law of Nationalist MP	Pro-Treaty
Count Plunkett	Former Parnellite candidate	Anti-Treaty

Party in the 1917 North Roscommon by-election. According to the count, the Treaty settlement was 'not reconcilable with the conscience of the Irish people'.[69] The other TDs with any connections to the Irish Party all supported the Treaty. However, while James Dolan's brother, Charles, had been an Irish Party MP, he had defected to Sinn Féin at an early stage in 1907; Peter Hughes, who had been a Nationalist councillor in County Louth, severed connections with the party in 1916. Joseph McGuinness, regardless of his brother Francis's early association with Longford Home Ruler J.P. Farrell, had fought in the Four Courts during the Easter Rising and later won a famous victory for Sinn Féin in the 1917 South Longford by-election.[70] McGuinness told the Dáil that he backed the Treaty for the good in it while Dolan did likewise, declaring there was no alternative and that it could be used to create the 'ideal' Gaelic state.[71]

Perhaps the most interesting of these home rule links, therefore, was Kevin O'Higgins. Although he has been categorised as belonging to the 'Roman Catholic establishment in waiting', O'Higgins denied the suggestion of Seán MacEntee during the debates that he was a relative of the former MP Tim Healy (objecting that he was 'not alive when Mr. Healy married my aunt').[72] O'Higgins's defence of the Treaty was pragmatic, saying he 'hardly hope[d] that within the terms of this Treaty there lies the fulfilment of Ireland's destiny'.[73] In doing so, however, he also made several allusions to the parliamentary movement. He did not want to make 'a stronger advocacy of the Treaty than I feel. I will not call it, as Mr Devlin called the Home Rule Act of 1914, a Magna Charta of liberty. I do not hail it, as the late Mr Redmond hailed it, as a full, complete, and final settlement of Ireland's claim. I will not say, as Mr Dillon said, that it would be treacherous and dishonourable to look for more'.[74]

However, O'Higgins maintained that the Treaty 'represents such a broad measure of liberty for the Irish people and it acknowledges such a large proportion of its rights, you are not entitled to reject it without being able to show them you have a reasonable prospect of achieving more'.[75] O'Higgins acknowledged defects in the Treaty, particularly the threat of force over the Free State entering the Commonwealth, yet he further added that if Irish people did go into the empire, they did so with their 'heads up'.[76] He also articulated an early desire to represent all aspects of Irish society, including former Home Rulers:

I would impress on members that they sit and act here to-day as the representatives of all our people and not merely as the representatives of a particular political party within the nation (hear, hear). I acknowledge as great a responsibility to the 6,000 people who voted against me in 1918 as to the 13,000 who voted for me (hear, hear). The lives and properties of the former are as much at stake on the vote I give as the lives and properties of the latter. I cannot simply regard myself as the nominee of a particular political party when an issue as grave as this is at stake.[77]

Despite O'Higgins's relation to the prominently home rule Sullivan family: he was the grandson of IPP MP T.D. Sullivan (and his aforementioned connection to Healy), his adolescent poetry had mocked John Redmond and private correspondence in 1918 revealed that while 'not a doctrinaire republican', he subscribed fully to 'the doctrine of Sinn Féin'.[78] Nevertheless, his allusion to the 1918 election, which drew barbs from opponents in the Dáil, was the clearest reference to the views of Irish Party supporters and anticipated the requirement for Irish Party and Sinn Féin supporters alike to accommodate themselves to the Treaty settlement.[79]

The Reaction of Irish Party Members and Followers

So what of those who had once led and supported the Irish Party itself? Irish Party veterans did not take part in the Treaty debates and many politicians, so prominent up to 1918, were mere observers during the months of December and January 1921–2. The First Dáil had been convened by Sinn Féin members who had been successful at the 1918 election and, as has been noted, the Second Dáil was exclusively Sinn Féin in character. Six 'Nationalist' members were returned for the Northern Irish parliament established under the Government of Ireland Act, but along with their Sinn Féin colleagues, they did not attend parliament.[80] The Irish Party had been essentially allowed to die outside Ulster by Dillon and other Irish Party leaders as the UIL and AOH received little encouragement. This was partially due to Dillon's ill health in early 1919. However, as violence spread during the War of Independence, there was a clear desire to allow Sinn Féin to have its chance and a desire not to be associated with support for the Crown forces.

The result of the party's defeat and this inaction meant that the remnants of the old Home Rule movement were completely sidelined by the time of the truce in July 1921.[81] The remaining Home Rule MPs at Westminster were an enfeebled grouping in parliament. The party's Liverpool MP T.P. O'Connor maintained contact with his old confidante Dillon, but he was insistent that O'Connor, Devlin and other Irish Party individuals should not contribute lest they be blamed for British and Sinn Féin failings. The once famed unity of the party no longer applied and Dillon was rarely impressed by the behaviour of MPs such as Edward Kelly and Jeremiah MacVeagh, who did not act in consort with O'Connor and Devlin in the House of Commons.[82] Devlin interested himself in issues affecting Ulster in debates; however, the West Belfast MP announced himself absent from the first stage of the House of Commons debate on the Treaty in December, recognising that the real decision would come in Dublin.[83] Four of the seven Irish Party representatives (Kelly, MacVeagh, O'Connor and John Redmond's son, Captain William Redmond) voted for the measure while former Unionist leader, Sir Edward Carson, condemned the Treaty bitterly in the House of Lords.[84]

The correspondence between Dillon and O'Connor as the Treaty was signed and later debated shows that both men were broadly supportive of the settlement. On 30 December, O'Connor wrote that he could not 'believe Dev's stupidity' in opposing it. However, as O'Connor had no motivation to speak out at that point, he decided against sending any pro-Treaty messages from the United States to the *Freeman's Journal* as 'any indication of the support of the Treaty by me or indeed by any of our party would possibly only harden some of its opponents to stronger opposition'.[85] Dillon had a strong dislike for de Valera as he observed a developing division which he felt would be 'quite as ferocious as the Parnellite split'.[86] Dillon feared the minority supporting the Treaty and did not agree with O'Connor's optimism at the end of British rule but shared O'Connor's feelings that they should not get involved: 'we should for the present stand absolutely aloof and take no … responsibility for this Treaty'.[87] Dillon added that the Treaty was a 'very good settlement' and, if handled properly, could provide the basis for a 'united and free Ireland'.[88]

O'Connor broke from Dillon's stance and voted for the Treaty, apparently on advice from friends in Ireland and a desire to avoid factionalism. He worried that this might upset Dillon, but the party's last leader privately agreed with O'Connor and had merely felt they could gain no credit from endorsement. By late January 1922, Dillon felt the UIL now belonged to a 'closed chapter' in history and wrote: 'my advice to all who contact me is to support the new Government – and do all in them to give it a fair chance to restore order and show what policy it proposes to carry out'.[89] After the Dáil had ratified the Treaty, Nationalist MPs at Westminster (including Devlin) subsequently voted for the Treaty and opposed amendments made against the settlement at the second and third stages of the Irish Free State (Agreement) Bill.[90] William Redmond gave a conciliatory speech on 8 March which expressed the view that 'properly accepted and properly worked', the Treaty could bring 'contented self-government'.[91]

The Irish Party's parliamentary opponents, on the other hand, had been instinctively better disposed to Sinn Féin since 1918. William O'Brien, and his old ally Tim Healy, in particular, were therefore less marginalised than Dillon and others.[92] Healy maintained contact with both sides from July 1921 up to the signing of the Treaty. Although he was arguably closer to the *Daily Express* owner Max Aitken, Lord Beaverbrook, than to anyone on the Irish side, he met with both sides in London during the Treaty negotiations.[93] Healy was subsequently a supporter of the settlement, but O'Brien grew to dislike the Treaty on the grounds that it entrenched partition and the former All-for-Ireland League leader became more sympathetic to de Valera and later Fianna Fáil in the Free State period.

Nevertheless, the sentiments of Dillon and O'Connor seem to have largely chimed with most remaining grassroots Home Rulers. The Cork County Board of the AOH looked to become more a social than a political organisation but opted to support Griffith's government.[94] Local newspapers formerly loyal to the Irish Party also backed the Treaty. A return to peace and constitutionalism proved attractive to individuals like T.F. McGahon of the *Dundalk Democrat* or John Hayden of the *Westmeath Examiner*, while even the Devlinite *Irish News* in Belfast gave the settlement a 'cautious welcome' in December 1921 ahead of the establishment of the Boundary Commission to rule on the border.[95] For some of the new moderate nationalist organisations like the IDL, the Treaty settlement granted self-government broadly on the lines they had wished.[96]

Conclusion: Supporting the Free State

In the Irish Free State, many old Home Rulers thus joined the ranks of
Treaty supporters from 1922. John M. Regan encompassed Home Rulers
who made such a transition in the 1920s within his 'counter-revolution'
thesis while Ciara Meehan's history of Cumann na nGaedheal characterised
it as taking up the 'tradition of constitutionalism' from the IPP.[97] However,
it should be noted that many did not want to renounce an Irish Party
identity. 'Old Nationalism' remained a political force in Northern Ireland
and, further south, the journey to accepting a pro-Treatyite label was a
circuitous and often difficult one for many former Home Rulers.[98] Old
Irish Party members and supporters were mere observers as the Treaty
and the Free State were brought to fruition; as Eoin MacNeill declared,
home rule was 'dead' by 1921. The Irish Free State was to be a dominion
and part of the Commonwealth rather than remaining within the United
Kingdom. The language of pro-Treatyites was understandably different
from that used by Irish Party members to defend previous legislation. As
Jason Knirck has argued, pro-Treaty Sinn Féin displayed little enthusiasm
for the empire as it had to distinguish its arguments from Redmond's
'imperial rhetoric' while still 'refuting republican arguments'.[99] Not all pre-
war Irish Party supporters had been as imperially minded as Redmond
and there was an evolution too in the demands of even some loyal party
followers during the First World War.[100]

Support for the Treaty may have seemed a logical step for remaining
Irish Party followers. Nonetheless, for the most part, the perspective of
former Home Rulers on the Treaty debates can be viewed simply as an
appreciation of the coming of self-government and a chance to end the
violence which had frightened and bewildered many supporters of the
once mighty but dispossessed party. All bar the most radical elements of
the old parliamentary movement were content to accept a deal. Many of
them, especially the more recalcitrant ones, were Treaty supporters, but
would be slow to endorse the Cumann na nGaedheal party subsequently
founded by pro-Treaty supporters. William Redmond won a Dáil seat
as an Independent in 1923, but by then he claimed that he was not 'in
ecstasies' about the Treaty and he later founded a new party (the Irish
National League) aimed at attracting old Irish Party followers in 1926
before eventually joining Cumann na nGaedheal in 1931.[101] Even the

retired John Dillon lost his admiration for the pro-Treatyites after the deaths of Collins and Griffith and he became a bitter critic of the nascent government over partition and other terms of the Treaty settlement.[102] His son James, on the other hand, was initially sceptical about the Treaty, but would later enter the Dáil and eventually become a leader of Fine Gael.[103] Such instances highlight the degree of fluidity in political identity in post-independence Ireland. However, the difficulties in reconciling some former Home Rulers to a regime led by individuals who had displaced the Irish Party, which introduced violence and pushed the old parliamentarians from the forefront of nationalist politics, were foreshadowed by the few references to the party in the Treaty debates. As Kevin O'Higgins alluded to in the Dáil, the pro-Treaty majority would be built on more than just followers of Collins or even pro-Treaty Sinn Féin; this variety of opinion would contribute to difficulties faced by the new government and provide electoral challenges for Cumann na nGaedheal as it sought to defend and consolidate the Treaty settlement throughout the 1920s.[104]

Notes

1   *Irish Press*, 10 June 1946.

2   David Fitzpatrick, *Politics and Irish life: provincial experiences of war and revolution* (London, 1977); Martin O'Donoghue, 'The legacy of the Irish Parliamentary Party in independent Ireland, 1922–49' (Ph.D. thesis, National University of Ireland, Galway, 2016).

3   This figure includes candidates who stood as 'Independent Nationalists' but excludes the two university constituencies. Michael Laffan put the IPP's vote count at 220,226 (idem, *The resurrection of Ireland: the Sinn Féin party, 1916–1923* (Cambridge, 1999), p. 166).

4   James McConnel, *The Irish Parliamentary Party and the third home rule crisis* (Dublin, 2013); Conor Mulvagh, *The Irish Parliamentary Party at Westminster, 1900–18* (Manchester, 2016); Michael Wheatley, *Nationalism and the Irish Party: provincial Ireland, 1910–1916* (Oxford, 2005).

5   Philip Bull, 'Butt, Isaac' in James McGuire and James Quinn (eds), *Dictionary of Irish Biography* (Cambridge, 2009) (http://dib.cambridge.org/viewReadPage.do?articleId=a1311) (12 Jan. 2018).

6   Colin Reid, '"An experiment in constructive unionism": Isaac Butt, home rule and federalist political thought during the 1870s' in *English Historical Review*, cxxix, no. 537 (2014), pp. 332–61.

7   Alan J. Ward, *The Irish constitutional tradition: responsible government and modern Ireland, 1782–1992* (Dublin, 1994), pp. 63–4.

8   While Ireland would have its own 164-member House of Commons, the lord lieutenant would nominate a 40-member upper house although this was amended in committee before the 1914 Act. The 1886 legislation had proposed a unicameral model with 'two orders' (ibid., pp. 67–9).

9   Daithí Ó Corráin, '"Resigned to take the bill with its defects": the Catholic Church and the third home rule bill' in Gabriel Doherty (ed.), *The home rule crisis 1912–14* (Cork, 2014), pp. 199–200; Dermot Meleady, *John Redmond: the national leader* (Dublin, 2014), p. 213.

10   Ward, *Irish constitutional tradition*, p. 69; Alvin Jackson, *Home rule: a history* (London, 2003), pp. 109–11.

11   Wheatley, *Nationalism and the Irish Party*.

12   Ronan Fanning, *Fatal path: British government and Irish revolution, 1910–1922* (London, 2013), pp. 132–5.

13   These included the authority to declare martial law and powers under the Defence of the Realm Act, 1914 (John Redmond to John Dillon, 2 July 1916 (Trinity College Dublin Library (TCDL), John Dillon Papers, 6749/633)).

14   Eamon Phoenix, *Northern nationalism: nationalist politics, partition and the Catholic minority in Northern Ireland, 1890–1940* (Belfast, 1994), pp. 21–35; Meleady, *John Redmond*, pp. 382–4.

15   Stephen Gwynn, *John Redmond's last years* (London, 1919), p. 302.

16   William O'Brien to Reverend James Clancy, 29 June 1916 (National Library of Ireland, William O'Brien Papers, MS 8506). For a full account of the convention, see R.B. McDowell, *The Irish Convention* (London, 1970).

17   Colin Reid, *The lost Ireland of Stephen Gwynn: Irish constitutional nationalism and cultural politics, 1864–1950* (Manchester, 2011), p. 158.

18   O'Leary later worked for the neo-Redmondite party, the Irish National League (1926–31), led by former Irish Party MPs Thomas O'Donnell and Captain William Redmond (O'Donoghue, 'The legacy of the Irish Parliamentary Party', pp. 179, 184–5). On O'Leary's relationship with the IPP leadership, see Laffan, *Resurrection of Ireland*, pp. 73–4.

19   Daniel O'Leary to Matthew Keating, 18 July 1917; O'Leary to Redmond, 14 July 1917 (TCDL, John Dillon Papers, 6749/657).

20   O'Leary to Redmond, 14 July 1917.

21   Ibid.

22   Maurice Walsh, *Bitter freedom: Ireland in a revolutionary world 1918–23* (London, 2013), p. 36; *Freeman's Journal*, 11 Nov. 1918.

23   F.S.L. Lyons, *John Dillon: a biography* (London, 1968), pp. 444–55; John Borgonovo, *The dynamics of war and revolution: Cork city 1916–1918* (Cork, 2013), pp. 224–5; J.J. Horgan, 'The world policy of President Wilson' in *Studies: An Irish Quarterly Review*, vii, no. 28 (1918), pp. 553–63.

24   Erskine Childers, 'Law and fact in Canada', 29 Nov. 1921 (University College
      Dublin Archives (UCDA), Éamon de Valera Papers, P150/1555), cited in Thomas
      Mohr, 'The Irish question and the evolution of British imperial law, 1916–1922',
      University College Dublin Working Papers in Law, Criminology & Socio-Legal
      Studies, research paper no. 12 (2016), p. 25.
25   *Nationality*, 7 Dec. 1918. On Griffith and dual-monarchy, see Arthur Griffith, *The
      resurrection of Hungary: a parallel for Ireland* (Dublin, 2003).
26   *Hansard 5 (Commons)*, cxlix, 31 (14 Dec. 1921); Ivan Gibbons, 'The Anglo-Irish
      Treaty 1921: the response of the British parliamentary Labour Party and Labour
      press' in *Labour History Review*, lxxvi, no. 1 (2011), p. 8.
27   Mohr, 'Irish question', pp. 3–4.
28   Ibid., p. 8. Gladstone used elements of the Canadian colonial constitution in
      drafting home rule legislation (Ward, *Irish constitutional tradition*, pp. 63–9).
29   Mohr, 'Irish question'; the dominions increased their claims to autonomy as the
      war progressed and secured separate representations at the Paris Peace Conference.
30   Laffan, *Resurrection of Ireland*, pp. 250–1.
31   Ibid., p. 327.
32   For complete figures in all four provinces, see *Freeman's Journal*, 12 June 1920.
33   Colin Reid, 'Stephen Gwynn and the failure of constitutionalism in Ireland, 1919–
      21' in *Historical Journal*, liii, no. 3 (2010), p. 724.
34   On 21 March 1914, when given the option of taking action against Ulster unionist
      resistance or accepting dismissal, many British army officers chose the latter course
      (Meleady, *John Redmond*, p. 268).
35   Reid, 'Gwynn and the failure of constitutionalism', p. 729; Senia Pašeta, 'Ireland's
      last home rule generation' in John M. Regan and Mike Cronin (eds), *Ireland: the
      politics of independence, 1922–49* (Basingstoke, 2000), p. 21.
36   See Dillon's letter, *Hibernian Journal*, Apr. 1920, p. 201.
37   Government of Ireland Act, 1920 (http://www.legislation.gov.uk/ukpga/1920/67/
      pdfs/ukpga_19200067_en.pdf) (4 Feb. 2017).
38   Jackson, *Home rule*, pp. 196–9.
39   Reid, *Lost Ireland*, pp. 181–5.
40   Pašeta, 'Ireland's last home rule generation', p. 25; Dillon's notes on Irish politics,
      30 Apr., 18 May 1921 (TCDL, John Dillon Papers, 6582).
41   Laffan, *Resurrection of Ireland*, p. 339.
42   *Freeman's Journal*, 9 May 1921.
43   Alvin Jackson, *Ireland 1798–1998: war, peace and beyond* (London, 2010), p. 255.
44   Mohr, 'Irish question', p. 3.
45   Jason Knirck, 'The dominion of Ireland: the Anglo-Irish Treaty in an imperial
      context' in *Éire Ireland*, xlii, no. 1 (2007), pp. 234–8.
46   *Dáil Éireann deb.*, T, no. 11, 227–34 (4 Jan. 1922).
47   Knirck, 'Dominion of Ireland', p. 230.
48   Maureen Wall, 'Partition: the Ulster question (1916–1926)' in T.D. Williams (ed.),
      The Irish struggle, 1916–1926 (London, 1966), pp. 79–93.

49 *Dáil Éireann deb.*, T, no. 4, 195 (16 Dec. 1921).
50 Ibid., no. 5, 242 (17 Dec. 1921).
51 Ibid., 231.
52 Ibid., no. 4, 192 (16 Dec. 1921); Knirck, 'Dominion of Ireland', p. 231; Pádraig de Búrca and John F. Boyle, *Free state or republic?* (Dublin, 2015), p. xvii.
53 *Dáil Éireann deb.*, T, no. 7, 75 (20 Dec. 1921).
54 Ibid., no. 10, 181 (3 Jan. 1922).
55 Ibid., no. 7, 54 (20 Dec. 1921).
56 Ibid., no. 11, 222 (4 Jan. 1922).
57 Dorothy Macardle, *The Irish Republic* (London, 1937), p. 78.
58 *Dáil Éireann deb.*, T, no. 9, 130 (22 Dec. 1921).
59 Ibid., no. 3, 159–60 (15 Dec. 1921).
60 *Nationality*, 7 Dec. 1918.
61 *Dáil Éireann deb.*, T, no. 3, 175 (15 Dec. 1921).
62 Others included Griffith's invocation of Thomas Davis (de Búrca and Boyle, *Free state or republic,* pp. 12, 37).
63 *Dáil Éireann deb.*, T, no. 6, 41 (19 Dec. 1921).
64 See for example ibid., no. 8, 110 (21 Dec. 1921); no. 14, 299 (6 Jan. 1922).
65 Ibid., no. 11, 230–32 (4 Jan. 1922).
66 Ibid., no. 5, 208 (16 Dec. 1921).
67 Ibid., no. 7, 76–7 (20 Dec. 1921).
68 Wheatley, *Nationalism and the Irish Party*; Mulvagh, *Irish Parliamentary Party.*
69 *Dáil Éireann deb.*, T, no. 6, 28 (19 Dec. 1921).
70 L.W. White, 'Dolan, James Nicholas' in McGuire and Quinn (eds), *Dictionary of Irish Biography*; Marie Coleman, 'Hughes, Peter' in ibid.; eadem, 'McGuinness, Joseph ("Joe")' in ibid.
71 *Dáil Éireann deb.*, T, no. 10, 204 (3 Jan. 1922).
72 John M. Regan, *The Irish counter-revolution: Treatyite politics and settlement in independent Ireland* (Dublin, 1999), p. 83; *Dáil Éireann deb.*, T, no. 5, 199 (16 Dec. 1921).
73 *Dáil Éireann deb.*, T, no. 6, 47 (19 Dec. 1921).
74 Ibid., 45–6; John P. McCarthy, *Kevin O'Higgins: builder of the Irish state* (Dublin, 2006), p. 41.
75 *Dáil Éireann deb.*, T, no. 6, 45 (19 Dec. 1921).
76 Ibid.
77 Ibid., 45–6.
78 O'Higgins to Sheridan, 20 Oct. 1918; poem, 'Redmond the Superman', *c.* 1910s (UCDA, Kevin O'Higgins Papers, P197/102; P197/134).
79 Patrick Maume, *The long gestation: Irish nationalist life, 1891–1918* (Dublin, 1999), p. 215.
80 Mary Harris, *The Catholic Church and the foundation of the Northern Irish state* (Cork, 1993), pp. 170–5.
81 T.P. O'Connor to John Dillon, 17 Oct. 1921 (TCDL, John Dillon Papers, 6744/860).

82 Dillon to O'Connor, 4 Apr. 1920 (ibid., 6743/754).
83 Phoenix, *Northern nationalism*, p. 159.
84 *Hansard 5 (Commons)*, cxlix, 363 (16 Dec. 1921); *Hansard 5 (Lords)*, xlviii, 36–53 (14 Dec. 1921); xlvix, 647–9 (21 Mar. 1922); A.T.Q. Stewart, *Edward Carson* (Belfast, 1981), pp. 124–7.
85 O'Connor to Dillon, 30 Dec. 1921 (TCDL, John Dillon Papers, 6744/865).
86 Dillon to O'Connor, 5 Jan. 1922 (ibid., 6744/866).
87 Ibid.
88 Ibid.
89 Dillon to O'Connor, 27 Jan. 1922 (TCDL, John Dillon Papers, 6744/870).
90 *Hansard 5 (Commons)*, cl, 1473 (17 Feb. 1922); xli, 1408, 1433 (8 Mar. 1922).
91 *Hansard 5 (Commons)*, cli, 1408 (8 Mar. 1922).
92 Frank Callanan, *T.M. Healy* (Cork, 1996), p. 552.
93 Ibid., pp. 552–84.
94 Minutes of AOH Cork county convention, 15 Jan. 1922 (Cork City and County Archives, u389a/25).
95 Phoenix, *Northern nationalism*, p. 155.
96 Pašeta, 'Ireland's last home rule generation', p. 25; Reid, 'Gwynn and the failure of constitutionalism', pp. 181–2.
97 Regan, *Irish counter-revolution*; Ciara Meehan, *The Cosgrave party: a history of Cumann na nGaedheal, 1923–33* (Dublin, 2010), p. xvi; Mel Farrell, *Party politics in a new democracy: the Irish Free State, 1922–37* (London, 2017).
98 O'Donoghue, 'The legacy of the Irish Parliamentary Party'.
99 Knirck, 'Dominion of Ireland', p. 247.
100 Wheatley, *Nationalism and the Irish Party*; idem, 'John Redmond and federalism in 1910' in *Irish Historical Studies*, xxxii, no. 127 (2001), pp. 343–64.
101 *Irish Independent*, 18 Aug. 1923.
102 Dillon was critical of the Free State in his rare public appearances in the 1920s, perhaps most famously in his National Club speech of 9 January 1925 (Lyons, *John Dillon*, pp. 476–7).
103 Maurice Manning, *James Dillon: a biography* (Dublin, 1999), p. 33.
104 I am grateful to Conor McNamara and anonymous reviewers for their comments on earlier drafts of this chapter.

CHAPTER 3

Republican Representations of the Treaty: 'A Usurpation Pure and Simple'

John Dorney

Those voting against the Treaty in the Dáil on 7 January 1922 comprised fifty-seven TDs. From this minority, Éamon de Valera, hitherto president of the Republic, created an anti-Treaty bloc, at first named Cumann na Poblachta and later anti-Treaty Sinn Féin, splintering the unity of the Irish republican movement. On 14 March 1922, the anti-Treaty officers of the Irish Republican Army (IRA) held their own convention at the Mansion House, and they rejected not only the Treaty but also the Dáil's ratification of it, along with the authority of IRA general headquarters (GHQ), led by Richard Mulcahy and Michael Collins. Taken together, this political and military split eventually triggered the Irish Civil War, a conflict that has done much to define the politics of the Irish state ever since. The anti-Treaty or, as they termed themselves, republican opposition to the Treaty settlement has often been caricatured and misunderstood. The anti-Treaty TDs, particularly their leader Éamon de Valera, have sometimes been portrayed as self-serving and hypocritical, at other times as impractical zealots irrevocably committed to the defence of an abstract republic against concrete Irish self-government as represented in the Treaty. The anti-Treaty faction of the IRA has had an even more hostile press, derided not only as fanatics but also as a cohort of anti-democratic militarists, prepared to strangle the young Irish democracy in the womb.

This chapter will attempt to show how anti-Treaty republicans represented themselves, both in the debates on the Treaty and afterwards. It will focus on three strands of the anti-Treaty movement that coalesced in the first half of 1922: the position of the anti-Treaty elite such as Éamon de Valera, the arguments against the Treaty voiced by anti-Treaty TDs and the position of rank and file anti-Treaty republicans, both in the political movement and in the IRA. Finally, this chapter will consider the question of whether the anti-Treaty position amounted to an ideological hostility to civilian rule and democracy in Ireland.

The Treaty

The Anglo-Irish Treaty allowed for the creation of the Irish Free State, a self-governing dominion of the British Commonwealth on the territory of 'Southern Ireland' – the area delineated in the Government of Ireland Act of 1920, comprising twenty-six of Ireland's thirty-two counties. The remaining six counties would remain in the United Kingdom as an autonomous region – Northern Ireland – and would be given one year to decide if they wanted to enter the Free State. The Free State would have its own parliament, army and police force and would control its own judicial and fiscal affairs. Against that, the British retained three naval bases in the Free State, retained a veto over a still-undrafted Free State constitution and insisted that that constitution must contain an oath of fidelity to the British monarch.[1]

The Treaty was a major step forward for Irish self-determination compared to previous initiatives such as the Home Rule Act of 1914 and the Government of Ireland Act of 1920, both of which had envisaged limited self-government for an Irish parliament within the United Kingdom. The partition of Ireland, on the face of it one of the Treaty's main drawbacks for Irish nationalists, had already been implemented; first when the northeast was excluded from the 1914 Home Rule Act, and later formalised with the creation of Northern Ireland in 1920. The Treaty gave away no more ground on the unity of Ireland than had already been lost and gave the southern Irish state a level of independence unthinkable before 1914. For many republicans, however, it represented a humiliating retreat from their goal of an all-Ireland independent republic. Aside from the question of partition, there were significant material problems with the

Treaty. It placed the sovereignty of the Irish Free State under the British Crown, to be represented in Ireland by a governor general, and members of parliament would have to swear an oath of fidelity to the king as well as an oath of allegiance to the Irish constitution. British retention of three naval bases threatened to drag Ireland into any future British wars. Irish citizens would have the right to appeal to the British Supreme Court, and it was not clear in 1922 whether the Imperial parliament at Westminster could still override the rulings of the Irish parliament in Dublin. All of these factors threatened to limit the practical independence of the future Irish state.

Almost as powerful as any cold-eyed considerations of national sovereignty, however, were the symbolic factors. The whole nationalist revolution had been based on a total rejection of the right of Britain to rule Ireland. Now, anti-Treaty republicans argued that Ireland was, for the first time, voluntarily accepting the sovereignty over them of the British king, to whom members of the Dáil would have to swear an oath of fidelity.

Initial Reactions to the Treaty

Indeed, when many republicans, even those who went on to support the Treaty, first heard of its terms, their first emotion was shock and bewilderment. Ernie O'Malley, the commander of the IRA's Second Southern Division, recalled that when he heard of the Treaty's terms 'I cursed long and loud, so this was what we had fought and died for, what we had worn ourselves out for during the truce'.[2] Similarly C.S. 'Todd' Andrews, a low-ranking IRA officer in Dublin, on reading of the oath of allegiance, the ports to be retained by the British and the Irish state 'paying the pensions of the hated RIC', 'thought there must be something wrong with the newspaper report, [Michael] Collins would never have agreed to this'.[3] He felt sick 'with rage and disappointment'.[4] Máire Comerford, a leading member of the women's republican group Cumann na mBan, was having tea with fellow republican Molly Childers at her home when the news of the Treaty arrived: '[when I] heard the hateful facts, I went home and cried on my bed'.[5] 'Ireland would have to bow to the government of England and abandon the Republic', she later wrote.[6] Even Eoin O'Duffy, hitherto commander of the IRA in County Monaghan, now GHQ Director of Operations and a close ally of Collins and Richard Mulcahy, at first reacted with anger and disappointment. He was with Mulcahy in a house in the Ranelagh area of Dublin when the terms of the Treaty came out and as one eyewitness recalled, 'O'Duffy was dead against it. "The Army won't stand for this Dick", he said.[7] Mulcahy eventually calmed him down by saying 'wait until you see Collins'.[8] Collins did eventually talk O'Duffy round but outside his own personal circle, the feeling of betrayal within the republican movement was widespread among republican activists, both political and military.

Anti-Treatyites and the 'IRB Clique'

One problem anti-Treaty republicans had with the Treaty was that they considered it had been signed by the plenipotentiaries, in particular Michael Collins, behind the back of President Éamon de Valera and presented as a *fait accompli*. Liam Mellows argued in the Dáil:

> The Dáil had no chance of discussing this Treaty as it should be discussed because the ground was cut from under the feet of the Dáil with the publication of this Treaty to the world before the Dáil had a chance of discussing it. The delegates, I repeat, had no power to sign away the rights of Ireland and the Irish Republic. They had no mandate to sign away the independence of this country as this Treaty does. They had no power to agree to anything inconsistent with the existence of the Republic. Now either the Republic exists or it does not. If the Republic exists, why are we talking about stepping towards the Republic by means of this Treaty?[9]

It was alleged within anti-Treaty republicanism that Collins had used the supposedly omnipotent power of the secret society the Irish Republican Brotherhood (IRB), of which he was president, to get the Treaty passed in the Dáil. Leading anti-Treatyite Cathal Brugha alleged that up to forty TDs voted for the Treaty as result of their IRB affiliation.[10]

The IRB was the Irish wing of the 'Fenian' movement – the other being the American wing Clan na Gael – founded in 1858 with the express aim of securing an Irish republic by force if necessary. Members swore an oath to the Republic, 'virtually established', and to follow the orders of the brotherhood's Supreme Council and its president.[11] The IRB had been a mass movement back in the 1860s but, by the early twentieth century, it more closely resembled a secret, 'vanguard', revolutionary society. It had only around 1,500 members and its *modus operandi* was to infiltrate and to guide mass organisations towards the brotherhood's goals. By this means it had effectively co-opted the Irish Volunteers in 1913–14 – a militia that had initially been formed merely as a guarantor of home rule – and used it to launch the insurrection of Easter 1916.

The executions of the 1916 Rising's leaders had torn a swathe through the pre-Rising Supreme Council of the IRB, exacerbated by the death on hunger strike of the next president of the organisation, Thomas Ashe, in 1917. From then until his death in August 1922, the president of the brotherhood was Michael Collins and he, even after the Treaty, was clear that the work of the brotherhood was not finished. When drafting a new constitution for the IRB 'after a duly elected [Irish] government has been established', in 1922, Collins appeared to believe that even after the Treaty, the Supreme Council could still function in secret as a kind of shadow government, parallel to the formal, elected government. He wrote: 'while accepting the present government of the Saor Stait [Free State] the Supreme Council of the IRB is declared the sole government of the Irish Republic until full independence is achieved and a permanent Republican government is established. The authority of the Supreme Council shall be unquestioned by members.'[12] In short, the idea of parallel secret IRB structures was not an anti-Treatyite fantasy.

With the exception of Minister for Defence Cathal Brugha, all of the men on the IRA GHQ staff were members of the IRB. Moreover, those who resigned over the Treaty were generally replaced with other high-ranking IRB members such as Seán Ó Muirthile, Desmond FitzGerald and Diarmuid O'Hegarty. Even in the negotiations for the truce in 1921, one IRA officer, Liam Nugent, recalled that British representative Alfred Cope met Collins alone in rooms on Dublin's Abbey Street:

It was strange that Mick [Collins] carried on these talks on his own as both Dev [Éamon de Valera] and Cathal Brugha were available. But neither of them were members of the I.R.B., and it was the I.R.B. who decided whatever peace was to be made, and men were being executed and losing their lives during these negotiations. While peace

talks were in progress the Central Council of the I.R.B. were anxious
to get [Dáil minister and later senior anti-Treatyite] Austin Stack out
of Dublin. He was definitely opposed to any backdoor negotiations.[13]

As far as anti-Treaty republicans were concerned, their loyalty was to the
institution of the Republic as declared in 1919 and its army, and neither
to Collins personally nor the IRB Supreme Council.

There is no doubt that the IRB, with Collins at its head, had
disproportionate influence in high places within the republican
movement, in ways that often bypassed the formal structures both of the
republican Dáil and of the IRA.

Senior IRB figure Seán Ó Muirthile later admitted that 'Collins
kept the IRB Supreme Council informed of peace negotiations with the
British [and] was glad to have the approval of his IRB colleagues before
accepting the Treaty'.[14] This was a startling admission given that they had
signed the document without waiting for the approval of the republican
cabinet or its president, de Valera himself. The brotherhood was not a
monolith, however. IRB connections were not enough, as Collins had
probably hoped, to secure unity within Sinn Féin and the IRA. Indeed,
Liam Lynch, who would go on to lead the anti-Treaty IRA, was also a
member of the IRB Supreme Council. Within anti-Treaty republican
circles, however, it was widely believed that only the unseen influence of
the brotherhood could explain the abandonment of republican principles
that the Treaty represented. Many anti-Treaty republicans, as a result,
blamed 'an IRB clique' for the acceptance of the Treaty at the top of the
IRA and by extension blamed the IRB for the ensuing Civil War. There
were even allegations that Collins and his 'IRB clique' formed a kind
of military 'junta' or dictatorship. To understand why this was such a
common reaction among anti-Treatyites, it is necessary to look at both
grassroots and elite representations of the Treaty.

Grassroots Republican Reactions: The Case of County Cavan

An idea of the emotional strength behind the feelings of betrayal among
some republicans at the Treaty can be gleaned from a look at the Treaty
debates in County Cavan in late 1921 and early 1922, when the settlement's

merits were argued about across town and county council chambers, Irish Farmers' Union meetings and Sinn Féin clubs. Cavan as a county is significant for a number of reasons. For one thing, while not among the most militant of counties in terms of IRA activity, it had been among the first to be mobilised politically by the separatist movement. As early as November 1917, the Sinn Féin 'counter-state' was beginning to make its presence felt in County Cavan. The Sinn Féin clubs in Cavan were among the first to pass a motion to set up Dáil courts, to 'deny law costs to the Crown or any traffic at all avoidable in English courts'.[15] By October 1917, these were operating in the towns of Ballyconnell, Kingscourt and Swanlinbar. By the time the Dáil courts were formally instituted in early 1920, in Cavan they had largely regularised what was happening already. Cavan also was among the first counties to elect a Sinn Féin TD, in July 1918, electing Arthur Griffith for East Cavan in a by-election over a year before Sinn Féin's ultimate victory in the general election of 1918.

For another thing, Cavan was situated along the very recently installed border with Northern Ireland, a border that was left unmoved by the Treaty, and which promised both to disrupt the local economy and also to harden sectarian divisions in the area. Since Irish republicanism in modern times has come to be associated with hostility to the partition of Ireland, it might be assumed that Cavan was a focal point for anti-Treaty sentiment. All the evidence suggests, however, that County Cavan was majority pro-Treaty in sympathy in early 1922. Paul Galligan, TD for West Cavan as well as commander of the West Cavan IRA Brigade, received a host of telegrams and letters from public bodies and parish councils in Cavan in the weeks leading up to the Dáil vote on the Treaty urging him to ratify it.[16] In the election of June 1922, Arthur Griffith, the pro-Treaty candidate and president of the Dáil, won over 13,000 first preference votes out of 25,000 cast in the constituency, more than those of the other candidates combined.[17] The anti-Treatyites were a minority in the area, even more so than they were nationally, and they knew it. Examining the arguments of local anti-Treatyites, therefore, gives us an insight into republican thinking.

At the Cavan County Council meeting of 1 January 1922, in response to a motion by Mr Fitzsimons to endorse the Treaty, on the grounds that 'Whilst it does not realise all the hopes of the Irish nation it safeguards the best interests of the Gaelic nation. Also there is no alternative,' Mr Boylan, an anti-Treatyite, responded with a counter-motion: 'As Republicans we do not approve of the Treaty.'[18] Fitzsimons and several others responded with a reiteration of the pro-Treaty case, Fitzsimons stating: 'I am as convinced a Republican today as at any time over the last 4 or 5 years. The Treaty is not a final settlement. I swore an oath to the Irish Republic but have no qualms about transferring that allegiance to the Irish Free State.'[19] Similarly a pro-Treaty Sinn Féin councillor, Mr O'Reilly, declared: 'I also took an oath and have no problem with transferring that allegiance to the Free State.'[20] Boylan, however, was not to be moved: 'I don't wish to say anything. The resolution speaks for itself. We were elected as Republicans. That is all.'[21]

Boylan's obdurate insistence that the Treaty, under which members of the Free State's parliament would have to take an oath of fidelity to the British king, was a violation of the oath they had taken to uphold the Republic, was also taken up in the Treaty debates in the Dáil. For instance, Margaret Pearse (mother of the executed 1916 Rising leader Patrick Pearse) declared: 'All I can say is what our catechism taught us in my days was: it is perjury to break your oath. I consider I'd be perjuring myself in breaking the oath I had taken to Dáil Eireann. An oath to me is a most sacred vow made in the presence of Almighty God to witness the truth, and the truth alone.'[22]

At this early stage, the anti-Treatyites' arguments were often emotional; men, in some cases their friends and families, had died for the Irish Republic and they were not going to settle for anything less than its perpetuation.

The debate at Cavan Farmers' Union on 3 January 1922, for example, highlighted the point evocatively. At Cavan Town Hall, Thomas Smith, a pro-Treaty Sinn Féin member, argued that the Treaty gave 'freedom to achieve freedom', quoting Michael Collins. Michael Sheridan took up the anti-Treaty argument.[23] 'Freedom', he declared, 'was won by a sacrifice of lives. It was wrung from England ... John Redmond, Lord rest him, could have had this in 1914 if he had utilised his own forces [Heckler: 'then why didn't he?'] without Easter Week, or 1920 or 1921'.[24] 'The Treaty', Sheridan went on, 'is not the freedom of [Patrick] Pearse or [Theobald Wolfe] Tone [who talked about] 'the "blood of Irishmen to redeem the soul of Ireland"'.[25] Then came the crux of the debate. A heckler shouted: 'Are you going to shed it?'[26] Sheridan was taken aback. 'That', he responded, 'is hardly fair. My family were prepared to shed blood and did shed it, the only sacrifice of life in Cavan and I am not ashamed of it'.[27] Michael Sheridan's brother Thomas had been shot dead by the Royal Irish Constabulary (RIC) in an arms raid in 1920, one of only three IRA Volunteers to be killed in the county during the conflict.[28] The Sheridan family home was also burnt by the RIC as a reprisal. As a result, Michael Sheridan was in no mood for compromise. He resumed: 'The threat of force is not a good argument for the Treaty and anyway it is mere bluff'.[29] What he said next, however, is the most revealing insight into the anti-Treaty republicans' stance:

> England may in the future subject Ireland to the same tyranny if a Republic is proclaimed. I am not a doctrinaire Republican, strictly speaking I am not saying what form of government Ireland should have, but I implicitly believe in complete and absolute independence from England. I will never consent to the Treaty. I have been through the mill, I saw England's paid assassins put my father against a wall with a revolver against his breast and the abuse of my aged mother looking for my wounded brother. I have looked down the barrel of revolvers. We must forgive but we won't forget. We must break the last link with England.[30]

What Did 'The Republic' Mean?

While the debates in County Cavan were of strictly local significance politically, they nevertheless shed an important light on a number of concepts that were central to anti-Treaty republican thinking. One was related to the term republicanism itself. Michael Sheridan stated that he was 'not a doctrinaire Republican' but believed in 'absolute and complete independence from England'. This attitude was in evidence across the anti-Treaty movement. 'The Republic' signified total Irish independence, not an abstract political ideal. Irish republicanism was not without a historical basis in wider republican thought. The IRB declared on the eve of its failed uprising in 1867 that

> All men are born with equal rights, and in associating to protect one another and share public burdens, justice demands that such associations should rest upon a basis which maintains equality instead of destroying it. We therefore declare that, unable longer to

endure the curse of Monarchical Government, we aim at founding a Republic based on universal suffrage, which shall secure to all the intrinsic value of their labour.[31]

In 1910, moreover, *Irish Freedom*, the newspaper of the IRB, wrote that a member of the brotherhood had to be 'a disciplined soldier for Ireland' but also 'a true and staunch Republican', which meant subscribing to 'personal liberty, equality of all men in the eyes of the state and denial of rights unless they are accompanied by an acceptance of duties'.[32] In 1922, however, there was very little evidence of such rhetoric. 'The Republic' simply meant full Irish independence to most anti-Treatyites.

The second important point that Michael Sheridan highlighted in his speech to Cavan County Council was the idea that the Treaty, by stopping short of full independence, would be a betrayal of the dead. This again was a very widespread sentiment. The volunteers of the IRA, as far as anti-Treatyites were concerned, had fought the British to a standstill, their friends and comrades had sacrificed their lives for the Republic. To give it away would be a kind of sacrilege. Liam Lynch, who went on to lead the anti-Treaty IRA as chief of staff during the ensuing Civil War, wrote to the then IRA chief of staff (and pro-Treatyite) Richard Mulcahy 'What am I to do with thousands of men who sacrificed everything during the war?'[33] It would be 'too degrading and dishonourable', Lynch wrote in April 1922, after the loss of hundreds of his comrades' lives in 1919–21, 'for the Irish people to accept the Treaty and enter the British Empire even if it were only for a short period'.[34] Mary MacSwiney, sister of Terence MacSwiney, the late lord mayor of Cork who had died on hunger strike in protest against his imprisonment by the British, asked the Dáil 'in the name of the dead to unite against this Treaty and let us take the consequences'.[35]

In short, the anti-Treaty position in 1922 was based on the idea that the Treaty did not represent the full independence of Ireland, even that of the twenty-six counties of the prospective Irish Free State, and that it was a betrayal of what those republicans who had died from 1916 to 1921 had lost their lives for. The oath of fidelity to the British monarch amounted to perjury, as it contradicted the oath they had already taken to the Irish Republic.

Éamon de Valera said the oath to the British king would 'disenfranchise every honest Republican like the Test Acts against Catholics and dissenters in the past'.[36] The Test Acts were part of the Penal Laws, applying from the early eighteenth century up to 1829, whereby any man serving in public office had to recognise the king as head of his church as well as head of his state. This had the effect of excluding all but members of the established Anglican Church from public office.[37] This was the basis on which the anti-Treaty faction of the IRA rejected the authority of the Dáil to approve the Treaty. The anti-Treaty IRA executive elected in March 1922, Richard Mulcahy reported, 'contended that the Dáil support of the Treaty subverted the Republic and relieved the Army of its allegiance to the Dáil'.[38] Joseph O'Connor, head of the IRA Dublin Brigade's Third Battalion, expressed its position thus: 'I felt that it was wrong to accept any settlement with England for less than the absolute freedom of our whole country. Now that the Dáil had accepted the new position I deemed that they had exceeded their powers, and that it was my duty to continue striving until England withdrew all her forces and we had complete control of our affairs'.[39]

Elite Republican Depictions of the Treaty

The sentiments found in grassroots republicanism were also strongly in evidence among 'elite' anti-Treaty activists, that is those in leadership positions and who held elected office. The Treaty for them simply did not mean full independence and its signing and passing was, in their eyes, the result of a series of nefarious and underhanded acts by the pro-Treatyites. Republican propaganda during the Civil War summed up their arguments: 'The Treaty was a betrayal, signed behind the back of the President' and it 'makes England's King Ireland's King'.[40] While some such arguments, just as much as those of grassroots activists and fighters, were based on emotion – 'the memory of the dead' – they did contain concrete, material points. In the Treaty debates in the Dáil, for instance, Dónal Buckley of Kildare argued that because of the British retention of three naval ports with military garrisons, the British military evacuation promised under the Treaty was not genuine:

How can it be said that we have freedom if we picture to ourselves John Bull standing four square in this country of ours, with a 'crúb' [claw/hoof] of his firmly fastened in each of our principal ports? We are told that in each of these ports there will be what is called a 'care and maintenance party' – a very nice mild term. What does it really mean – this care and maintenance party? It means a British Garrison in each of these ports with the Union Jack – the symbol of oppression and treachery and slavery in this country, and all over the world, in Ireland especially – that this symbol of slavery will float over each of these strongholds, blockhouses of John Bull.[41]

This was echoed in the republican press, which argued that because of British control of the ports, 'Ireland will be dragged into every British war and burdened with Imperial war debt'.[42]

Liam Mellows dismissed arguments that the Treaty was the 'will of the people' as pro-Treaty deputies maintained. Rather, he argued the people wanted a republic and full independence but had been 'stampeded' by Lloyd George's threats of 'immediate and terrible war' into accepting the Treaty:

> The people are being stampeded: in the people's minds there is only one alternative to this Treaty and that is terrible, immediate war. During the adjournment I paid a trip to the country and I found that the people who are in favour of the Treaty are not in favour of the Treaty on its merits, but are in favour of the Treaty because they fear what is to happen if it be rejected. That is not the will of the people. That is the fear of the people. The will of the people was when the people declared for a Republic.[43]

It has become a commonplace in Irish historiography to say that the Treaty debates avoided the issue of partition in favour of arguing over how independent the southern Irish state would be. Strictly speaking, this was largely true, though some anti-Treatyites did bring it up in the Dáil debates. Seán MacEntee, a native of Belfast representing Monaghan, argued that the Treaty was a 'double betrayal', in that it surrendered the Republic and made Ulster 'England's fortress'.[44] Later, anti-Treaty propaganda reiterated that under the Treaty, 'our hitherto undivided country was partitioned' and Northern nationalists had been 'put under a ruthless tyranny'.[45]

By 1923, ending partition was the first item that many anti-Treaty candidates in the general election of that year were putting at the top of their agenda. The republican candidate for Cavan, for instance, Patrick Smith (who was in jail in Dundalk at the time) campaigned under the slogan 'No partition, no oath, no foreign king'.[46] The lack of mention of partition during the Treaty debates was not because the anti-Treatyites did not care about it but rather that the pro-Treatyites successfully managed to portray themselves, in 1922, as the leaders on the question of ending partition. Collins had always championed the Northern nationalists' cause and had also assured the Northern IRA that he had no intention of accepting partition in the long-term. In March 1922, he told Northern IRA leaders that 'although the Treaty might have been an outward expression of partition, the Government had plans whereby they would make it impossible and that partition would never be recognised even if it meant smashing the Treaty'.[47] It was the pro-Treatyites who made the greater mention of the North during the Treaty debates. Collins himself, who represented Armagh, specifically linked the Treaty with the ending of partition, while Ernest Blythe, a pro-Treaty deputy from the North, said that he 'would not be opposed to the coercion of Ulster if it were necessary'.[48] Similarly Eoin O'Duffy asked the Dáil if it knew of any better means than the Treaty to 'bring Ulster into an All-Ireland Parliament, let that means be brought forward'.[49]

De Valera

Many senior pro-Treaty figures blamed Éamon de Valera, president of the self-declared Irish Republic between 1919 and 1922, for the split over the Treaty and for the ensuing Civil War. They contended that without his political stature, anti-Treaty elements of the IRA would never have mounted an armed challenge to the Treaty settlement. However, de Valera's position was more nuanced than has usually been painted. He was not really leading the anti-Treaty militants in early 1922 but scrambling to try to regain influence over them after they had disavowed the Dáil's authority. He had assumed, during the Treaty negotiations in late 1921, that the talks with the British could not deliver a republic. What he had proposed was that 'we will have proposals brought back to us [the cabinet] that cannot satisfy everybody … when such a time comes, I will be in a position … to come forward with such proposals as we think just and right'.[50] In other words, while de Valera understood the need for compromise in December 1921, he wanted to be able to sell any deal made with the British to the republican militants as a victory rather than as a concession, with him taking the credit for the final draft. Clearly, this would have been difficult for the Treaty negotiating team to accept. They would have been responsible for the 'bad deal' and de Valera for the 'good one'; but it was nevertheless an error, committed under British pressure, for them to sign the Treaty without, as had been agreed, cabinet consent.

In early 1922, after Sinn Féin split over the Treaty, de Valera set up his own party, Cumann na Poblachta, with an office on Dublin's Suffolk Street. In February 1922, he led it back into the Dáil, though without explicitly accepting the parliament's decision on the Treaty. De Valera proposed, as an alternative to the Treaty, 'Document No. 2', a re-negotiation of the agreement with the British, inserting a face-saving (for Irish republicans) formula whereby Ireland would have 'external association' with the British Empire, and in which an Irish constitution would acknowledge membership of the empire with the British monarch at its head, but not acknowledge that monarch as the Irish head of state. This was also a compromise on the idea of an independent Irish republic, equally as unacceptable to the militants in the IRA as the Treaty itself. Moreover, in the conditions of early 1922, with British forces evacuating southern Ireland and no ready-made Irish military or police force to take their place, it was the military wing of the republican movement that was driving events; taking over barracks and effectively administering parts of the country on its own.

The key to understanding de Valera's position in the Civil War is that he was following the republican militants, attempting to win back control over them by appearing to support their position, while actually trying to lead them towards a new compromise. De Valera's gamble, that he would win back leadership of the anti-Treatyite movement by militant rhetoric and then lead it back towards compromise, failed disastrously, however. Instead, during the Civil War, he found himself beholden to anti-Treaty military leaders, in particular IRA chief of staff, Liam Lynch, whose policy was quite simple: 'we are finished with a policy of compromise and negotiation unless based on recognition of the Republic ... We have no intention of setting up a government but await such time as An Dáil will carry on as Government of the Republic ... In the meantime, no other Government will be allowed to function.'[51] In other words, it was the Republic or nothing.

Democracy, Dictators and Civil War

The debate over the Treaty itself was soon overtaken by the bitter and ultimately bloody schism that the Treaty caused, and the ten-month period of Civil War. This, in many ways, contributed more to the ultimate trajectory of Irish politics than did the Treaty debate itself. For the pro-Treaty side, organised by mid-1922 into the Provisional Government with its own armed forces, the National Army, and an embryonic police force, the Civic Guard, what was at issue was the maintenance of Irish democracy. For them, the Treaty, whatever its intrinsic merits, had been approved by the Dáil and, subsequently, their party (pro-Treaty Sinn Féin) had won the majority of votes in the Free State's first election of 16 June 1922. Subsequent armed defiance by the anti-Treaty IRA of the settlement and of the Provisional Government whose duty it was to implement it, was therefore armed opposition to the democratic 'will of the people' and the government was fully justified in using force to dissolve it, starting at the Four Courts in Dublin on 28 June 1922. The anti-Treatyites, in their eyes, were aspirant military dictators.

It was a theme taken up in the press of the day; the *Freeman's Journal* in the first week of the Civil War, for example, thundered against the 'hopeless and reckless' attempt of the 'mutineers' to 'rush the Irish capital and establish a military dictatorship.'[52] Similarly, the *Irish Independent* felt that 'The Irish government was obliged to take action against the Irregulars who had defied, not British but Irish government.'[53] It was also the principal theme of Tom Garvin's 1996 book *1922: the birth of Irish democracy*, which argued that the IRA represented a militaristic 'public band' contemptuous of democracy.[54]

However, as Peter Hart argued of the anti-Treatyites, their stance was defensive, not offensive in nature: 'Theirs was a deterrent posture, not an aggressive one ... to maintain their position as a standing army and to keep the Free State at bay ... The Volunteers were ademocratic, not antidemocratic. They typically felt themselves to be above the political process, but they never sought to change it or to end it in the name of a fascist, communist or militarist alternative, or even in the name of national emergency'.[55] The distinction between ademocratic and anti-democratic is important. The anti-Treaty IRA was prepared not to abide by the Dáil's decision but not prepared to overthrow it by force. The fine distinction no doubt meant little to Collins, Griffith and their beleaguered colleagues in the Provisional Government, but it is critical to an understanding of the anti-Treatyite position in 1922. They believed they were not the aggressors in the Civil War but the aggrieved party. According to their lights, they had never defied the democratic will of the people but had been attacked without provocation on British orders.

Both Liam Lynch and Éamon de Valera had entered into agreements with Collins in May 1922, the former joining a council of four men set up to maintain unity between pro- and anti-Treaty IRA factions, making sure that the 'Republican aim shall not be prejudiced', and de Valera entering into an election pact with Collins, whereby pro- and anti-Sinn Féin factions would jointly fight the election of June 1922.[56] The 'pact' held in some areas but generally did not survive to polling day. Collins urged voters on the eve of the election to vote for the candidate of their choice. More importantly, on the morning of the election, the kernel of the compromise, that the Free State constitution would not contain an oath of fidelity to the British monarch, was collapsed when the constitution was published and did indeed contain such an oath. The pro-Treaty Sinn Féin party won the election but, while the anti-Treatyites maintained their defiant posture and a particularly militant IRA faction in the Four Courts in central Dublin declared it would 'declare war on Britain', it appears as if de Valera for one contemplated political opposition to the Treaty only.[57] He lamented that the election was

a triumph for methods of imperial pacification – outrage, murder, massacre and then threat and concession ... By threat of infamous war ... our people have voted as England wanted but their hearts and aspirations are unchanged ... England's gain is for the moment only. The men and women who have been rejected by the electorate went down with flags flying, true to their principles.[58]

He said he looked forward to the Dáil opening and expressed the opinion that it would not approve the proposed Free State constitution with its oath to the British king.[59]

In late June, however, a fatal confluence of events: the assassination of the British field marshal Henry Wilson in London, a British ultimatum to the Provisional Government to act against the 'irregulars' and the rival arrests of IRA officer Leo Henderson and National Army general J.J. O'Connell, led to the Provisional Government opening fire on the anti-Treaty IRA stronghold of the Four Courts. Anti-Treaty republicans maintained that 'war was opened at Britain's command' in spite of the pact, which allowed the Provisional Government 'to strike unexpectedly in the back'.[60] De Valera told the press: 'At the last meeting of the Dáil we had an agreement to work for internal peace [but now] at the bidding of the English it is broken and Irishmen are shooting down brother Irishmen in the face of English threat'.[61] Éamon de Valera, by 2 July, was openly calling the Provisional Government a dictatorship:

> The so-called Provisional Government is not the Government. The legitimate government is Dáil Eireann which is the government of the Republic. The Republic has not been disestablished. Since January the President and ministers of the Dáil have assumed dictatorial powers. The IRA are soldiers who took an oath of allegiance to the Republic and are acting in accordance with its explicit terms and intentions ... The soldiers of the Republic have been attacked at the instigation of English politicians. The Pact which secured peaceful elections has been torn up. The Dáil has not been allowed to meet. [This is] a military dictatorship with English guns and armoured cars. The Irish people want a Republic, they do not want an English King. Some have been induced to give the appearance of submission by the threat of war.[62]

Thus, for the anti-Treaty republicans, they were not fighting to take power but merely defending themselves and the Republic against an unprovoked attack and what they characterised as a pro-Treaty military junta.

De Valera characterised the Provisional Government as a British-installed 'coup d'etat' put in power by 'a series of unconstitutional and illegal acts prompted by the threats of the enemies of our country'.[63] The Second Dáil had never been dissolved and war had been declared on the 'soldiers of the Republic' before the Third Dáil – elected in June 1922 – ever got a chance to meet.[64] While this should be read partly as war propaganda, it was not entirely empty rhetoric. The Dáil which was elected in June 1922 had not met by the time Michael Collins made the decision to attack the Four Courts, and he never consulted it before opening hostilities with the anti-Treatyites. Moreover, in the following month he prorogued it three more times. It only finally met after his death in late August 1922. John M. Regan has argued that by his position as head of the Provisional Government and assumption also in July 1922 of the position of National Army commander-in-chief, Collins 'appeared to exert control over the civil, military and extra-constitutional powers within the Treaty regime' and 'vetoed civilian ministers' demands to have the parliament meet' in August 1922.[65] However, after Collins's death, and under severe pressure from the Labour Party, the government finally allowed the Third Dáil to meet on 9 September 1922. While no anti-Treaty TDs were willing (or able in many cases, many being in prison or liable for arrest) to attend, the Labour Party provided a 'loyal opposition' to the pro-Treaty government.

To the anti-Treatyites, the opening of the Third Dáil was, in many respects, a political setback. Before the Dáil met, they could characterise the pro-Treaty government as a de facto British imposed dictatorship – or, as de Valera put it – 'a usurpation pure and simple'.[66] Now with the Dáil in session, they had to fall back on more technical, legalistic arguments. De Valera, for instance, told Labour TD Patrick Gaffney, who wrote to him trying to arrange peace talks, that 'The Second Dáil has not been dissolved'; the purported Third Dáil, elected in 1922, was merely the 'Parliament of Southern Ireland' – a British imposed, 26-county assembly.[67] He reiterated the point in correspondence with Senator James Douglas in December 1922: 'the only legitimate government is the Second Dáil'.[68] The point was eventually to become the basis of militant republican rejection of the Irish state, right throughout the twentieth century and beyond.

Technically speaking, there was some basis to what de Valera said. The Second Dáil was supposed to have met for the last time on 30 June 1922 to dissolve itself but had not, due to the opening of hostilities on 28 June. Arthur Griffith, for one, had wanted it to meet and formally dissolve itself before the new, Third Dáil, elected in June 1922, sat but it never did.[69] Whatever the strict legalities, the purist case for republican continuity advocated by de Valera in late 1922 was a weak one. The First

Dáil of 1919–21 had been elected in a British general election and it had never been formally dissolved either.[70] The Second Dáil was elected in polls held under the 1920 Government of Ireland Act for the proposed parliament of southern Ireland in May 1921. Unlike the Third Dáil of 1922, which, notwithstanding British threats, had been popularly elected, the 124 Sinn Féin deputies elected in May 1921 had all been returned unopposed. The Second Dáil was, in truth, therefore, a poor basis on which to place popular republican sovereignty. Furthermore, as late as early September 1922, de Valera had actually been calling for the opening of the Third Dáil as one of his peace proposals. Nevertheless, for the anti-Treaty republicans, their position remained unchanged. They stood for the self-determination of the Irish people without outside interference and they maintained that the Civil War amounted to an unprovoked attack on them by agents of the British.

In response to peace initiatives in late 1922, de Valera wrote: 'we are fighting for the right of the people of this nation to determine without foreign dictation what shall be their government'.[71] He told Patrick Gaffney that 'I cannot ask the soldiers of the Republic to be loyal to such a usurpation', a point he repeated in correspondence to the trade unionists of the Wexford Workers' Council. The ratepayers asked for peace and a coalition government, to which de Valera responded that 'a coalition government was formed last June [in the pact election], there is no such hope now'.[72]

The Republican 'Government' in the Civil War

With the Civil War dragging on, in October 1922, to formalise their position and to counter the allegation of a prospective anti-Treaty IRA dictatorship, de Valera, at Liam Lynch's suggestion, set up a civilian republican government to which the IRA executive pledged its allegiance. Its stated aim was to 'preserve the continuity of independent Irish government' until 'the people are rid of external aggression to decide freely how they are to be governed'. De Valera was nominated as president of the phantom Republic, with a 'Council of State' of nine men and two women republican TDs.[73] Lynch himself, the head of the anti-Treaty guerrilla forces, declined to take a position in the republican shadow government as minister for defence as he was not a TD, citing fears that it could be used to maintain the line of a proposed IRA dictatorship: 'the enemy would be keen to use it as "dictatorship propaganda"', he wrote to de Valera.[74] However, the IRA was the senior partner in the anti-Treaty republican movement. The civilian republican government had arisen from a suggestion made at an IRA executive meeting and while Éamon de Valera was highly influential as the republican 'President', it was Liam Lynch as IRA chief of staff who was unquestioned commander of the military organisation, and along with the IRA executive (of which de Valera was not a member) the setter of military and strategic policy.

While the anti-Treaty republicans claimed to be 'interpreting the desires of all true citizens of the Republic', the reality was, as they knew, they did not have the backing of the majority. De Valera, in private, wrote to Lynch that 'the only public policy is maintaining the Republic and the sovereignty and independence of the nation', but he also advised that they may have to accept something less, though not 'explicitly accepting loss of sovereignty or partition'.[75] The short-term aim had to be, according to de Valera, to 'win back the allegiance of the people'.[76] In early February 1923, de Valera tried to resurrect Document No. 2, writing to Lynch that 'we need to get the constitutional way adopted … we need to take the lead on peace, it would be a victory'.[77] But his wavering on republican purity was curtly dismissed by Lynch.[78] It was not until the latter's death in a skirmish in County Tipperary in April 1923 that de Valera managed to regain control over the IRA leadership, in the person of Frank Aiken. In the years that followed, de Valera would eventually lead most of the anti-Treaty republican movement towards what he regarded as the dismantling of the Treaty settlement by constitutional means in Fianna Fáil. Many of the former anti-Treaty IRA and Sinn Féin activists followed him into what Seán Lemass referred to as a 'slightly constitutional party' in 1926.[79] Some members of the republican movement, though, principally those who remained within the IRA throughout the 1920s and 1930s, clung to the same republican legitimism that had characterised the anti-Treaty position during the Civil War – the Free State was an illegitimate, British-imposed entity, the last legitimately elected Dáil was the Second Dáil of 1921–2 and no free popular vote on the constitutional settlement in Ireland could take place unless it was on an all-Ireland basis and without the threat of British aggression. Adding a further layer of unreality, in 1938, some anti-Treaty (and anti-Fianna Fáil) TDs from the Second

Dáil agreed to vest what they considered to be the authority of that long-dissolved parliament in the IRA Army Council. Thus, the IRA of subsequent decades actually claimed to be the legitimate government of Ireland, pending the re-establishment of the Republic declared in 1919. It is worth noting that this was a position the IRA never claimed for itself, and indeed disavowed, during the Civil War.[80]

Conclusion: The Purist Republican Dead End

Irish republican opposition to the Anglo-Irish Treaty was not based on abstract republican ideology but on real fears that the settlement would not deliver full Irish independence, even for a 26-county Irish state. While the oath of fidelity to the British monarch that TDs would have to take was indeed of huge symbolic importance, there were also rational, concrete objections. The most important of these were the ports that the British retained under the Treaty, giving Britain a vestigial garrison in Ireland and an unacceptable influence in Irish foreign policy. The partition of Ireland did not figure prominently during the Treaty debates, not because anti-Treaty republicans were not interested in the issue, but because it appeared as if the pro-Treatyites, and in particular Michael Collins, were also committed to ending partition in early 1922. When, by 1923, it became apparent that the Treaty would not mean the end of Northern Ireland, this became a central feature of anti-Treaty republican rhetoric. Republican opposition to the Treaty also had an undeniably emotional element. Many republicans argued that because their friends, family members and comrades had died for the Irish Republic it simply could not be given away.

Pro-Treatyites consistently argued that the Treaty was the 'will of the people' and that it was democratically endorsed by both the Dáil in January 1922 and by the electorate in June of that year. They, therefore, characterised the anti-Treatyites as anti-democratic and potential military dictators. The anti-Treatyites certainly acted in defiance of the Dáil in early 1922. However, they were at pains throughout the Civil War period to emphasise that they had no intention of installing a military government. Rather, they claimed through a series of rather convoluted arguments that because of the British threat of war, the election of 1922 did not constitute a free choice, but, as Liam Mellows put it, simply

showed 'the fear of the people' at rejecting the Treaty.[81] Moreover, while
the pro-Treaty side depicted the Civil War that broke out in late June
1922 as a war to defend Irish democracy, the anti-Treatyites depicted it
as a defensive struggle on their part to uphold the Irish Republic against
the Provisional Government, a British-installed 'usurpation' in de Valera's
words, which had attacked their forces without provocation or orders
from the British.

Ultimately, in the years after the Civil War, it took all of Éamon de
Valera's political skills to rescue anti-Treaty republicanism from the dead
end of its purism in 1922. He would insist that, henceforth, republicans
engage with the institutions of the southern state to win popular support
and not, as in 1922, simply declare that popular opinion was misled or
mistaken. It was a lesson some in the republican movement took far
longer to learn.

Notes

1   For the Treaty terms, see Cormac K.H. O'Malley and Anne Dolan (eds), *No
     surrender here! The Civil War papers of Ernie O'Malley, 1922–1924* (Dublin, 2007),
     Appendix I, pp. 483–7.
2   Ernie O'Malley, *The singing flame* (Dublin, 1978), p. 41.
3   C.S. Andrews, *Dublin made me: an autobiography* (Dublin, 2002) p. 217.
4   Ibid.
5   Máire Comerford, Unpublished memoir (University College Dublin Archives
     (UCDA), Máire Comerford Papers, LA18/35).
6   Ibid.
7   Fearghal McGarry, *Eoin O'Duffy: a self-made hero* (Oxford, 2007), p. 88.
8   Ibid.
9   *Dáil Éireann deb.*, T, no. 11, 228 (4 Jan. 1922). The 'stepping stone' is a reference to
     Michael Collins's characterisation of the Treaty as a stepping stone.
10   Michael Hopkinson, *Green against green – the Irish Civil War: a history of the Irish
     Civil War, 1922–1923* (Dublin, 2004), pp. 44–5.
11   See, for instance, Witness statement of Diarmuid Lynch, 2 May 1947 (Bureau of
     Military History (BMH), WS 04), who discusses the election in 1915 of a new
     Supreme Council and of Dennis McCullough as 'President of the Irish Republic
     virtually established by the IRB'.
12   John M. Regan, *Myth and the Irish state: historical problems and other essays*
     (Dublin, 2013), pp. 126–7.
13   Witness statement of Lawrence Nugent, 12 Nov. 1953 (BMH, WS 907).
14   Seán Ó Muirthile testimony to army inquiry (UCDA, Mulcahy Papers, P7/C/13).

15 Dermot McMonagle, 'Cavan's forgotten contribution to the War of Independence' in *History Ireland*, xv, no. 6 (Nov.–Dec. 2007), pp. 12–13.

16 Correspondence of Cavan Urban District Council, Swanlinbar Sinn Féin Club, Belturbet District Council to Peter Paul Galligan TD, Dec. 1921 (UCDA, Peter Paul Galligan Papers, P25/1).

17 *Anglo-Celt*, 24 June 1922. Although due to the 'pact' between the pro- and anti-Treaty Sinn Féin wings there were not anti-Treaty candidates in Cavan in the election. Patrick Smith, the 'Republican' or anti-Treaty candidate in the election of August 1923 polled over 6,000 votes in that election, coming second to the Farmers' Party candidate and putting Seán Milroy, the pro-Treaty Cumann na nGaedheal candidate, into third place. This indicated that, by that time at least, opinions had swung against the pro-Treatyites somewhat in the county (ibid., 1 Sept. 1923).

18 *Anglo-Celt*, 7 Jan. 1922.

19 Ibid.

20 Ibid.

21 Ibid.

22 *Dáil Éireann deb.*, T, no. 11, 223 (4 Jan. 1922).

23 *Anglo-Celt*, 7 Jan. 1922.

24 Ibid.

25 Ibid.

26 Ibid.

27 Ibid.

28 For IRA fatalities in County Cavan, see IRA monument, the Courthouse, Cavan town.

29 Ibid.

30 Ibid.

31 1867 IRB proclamation (https://www.wsm.ie/content/fenian-proclamation-1867) (8 June 2017).

32 *Irish Freedom*, Dec. 1910.

33 Richard Mulcahy statement on army situation, 4 May 1922 (UCDA, Mulcahy Papers, P/7/B/192).

34 Liam Lynch to Mrs Cleary, 10 Apr. 1922 (National Library of Ireland, Florence O'Donoghue Papers, MS 31,242).

35 Hopkinson, *Green against green*, p. 37.

36 Éamon de Valera's reaction to election, 21 June 1922 (UCDA, Éamon de Valera Papers, P150/1588).

37 Ibid.

38 Mulcahy statement on army situation, 4 May 1922.

39 Witness statement of Joseph O'Connor, 28 June 1951 (BMH, WS 544).

40 'Address From the Soldiers of the Republic to their former comrades in the Free State Army', Dec. 1922 (UCDA, Moss Twomey Papers, P69/76).

41 *Dáil Éireann deb.*,T, no. 11, 214 (4 Jan. 1922).

42   'Address From the Soldiers of the Republic to their former comrades in the Free State Army', Dec. 1922.

43   *Dáil Éireann deb.*, T, no. 11, 30 (4 Jan. 1922).

44   Pádraig de Búrca and John F. Boyle, *Free state or republic?* (Dublin, 2016), p. 33.

45   'Address From the Soldiers of the Republic to their former comrades in the Free State Army', Dec. 1922.

46   *Anglo-Celt*, 11 Aug. 1923.

47   Cited in Kieran Glennon, *From pogrom to civil war: Tom Glennon and the Belfast IRA* (Cork, 2013), p. 147.

48   De Búrca and Boyle, *Free state or republic?*, p. 40.

49   Ibid., p. 45.

50   John M. Regan, *The Irish counter-revolution, 1921–1936* (Dublin, 1999), p. 12.

51   Liam Lynch to Ernie O'Malley, 25 July 1922, in O'Malley and Dolan (eds), *No surrender here!*, p. 68.

52   *Freeman's Journal*, 3 July 1922.

53   *Irish Independent*, 5 July 1922.

54   Tom Garvin, *1922: the birth of Irish democracy* (Dublin, 2005), p. 134.

55   Peter Hart, *The IRA at war 1916–1923* (Oxford, 2003), pp. 97, 105.

56   Witness statement of Joseph O'Connor, 28 June 1951.

57   Seán MacBride notes on IRA convention, 18 June 1922, cited in O'Malley and Dolan (eds), *No surrender here!*, pp. 26–7.

58   De Valera's reaction to election, 21 June 1922.

59   Ibid.

60   'Address From the Soldiers of the Republic to their former comrades in the Free State Army', Dec. 1922.

61   Statement by Éamon de Valera to the press, 28 June 1922 (UCDA, De Valera Papers, P150/1588).

62   Statement by Éamon de Valera to US journalists, 2 July 1922 (ibid.).

63   Éamon de Valera to Patrick Gaffney TD, 23 Oct. 1922 (ibid., P150/1647).

64   Ibid.

65   Regan, *Myth and the Irish state*, pp. 9–10.

66   De Valera to Gaffney, 23 Oct. 1922.

67   Ibid.

68   Éamon de Valera to Senator James Douglas, Dec. 1922–Jan. 1923 (UCDA, De Valera Papers, P150/1647).

69   Regan, *Irish counter-revolution*, pp. 75–6.

70   Under the pressures of the War of Independence it met only sporadically in any case. De Valera himself had moved that the 1921 elections be regarded as Dáil elections and that the 'present Dáil dissolve automatically as soon as the new body has been summoned' and that 'the Ministry remain in power until the new Dáil has met'. The logic of this surely legitimised also the Third Dáil of 1922 (Brian Murphy, 'The First Dáil Éireann' in *History Ireland*, ii, no. 1 (spring 1994) (http://www.historyireland.com/20th-century-contemporary-history/the-first-Dáil-eireann/) (31 Mar. 2017)).

71   De Valera to Gaffney, 23 Oct. 1922.

72   Ibid.

73   Creation of republican government, Oct. 1922 (UCDA, De Valera Papers, P150/1695). The members of the council were Austin Stack, Seán T. O'Kelly, Robert Barton, Laurence Ginnell, Mary MacSwiney, J.J. O'Kelly, Kathleen O'Callaghan, M.P. Colivet, P.J. Ruttledge and Seán Moylan. Moylan was the only senior IRA figure on the council.

74   Liam Lynch to Éamon de Valera, 23 Oct. 1922 (UCDA, De Valera Papers, P150/1749).

75   Éamon de Valera to Liam Lynch, 16 Oct. 1922 (ibid., P150/1695).

76   Ibid.

77   Ibid.

78   Éamon de Valera to Liam Lynch, 7 Feb. 1923 (UCDA, De Valera Papers, P150/1749).

79   See J. Bowyer Bell, *The secret army: the IRA* (3rd ed., New Brunswick, 2008), p. 74.

80   Brian Hanley, *The IRA: a documentary history 1919–2005* (Dublin, 2010), p. 101.

81   *Dáil Éireann deb.*, T, no. 11, 230 (4 Jan. 1922).

CHAPTER 4

'Merely Tuppence Half-Penny Looking Down on Tuppence'? Class, the Second Dáil and Irish Republicanism

Brian Hanley

This chapter discusses whether social background was significant in the division over the Treaty and in terms of the broader question of class and the Irish Revolution. It engages with the view that socio-economic issues partly explain the Treaty split and the makeup of the two chief opposing factions during the Civil War. Many have tended to agree with Kevin O'Higgins's assertion that he and his colleagues were the 'most conservative-minded revolutionaries that ever put through a successful revolution'.[1] However, there remains a strong tendency to see social radicalism as implicit in the anti-Treaty stance, some even claiming that 'the logic of republicanism has tended to be anti-capitalist'.[2] This chapter attempts to unravel how contemporary republicans, that is supporters of Sinn Féin, the Irish Republican Army (IRA) and those who sought an independent Ireland, viewed themselves and their opponents in terms of social class.

'A Very Clear Idea of Their Place'

In the nineteenth century, Virginia Crossman commented:

> [Irish] people had a very clear idea of their place in society relative to other people, and the importance of maintaining this. If landowners

tended to see all tenants as members of the lower classes broadly defined, middling and large tenant farmers regarded themselves as belonging to a very different social category from small tenants and labourers, and were anxious to enforce this sense of difference through adherence to concepts such as respectability. The poor, and more particularly the destitute, were regarded by the better off as almost beyond class.[3]

IRA leader Ernie O'Malley reflected of Ireland in the early 1900s that 'in the towns tuppence-ha'penny looked down on tuppence, and throughout the country the grades in social difference were as numerous as the layers of an onion'.[4] During the same period, Irish-Irelander D.P. Moran complained that in Ireland class distinctions were 'ridiculously minute and acute'.[5] These observations suggest that Irish people were acutely aware of class division. However, the anti-Treatyite C.S. (Todd) Andrews later asserted that 'the ethos of the Republican Movement before the Treaty had been egalitarian. We assumed that apart from the usual tendency of tuppence-halfpenny to look down on tuppence, the Irish nation in the mass was a classless society. There was no social immobility based on birth or inherited wealth'.[6] Instead, Andrews tended to associate class distinction only with the 'landed gentry and wealthy unionists'.

Religion and Power

The assumption that class distinction was derived largely from the Anglo-Irish or British connection would remain an influential one in Irish political discourse.[7] In part, this view reflected the reality of sectarian privilege prior to independence. As Fergus Campbell has illustrated, to a great extent power and wealth in pre-independence Ireland remained largely in the hands of Protestant unionists. Catholics made up 37 per cent of higher civil servants but 61 per cent of clerical officers and clerks. In the police only 9 per cent of senior officers were Catholic in contrast to around 70 per cent of the rank and file. Of Ireland's major businessmen, around 20 per cent were Catholic in 1911.[8] The cultural division between the Anglo-Irish and Irish nationalists remained very wide. Part of the enthusiasm engendered by home rule was the belief that self-government would deliver real changes to Irish society. Hence John Dillon, the Irish

Parliamentary Party's deputy leader, could tell cheering crowds in 1912 'we have undone, and are undoing, the work of three centuries of confiscation and persecution … the holy soil of Ireland is passing back rapidly into the possession of the children of our race … and the work of Oliver Cromwell is nearly undone'.[9] As republican activist Laurence Nugent explained, 'outside of the professional politicians, Home Rule meant to the ordinary citizen freedom for Ireland without any qualifications'.[10] For many this 'freedom' also meant an end to Protestant economic and social dominance.

Campbell also explained that since the Famine 'a seismic shift in power-holding had taken place in provincial Ireland'.[11] During this period, the:

> Large farmers and provincial shopkeepers replaced the landlords as the most wealthy and politically influential class in Irish society. As individuals, their wealth may have been miniscule compared with the great landlords or the big businessmen, but collectively the thousands of provincial merchants, small businessmen, shopkeepers, and large farmers were the most powerful section of Irish society by 1914. These men and women ran local government in nationalist Ireland; they were extremely influential in nationalist political organizations and in the Irish Parliamentary Party … and together with the Catholic Church effectively controlled political, economic, cultural and moral life in rural Ireland.[12]

'No Claim to be a Cross-Section of the Whole Community'

A large number of those taking part in the Treaty debates, though they had rejected the politics of the home rule movement, were the sons and daughters of this rising Catholic bourgeoisie. On either side of the Treaty divide there were people from humble and from relatively privileged backgrounds. There is no doubt that the majority of them took their stance for sincere reasons. Several paid for that decision with their lives. However, their social status seems to have had little bearing on their views about the Treaty. In his study *Representative government in Ireland*, J.L. McCracken contended that the majority of the Second Dáil's TDs came from the professional and commercial classes. He calculated that there were thirty-eight professionals among the TDs. These included doctors (eight), barristers, lecturers, teachers (at least fifteen), accountants, journalists and engineers.[13] Another 15 per cent of TDs were involved in commercial occupations such as finance and insurance or were publicans, merchants or shopkeepers. This was a major over-representation of these classes who then made up about just over 13 per cent of the working population. About 18 per cent of TDs were farmers or involved in agriculture (approximately eleven), a relatively small number given the prominence of agriculture in Irish society, with 43 per cent of the population engaged in work on the land.[14] However, the number of farmers' children among TDs was quite high, approximately thirty-three. The category 'farmer' is, of course, subject to qualification about size of farm, what type of farmer, how many people were employed on it and so on. When first elected in 1918, Frank Lawless was described as an 'extensive farmer' but that could mean different things from region to region.[15] A number of TDs had more than one occupation. There were individuals with Anglo-Irish backgrounds as well as representatives of the Catholic upper-class but also several skilled workers or tradesmen. Erhard Rumpf and A.C. Hepburn asserted that the 'the Sinn Féin politicians elected in 1918 and 1921 came predominantly from the lower stratum of the urban and small-town middle class'.[16] They pointed out that 'the distinctions are not sufficiently clear-cut, however, to permit any general conclusions to be drawn'.[17] Indeed, it is unclear what exactly the profession of some TDs was, and in any case, several were essentially full-time revolutionaries. Nevertheless, as McCracken asserted, the Dáil 'had no claim to be a cross-section of the whole community'.[18]

The Unskilled

The most glaring omission from the Dáil's membership was unskilled workers. There were about 200,000 agricultural labourers in the country according to the 1911 census. Over 600,000 people worked in industry, both skilled and unskilled, of whom 63,000 were regarded as engaged in transport work. In Dublin alone there were 18,000 unskilled workers. Over 170,000 people (mainly women) worked in domestic service of various types.[19] But not one TD was an unskilled worker. There were TDs who associated with organised labour, Richard Corish (Wexford), Joseph McGrath (Dublin North-West), and Seán Etchingham (Wexford) among them, but the class that made up the Irish Transport and General Workers' Union (ITGWU) was not itself represented in the Dáil. By 1920, that union had around 120,000 members, around half of them rural labourers, so it was a substantial force in society.[20]

There were a number of skilled tradesmen or artisans in the Dáil (approximately ten). These included a blacksmith, an electrician, two tailors, two coach-builders and a fitter. But in almost all cases these men were self-employed or running their own businesses by 1921. There was also a significant number of teachers, clerks and other white-collar workers. Many of those who were professionals were the children of business people or farmers and some of the skilled and white-collar workers were the children of urban or rural workers from lower down the social scale.[21] It should be noted, in that era, a skilled worker was regarded as very different from a labourer, and a white-collar worker very different again from them both. The social distance between these categories was often very great. As Aidan Kelly notes of the white-collar worker, 'prestige was the dominant element in his social profile; unable to reach or match the social plane of his superiors he responded by establishing a clear gap between himself and the great mass of manual workers'.[22] Of the division between the skilled trades and unskilled, J.J. Lee describes how craftsmen 'were a class apart from the great mass of unskilled workers [and] were peculiarly vulnerable to the threat of downward social mobility'.[23] They had secured a 'foot-hold on the slippery slope of respectability' and could 'glimpse the awful chasm gaping below them' if they lost their grip.[24] Therefore, the tradesman 'clung to his job, and to his children's right of succession, with something of the tenacity with which the tenant farmer clung to his holding'.[25]

Education

The class basis of the Dáil was also reflected in its members' educational background. A large number, 39 per cent (forty-nine), had been educated to national school level only. But 59 per cent of TDs (seventy-four) had attended secondary school and 26 per cent (thirty-three) had gone to university or had some form of professional training. The secondary schools attended included Clongowes Wood College, Blackrock College, Belvedere College, Castleknock College, St Eunan's College, Letterkenny, St Columb's College, Derry, St Malachy's College, Belfast, Mungret College in Limerick, St Angela's Ursuline College in Cork and Loreto College in Mullingar (all but one of the female TDs were educated at secondary level) and a number of the Christian Brother colleges.[26] Thus, they were broadly representative of the upwardly mobile Catholic middle class but not of the mass of the population. Of the universities attended, not surprisingly, there were several graduates of University College Dublin (UCD) and St Patrick's College, Drumcondra, but there were also some Trinity College Dublin graduates and Cambridge University and the Royal University, Edinburgh, were also represented. A number of those who attained education at secondary and third level had benefitted from scholarships, despite, like Éamon de Valera, coming from relatively humble backgrounds.[27]

'No Corner Boys or Criminals'

Republicans' social perceptions of themselves were also important. Imprisoned after the Easter Rising, Gerald Doyle described his comrades as 'doctors, solicitors, chemists and men who were prominent in the public life of the city, civil servants, tradesmen and school masters, as well as farmers, all of whom make up the decent citizens of a country'.[28] Indeed, their British enemies were often impressed by how respectable the rebels were. An official of the Prison Commission at Dartmoor 'was struck by their demeanour which was always respectful and courteous. Their attitude was almost dignified ... They were drawn from all classes – shop assistants, small tradesmen, labourers, two or three farmers from Galway, students, civil servants, journalists, clerks – and amongst them was a doctor, a Professor of Mathematics, and a writer of fiction – no corner boys or criminals'.[29] Ernie O'Malley's worries on the eve of the Civil War that if the IRA did not move against the Free State then 'slowly our men would either be absorbed or would return to their farms, business or universities' is illuminating in terms of his assumptions about where IRA volunteers came from.[30] Indeed, some of O'Malley's anti-Treaty comrades came from privileged backgrounds. Frank Aiken, who became the anti-Treaty IRA's chief of staff in 1923, was from a family of prominent farmers, building contractors and landlords in south County Down and County Armagh.[31] Fellow anti-Treatyite Dr Jim Ryan was raised on a 150-acre farm at Tomcoole, County Wexford, where his family employed both domestic and farm servants. Eight of the twelve Ryan siblings opposed the Treaty, including several of his sisters, whose achievements as women were remarkable in that era. However, the Ryans also clearly benefitted from their position in society; all but one of them went to university.[32] Several of the Ryans were part of the influential republican stratum at UCD, many of whom resided in the suburbs of Ranelagh, Rathmines and Pembroke. A significant number of IRA activists during the Civil War were UCD graduates or students.[33] IRA leader Ernie O'Malley was eventually captured in the Ailesbury Road home of Ellen Humphreys, republican activist and sister of The O'Rahilly. Her daughter Sighle, educated at Mount Anville Secondary School and at the University of Paris, was an anti-Treaty activist; Sighle's brothers Emmet and Dick had been 'out' (i.e. involved in the Rising) in 1916. Emmet had gone to school at the Crescent College in Limerick and Clongowes Wood College and then on to UCD.

Servants

Among those injured during O'Malley's capture was Eileen Flanagan, the Humphreys's family maid.[34] Many republicans were sufficiently prosperous to employ domestic servants. In 1911, living with his wife Sinéad and their young son Vivien at Morehampton Terrace in Pembroke, Éamon de Valera employed a servant, 25-year-old Dubliner Mary Coffey.[35] Áine Heron of Cumann na mBan, whose husband owned a shop in Dublin's Phibsborough, remembered that 'during the whole of the Black and Tan period I continued being busily engaged at these [republican] activities ... fortunately I had a good maid who freed me from all domestic preoccupations and anxiety about the children'.[36] Explaining why she was unable to leave her home during the Rising, Kitty O'Doherty of Cumann na mBan claimed that 'on Holy Saturday my maid went away for the day and never came back'.[37] There are numerous references to republicans employing domestic staff in the Bureau of Military History witness statements.[38] The politics of the domestic servants, who made up nearly

10 per cent of the workforce, were diverse of course, with many aiding the IRA and others being suspected of working for the British; but none were to the fore in republican politics.[39]

Sinn Féin tended to be substantially more middle class than the IRA volunteers, whose makeup was more mixed. But while there were unskilled workers involved in the IRA, in proportion to their numbers in society they were still underrepresented, particularly among the officer class. In the 1916–21 period, IRA officers tended to be 'upwardly mobile members of the skilled working class, white-collar workers and lower professions', with a sprinkling of students.[40]

Poverty

Many republicans saw poverty as an indictment of British rule and some were sympathetic to labour radicalism. Others held the conventional views of their class. Writing to Austin Stack during May 1921, W.T. Cosgrave (a publican) reflected that:

> people reared in workhouses, as you are aware, are no great acquisition to the community and they have no ideas whatsoever of civic responsibilities. As a rule their highest ambition is to live at the expense of the ratepayers. Consequently it would be a decided gain if they all took it into their heads to emigrate. When they go abroad they are thrown on their own responsibilities and have to work whether they like it nor not.[41]

But, as a Dublin councillor, Cosgrave had been notably concerned with housing reform, and during 1917, a fellow prisoner remarked that 'Cosgrave is as much interested in the housing of the working classes as if he were at home in Dublin'.[42] Perhaps his attitude towards workhouse inmates suggested hostility towards a certain section of the poor, as Seán Lucey has outlined in his study of the Poor Law and workhouses during the revolutionary era.[43] A less harsh, but somewhat paternalistic attitude was expressed by university lecturer Eoin MacNeill to his daughter Eibhlín:

> Máthair wrote about how patient the poor are under their present great afflictions. Just think what they must have to bear, & how

others who are better off make so much of troubles that are slight in comparison. I hope Máthair succeeded in seeing young Cullen, & that she will see Mr. Partridge when he comes to Dublin. Do you ever come across the very poor people? If you don't you should try to see them. Perhaps Máthair & Madame O'Rahilly could arrange that you could visit some poor homes. Madame O'R(ahilly) is a great lover of the poor.[44]

Only a few separatists shared the views expressed in the *Catholic Bulletin*, which saw poverty as honourable in comparison to Anglicisation. During the 1913 Lockout, the *Bulletin*, edited by Sinn Féin's J.J. O'Kelly (by 1921 deputy speaker of the Dáil and TD for Louth-Meath), complained how 'English Socialists [had] succeeded in filling the heads of Irish workmen with half-baked paganism [and] as a reward and tie for future allegiance, they proceeded to fill their stomachs with bread'.[45] The *Bulletin* warned that these socialists

> would not only load a ship but an armada if by so doing they could loosen the strong hold Christianity has upon our people. The sight of what was once a proud and self-respecting people, whose grandfathers gladly died on the roadside rather than accept the poorhouse taint, crunching the beggar's crust thrown by English Socialists [was] the most sickening spectacle witnessed in our generation.[46]

In general, however, most republican radicals sympathised with the locked-out workers, though there was much suspicion of Jim Larkin and syndicalism.[47]

'The Scum of the City'?

A feature of politics between 1914 and 1918 was the number of clashes between republicans and the urban poor. Many are familiar with the hostility expressed by some Dubliners towards the rebels in 1916. W.J. Brennan-Whitmore remembered how as they 'hobbled down the quays, under heavy escort, we were pelted with garbage and filthy epithets by the scum of the city'.[48] But such conflicts were not confined to Dublin or to the Easter Rising. They were a particular feature of the election campaigns of 1917 and 1918 and happened right across Ireland.[49] Republicans usually blamed these conflicts on those with relatives in the British army, especially the so-called 'separation women'. In 1915, an Irish Volunteer parade, made up of men from across Munster, was attacked as it paraded through Limerick's lanes. Mick Quirke recounted how 'we got an awful hiding ... from the mob of the city, who used bottles, bricks and stones, and pots full of urine.'[50] Tom Clarke reputedly remarked that he had 'always wondered why King William couldn't take Limerick. I know now.'[51] Denis F. Madden claimed that in Waterford during 1918, 'drink was flowing ... to see that fanatical, separation-money mob, one could not help thinking what Daniel O'Connell thought when he said: "You should know the animals I was supposed to make a nation out of".'[52] Michael S. O'Mahony described those who clashed with republicans in Tullamore as 'the rabble of the town – wives whose husbands were in the British army and people like that.'[53] Laurence Nugent explained how

> the women and children in two districts of the town of Longford were very rough. There were also a goodly number of young men (roughs) who had not yet joined the British Army. The people here mentioned were in receipt of Separation Allowances. Their husbands (mostly tinkers or militia men) were in the British Army. These people were violent supporters of the I.P.P.[54]

This helps contextualise the well-known examples of hostility encountered by the 1916 rebels in inner-city Dublin. Many of those who took part in the Rising spoke of being attacked by 'the rabble of the city'.[55] There were, in fact, fatalities during Easter week when republicans fired on their assailants.[56]

John Dorney suggests that, by 1919, many of the urban poor had been won over to Sinn Féin.[57] Nevertheless, there seems to have been a real hostility between republicans and sections of the working class. Some of the violence may have been due to suspicion of outsiders. Many of the Irish Volunteers parading through Limerick's poorest areas in 1915 were from the Munster countryside. In 1917–18 Sinn Féin's canvassers came from across Ireland to campaign in elections but the Home Rule Party's supporters seem to have been predominantly local. However, republican descriptions of drunken separation women were certainly influenced by class and gender prejudice, and we lack any perspective from the side of the 'rabble'.[58] Many of the people involved may have had relatives serving in the British military but this did not mean they were pro-British per se; but republicans, who in general did not come from this class themselves, tended to assume either depravity or financial seduction on behalf of those who opposed them.

Republicans and Labour

There were also, of course, republicans active in the labour movement. The prominent ITGWU leader Cathal O'Shannon had been 'out' in 1916 and interned. Paddy Gaffney in Carlow was a Volunteer organiser and president of the local ITGWU.[59] During 1919, Martin Conlon, a Dublin Corporation sanitary officer and member of the Irish Republican Brotherhood (IRB) Supreme Council, was put in charge of a 'Secret Service Unit' known as the 'Labour Board' by Michael Collins. This body also included Thomas Maguire of the Stationary Engine Drivers' Society, Joseph Toomey of the Amalgamated Society of Engineers and Luke Kennedy, an electrician. Conlon described how their

> duty was to use our influence in our various Trade Unions, and in the Labour Movement generally on behalf of the Republic: to get hold of men in important key positions, such as Power Stations, Railways, and Transport Dockworkers etc; and most important of all, to undermine the Amalgamated and Cross Channel Unions, and where possible to organise breakaways from these Unions, and establish purely Irish Unions instead.[60]

The formation of the Irish Engineering, Shipbuilding and Foundry Trades Union in 1920 was part of this process.[61] Seán O'Duffy, secretary of the pre-1920 Electrical Trades Union and a 1916 veteran, was involved in supplying men to do maintenance work in various British army barracks. O'Duffy was able to convince the authorities to give him a special pass that allowed travel after curfew, which he then provided for the use of Michael Collins and others.[62]

In early 1917, a group of activists, many of them IRB men, took control of the Dublin Municipal Officers' Association (DMOA). They then used the DMOA to launch the Irish Local Government Officers' Trade Union (ILGOU) as a national trade union of local government officials that supported Dáil Éireann as the only legitimate authority in Ireland. Members of this group included Henry Mangan, the city accountant, and Joseph Hutchinson, also in the city accountant's office; and Thomas Gay of the Capel Street library. At their head was 1916 veteran Harry Nicholls.[63] Organised republican strength seems to have been based among white-collar and skilled workers but the greatest expansion of union membership in that era was among the unskilled, especially in rural areas, who joined the ITGWU in large numbers. These people were not present in the republican movement in numbers in proportion to their presence in society.

Class and the Treaty Debates

There was relatively little explicit reference to class concerns in the Treaty debates themselves. Liam Mellows (Galway) criticised the Treaty's concessions to imperialism, arguing that

> The British Empire represents to me nothing but the concentrated tyranny of ages ... the thing that has crushed this country; yet we are told that we are going into it now with our heads up. We are going into the British Empire to participate in the Empire's shame ... the crucifixion of India and the degradation of Egypt. Is that what the Irish people fought for freedom for?

But he also argued that

> we do not seek to make this country a materially great country at the expense of its honour ... we would rather have this country poor and indigent, we would rather have the people of Ireland eking out a poor existence on the soil; as long as they possessed their souls, their minds, their honour. The fight has been for something more than the fleshpots of Empire.[64]

Countess Markievicz (Dublin South) asserted that she was standing by 'James Connolly's ideal of a Workers' Republic' and that the Treaty would 'uphold the capitalists' interests in Ireland'.[65] She claimed that the Treaty benefitted most what she called the 'anti-Irish Irishmen ... that class of capitalists who have been more crushing, cruel and grinding on the people than any class of capitalists of whom I ever read in any other country'.[66] She also associated capitalist values with Britain claiming that 'love of luxury, love of wealth ... trample on your neighbours to get to the top, immorality and the divorce laws of the English nation' would follow from the Treaty's acceptance.[67] However, most republican objections to the Treaty centred around its concessions to imperialism and its betrayal of the 1916 declaration of a republic rather than on social grounds.

Some of those who supported the Treaty raised social and economic concerns themselves. Piaras Béaslaí (Kerry-Limerick West) claimed that he knew the Irish people of 'all types and all classes, good, bad or indifferent' and that Michael Collins and Arthur Griffith knew the people as well: 'sailors, fishermen, farmers, labourers, shopkeepers, cattle dealers, as well as university professors and international law experts (laughter)' and that the real interests of these people would be served by the Treaty not by abstract debates about sovereignty.[68] Joseph McGrath (Dublin North-West), former manager of the ITGWU insurance section, quoted from the Dáil's Democratic Programme of 1919 on the need for the state to ensure no child suffered from hunger, want or lack of shelter and argued that 'under this Treaty every single thing in this Democratic Programme can be put into force'.[69] Clare TD and IRA leader Patrick Brennan told that Dáil that he was 'a member of the Irish Clerical Workers' Union; therefore I am a Trades Unionist'.[70] However, he emphasised that he did not speak for 'any particular class' when he called for support for the Treaty.[71] Richard Corish (Wexford), who had been a leading activist in the bitter Wexford lockout of 1911–12 and a prominent ITGWU official, also supported the Treaty. Corish argued that he was voting for the Treaty not because it was in accordance with his views but because it was 'the best thing for my country at the moment' and because 'the people of my constituency want me to vote for it'.[72] Some pro-Treatyites did sound a note of fear regarding the potential for social disorder. Alexander McCabe (Sligo-Mayo East) warned that if war was resumed then 'life will become cheap ... the striker will abandon the peaceful method of picketing for the bomb and the torch. The landless workers will have recourse to more deadly weapons than hazel sticks in attacking the ranches'.[73] McCabe's worries reflected the widespread industrial and agrarian struggles that were taking place throughout the country.[74] In retrospect, some republicans suggested that those involved in such activities were ready to support the anti-Treaty cause but were held back by the IRA's lack of social thinking. However, evidence also suggests both working class support for, and also apathy about, the Treaty itself.

Working Class Opinion and the Treaty

Patrick Magee of the South Wexford branch of the ITGWU wrote to local TD Jim Ryan in early 1922, asking that he note that the 'organised workers ... call upon our Deputies representing Wexford in An Dáil to vote for the anglo-Irish treaty'.[75] While Magee noted that the objects

> For which so many of our comrades suffered and died have not been secured ... We are of opinion that the present treaty is a step in that Direction, We may state that we have not been stampeded by Press reports or speeches of outside individuals ... but we consider with an unratified treaty and a divided country there appears nothing before us but stress and disorder in the country and misery in our homes. We believe that with the control of education and finance etc that social conditions can be so improved that ultimately the goal for which our Union aims for which James Connolly died will become an accomplished fact namely A Workers Republic.[76]

While only a local snapshot of opinion, the support for a general strike against militarism and the vote secured by the Labour Party at the 1922 election also point toward working class unease with both sides of the debate.[77]

Labour Successes

On 24 April 1922, the executive of the Labour Party called a general strike in protest at the drift towards civil war. It was perceived by many as directed mainly at the anti-Treaty IRA and received positive coverage in the Dublin (pro-Treaty) press. Nevertheless, it was widely supported and labour leaders were critical of the actions of both the IRA and the new national forces.[78] In the June general election, seventeen out of eighteen Labour candidates were elected, five of them topping the poll. Two seats were won in each of the Waterford-East Tipperary, Wexford, Kildare and East Cork constituencies. In Wexford, anti-Treaty TD Jim Ryan lost his seat, while Richard Corish, now a Labour candidate, topped the poll and brought in a running mate. In other areas, Labour probably would have won more seats had extra candidates stood. Labour took 50 per cent of the vote in Leix-Offaly, 35 per cent of the vote in Carlow and, in Louth-Meath, Cathal O'Shannon received more than two quotas of first preference votes.[79] In Galway, Liam Mellows lost his seat, while Thomas J. O'Connell gained one for Labour.[80] Rumpf and Hepburn noted that 'Labour's vote came first and foremost from farm labourers in the eastern and south-eastern counties'.[81] In contrast, 'republican support was below average in the cities, whereas support for the pro-treaty wing of Sinn Féin was above average.'[82] However, they concluded that 'it seems clear that the "working class" as such had no identifiable voting preference in these elections. Than [sic] as now, class consciousness (as distinct from status consciousness) was not an important factor in Irish politics or Irish society.'[83] But this is incorrect. Labour may indeed have gained support from former Home Rulers or from voters who resented the lack of choice presented to them by rival Sinn Féiners.[84] Indeed many of the Independents elected were former Home Rulers. In Mid Dublin, an area of dense working-class population, Laurence O'Neill topped the poll with 9,465 votes followed by Alfred Bryne on 7,899, both men coming in well ahead of both pro- and anti-Treaty candidates.[85] Byrne would retain a popular base in Dublin for decades. But much of Labour's vote came in areas where there had been strikes among farm workers, with ITGWU organisers associated with them elected in Carlow, Waterford, Tipperary and Cork.[86] Moderates were unlikely to vote for a party associated with such militancy.[87] Clearly the Labour vote had a class aspect and suggested working class interest in social and economic issues even in the midst of the great national debate.

'Apathetic to the Struggle'?

On the far-left, the Communist Party (hostile to both the Treaty and the Labour Party) suggested that when it came to the Treaty 'a big percentage of the Irish are apathetic to the struggle; this is particularly true of the landless peasants and the workers in the cities and big towns.'[88] That party's ideas about how republicans could win workers' support would profoundly influence the thinking of Liam Mellows among others (whose explicit appeals to the 'men of no property' were not made during the Treaty debates themselves), and, thereafter, frame left-republican thinking on the Civil War.[89] But the communists were also asserting that many workers were actually not interested in the Treaty debate. Republicans have tended to ignore this, assuming that because the 'stake-in-the-country people' supported the Treaty, that the poor would automatically oppose it. That they did so is far from clear. Anti-Treaty TDs certainly did not represent a more working-class group than their opponents. Neither was the IRA much more working class than its enemies in the National Army, which recruited heavily from among the urban poor. Limerick anti-Treatyite Mossie Hartnett noted that recruits to the Free State army 'were paid the then generous wage of 25 shillings per week and their keep. It had a staggering impact on poor needy labourers and ex-British soldiers, all without money and work. So it was goodbye to republicanism, which most [of them] did not understand anyway.'[90]

'Tramps and Misfits'?

The debate on the class character of the Civil War is on-going, with Gavin Foster's work revealing the importance of concepts such as social respectability and status to the participants. Class informed the views of both sides about each other. Republicans could describe the Free State army as being made up of 'the tramp, the tinker and the brute', 'low caste hirelings', 'tramps and misfits of every conceivable type' and recruits from 'off the street corners'.[91] The use of the terms 'tramp' and 'tinker' was also suggestive of deeper prejudices. Republican police had seen the control of this section of the population as part of their work before 1922, one recalling that the 'Tramp or Tinker class, who often gave a bit of trouble … became very quiet. They knew what to expect when arrested by the RIC but what happened when arrested by the IRA was an unexplored region to them and they were not taking any chances'.[92] Suffice to say there were no prominent republicans from the Travelling community.

But as Foster also shows, terms such as 'riff-raff', 'tramps and wasters', 'corner boys' and 'the dregs of society' were also used to describe republicans.[93] Certainly there was a sense in which many pro-Treatyites *thought* themselves a cut above their opponents, encapsulated in Cumann na nGaedheal Minister for Agriculture Patrick Hogan's later claim that republicans were 'incapable of governing', because after all 'you must have breeding to govern'.[94] Many of the urban-reared Free State troops also displayed contempt for the 'Paddy-Joes' or 'padjoes'; the rural anti-Treatyites who they assumed were ignorant 'culchies'.[95] It is clear that while class-based discourse played a real part in the perceptions of both sides of the Treaty split, there was no simple socio-economic dividing line between them.[96]

Republicans and Class

In the years after the Civil War, the republican movement became noticeably more proletarian. By the 1930s, most rank-and-file IRA members seem to have been drawn from among the urban and rural poor. In Dublin, its officers were largely workers (both skilled and unskilled) or unemployed. In Belfast, IRA officers were almost completely from the manual working class. In rural areas the picture was still more diverse with several farmers and schoolteachers among local commanders.[97] It is notable that in 1934, a Tipperary garda would describe local Cumann na mBan members as being the 'domestic servant type', something which their predecessors in 1919–21 usually were not.[98]

By the 1970s, there was also a far more explicit republican identification with class as a basis for support. In 1977, *An Phoblacht* contended that while 'there are good and courageous Irish people in the various classes in Ireland today ... our experience tells us that the most obvious support for the armed struggle and those elements which back it against imperialism comes largely from the most deprived and oppressed, whose instinct remains uncorrupted'.[99] Popular perceptions of republicanism have, in many ways, come full circle. Today the urban poor are regarded as the people most likely to support Sinn Féin (or other republican groups). In a typically uninformed critique of that party, journalist John Drennan echoed earlier prejudices when he contended that most Sinn Féin supporters existed on a diet of 'Dutch Gold, batter burgers and chips'.[100] But it is a mistake to read this modern basis for republican support back onto the Treaty split.

'Inherently Unirish'

There are still those who assume Irish society is somewhat classless. The idea that class is something primarily identified with the Anglo-Irish was reflected in Fine Gael's Dr James Reilly's assumption that purchasing a Georgian mansion and sleeping in a bed made for King George IV's visit to Ireland in 1821, represented a triumph for the plain people against the ascendancy; 'Feck you, Your Majesty; Paddy is back.'[101] The idea was even more central to the ethos of Fianna Fáil. One could possess substantial wealth and yet still be 'of the people'. C.S. Andrews claimed that he and his colleagues 'were the children of unimportant people – the men of no property of whom Wolfe Tone spoke' but Andrews (whose parents owned a shop and who was educated at UCD) and his colleagues were not largely manual workers or rural labourers but broadly part of the middle class.[102] Richard Dunphy has described this belief as part of the 'flattering self-image' of those who became 'modestly wealthy through their own enterprise and industry and through government policy' that they were patriots and not in any way similar to the aristocracy who inherited their wealth.[103] During 1972, Fianna Fáil's Brian Lenihan would contrast Northern Ireland with 'the type of society which we have evolved here ... which is almost totally nonsectarian, classless and devoted to the common good and the achievement of justice'.[104] Charles Haughey could dismiss socialism as 'an alien gospel of class warfare, envy and strife ... inherently unIrish and therefore unworthy of a serious place in the language of Irish political debate'.[105] In part they could do this because, in the eyes of their supporters at least, Fine Gael was descended from the 'stake in the country' people and Fianna Fáil from the anti-Treatyite dispossessed.

A Struggle for Self-Determination

The Irish Revolution was led by people who were broadly middle class and who held diverse views on social and economic matters.[106] Many of them believed in a more equal society, but they did not usually see this in terms of class conflict. The key issue that united them was self-determination. Facing the most powerful empire in the world and attaining even limited independence was a considerable achievement. What compromises were necessary to gain this measure of independence informed their stances on the Treaty far more than any concerns with social justice. This is not to suggest that class or class struggle were not part of the story of the revolutionary era but they were not the key factors for republicans in either acceptance or rejection of the Treaty.

Notes

1   J.J. Lee, *Ireland 1912–1985: politics and society* (Cambridge, 1989), p. 105.
2   David Lloyd, 'On republican reading' in Cormac K.H. O'Malley and Nicholas Allen (eds), *Broken landscapes: selected letters of Ernie O'Malley, 1924–1957* (Dublin, 2011), p. 386.
3   Virginia Crossman, 'Middle-class attitudes to poverty and welfare in post-Famine Ireland' in Fintan Lane (ed.), *Politics, society and the middle class in modern Ireland* (Basingstoke, 2010), pp. 130–47.
4   Ernie O'Malley, *On another man's wound* (Dublin, 1979), p. 24.
5   Tony Farmar, *Ordinary lives: three generations of Irish middle class experience* (Dublin, 1991), p. 12.
6   C.S. Andrews, *Man of no property* (Dublin, 2001), p. 7.
7   Lindsey Earner-Byrne, *Letters of the Catholic poor: poverty in independent Ireland, 1920–1940* (Cambridge, 2017), p. 7.
8   Fergus Campbell, *The Irish establishment 1879–1914* (Oxford, 2009), pp. 298–320.
9   *Irish Independent*, 1 Apr. 1912.
10   Witness statement of Laurence Nugent, 12 Nov. 1953 (Bureau of Military History (BMH), 907).
11   Campbell, *Irish establishment*, p. 3.
12   Ibid.
13   J.L. McCracken, *Representative government in Ireland: a study of Dáil Éireann 1919–48* (Westport, CT, 1976), pp. 93–101.
14   L.P. Curtis Jr, 'Ireland in 1914' in W.E. Vaughan (ed.), *A new history of Ireland*, vi: *Ireland under the union, ii: 1870–1921* (Oxford, 2005), pp. 151–4.
15   *Irish Independent*, 28 Dec. 1918.
16   Erhard Rumpf and A.C. Hepburn, *Nationalism and socialism in twentieth-century Ireland* (Liverpool, 1977), pp. 34–5.
17   Ibid.
18   Ibid., pp. 33–4.
19   Curtis Jr, 'Ireland in 1914', pp. 151–4.

20   Emmet O'Connor, *A labour history of Ireland 1824–2000* (Dublin, 2011), pp. 102–5.

21   See Appendix 2.

22   Aidan Kelly, 'White-collar trade unionism' in Donal Nevin (ed.), *Trade unions and change in Irish society* (Dublin, 1980), pp. 65–81.

23   J.J. Lee, 'Workers and society in modern Ireland' in Nevin (ed.), *Trade unions*, pp. 11–25.

24   Ibid.

25   Ibid.

26   See Appendix 2.

27   David McCullagh, *De Valera,* i: *rise 1882–1932* (Dublin, 2017), pp. 25–8.

28   Witness statement of Gerald Doyle, 15 Oct. 1956 (BMH, 1511).

29   David Fitzpatrick, *Harry Boland's Irish revolution* (Cork, 2004), p. 47.

30   Michael Hopkinson, *Green against green: the Irish Civil War* (Dublin, 1989), p. 61.

31   Eoin Magennis, 'Frank Aiken: family, early life, and the revolutionary period, 1898–1921' in Bryce Evans and Stephen Kelly (eds), *Frank Aiken: nationalist and internationalist* (Dublin, 2014), pp. 60–1.

32   'Seán T. Ó Ceallaigh and the Ryans of Tomcoole' (National Library of Ireland, Collection List 178).

33   John Dorney, *The Civil War in Dublin: the fight for the Irish capital 1922–1924* (Dublin, 2017), p. 14.

34   *Irish Times*, 6 Nov. 1922.

35   Census, 1911 (http://www.census.nationalarchives.ie/pages1911/Dublin/Pembroke-West/Morehampton_Terrace/11618/) (12 Feb. 2017). According to the census returns Coffey was unable to read.

36   Witness statement of Áine Heron, 16 Sept. 1949 (BMH, 293).

37   Witness statement of Kitty O'Doherty, 17 Feb. 1950 (BMH, 355).

38   See, for example, witness statement of Michael Kilroy, 15 Apr. 1955 (BMH, 1162); witness statement of Kate O'Callaghan, 14 June 1952 (BMH, 688); witness statement of Robert Brennan, 28 Oct. 1952 (BMH, 125); witness statement of Maeve McGarry, 31 Mar. 1953 (BMH, 826); witness statement of Tom Treacy, 11 Feb. 1950 (BMH, 1093); witness statement of Patrick Doyle, 22 Nov. 1955 (BMH, 1298); witness statement of Máire Ó Brolcháin, 28 Oct. 1949 (BMH, 321); witness statement of Joseph Kenny, 2 Jan. 1950 (BMH, 332); witness statement of Áine O'Rahilly, 2 Jan. 1950 (BMH, 333); witness statement of J.J. O'Kelly, 1 May 1950 (BMH, 427); witness statement of Mary Flannery Woods, 13 Dec. 1951 (BMH, 624); witness statement of Michael Joseph Ryan, 25 Dec. 1951 (BMH, 633); witness statement of Eithne Coyle, 10 Nov. 1952 (BMH, 750); witness statement of Daniel O'Keeffe, 21 Jan. 1957 (BMH, 1587); witness statement of Matthew Connolly, 27 Nov. 1958 (BMH, 1746); and witness statement of Eithne MacSwiney, 17 Apr. 1948 (BMH, 119).

39   170,749 people were employed in domestic work. The majority were women (Curtis Jr, 'Ireland in 1914', p. 152).

40   Pádraig Yeates, *Dublin: a city in turmoil, 1919–21* (Dublin, 2012), p. 229.

41   Diarmaid Ferriter, *A nation not a rabble: the Irish Revolution 1913–23* (London,

2015), p. 223.

42   Eoin MacNeill to Mór MacNeill, 26 Mar. 1917 (University College Dublin Archives (UCDA), Eoin MacNeill Papers, LA1/G/150).

43   D.S. Lucey, *The end of the Irish Poor Law? Welfare and healthcare reform in revolutionary and independent Ireland* (Manchester, 2015), pp. 13–40.

44   Eoin MacNeill to Eibhlín MacNeill, 17 May 1917 (UCDA, MacNeill Papers, LA/G/153).

45   *Catholic Bulletin*, Nov. 1913.

46   Ibid.

47   Michael Laffan, *The resurrection of Ireland: the Sinn Féin party 1916–1923* (Cambridge, 1999), pp. 252–9.

48   W.J. Brennan Whitmore, *Dublin burning: the Easter Rising from behind the barricades* (Dublin, 1996), p. 125.

49   John Borgonovo, *The dynamics of war and revolution: Cork City, 1916–1918* (Cork, 2013), pp. 62–5, 142–4.

50   John O'Callaghan, *Revolutionary Limerick: the republican campaign for independence in Limerick, 1913–1921* (Dublin, 2010), p. 37.

51   Witness statement of Michael Brennan, 11 Jan. 1955 (BMH, 1068).

52   Witness statement of Denis F. Madden, 17 Feb. 1955 (BMH, 1103).

53   Witness statement of Michael S. O'Mahony, 9 Dec. 1951 date (BMH, 669).

54   Witness statement of Laurence Nugent, 12 Nov. 1953 (BMH, 907).

55   Witness statement of Thomas McCarthy, 18 Oct. 1949 (BMH, 307); witness statement of Bernard McAlister, 1 Oct. 1948 (BMH, 147).

56   Joe Duffy, *Children of the Rising: the untold story of the young lives lost during Easter 1916* (Dublin, 2016), p. 102.

57   John Dorney, 'The rabble and the republic' in *Saothar*, xli (2016), pp. 101–9.

58   Similar prejudices were also expressed in contemporary publications such as the *Soldier Hunter*, 2 Mar. 1918.

59   Charles Callan and Barry Desmond (eds), *Irish Labour lives: a biographical dictionary of Irish Labour Party deputies, senators, MPs and MEPs* (Dublin, 2010), pp. 109–10, 225–7.

60   Pádraig Yeates, 'Article' in *Saothar*, xxxix (2014), pp. 126–7.

61   Éamon Devoy and Pádraig Yeates, *Gardiner Row and Irish craft workers in a time of revolution* (Dublin, 2009).

62   Witness statement of Seán O'Duffy, 13 Nov. 1951 (BMH, 619).

63   Martin Maguire, 'The Dublin Municipal Officers' Association, local government trade unionism & the 1916 Rising' in *Saothar*, xli (2016), pp. 277–81.

64   *Dáil Éireann deb.*, T, no. 11, 232 (4 Jan. 1922).

65   Ibid., no. 10, 182 (3 Jan. 1922).

66   Ibid.

67   Ibid., 183.

68   Ibid., 179.

69   Ibid., no. 15, 306 (7 Jan. 1922).

70   Ibid, 310. My thanks to Tony Varley for drawing my attention to this.

71   Ibid.

72   Ibid., no. 14, 300 (6 Jan. 1922).

73   Ibid., no. 11, 222 (4 Jan. 1922).

74   O'Connor, *Labour history of Ireland*, pp. 102–27.

75   Patrick Magee to James Ryan, 1 Jan. 1922 (UCDA, James Ryan Papers, P88/338).

76   Ibid.

77   Incidentally Ryan told the Dáil that not a single person in Wexford had asked him to support the Treaty (*Dáil Éireann deb.*, T, no. 15, 310 (7 Jan. 1922)).

78   Arthur Mitchell, *Labour in Irish politics: the Irish labour movement in an age of revolution* (Dublin, 1974), pp. 156–7.

79   Niamh Puirséil, *The Irish Labour Party, 1922–73* (Dublin, 2007), pp. 12–13.

80   Brian W. Walker (ed.), *Parliamentary election results in Ireland 1918–92* (Dublin, 1992), p. 105.

81   Rumpf and Hepburn, *Nationalism and socialism*, p. 67.

82   Ibid.

83   Ibid.

84   Puirséil, *Irish Labour Party*, p. 13; Mitchell, *Labour in Irish politics*, p. 162.

85   Walker (ed.), *Parliamentary election results*, p. 105.

86   John Butler, Nicholas Phelan, Thomas Nagle, Patrick Gaffney and Michael Bradley among them (Callan and Desmond (eds), *Irish Labour lives*, pp. 31–2, 235, 195–6, 109–10 & 16–18).

87   O'Connor, *Labour history of Ireland*, pp. 125–6.

88   *Workers' Republic*, 29 July 1922.

89   Emmet O'Connor, *Reds and the green: Ireland, Russia and the Communist Internationals 1919–43* (Dublin, 2004), pp. 65–75.

90   Dorney, 'Rabble and the republic', p. 108.

91   G.M. Foster, *The Irish Civil War and society: politics, class and conflict* (Basingstoke, 2015), pp. 60–1.

92   Witness statement of Thomas Lavin, 2 Sept. 1954 (BMH, 1001). For a romanticised but perhaps revealing hint of the relationship between republicans and Travellers, see Sigerson Clifford, 'The ballad of the tinker's son' in Terry Moylan (ed.), *The indignant muse* (Dublin, 2016), pp. 648–50.

93   Foster, *Irish Civil War*, pp. 37–8.

94   Lee, *Ireland 1912–1985*, p. 169.

95   Foster, *Irish Civil War*, p. 41.

96   The support of former unionist and home rule business interests for the pro-Treatyites, in many cases out of necessity more than enthusiasm, is significant of course but this chapter is primarily examining the republican movement.

97   Brian Hanley, *The IRA 1926–1936* (Dublin, 2002), pp. 20–4.

98   Ibid., p. 99.

99   *An Phoblacht*, 5 Oct. 1977.

100   *Sunday Independent*, 1 Dec. 2013.

101   *Irish Times*, 26 Aug. 2016.

102   Tom Garvin, 'Andrews, Christopher Stephen ('Todd')' in James McGuire and James Quinn (eds), *Dictionary of Irish Biography* (9 vols, Cambridge, 2009), i, pp. 112–13.

103   Richard Dunphy, *The making of Fianna Fáil power in Ireland, 1923–1948* (Oxford, 1991), pp. 46–9.

104   *Irish Times*, 4 Feb. 1972.

105   Diarmaid Ferriter, *The transformation of Ireland, 1900–2000* (London, 2004), p. 697.

106   J.M. Regan, 'Strangers in our midst: middling people, revolution and counter-revolution in twentieth-century Ireland' in *Radharc*, ii (Nov. 2001), pp. 35–50.

CHAPTER 5

'Between Two Hells': The Social, Political and Military Backgrounds and Motivations of the 121 TDs Who Voted For or Against the Anglo-Irish Treaty in January 1922

Eunan O'Halpin and Mary Staines

This chapter explores the personal and occupational backgrounds of two TDs in the Second Dáil, P.J. Moloney (1871–1947) of Tipperary town and Michael Staines (1885–1955) of Dublin. The chapter examines them in the context of what is known about all those 121 TDs who participated in the decisive Treaty vote on 7 January 1922, when the Dáil resolved to accept the Treaty by a narrow 64–57 margin.

We have chosen Michael Staines TD and P.J. Moloney TD for detailed discussion because of family links. Michael Staines was Mary Staines's grandfather, and voted for the Treaty; P.J. Moloney was Eunan O'Halpin's great-grandfather, and voted against it.

We draw particularly on data from Dáil proceedings, and also use material derived from newly released sources on the Irish Revolution, such as the Bureau of Military History (BMH) witness statements, first opened to research in 2003, and the enormous archive of the Military Service Pensions Collection, the phased release of which began in 2014.

Michael Staines gave one statement to the BMH in 1947, a vivid account of his experiences from the foundation of the Irish Volunteers in 1913 to the events of the 1916 Rising.[1] In 1954, the year before his death, he gave another lengthy statement covering the post-Rising era up to December 1921. This was accompanied by a separate statement attacking a wildly inaccurate Radio Éireann broadcast about events in Dublin during the Rising by another veteran, Peter Reynolds. Staines thought Reynolds's account dishonest and misleading, and quoted the view of another comrade that it was 'the most awful tripe'.[2]

Staines, who features in the testimonies of many other veterans due to his organisational roles between 1913 and 1922 in both the military and political wings of the independence movement, had a reputation as a very capable and cool-headed individual who was not afraid to speak his own mind. A key figure in the mobilisation of the Irish Volunteers in Dublin to participate in the Rising on Easter Monday 1916, during which he worked closely with the rebel leaders Patrick Pearse and James Connolly, he became a close associate of Michael Collins after the Rising. Staines was also relied upon by Richard Mulcahy, the military leader of the separatist movement from 1918 to 1921, and by political figures including Arthur Griffith and Éamon de Valera. Along with Griffith, Éamonn Duggan and Eoin MacNeill, he was one of four senior figures released from Mountjoy Jail on 30 June 1921 to facilitate conclusion of the negotiations which culminated in the truce that came into effect nine days later.[3] Unlike some other leading men who took the pro-Treaty side in the Civil War of 1922–3, furthermore, Staines seems to have retained the respect of many former comrades who fought on the other side, probably a reflection of his long record of military and political organisational work before and after 1916, and also of his activities as the Dáil government's liaison officer for prisoners in the autumn of 1921.

P.J. Moloney had no comparable national roles in the independence struggle after his release from detention in 1916. He died in the year that the BMH was established and so had no opportunity to provide a witness statement. It was only in 2001 that a lengthy account of his ideological development up to 1916, and his arrest and detention after the 1916 Rising, was discovered in a Home Office file in London. Moloney, 'having plenty of leisure' in Barlinnie Jail in Glasgow in June 1916, decided to 'occupy myself by writing in plain language, without exaggeration or pretence of literary embellishment, my experience of military law and usage since my arrest in Tipperary on the morning of May 3rd'.[4] He submitted the document to the Sankey Commission in 1916, which had been established to review the cases of men in detention. When he was released in July 1916, the Home Office refused to return what one official loftily termed 'a jeremiad, a dreary catalogue of complaints, correct in grammar and [which] shows the author to be a person of some education', on the grounds of its seditious sentiments.[5] This arbitrary act was a stroke of luck for posterity. Moloney's account has remained safe in British hands for over a century, whereas his Tipperary premises, family home and personal effects were destroyed by fire in an unofficial reprisal in November 1920.

This paper thus reflects an intersection between a scientific question, and a familial one. The first question is simple: why did someone such as P.J. Moloney, a modestly bourgeois middle-aged man who had already lost much but who still had much to lose, go against the Treaty? And how typical was his background amongst anti-Treatyite leaders at local level? Should he, by rights, have been on the pro-Treaty side? By the same token, should Michael Staines, the son of an impoverished ex-policeman living in overcrowded circumstances in inner-city Dublin, in terms of class, not have been an anti-Treatyite?[6]

A number of contributors to this volume discuss the complex question of why individual TDs chose to support or to oppose the Treaty. Personal allegiance to one or other of the divided separatist leadership appears to have been at least as significant a factor as ideology or class origins. Many years ago Erhard Rumpf and A.C. Hepburn cautioned in *Nationalism and socialism in twentieth-century Ireland* that the social and economic 'distinctions ... are not sufficiently clearcut ... to permit any general conclusions to be drawn' about the divide within the revolutionary elite.[7] Tom Garvin wrote that 'older leaders supported the Treaty more firmly than did the young' within the Dáil.[8] Gavin Foster has recently argued for the significance of social differences between pro- and anti-Treatyites, maintaining essentially that the anti-Treatyites were a less bourgeois collectivity and pointing to pro-Treaty propaganda dismissing anti-Treatyites as unprincipled 'thrill-seeking, ignorant youths'.[9] Whatever about their foot-soldiers and supporters, however, such an analysis is an oversimplification in terms of the respective pro- and anti-Treaty elites, whether in terms of those who actually did the fighting in 1916, and between 1919 and 1923, or of those who engaged in the political sphere during and after the Civil War.

A Profile of the Membership of the Second Dáil

Biographical data was sought on all the TDs of the Second Dáil, in order to ascertain whether the cohort could be regarded as truly representative of the nationalist people of Ireland and also whether their positions on the Treaty were grounded in the views of their constituents. An attempt was also made to see whether factors including age, gender, occupation, a long-standing association with a constituency, revolutionary activity, experience of imprisonment and membership of the First Dáil could reasonably be assumed to be factors influencing their decisions on whether to support or to oppose the Treaty.

The data indicate that, broadly speaking, pro- and anti-Treaty TDs cannot be distinguished by the extent of their direct experience of rebellion and incarceration; that significantly more pro-Treaty than anti-Treaty TDs came from or had long-standing links with the constituencies which they represented in the Dáil; that pro-Treaty TDs were, on average, three years younger than their anti-Treaty colleagues; that experience of incarceration, or the loss of a loved one during the struggle against Britain, were not determining factors in the Treaty position of male TDs; and that while pro-Treaty TDs were somewhat more likely to be in professional or commercial occupations, social class and economic circumstances were not obviously linked to their individual decisions to support or to oppose the Treaty.

For our purposes, the key measures are age, profession/occupation and relationship to the constituencies which deputies represented (with the obvious exceptions of the four National University of Ireland TDs and taking into account that four TDs were elected simultaneously for two constituencies).

For the 118 TDs whose years of birth have been established, the average age was 38.8 years. Of these 118, the average age of the sixty-five TDs who voted in favour of the Treaty was 37.5 years, while that of the fifty-three who voted against was 40.5 years. There was a greater spread of age in the anti-Treaty cohort: nine anti-Treaty TDs were over fifty years of age, as against five pro-Treaty TDs; seven pro-Treaty TDs, and eight anti-Treaty TDs, were under thirty years of age.

The place of birth of 119 TDs was ascertained. Of these, sixty-three voted in favour and fifty-six against. Sixty-nine of these TDs were born in or had spent most of their lives in the constituency which they represented. Of these, forty-two voted in favour of the Treaty and twenty-seven voted against it. This indicates that even in the extraordinary circumstances of the 1918 and 1920 general elections in Ireland, which were held under the British first-past-the-post electoral system in single-seat constituencies, the phenomenon of what Richard Sinnott terms 'the local candidate criterion' was evident.[10] Of the two TDs whose birthplaces have not been ascertained, one voted for the Treaty and one against.

The occupations of 118 TDs were ascertained. TDs were classified by reference to the categories employed in the General Report of the 1911 census.[11] This divides occupations into six classes, of which the TDs fell into three main groups – professional, commercial and farmers. TDs were allocated to the class most appropriate to their occupation. Sixty-six were in the professions, of whom thirty-six voted for the Treaty and thirty against it. Twenty pro-Treaty TDs were involved in the commercial sector

Table 6.1. Age of TDs in January 1922

Average Age of TDs	Pro-Treaty	Anti-Treaty
38.8	37.5	40.5

Note: N=118

Table 6.2. Connection to Constituency

Born in or raised in locality represented	Pro-Treaty	Anti-Treaty
69	42	27

Table 6.3. Occupation by 1911 Census Classifications

Occupation	Pro-Treaty	Anti-Treaty
Professional	36	30
Commercial	20	18
Agricultural	6	7

Note: N=117. Figures refer to absolute number of TDs.

and eighteen anti-Treaty TDs. The agricultural sector was almost equal with six pro-Treaty TDs and seven anti-Treaty. The remaining one of our 118 was classed as a 'gentlewoman'.

The data obtained on the age and occupations of TDs are indicated in Tables 6.1 to 6.3. These data challenge Garvin's generalisation that older TDs supported the Treaty 'more firmly than did the young'.[12] They also suggest that the Treaty split, while it undoubtedly defined party politics in independent Ireland, defies crude social or generational categorisation. As Michael Gallagher put it, the 1923 general election which immediately followed the Civil War demonstrated that 'this narrow political/ constitutional cleavage, rather than any socio-economic cleavage, was to be the dominant influence on the Irish party system'.[13]

Sixty-three TDs had been members of the First Dáil. There were seventy-three constituencies represented in the First Dáil, but four members had a dual mandate, so on its initiation, the First Dáil consisted of sixty-nine persons. Of these, two died in prison (Pierce McCann in 1919, Terence MacSwiney in 1920), three had resigned because of disagreement with aspects of the independence campaign (Diarmuid Lynch and Roger Sweetman in 1920, and James O'Mara in 1921), and one (J.J. Clancy) was not re-nominated for Sligo North in May 1921 due to differences with other local Irish Republican Army (IRA) leaders.[14] Of the sixty-three TDs who progressed to the Second Dáil, thirty-three voted for the Treaty and twenty-eight against, a very similar ratio to the overall voting figures for and against the Treaty.

We should note that two of those who voted for the Treaty – Robert Barton and Peter Paul Galligan – nevertheless supported the failed attempt to re-elect de Valera as president of Dáil Éireann on 9 January.[15] Another, Pádraic Ó Máille, destined to be wounded by IRA gunmen in a failed assassination attempt in Dublin on 7 December 1922, which instead claimed the life of another equivocal supporter of the Treaty, Seán Hales TD, ultimately switched to Fianna Fáil.[16] He sat as a senator from 1934 to 1936, and from 1938 to his death in 1946. Pro-Treaty TD Tom Kelly, who had missed the Treaty vote in 1921 due to illness, held a Dublin seat for Fianna Fáil from 1932 until he died in 1943. Such quirks reflected the tangled nature of the Treaty split.

Opponents Compared

Michael Staines and P.J. Moloney were men of very different backgrounds, personal circumstances, education, occupation, experience and outlook. One, engaged and due to be married only in November 1922, lived in the national capital and had been a full-time revolutionary since 1915; the other, a married man with eight children and step-children, lived in a small Munster town, where he built up his pharmacy business. But for the Rising and its aftermath, it is unlikely that they would ever have met. What they had in common were aspects of their revolutionary careers, including pre-Rising membership of the Irish Volunteers, periods of imprisonment between 1916 and 1921, the loss of loved ones killed during the conflict, election as MPs in the general election of December 1918 and membership of Dáil Éireann from 1919 to 1923.

Aged thirty-six when he took part in the Treaty debates, Michael Staines had been a full-time revolutionary for about six years. Born in Newport, County Mayo, he grew up first in Roscommon and then in Dublin, where the 1911 census records the family living at 63 Murtagh Road in Stoneybatter. Edward, the father, is listed as a fifty-year-old bacon curer. His wife Margaret bore nine children, all of whom, unusually, lived beyond infancy.[17]

Staines, who left school at fifteen to become an ironmonger's assistant, had been radicalised through the Gaelic League and he joined the Irish Volunteers on their formation in November 1913. By 1916, he was a significant figure: in his first BMH statement he recalled how at 2 a.m. on Monday 24 April 'Pearse and McDonagh called me aside and spoke to me. Pearse said "We are going into action at 12 o'clock today and as representative of the Dublin Brigade we want your consent".[18] His lengthy and vivid account of the occupation of the General Post Office during the Rising, culminating in his helping to evacuate the wounded James Connolly on a stretcher under fire, ends with his transfer to Wakefield Prison in Yorkshire on 30 April after two days in detention in Richmond Barracks (where P.J. Moloney was later held for some days).[19]

Staines was highly regarded as an organiser. He told the BMH that 'I was not in the IRB [Irish Republican Brotherhood, an oath-bound secret society] but they trusted me', a claim reflected in the key roles which he held after 1916.[20] These included serving as the Irish Volunteers' quartermaster general (until his arrest in December 1920), as director of the ill-conceived 'Belfast Boycott' (in which efforts were made to prevent the distribution and sale of goods originating in Belfast as a reprisal for sectarian attacks on Catholic workers) and, as noted above, as liaison officer for Irish prisoners from September 1921 up to the signing of the Treaty. As is discussed later, that last role in particular convinced Staines to accept the Treaty in January 1922, because it was a means of freeing all the men.

Michael Staines was the eldest of the family. Most of his siblings old enough to do so were also actively involved to varying degrees in the revolutionary movement. Mary, his sister, smuggled twenty-two .45 revolvers in a number of visits to Staines in Mountjoy Jail to aid in the planned escape of Seán Mac Eoin, who had been condemned to death, in 1921.[21] Humphrey, his brother, employed on the White Star liner *Baltic* which plied between Liverpool and New York, brought back about twenty revolvers for the IRA on each trip.[22] William (otherwise Liam) was severely wounded in the head by a grenade fragment during the 1916 Rising whilst fighting in the Mendicity Institute, losing part of his skull. He was considered fit enough to be interned in Kilmainham, Knutsford, Wandsworth and Frongoch, but his health never fully recovered and he died in 1918. Staines's mother sought compensation as a dependant under the Army Pensions Act, 1932, though officials ruled that the illness which killed him was not directly related to his wounds.[23] Vincent and James served in Na Fianna Éireann during the 1916 Rising and subsequently in the IRA during the War of Independence and were imprisoned in the Curragh in 1921. During the truce, Jim escaped by hiding under planks on a timber lorry, while Vincent 'got four stabs of a bayonet before he shouted' when detected trying to escape 'in a swill cart'.[24] On the other hand, their brother John, who had enlisted in the Royal Navy in 1912, served until his death in action in 1919.

While in Mountjoy Jail from December 1920 to 30 June 1921, Michael Staines saw six fellow prisoners go to their deaths on 14 March 1921: 'The six lads, Frank Flood and the others ... went to the scaffold very cheerfully. We were locked up that morning and we said the Rosary through the window for them'.[25] While acting as liaison officer for all prisoners in British custody during the truce – the period between 11 July 1921 and the completion of the Treaty on 6 December 1921 – he was present in Ballykinlar Camp in August 1921 when a trigger-happy young sentry killed internee Tadhg Barry from Cork, who 'was waiting at or near the car to have a chat with me'.[26]

Although peace came with surprising suddenness and longevity in 1923, Michael Staines had to deal with one further painful experience of violent death: in June 1919, his brother John had died aged twenty-five, one of two Irishmen killed when the British submarine L55 was forced into a minefield by Bolshevik destroyers and sunk in the Gulf of Finland, with all forty-two crew being lost.[27] The remains of most of the crew were recovered in 1927, when the submarine was salvaged and re-commissioned by the Soviet navy. They were carried back to Britain the following year in Union Jack-draped coffins and buried amidst much ceremony recorded by British Pathé News cameras. It fell to Michael to travel to Portsmouth to identify his brother before burial, a task which really shook him because the body was so eerily well-preserved.[28]

P.J. Moloney, who described himself as 'an ardent Nationalist, a follower of Parnell', was the founding president of the Irish Volunteers in Tipperary in 1915, a choice which he complained lost him many customers even before the Rising.[29] It is likely that he was also a member of the IRB, given his high regard for the IRB's national organiser Seán Mac Diarmada (McDermott): in June 1916, he recalled 'the bitter grief of us all' incarcerated in the temporary detention barracks at Richmond Barracks in Dublin, 'but particularly those of our party who had the privilege of Sean McDermott's friendship'. It was 'an unusually quiet solemn day' when news reached them of Mac Diarmada's execution: 'He was as brave & true-hearted a man as I ever want to know ... the favourite of all who knew him, to know him was to love him'.[30]

Moloney aligns with Tom Garvin's typology of Irish revolutionaries, 'assimilated to an ideological tradition that was non-socialist and separatist in the Fenian tradition', radical in terms of fighting to break away from British rule, but economically and socially conservative and strongly Catholic (though anti-clerical).[31] Unlike many significant figures in the revolutionary movement, he never joined the Gaelic League. Indeed, he recorded his embarrassment when visited in Barlinnie Jail by a Jesuit priest of Irish extraction who addressed him in Irish: 'I was ashamed that my laziness had prevented me from learning to speak and understand my own language'.[32]

Born in 1871, the second son of a substantial farmer from just outside Tipperary town, P.J. Moloney trained as a pharmacist in Limerick city. In November 1893, he married a widow with three children, Ellen Hannon (née O'Brien). One of her sons, Fr John, became a senior figure in the Society of Jesus, being adviser to the superior general on the English-speaking Jesuit provinces, and from 1938 to 1940, apostolic delegate to the Irish Christian Brothers' communities across the world, before his sudden death in Rome in 1947.[33] Moloney's youngest step-child William Hannon (1892–1946), who was less than two-years-old when his mother remarried, chose a career path much at odds with his stepfather's politics: he was commissioned as a lieutenant in the Royal Irish Rifles in 1914 and later transferred to the Royal Flying Corps (from April 1918, the Royal Air Force) as a pilot, seeing action in the Balkans. He remained in service until early 1923, when he resigned his British commission and joined the newly formed air corps of the National Army, against which his two surviving younger stepbrothers were fighting.[34] Whether this was a cause or consequence of a family rift is unknown.

Through her first marriage, Ellen had a family link to Hannah Bracken of Templemore, County Tipperary, mother of Brendan Bracken, the future British wartime cabinet minister and Churchill's close confidant. Moloney's eldest son Jim recalled how, when a boy in the 1900s, he and his mother stayed with Hannah Bracken and her family in Glasnevin in Dublin.[35]

P.J. and Ellen Moloney had one daughter, Mary Frances (Mai), and sons Jim, Con and Paddy. Mai qualified as a medical doctor, an unusual achievement for a young woman of those times, while the eldest son Jim received his secondary education in Mungret College, the Jesuit boarding school outside Limerick city, before training as a pharmacist in Dublin. His brothers Con and Paddy also seem to have spent some time in the school. All this indicates that the family was relatively prosperous.[36]

P.J. Moloney's role after 1916 was political rather than military, although the decision to form what became the 3rd Tipperary Brigade of the Irish Volunteers/IRA in 1918 was taken at a meeting in his Church Street premises attended by Chief of Staff Richard Mulcahy, and his home was 'Brigade headquarters at the time of the Solohead[beg] ambush' just outside Tipperary town in January 1919, where Seán Treacy and Dan Breen fired what are generally regarded as the first shots of the War of Independence, and which took place on the same day that Moloney attended the first meeting of Dáil Éireann in the Mansion House in Dublin.[37] Released in July 1916, less than two years later, Moloney was one of seventy-three prominent Sinn Féiners detained during the 'German Plot' scare of May 1918 (this round-up, in the midst of the popular uproar against the decision to impose conscription in Ireland, was on foot of what the British cabinet secretary contemptuously dismissed as 'evidence of the most flimsy and ancient description' suggesting post-Rising contacts between Irish separatists and Germany).[38] Freed once more in December 1918, Moloney was again arrested in January 1920: in May he and another prisoner were transferred from Wormwood Scrubs Jail in London to hospital after twenty-three days on hunger-strike, which cannot have been easy for a 47-year-old man on his third stint in prison: they were 'the last of the 175 hunger-strikers in the gaol ... with their release the great strike was brought to a triumphant conclusion.'[39]

Worse was to come. All four Moloney children had joined republican organisations after 1916, Mai serving in Cumann na mBan and her brothers in the IRA. In September 1920, Ernie O'Malley, an officer from IRA headquarters operating in County Tipperary, noted: 'reprisal notes received by PJ, so the house may go up at any moment': it was an obvious target for a revenge attack because of the Moloneys' IRA links.[40] By November, all the men of the family were on the run or in jail – the youngest, Paddy, had twice been jailed in 1920 'for minor acts of defiance', reportedly enduring four months of solitary confinement which severely affected his health.[41] On 14 November, the Moloney pharmacy (and home) was burned to the ground following the deaths of four policemen in an ambush by the 3rd Tipperary Brigade at Lisnagual (also known as Lisvernane) in the nearby Glen of Aherlow.[42] Ellen Moloney described the destruction of her home in a letter to her sister. During the night, three Royal Irish Constabulary (RIC) men armed with rifles forced their way in – although they wore masks, she easily recognised one of them as he 'was in our house every day'.[43] The arsonists ejected Ellen and a servant, the only people in the house, before sprinkling petrol everywhere. The inferno destroyed not only Moloney's pharmacy stocks but all the family's possessions and memorabilia. Damage was estimated at £10,000, the adjacent premises of Lipton's Grocers was destroyed and the entire terrace might have been consumed were it not for 'good work by the local police and the military fire brigade'.[44] The fire also consumed a collection of books belonging to Ernie O'Malley, who had given them to Con Moloney for safekeeping.[45]

On 1 May 1921, Paddy and his battalion commander Seán Duffy were surprised by a police raid on a farm outside the town, and in the ensuing fight, both were shot dead.[46] His older brother Jim, who had served in the Dublin Brigade while a pharmacy student in Dublin from 1918 to 1920, succeeded him as adjutant of the 4th Battalion, 3rd Tipperary Brigade. In 1922/3 he served on the staff of anti-Treaty IRA Chief of Staff Liam Lynch as director of communications. His brother Con, divisional adjutant of the 2nd Southern Division from March 1921 to the Treaty, was adjutant general from July 1922 and from January 1923 deputy chief of staff of the anti-Treaty IRA. In March 1923, he and Jim were captured following a fierce gunfight in the Glen of Aherlow, 'Con Moloney using a Thompson gun and his two companions rifles'.[47] Con was very badly wounded, which may explain his relatively early release from imprisonment in December 1923. Jim was among the last republican prisoners to be released, in July 1924.[48]

Moloney and Staines in the Dáil Debates

The first substantive Dáil discussion on the Treaty was held in private on 14 December. When public sessions commenced on 19 December, IRA officer C.S. (Todd) Andrews, a University College Dublin student, contrived to hear most of them by 'quiet inconspicuous leaning against the jamb of a door'.[49] He recalled that 'by this time the common assumption was that the Treaty would be accepted and worked. A manifestation of this was the total absence of crowds, even of the usual rubbernecks, outside Earlsfort Terrace'.[50] Proceedings were adjourned on 22 December for the Christmas break, an interlude which may have been decisive because it gave TDs time to test opinion in their constituencies – many local authorities had already called for acceptance, with Westmeath County Council stating that 'we are, perhaps, in more immediate touch' with local feeling 'than are the Dáil representatives of the county'.[51] On the other hand, the break also gave anti-Treatyites an opportunity to put pressure on TDs to oppose the Treaty root and branch.[52]

P.J. Moloney made only a brief contribution to the Treaty debates. He rose to speak on 22 December 1921, in a session chaired by the anti-Treaty diehard Brian O'Higgins TD. Moloney's remarks were brief, heart-felt and reflect what John Regan terms 'republican spiritualism'.[53] Speaking without rancour, he began:

It is with some diffidence I arise … Permit me, all you members of the Deputation, to address to you a tribute of my good faith in the great efforts you made to bring back to An Dáil of the Irish people a settlement of this very difficult, insoluble problem. I, as well as all the other members of this Dáil, am asked to approve of your work. I cannot do it. I don't want to inflict upon you my views. They are the views of a great many members of this House. Permit me though to say that I will not willingly consent to go back into the British Empire. I will not, willingly or otherwise, vote myself into the British Empire, but I say 'Damn the Treaty whatever about the consequences'. There is my position. It is the position of a great many men like me, men of average intelligence, men of average faith and principle, decent Irishmen who love Ireland and who are prepared to make sacrifices for Ireland every time, and through no fault of any of yours here, they are put in the position – we have been manoeuvred into a position where we have to choose between two hells. I refuse to choose between two hells. I ask here now publicly our leaders, or some leader, to point out to me some path by which a man such as I am – not pretending to be an orator or a statesman, but an ordinary man – can leave these two hells behind him with the vestige of my honour. I will not vote for the Treaty. I am waiting for guidance, and waiting for the path. That is all I have to say.[54]

Moloney again used conciliatory language in June 1922, during the 'pact election' campaign. Speaking from a platform of pro- and anti-Treaty candidates, he was applauded when he said that 'they were as united today as ever before against the common enemy of their country'.[55] While he termed himself no enemy of the Labour Party, he urged all sectional parties to stand aside 'in the interest of national welfare'.[56] Only through unity could the separatist movement get 'the last ounce due to Ireland by John Bull, who was … backing up the North East with guns and powder to be used against their fellow Catholics there'.[57]

In his sole contribution to the debate, on 6 January 1922, Michael Staines adopted a more matter-of-fact approach:

> Since fourteenth December I have listened to lectures, sermons and speeches. Well I won't lecture you, I won't preach; I will just say a few words. I will be brief for two reasons. The first is that I don't want to import any bitterness into this discussion; I want to have the Dáil and the country united if possible; if they are not united I sincerely hope that no word or action of mine will be responsible for disunion. The second reason is that there are 2000 Irishmen in Irish and English jails; they have got to stop there while we are talking and repeating the same things over and over again; there are forty one of these men in jails in this Republic of Ireland under sentence of death. I don't want and I'm sure these prisoners don't want me to bring up their case here in order that it would decide the vote one way or another; I am speaking for myself; but anyway for their sakes I think we ought to hurry up and finish this debate. I am declaring for the approval of the Treaty between Ireland and Great Britain; and in doing so I do it in accordance with the dictates of my own conscience; in accordance with the wishes of the majority of my constituents; and in accordance with the wishes of the majority of the people of Ireland.[58]

It is striking that, whereas Moloney dwelt entirely on his own response to the Treaty, Staines invoked what he said were the views of the majority both of his Dublin constituents and of Irish people generally, while also emphasising the need to secure the release of Irish prisoners.

What is also striking about the contributions of Staines and Moloney, and what applies to almost all the male TDs who participated in the Treaty debates, is that neither man made reference to their own experiences of imprisonment nor to the loss respectively of a sibling and a son. The majority of TDs had suffered terms of incarceration and at least eleven, including W.T. Cosgrave, whose half-brother Frank Gobben Burke had been killed fighting alongside him in 1916, had close relatives who had been killed or very seriously wounded during the struggle. Eight of these eleven, including two widows (Kathleen Clarke and Kate O'Callaghan), one mother (Margaret Pearse) and one sister (Mary MacSwiney), voted against the Treaty.[59] But, with the exception of the idiosyncratic and querulous George Noble, Count Plunkett, male TDs did not invoke the memory of fallen comrades or dwell on their own sufferings or losses (although Seán Mac Eoin did allude to 'his own past service for Ireland').[60] There was weight in Michael Collins's observation that 'we have too much respect for the dead' to bring them into the argument.[61]

The disinclination of Staines, Moloney and almost all other male pro- and anti-Treaty TDs to invoke dead relatives by name in the Dáil chamber contrasts with the approach of four of the six women TDs, all anti-Treaty, for whom the dead were everything. Those whom they mentioned by name were already famous in the separatist canon, particularly Patrick Pearse, Terence MacSwiney and Kevin Barry. Jason Knirck argues that while the Second Dáil 'was primarily composed of men who had fought for Ireland during her military struggle against English rule', women TDs were 'the shapers of their own rhetoric and discourse, choosing how to deploy the images of their martyred relations' just as they had been encouraged and expected to do during the struggle against British rule.[62] This was much resented amongst pro-Treatyites, not least because one woman TD, Mary MacSwiney, spoke at inordinate length.[63] The National University of Ireland TD Dr Ada English, in a concise contribution, defended her female colleagues against criticisms 'more freely because ... I have no dead men to throw in my teeth as a reason for holding the opinions I hold'.[64] But one must ask why women TDs claimed such proprietorial rights over the shades of the most famous of those who had died in the separatist cause since April 1916. Mary MacSwiney paid a back-handed tribute to the pro-Treaty TD Seán Mac Eoin, who had been saved from execution in Mountjoy Jail by the truce: 'if he were my brother, I would rather he were with Kevin Barry', that is, honourably and gloriously dead at British hands.[65]

What were the constraints on Moloney, Staines and other male TDs, both pro- and anti-Treaty, which prevented them from using such rhetoric? Was it because four of the six women TDs – MacSwiney, Kate O'Callaghan, Kathleen Clarke and Margaret Pearse – had been elected essentially as proxies for martyrs and felt obliged to justify their presence by reference to their lost menfolk? With the exception of Constance Markievicz, women TDs could not claim to have done battle because they simply were not allowed to fight. This is reflected in a Civil War letter to Jim Moloney from his fiancée, the republican activist Kathy Barry, recounting her experiences with Cathal Brugha, de Valera and other republican leaders in the besieged Hammam Buildings on Sackville (O'Connell) Street in early July 1922: 'I love those three days at the end because I felt I was nearly as useful as a man and you don't know how helpless a feeling it is to be a woman when you feel you ought to be a man.'[66]

Continuity or Contrivance? The Republican 'Second Dáil', 1922–1938

Both Staines and Moloney were re-elected in the June 1922 'pact election', conducted under an arrangement negotiated by Collins and de Valera under which pro- and anti-Treaty candidates were nominated in equal proportion to their presence in the Second Dáil. But neither man ran in the August 1923 general election, the first held under universal suffrage for men and women for an enlarged 153-seat Dáil Éireann representing only the twenty-six counties of the newly established Irish Free State. Nine other pro-Treaty TDs and five anti-Treaty TDs stood down in 1923. In addition, the forty-four Sinn Féin TDs elected in August 1923 did not take their seats, instead constituting themselves as the legitimate 'Second Dáil' on the strength of Éamon de Valera's technically accurate argument that the Second Dáil had not formally been dissolved before the June 1922 election. This rump 'Second Dáil' re-installed de Valera as president of the Irish Republic and, upon his release from prison in July 1924, appointed its own republican government.[67] These innovations took no account of, and had no impact on, the Free State, which by the end of the Civil War had proved itself a legitimate and viable entity both to the Irish public and to the international community. De Valera and some other republicans came to recognise this: in April 1926, he formed the powerful political party Fianna Fáil, and when circumstance demanded, he led it into the Dáil in August 1927. The residual 'Second Dáil', an embittered fundamentalist republican congeries now quite bereft of political talent and public support, limped along for over a decade until, in December 1938, it resolved to 'delegate the authority reposed in us to the Army Council of the IRA', which thus became the legislature and executive as well as the army of the Irish Republic.[68] In subsequent decades, it was this hand-me-down mantle of the Republic, unpicked and rewoven into a balaclava, which provided the ideological basis for Irish republican violence until the mainstream republican leadership, like de Valera before them, cast it aside, finally accepting the legitimacy of the real Republic of Ireland and its democratic institutions.

The August 1923 election marked 'a vigorous effort by interest groups' representing workers, farmers and businessmen 'to gain control of the Dáil, and to transform the whole basis of the Irish party system'.[69] The outcome demonstrated 'the continued vitality of the Treaty division' and was very disappointing particularly for Labour and the Farmers' Party.[70] Yet while the absence of the forty-four Sinn Féin TDs from Dáil Éireann after August 1923 temporarily deprived Irish politics of a significant bloc of political talent and revolutionary experience, it did create an opportunity for others to show their mettle. Labour by default became the official opposition.[71] There the party doggedly contributed, as Ciara Meehan has observed, to 'the creation of political stability and democratic normality' and ensuring that the executive was held to account in the Oireachtas.[72] Yet it transpired that Labour was effectively just warming up the opposition benches for de Valera and Fianna Fáil once they took the oath and entered the Dáil. The Treaty split found a natural home in the new Ireland.

Returning to Normalcy

Practical rather than ideological factors explain why neither Staines nor Moloney sought election to Dáil Éireann in 1923. It is likely that Staines, only recently married, thought it best to settle down and earn a living. He had served as the first garda commissioner in February 1922 but resigned in September after seven tumultuous months which saw a short-lived mutiny over pay and over the employment of ex-RIC men as officers in the new force.[73] In 1930, he returned to the Oireachtas when elected to Seanad Éireann to fill the seat vacated by the death of General Sir Bryan Mahon, and he remained a senator until the abolition of the second chamber in 1936. He made some pithy contributions. In 1933, he denounced the de Valera government's plans to impose pay cuts on the Garda Síochána, the force which he had helped bring into being, observing that when a similar measure was planned in 1930 by W.T. Cosgrave's Minister for Finance Ernest Blythe, the 'proposal in its stark nakedness was killed'.[74] In 1934, Staines argued successfully that the Military Service Pensions Bill, which was introduced to recognise the military service of anti-Treatyites between 1916 and 1923 on the same lines as had been granted in 1924 to those who had fought on the government side during the Civil War of 1922–3, should be extended to include, 'in this age of chivalry, this age of the equality of the sexes, the Cumann-na-mBan' who 'fought in Easter Week just as well as the Volunteers, the Hibernian Rifles, the Fianna Eireann and the Citizen Army. They fought as well and they are as well entitled to pensions'.[75]

In 1925, Staines was awarded a very substantial military service annual pension of £279 7s. 6d. He had already established himself as a hardware wholesaler, and for a time he also served as a director of the New Ireland Assurance Company. But despite his organisational talents he appears to have been hopeless with money, and he had chronic difficulty supporting his family of seven children (one of whom died suddenly in 1952).[76]

Michael Staines was clearly highly regarded across the Civil War divide. Upon his death, de Valera's *Irish Press* reported in very positive terms on his revolutionary career and achievements. Senior Fianna Fáil figures also attended his funeral alongside ministers of the Fine Gael-led John A. Costello coalition government, as well as other dignitaries and military and garda officers.[77]

P.J. Moloney played no direct role during the Civil War, though he bore the worry that his two surviving sons were hunted men serving on Liam Lynch's staff and likely to be killed or executed if captured. He had not yet rebuilt his pharmacy business and his main income appears to have come from part-time work as a 'medical compounder' for Tipperary Board of Guardians, with whom he engaged in lengthy correspondence in 1923 in an attempt to secure arrears of salary and better pay.[78] He was succeeded in the August 1923 election as Tipperary town's standard-bearer by the celebrated IRA man Dan Breen: anti-Treaty Sinn Féin took two of the seven Tipperary seats with 29 per cent of the poll.[79] Moloney later supported de Valera's move into conventional politics, becoming a member of Fianna Fáil. For many years he chaired the commemorative committee for Seán Treacy (1895–1920) and gave the annual graveside oration.[80] Moloney's funeral in September 1947, reported in the *Irish Press*, was attended by Taoiseach Éamon de Valera: 'The coffin was draped in the Tricolour, and members of the Third Tipperary Brigade … formed a guard of honour.'[81] In a tribute, Dan Breen TD said that

> Yes, PJ was with us in the fight. He also gave his three sons to the fight … The Ireland he worked and suffered for shall be realised and when that day dawns of a completely free and Gaelic Ireland, PJ Moloney's name will shine out on the list of those whom he has now joined in his eternal reward.[82]

Conclusion: Definitive Ambiguity

This brief study of two TDs, one pro- and one anti-Treaty, placed in the context of a wider effort to determine the backgrounds of all of the 121 Second Dáil TDs who deliberated and voted on the Treaty, is hardly definitive but it does provide a cautionary note for those who attempt to project onto the immediate Treaty split clear social and economic divisions within the revolutionary elite, characterising pro-Treatyite TDs as essentially more bourgeois and inherently more conservative than their opponents.

The data discussed here indicate that factors such as age, or military experience, or periods of imprisonment, or loss of a family member during the independence struggle, or class origins, or level of education, or occupation, or economic circumstances, do not satisfactorily explain the Treaty split in Dáil Éireann. The cases of the younger, single, penniless Michael Staines and the older, married, well-established P.J. Moloney are instructive not because they are anomalous but because they are not.

In seeking to explain the Treaty split, therefore, we must look to other factors, both personal and ideological. It is clear that many TDs took their line from leaders whom they trusted, 'Mick' or 'Dev'. But they did not do so blindly. The Treaty debates may appear inward-looking, and at times uncomfortably bitter and personal, but this was neither surprising nor reprehensible. Why should people not speak with feeling, and sometimes with venom, when presented with an Anglo-Irish settlement which almost everybody agreed was less than perfect, when the stakes were so high and the choices so stark, when the Treaty acknowledged the Crown and left the question of Irish unity hanging? All of the TDs who voted considered themselves Irish republicans as well as Irish separatists. What they could not agree on was how best to define an Irish republic, let alone how best to achieve it, in the prevailing circumstances. Those arguments have not yet fully run their course in Irish politics.

Notes

1   Witness statement of Michael Staines, 25 July 1947 (Bureau of Military History (BMH), 284).
2   Witness statements of Michael Staines, 10 May 1954 (BMH, 943, 944).
3   Witness statement of Michael Staines (BMH, 943).
4   P.J. Moloney's account of arrest and imprisonment, nd, c. late June 1916 (The National Archives, London (TNA), HO144/1457/313643). Eunan O'Halpin is very grateful to Professor Anne Dolan for drawing his attention to this document, referred to hereafter as 'Moloney journal'.
5   Nenagh Guardian, 20 Nov. 1920.
6   Census of Ireland, 1901, 1911 (National Archives of Ireland (NAI)).
7   Erhard Rumpf and A.C. Hepburn, Nationalism and socialism in twentieth-century Ireland (Liverpool, 1977), p. 34.
8   Tom Garvin, 'The formation of the Irish political élite' in Brian Farrell (ed.), The creation of the Dáil: a volume of essays from the Thomas Davis lectures (Dublin, 1994), p. 58.
9   Gavin M. Foster, The Irish Civil War and society: politics, class, and conflict (Basingstoke, 2015), pp. 6, 117–22.
10   Richard Sinnott, Irish voters decide: voting behaviour in elections and referendums since 1918 (Manchester, 1995), p. 172.
11   General report of 1911 census in Ireland (www.histop.org) (4 Nov. 2017).
12   Garvin, 'Formation of the Irish political élite', p. 58.
13   Michael Gallagher, Irish elections 1922–1944: results and analysis: i (Limerick, 1993), p. 24.
14   Michael Laffan, The resurrection of Ireland: the Sinn Féin party, 1916-1923 (Cambridge, 1999), p. 337.

15   Kevin Galligan, *Peter Paul Galligan: 'one of the most dangerous men in the rebel movement'* (Dublin, 2012), pp. 112–13.

16   Eunan O'Halpin, *Defending Ireland: the Irish state and its enemies since 1916* (Oxford, 1999), p. 79.

17   *Census of Ireland*, 1911.

18   Witness statement of Michael Staines (BMH, 284).

19   Ibid.

20   Witness statement of Michael Staines (BMH, 284).

21   Ibid.

22   Witness statement of Michael Staines (BMH, 284).

23   File of William F. Staines, Dec. 1918–11 Feb. 1937 (Military Archives of Ireland (MAI), Military Service Pensions Collection (MSPC), DP5788).

24   Witness statement of Michael Staines (BMH, 944); witness statement of Michael McCoy, 4 May 1951 (ibid., 1610).

25   Witness statement of Michael Staines (BMH, 944).

26   Ibid.

27   Register of Seaman's Services: stokers, John Patrick Staines (TNA, ADM/188/898/15531).

28   'L55. The ship that wouldn't die' (http://www.wokinghamremembers.com/l55-the-ship-that-wouldnt-die/) (18 Feb. 2018); family information from Dr Mary Staines.

29   Moloney journal.

30   Ibid.

31   Tom Garvin, *Nationalist revolutionaries in Ireland, 1858–1928* (Dublin, 1987), p. 10.

32   Moloney journal.

33   Fr John Hannon's statement, nd, *c.* 1902 (Jesuit Archives, Dublin, 'Informations of the Novices, 1897–1907').

34   William Hannon's army medal card and Royal Air Force service record (TNA, WO372/9 and AIR76/207).

35   Information from James Moloney (1896–1981), grandfather of Eunan O'Halpin, *c.* 1976. On Bracken, see Charles Lysaght, *Brendan Bracken* (London, 1979).

36   *Mungret Annual 1913*, pp. 142–3.

37   Transcript of interview with Senator Bill Quirke and Seán Fitzpatrick, 17 Apr. 1936 (MAI, MSPC, 4143) (James Moloney application, not yet released, but extracts in possession of Eunan O'Halpin); Desmond Ryan, *Sean Treacy and the 3rd Tipperary Brigade* (Tralee, 1945), p. 45.

38   Sir Maurice Hankey's diary entry, 21 May 1918, quoted in Eunan O'Halpin, *The decline of the Union: British government in Ireland 1892–1920* (Dublin, 1987), p. 162.

39   *Irish Independent*, 14 May 1920.

40   'Extracts from loose-leaf diary' of Captain Ernie O'Malley, 15 Sept. 1920 (King's College, London, Liddell Hart Centre for Military Archives, Foulkes Papers, 7/24, epitome G/3347/1).

41   *The Advocate*, 19 May 1921. Eunan O'Halpin is grateful to Elizabeth Ward for sending an extract from this source, an Australian Catholic weekly newspaper published in Melbourne, Victoria.

42   Witness statement of Paul Merrigan, 3 Sept. 1957 (BMH, 1667); transcript of James Moloney's interview with Military Service Pensions Board, 3 Mar. 1936 (MAI, MSPC, 4143) (not yet released, but extracts in possession of Eunan O'Halpin).

43   Eunan O'Halpin's recollection of a letter shown to him by James Moloney's relative Dr Pat Humphreys, Dublin, c. 1993.

44   *Nenagh Guardian*, 20 Nov. 1920.

45   Ernie O'Malley, *On another man's wound* (Cork, 2013), p. 400.

46   *Tipperary Star*, 3 May 1921.

47   *Irish Independent*, 9 Mar. 1923. University College Dublin Archives (UCDA) holds Con Moloney's papers (UCDA, P9), while correspondence between Jim and his wife Kathy Barry Moloney can be found in her papers (UCDA, P94).

48   *Nenagh Guardian*, 19 July 1924.

49   C.S. Andrews, *Dublin made me: an autobiography* (Dublin, 1979), pp. 205–6.

50   Ibid.

51   Westmeath County Council minutes, 15 Dec. 1921 (Westmeath County Library, WMCC10/17).

52   Bill Kissane, *The politics of the Irish Civil War* (Oxford, 2006), pp. 59–60; Laffan, *Resurrection of Ireland*, pp. 357–8.

53   John M. Regan, *The Irish counter-revolution 1921–1936: Treatyite politics and settlement in independent Ireland* (Dublin, 1999), p. 38.

54   *Dáil Éireann deb.*, T, no. 9, 147–8 (22 Dec. 1921).

55   *Nenagh Guardian*, 17 June 1922.

56   Ibid.

57   Ibid.

58   *Dáil Éireann deb.*, T, no. 14, 296 (6 Jan. 1922).

59   Mary Staines, 'The Anglo-Irish Treaty debate December 1921–January 1922: who decided and why?' (M.Phil. dissertation, Trinity College Dublin, 2016).

60   Jason Knirck, *Imagining Ireland's independence: the debates over the Anglo-Irish Treaty of 1921* (Lanham, MD, 2006), p. 128.

61   *Dáil Éireann deb.*, T, no. 8, 91 (21 Dec. 1921).

62   Jason Knirck, *Women of the Dáil* (Dublin, 2006), pp. 72, 78.

63   Ibid.

64   *Dáil Éireann deb.*, T, no. 11, 250 (4 Jan. 1922).

65   Ibid., no. 8, 122 (21 Dec. 1921).

66   Kathy Barry to Jim Moloney, 23 Feb. 1923, quoted by Eve Morrison in the *Irish Times*, 23 May 2013.

67   Brian P. Murphy, *Patrick Pearse and the lost republican ideal* (Dublin, 1991), pp. 141–6.

68   Second Dáil resolution, 8 Dec. 1938, quoted in ibid., p. 182.

69   Gallagher, *Irish elections*, pp. 23–4.

70   Ibid.

71   Ibid.

72   Ciara Meehan, 'Labour and Dáil Éireann, 1922–32' in Paul Daly, Ronan O'Brien and Paul Rouse (eds), *Making the difference? The Irish Labour Party 1912–2012* (Dublin, 2012), p. 53.

73   Witness statement of Michael Staines (BMH, 944); Michael Staines's military service pension record, 11 Feb. 1925–3 Feb. 1986 (MAI, MSPC, 24SP6787); Conor Brady, *Guardians of the peace* (Dublin, 1974), p. 72.

74   *Seanad Éireann deb.*, xvii, no. 8, 628 (25 July 1933).

75   Ibid., xix, no. 3, 296 (24 Aug. 1934).

76   *Irish Press*, 19 May 1952.

77   *Irish Independent*, 29 Oct. 1955.

78   Tipperary Poor Law Union minutes, 1922–3, entries for 27 Jan., 24 Mar., 28 Apr., 19 May, 28 July, 4 Aug., 29 Sept. and 10 Nov. 1923 (Tipperary County Library, Thurles).

79   Gallagher, *Irish elections*, p. 41.

80   See, for example, *Nenagh Guardian*, 19 Oct. 1940, 20 Oct. 1945.

81   Ibid., 13 Sept. 1947.

82   *Irish Press*, 8 Sept. 1947.

CHAPTER 6

Debating not Negotiating: The Female TDs of the Second Dáil

Sinéad McCoole

This chapter is an examination of the female TDs of the Second Dáil, their contributions to the Treaty debates in December 1921 and January 1922, and how these contributions were reported and portrayed during the early years of the Irish Free State. It is the author's intention to give readers a fuller understanding of the contribution of the female TDs by placing the debates in the context of women in politics in the lead-up to December 1921. This chapter brings together small biographical details for the first time. By examining each of the deputies individually, looking at their education and their experiences as activists, it is intended to bring new insights to their contributions to the Treaty debates. Central to this chapter are Mary MacSwiney's and Countess Constance Markievicz's ambitions to join the Treaty delegation. By exploring the documentation that survives, it is hoped that a more rounded view of these women emerges, providing some new insights into their thoughts and motivations.

The chapter opens and closes with the depiction of the women TDs of the Second Dáil by historians from the 1920s to the present and ends with a call for a re-reading of the Treaty debates through a gendered lens.

Women's Contribution to the Treaty Debates – Legacy Issues

In his book *Michael Collins and the making of a new Ireland* (1926), Piaras Béaslaí described Mary MacSwiney's contribution during the Treaty debates as a 'screeching tirade'.[1] Written in post-Civil War Ireland, when MacSwiney was an articulate opponent of the new government, one must conclude that it was expedient for political purposes to cast her thus as she continued her espousal of the legitimacy of the Second Dáil.[2] Indeed, TDs who opposed the Irish Free State often referred to the Second Dáil, which continued to meet under anti-Treaty Sinn Féin's auspices. A photograph of one of the gatherings, sold by the Dublin photography company Lafayette, and including Kate O'Callaghan, Mary MacSwiney and Dr Ada English, was mounted on a card with the title *Dáil Éireann: Easter 1928*.

Over the last century, the female activists have been described variously as eccentrics, disreputable and in Éamon de Valera's words, 'at once the boldest and most unmanageable revolutionaries'.[3] F.S.L. Lyons's *Ireland since the Famine* (1973), a standard textbook for second- and third-level history students for almost two decades, described Mary MacSwiney as a 'fanatical' republican and Countess Markievicz as 'bitter and intense'.[4] He went on to state that 'she had many attributes of a soldier … she was to play a man's part in and after 1916'.[5] Roy Foster's *Modern Ireland* (1989), a key Irish text of that decade which was read widely outside academia, does not mention the contributions of the female TDs in the Treaty debates, or indeed, crucially, their imprisonment along with other women in such large numbers during the Civil War. All six female members of the Second Dáil – Countess Markievicz, Mary MacSwiney, Ada English, Kathleen Clarke, Kate O'Callaghan and Margaret Pearse – rejected the Treaty. Cumann na mBan overwhelmingly rejected the Treaty by 419 votes to 63. Upwards of 700 women were imprisoned during the Civil War period 1922–3 including Mary MacSwiney, Countess Markievicz, Kate O'Callaghan and Kathleen Clarke. By the 1980s, knowledge of the mass arrest of women appeared to be all but lost to the mainstream narrative.[6] Interviews with those who were anti-Treaty were recorded elsewhere in the publications of non-academic historians: Uinseann MacEoin's *Survivors* (1980) and Kenneth Griffith and Timothy O'Grady's *Curious journey* (1982).

Anti-Treaty Stance

The president of the executive council of the Irish Free State, W.T. Cosgrave, stated that the women imprisoned in the Civil War could not be treated as 'ordinary women'.[7] Kevin O'Higgins, writing privately on

5 July 1923, described that 'the national hysteria is almost gone – a few ladies drumming their heels on the ground, but the acoustics for that kind of thing are not as good as they used to be'.[8]

Jason Knirck's key text *Women of the Dáil: gender, republicanism and the Anglo-Irish Treaty* describes the women TDs as the guardians of the revolutionary traditions and surrogates of memory; he suggests that they were replacing their male relatives. This dismisses the women TDs' roles in maintaining and indeed building support for the 'Sinn Féin' cause following the mass arrest of moderate and extremist nationalist men in the wake of the 1916 Rising. Ireland was a country that had experienced years of an unofficial, but at the same time brutal and intense, guerrilla war. Three of the Second Dáil's female TDs had spent time in prison – Countess Markievicz, Kathleen Clarke and Ada English, and two were widowed – Kathleen Clarke in 1916 and Kate O'Callaghan in 1921. In 1920, Mary MacSwiney's brother Terence had died on hunger-strike for political status. It also dismisses the idea that the women were independent thinkers. Mary MacSwiney said in the Treaty debates on 21 December 1921: 'I am not speaking as a young, ardent enthusiast. I am speaking as a woman who has thought and studied much, who realises, as only as a woman can, the evils of war and the suffering of war.'[9] In spite of this, even while the debates were on-going, the women of the Dáil were being linked to dead men. In response to this, on 4 January 1922, Ada English stated: 'I thank my God, I have no dead men to throw in my teeth as a reason for holding the opinions that I hold.'[10]

Women Politicised

In reviewing the contribution of the female TDs to the Treaty debates, it must be remembered that in May 1921, it was only the second time women could contest parliamentary elections in Ireland. To fully understand their contribution, it is important to examine their acceptance into the political realm and into party politics. Events in Ireland in the opening decades of the twentieth century fundamentally changed how the first generation of female voters, female candidates and the successful female parliamentarians conducted themselves.

Women who had been politicised in an earlier period, that is those who had served as Poor Law Guardians, urban district councillors and rural district councillors, never entered the Dáil. They remained outside politics in the post-1916 era. Women who supported the Irish Parliamentary Party (IPP) and home rule did not stand for election in 1918. Louie Bennett, one of the founders of the Irishwomen's Reform League, was the first woman nominated for election in 1918 by the Labour Party but declined to stand. While she continued in public service, making her contribution in trade unionism and rising to the position of president of the Irish Trade Union Congress in 1932, she never served in the Dáil.

Unlike their male counterparts, the 234,046 Ulster unionist women who signed the Women's Declaration in support of the Union in 1912 (including those who had signed in Dublin who could prove they were born in Ulster) had not been required to take up arms or give their support to an armed conflict in a realisation of their pledge. In the new House of Commons of Northern Ireland established under the Government of Ireland Act of 1920, two members of the Ulster Women's Unionist Council were elected in 1921 – Dehra Chichester and Julia McMordie. They were able to enter the political arena and focus on issues. In her earliest speech in the House of Commons, McMordie defended the appointment of female police officers. This was at a time when there were two women in a force of 3,000 officers. McMordie opposed the Constabulary Bill of 1922 as there was no clause dealing with women officers. While Chichester entered politics as a widow, she was not defined by it. From the outset she was an important force in her party and was the first woman to sit in the Northern Ireland cabinet, albeit two decades later.

Another Ulster woman, Winifred (Winnie) Carney stood unsuccessfully for election in 1918 in the 'unpromising wards for Sinn Féiners, the Central/East Belfast Victoria Division'.[11] Born in County Down and raised in Belfast, Carney was a confidant of James Connolly and had served in the General Post Office headquarters garrison in 1916. Carney did not contest the election in 1921. Her biographer records that following her election defeat in 1918, she had commented: 'I am determined that I too shall one day share the responsibility in directing the government of the country'.[12] This was not to be. Her desire for a socialist republic was unfulfilled and she lived out her days in Belfast.

In 1918, Countess Markievicz was elected the only female member of the First Dáil Éireann. In accordance with Sinn Féin's policy, she did not take up her seat in Westminster. Markievicz became minister for labour, a position for which she had not been proposed; she had bullied her way to the position, claiming that she had earned the right to be a minister as well as any of the men, and if she was not made minister she would go over to the Labour Party, as Kathleen Clarke details in her autobiography.[13] Markievicz was imprisoned for much of the campaign for independence in 1919, and again from September 1920 to July 1921. This compromised her ability to run her department (in addition to the other complications of her being part of an illegal organisation trying to fulfil the functions of an underground government during an armed conflict). This also meant putting aside issues to focus on attaining independence. Markievicz described women during this period: 'We have been in a difficult position in Ireland because we were on the run … War measures were the only measures that were attended to and naturally the women did not push forward at this time'.[14] Both by education and upbringing these women were schooled to be reserved. Acceptance into a male world of politics was now complicated by the highly charged atmosphere of war. Latterly, with so many women not taking their seats in the Dáil because of their opposition to the Irish Free State, this had a significant consequence at a time when a new party political system was being founded. The Third Dáil, resulting from the 'pact election', was formed by Michael Collins and Éamon de Valera in May 1922. Two of the women candidates were returned: Mary MacSwiney and Kate O'Callaghan. Margaret Pearse, Ada English and Kathleen Clarke were defeated. The Dáil, which was due to have its first session on 30 June, did not sit as hostilities commenced. Michael Collins was killed in the conflict that followed. The general election of August 1923 lead to the formation of the Fourth Dáil. Cáitlín Brugha, Dr Kathleen Lynn and Countess Markievicz were elected but refused to take their seats. Margaret Collins-O'Driscoll was the only female who took her seat. She was a Cumann na nGaedheal TD for Dublin North and Michael Collins's sister.

Republican Tradition

In his study of the Treaty debates, Jason Knirck argues that this period allowed for a feminisation of the republican tradition. Certainly, all the women who entered the Dáil were republican. Cumann na Saoirse (the women's group that accepted the Treaty) did not become a vehicle by which pro-Treaty women entered the political arena. What is really meant by a feminisation of the republican tradition? As Dorothy Macardle discusses in *The Irish Republic*: 'Whether the Irish Republic ever existed has been disputed not only by jurists and not only with words. For the Irish people the Republic was for a few tense years, a living reality which dominated every aspect of their lives. Its existence was a fact of human history, if not of logic or law.'[15]

Some of the female TDs would have been well-read in the republican tradition that originated with Theobald Wolfe Tone, who had been inspired by ideals of the French Revolution. Countess Markievicz's book collection in 1901/1902 included Colonel Philip Roche Fermoy's *Commentary on the memoir of Theobald Wolfe Tone* (1846).[16] However, the 'republican' tradition for most anti-Treaty women was simply the 1916 Proclamation which had been addressed to Irishmen and Irishwomen and promised 'equal rights and equal opportunities'. The proclamation was often quoted by women in private and public declarations in those years. In 1917, 25,000 copies of a leaflet urging women to assert the political rights given to them by the republican proclamation were published.[17] A miniature copy of the proclamation was pasted into the minute book of the Committee of the Women Delegates to the All-Ireland Conference (on 19 April 1917; as if to serve as a reminder of its contents).[18] To women TDs during the Treaty debates, the Proclamation of the Provisional Government of the Irish Republic was more than a manifesto, it was a statement that the Republic they had been fighting for was a place in which they were equal citizens. Within a year of the Rising new male activists came to the fore. They had a different outlook from the men who had put their names to the 1916 Proclamation. As Margaret Ward has argued: 'the realisation began to dawn that if they did not insist upon a voice in this process their male comrades would have reorganised and determined future polices without consultation or inclusion of their female colleagues.'[19]

Exclusion From the Political Centre

On 19 April 1917, one year after the Rising, a meeting was convened by George Noble, Count Plunkett, to ascertain if the 'Liberty Clubs' and 'Arthur Griffith's Sinn Féin' would become the nucleus of the new nationalist political movement. A council of nine was formed and Plunkett's wife Josephine was the only woman involved. Countess Plunkett had been selected rather than elected and many believed she was not the most qualified. As outlined by Margaret Ward: 'Many women were unhappy with this situation and doubtful if the elderly countess was suitable for the task and angry that women had only been given one representative.'[20] Josephine Plunkett's daughter, Geraldine Dillon (who it must be noted was one of her mother's strongest critics), wrote in her memoirs of her mother's poor grasp of the political situation in this period and of how she was prevented from giving interviews.[21] One month after her co-option, a deputation of women representing Inghinidhe na hÉireann (Maud Gonne's Daughters of Ireland), the Irish Women Workers' Union and the Irish Citizen Army came together. These were the most vocal and political women of the period. They worked together across many causes. They formed the 'League of Women's Delegates' (later known as Cumann na Teachtaire) and instigated a number of actions. They held meetings to ensure that women were fully represented in politics but at no point did they consider forming themselves into a political party.

One action was to write (a rather circuitous route) to Countess Plunkett's son-in-law Tom Dillon, asking him to include that 'women were equal to be delegates on all councils' when writing to nationalists around the country.[22] By June 1917, the 1916 Rising prisoners were being released. The council of nine was expanded but no more women were included. When Countess Plunkett was ill, Kathleen Lynn was put forward as a substitute. Lynn was a medical doctor and the chief medical officer in the Irish Citizen Army during the 1916 Rising. She was astute and capable but as the sole female representative, her impact would have been limited. (Her contributions to this group are undocumented.)

There were more setbacks for the women when the Sinn Féin executive committee was formed. Men from the Irish Volunteers were automatically co-opted, but not Cumann na mBan members. Countess Markievicz was co-opted following her release from prison. She was probably the best-known female politician in Ireland and Britain, with frequent appearances in the popular press as 'the rebel countess'. An advocate of the rights of women and workers, Markievicz was the only woman sentenced to death for her part in the Rising, but her sentence had been commuted to life in prison (she served just over one year).

At the Sinn Féin convention in 1917, members of the League of Women's Delegates succeeded in getting a resolution passed to have the equality of men and women emphasised in all speeches and leaflets. The other resolution to have women form half of those on the Sinn Féin executive committee was ruled out of order. The League of Women's Delegates held meetings but not always as public forums. The group's minute book records a meeting in December 1917 in the bathroom at the Mansion House, next to the Round Room.[23] The significance of those prominent women meeting in such circumstances does not suggest a strong political movement, but a secretive, behind-the-scenes action group, planning how to approach negotiation without bringing attention to their actions.

The minute book records of the League of Women's Delegates seem to suggest that the group ceased to meet after 1919. This may be explained by the onset of the hostilities which became known as the War of Independence. It had certainly not disbanded because its list of requirements had been attained. Indeed, after the truce, the situation for women within the party structure was not greatly altered. In her capacity as director of organisation for Sinn Féin, Hanna Sheehy Skeffington concluded her overview of the party: 'An impression exists in some districts that membership ... is confined to men. This is a mistake and every effort should be made ... women shall not only be on the roll as members but take an active share in the work of ... the Sinn Féin movement generally'.[24] Sheehy Skeffington was never elected to the Dáil. When she stood as a candidate of the Women's Social and Progressive League in Dublin South in the general election of 1943, she received 917 first preference votes.[25] Her ability had been acknowledged by P.H. Pearse, Tom Clarke, Éamonn Ceannt, Joseph Plunkett, Thomas MacDonagh, Seán Mac Diarmada and James Connolly. When they had established themselves as the Provisional Government of the Irish Republic in 1916, their plan for a five-member civil provisional government had allocated one position to a woman, and that woman had been Sheehy Skeffington.[26]

In August 1921, when the Dáil cabinet was reorganised, Countess Markievicz was reappointed but she was left out of the inner circle of decision-making ministers. She was the most seasoned female politician in the Dáil in 1921. Her many speeches inside and outside the chamber demonstrated her ability. One of her well-crafted speeches was published as a pamphlet in 1909: *Women, ideals and the nation*. Markievicz had been educated by private tutors and had received art training in Britain and France. She referred to her lack of formal education in the speech on extending the franchise in March 1922: 'I have a vote myself to send men and women to the Dáil and I wish to have that privilege extended to the young women of Ireland, who I count in every way as my superiors … they had the education denied me in my youth.'[27] She was quickly referenced in the history books for her central role but was not immune to negative portrayal. Her first biographer, Seán Ó Faoláin, was highly critical. *The average revolutionary* (1934) outraged Markievicz's contemporaries. Their counterblast came from Helena Molony, member of the Irish Citizen Army, city hall garrison, trade unionist and editor of *Bean na hÉireann*. Molony wrote in the 1930s: 'any serious thing a woman does (outside nursing babies or washing pots) is the result of being in love with some man or disappointment in love of some man or looking for excitement, or limelight or indulging their vanity.'[28]

It has been suggested by Jason Knirck that Mary MacSwiney would not have achieved prominence on her own without the circumstances that befell her. He quotes a letter sent to Cumann na mBan headquarters: 'If anyone had told me twelve months ago what I should be doing today I should have advised him to take a bee-line for the nearest lunatic asylum.'[29] Many events that shaped MacSwiney's life were not of her making and not of her choice. The eldest of nine MacSwiney children, she was born in London and, in 1904, was teaching in a British boarding school. Her mother's death brought her back to Cork to oversee the upbringing and welfare of her younger siblings. When her younger brother Terence was dying on hunger-strike in Brixton Prison in 1920, it is not surprising that, in *loco parentis*, his spinster sister would travel there. Her ability as a press spokesperson placed her in the public realm. She maintained an international focus on her brother until his death after seventy-four days on hunger-strike. She travelled to the United States on a speaking tour at the request of Éamon de Valera and was there when elected as a TD. She wrote to de Valera from Philadelphia on 20 July 1921, the day he set out for London for the first negotiations with Prime Minister David Lloyd George:

It is now nearly eight months since I took up, at your special request, the task of touring this country. And in view of possible new developments I want to write you for further orders. Needless to say, how we are longing for a peep at the inside negotiations ... I feel very strongly that Lloyd George being a very clever man ... in view of England's big troubles all over the World, – the wisest course for her Government would be to acknowledge our Republic at once and make friends with us. Whether he can persuade the Tories to agree with him or not remains to be seen.[30]

In the same letter, she told de Valera that she would oppose the settlement: 'If by any chance there should be a question of putting the matter before the Country I shall take the first boat home to add my voice to the "No Surrender" side'.[31] At the first stage of the negotiations she had already defined her position. She concluded her letter:

As for having 'done my bit', that plea is out of course, for none of us can be said to have done our part fully till Ireland is free or we are dead. If I leave here it will only be to do something else at home and the question is where I can be most use. I do not ask for any option in the matter being I hope as good a soldier as the next.[32]

What has not been fully explored to date is MacSwiney's own political ambitions, most particularly her desire to be on the delegation team to broker a peace deal. In later years, she told a friend that when she asked de Valera if she might join the negotiation team he told her that she was 'too extreme'.[33] De Valera gives no indication of this when he wrote of her to Joseph McGarrity on 27 December 1921: 'Miss MacSwiney I would have liked to see facing Lloyd George across the table not merely because of her own personality and her political ability, but Lloyd George could not fail to see beside her the spirit of her dead brother'.[34]

In 1924, P.S. O'Hegarty published a personal exchange between himself and Mary MacSwiney in his *The victory of Sinn Féin*. This took place when she returned from her tour of the United States. He reproduces his conversation, in which he admonishes MacSwiney for thinking that de Valera could achieve a republic. He told her 'use your own intelligence' and she replied that she thought de Valera could achieve a 'semi-independent connexion with England which we could accept'.[35] This exchange was written when both de Valera and MacSwiney were not elected members of the Dáil. It has to be assessed as a pro-Treaty view, based on a past conversation with an opponent who was still a threat to the stability of the state. It is important also to see it as a more compromising depiction of MacSwiney at this juncture, which contrasts with her delivery at the Treaty debates, where she reverted to her desire for a full republic. In a public session on 21 December 1921, she told the assembled TDs: 'You have told us it is between the acceptance of that document and war. If it were, with every sense of deep responsibility, I say then let us take war'.[36] MacSwiney was considering 'Document No. 2', de Valera's solution to the terms of the Treaty, which was withdrawn.

On 22 February 1922, Jennie Wyse Power, now pro-Treaty, wrote of MacSwiney as 'the virtual leader' and of how de Valera 'is completely in her hands'.[37] She concluded: 'It is a great tribute to her strength.'[38] Wyse Power was the woman with the longest career in active politics; from the Ladies' Land League she had moved on to become a founding member of the Irish Women's Franchise League, vice-president of Inghinidhe na hÉireann, a Poor Law Guardian and a founder member and vice-president of Sinn Féin and an executive committee member of Cumann na mBan and vice-president of Cumann na Saoirse, the short-lived pro-Treaty group. The private coded message, quoted above and sent, it is believed, to her daughter Nancy, does not conceal her admiration for MacSwiney. It is important to note that at this moment, women, even those in opposition, saw MacSwiney as a woman in power showing steadfastness in the face of opposition. In October 1922, MacSwiney was appointed as one of de Valera's council of state. Her decision to go on hunger-strike, first in November 1922 and again when she was arrested for a second time in April 1923, is linked with her brother's actions but must also be seen as the action of a woman prepared to stand by her principles regardless of the consequences, not merely as a copycat action. She had stated that she would take this stance on 21 December 1921, in public session: 'If this country should be so false to itself as to adopt the so-called Treaty, I have already told some of the Ministers on the other side of the House that I will be their first rebel under their so-called Free State, that they will have the pleasure or the pain as it pleases them, of imprisoning me as one of their first and most deliberate and irreconcilable rebels.'[39]

Countess Markievicz also expressed her desire to be part of the negotiating team; she cited a fuller understanding of the British because of her upbringing and family links. At the public session on 3 January 1922, she stated: 'Now you all know me, you know that my people came here in Henry VIII's time, and by that bad black drop of English blood in me I know the English – that's the truth. I say it is because of the black drop in me that I know the English personally better perhaps than the people who went over on the delegation.'[40] This contribution was greeted with laughter. She continued: 'Why, didn't you send me? I tell you, don't trust the English with gifts in their hands ... I tell you, you will come out of this a defeated nation ... I am pledged as a rebel, an unconvertible rebel, because I am pledged to the one thing – a free and independent Republic.'[41]

Looking Beyond the Treaty Debates: Was the Women's Ability Underestimated?

The women of the Dáil were very well educated by the standard of the day and would have been an asset to the negotiating team. Jim Kemmy, Limerick Labour TD and local historian (someone who would have had the advantage of first-hand accounts), described Kate O'Callaghan: 'Kate added an intellectual spur to her husband's aspirations for culture and national self-determination.'[42] Contemporaries recall her 'brilliant mind imbibed with a wide knowledge of European culture.'[43] Madge Daly described her as 'refined, cultured and learned' and the Reverend Dr I. Cotter, who had known Kate and Michael O'Callaghan before 1921, described how he had never been in a house 'where husband and wife so supplemented intellectual activities on behalf of their dear country.'[44]

Born Kate Murphy in County Cork in 1885, she was one of eleven children surviving to adulthood. Along with her sisters Mary, Bridget and Ellen, she attended university. O'Callaghan attended St Mary's University College at the Dominican College on Eccles Street in Dublin. There she studied Irish (then described as Celtic), English Language and Literature, Elementary Mathematics and Natural Philosophy, before taking the Cambridge teacher-training examinations.[45] She went on to work in Mary

Immaculate College, Limerick, as a lecturer on Methods of Teaching from
1912 until her marriage to Michael O'Callaghan in 1914.[46]

O'Callaghan became a public figure in her adopted home of Limerick
city following the shooting of her husband Michael O'Callaghan on 7
March 1921. He had been mayor of Limerick during the height of the War
of Independence. O'Callaghan became one of the so-called 'Black Widows'
and was elected by the people of Limerick City-Limerick East. Madge Daly
described her vote as 'a huge vote' but the exact figures were not recorded.[47]
Her rise to prominence was ensured when she published her account of her
husband's murder by an unknown assassin entitled: *The Limerick curfew
murders of March 7th 1921: the case of Michael O'Callaghan, councillor and
ex-mayor, presented by his widow*. There was precedent for this, as Hanna
Sheehy Skeffington had published *British militarism as I have known it* in
1917, dealing with the events that surrounded the shooting of her husband
during the Rising. Sheehy Skeffington's account was in direct contradiction
to the official accounts. So too O'Callaghan wrote to counter the official
report that the shooting was by members of the Irish Republican Army
(IRA). O'Callaghan refused to attend the military court of inquiry, stating
that she would appear before a jury of her countrymen. On 10 March 1921,
she wrote: 'I shall not attend any Military Court of Inquiry, as I believe
that these courts are but a farce and a travesty of justice.'[48] When her
letters to the press were censored, she wrote her own account. Her vivid
retelling of witnessing her husband's death in the hallway of their home
put a public voice to her tragedy. As she wrote: 'I had never seen anybody
die, so I continued to hope; whereas from the first shot there was no hope
at all.'[49] As she described in the Dáil: 'My political views have always been
known in Limerick, and the people of Limerick who elected me Deputy
of this Dáil two months after my husband's murder, and because of that
murder, know I will stand by my convictions and by my oath to the Irish
Republic.'[50]

During the debates, it was clear that O'Callaghan was well informed
of the Treaty's contents and had a clear understanding. When describing
her reading of the documents, she did admit that she had read the
contents: 'with a mind sharpened by sorrow.'[51] The 37-year-old childless
widow had been politicised from an early age. She was an advocate of the
franchise for women and active in the suffrage movement. As she stated
during the debates:

For myself, since girlhood I have been a separatist, I wanted, and I want, an independent Ireland, an Ireland independent of the British Empire, and I can assure you that my life in Limerick during 1920, culminating in the murder of my husband last March – my life and that event have not converted me to Dominion Status within the British Empire.[52]

Madge Daly described her as 'incapable of being deflected from her high ideals'.[53] O'Callaghan addressed this when she stated, on 20 December 1921: 'When it was found that the women deputies of An Dáil were not open to canvas, the matter was dismissed with the remark: "Oh, naturally, these women are very bitter." Well, now I protest at that. No woman in this Dáil is going to give her vote merely because she is warped by a deep personal loss.'[54] She continued: 'The women of Ireland so far have not appeared much on the political stage. That does not mean that they have no deep convictions about Ireland's status and freedom.'[55] In her contributions of 20 December 1921, she acquitted herself as a woman capable of her own judgements and forming her own beliefs. When others evoked Michael O'Callaghan's name she told them 'leave my husband's name out of this matter'.[56] It is important to highlight that O'Callaghan played down her own abilities during these debates. Despite being one of a small number of Irish women graduates and a former lecturer in a teacher-training college, she described herself as 'a plain person, a person of plain intelligence' when discussing the sequence of events and the instructions of the plenipotentiaries.[57]

Another of the first Irish women graduates, Dr Adeline (Ada) English, was one of Kate O'Callaghan's fellow deputies. English was born in Cahersiveen, County Kerry, on 10 January 1875, the daughter of an apothecary, Patrick English. She was raised in Mullingar where her father established his business, English's Medical Hall. Aged forty-four when elected to the Second Dáil, her constituency was the National University of Ireland (which had had four seats since 1918). In 1904, English qualified as a doctor, having completed her education at the Catholic University of Medicine on Cecilia Street in Dublin. In 1914, she became the first statutory lecturer in 'mental diseases' at University College Galway.[58] English had become a fluent Irish-speaker and in 1899, had been a pupil in P.H. Pearse's Gaelic League Irish class.

A Dublin Castle file dated 3 March 1918 recorded English as the president of the local Cumann na mBan in Ballinasloe. On 9 June 1918, she was recorded as chief organiser of a women's anti-conscription demonstration at Ballinasloe.[59] The report on her activities recorded that she had sheltered members of the IRA in the asylum in Ballinasloe, her place of work. She was arrested on 19 January 1921 because she had been found in possession of 'various documents relating to Sinn Féin'.[60] On 24 February 1921, English was tried by 'Field General Court Martial' in Galway under regulation 79, sub-section 3, of the regulations of the Restoration of Order in Ireland Act of 1920. English was sentenced to nine months in prison with 'hard labour' although hard labour was not imposed.[61]

While still in jail, English was elected as a TD. As she was suffering from food poisoning, she was released early from prison on 15 May 1921, on condition that she would reside outside the counties of Galway and Mayo. She obeyed this diktat in the short-term and in June was reported in the local press as recuperating in the south of France.[62] As she said in the Treaty debates on 4 January 1922:

> when I was selected as Deputy in this place I was very much surprised and, after I got out of jail, when I was well enough to see some of my constituents, I asked them how it came they selected me, and they said they selected me, and they told me they wanted someone they could depend on to stand by the Republic, and who would not let Galway down ... (cheers). That is what my constituents told me they wanted when they sent me here, and they have got it (cheers).[63]

Her objection was to the oath as reported in the Irish Times:

> If the oaths were omitted from the Treaty she could accept it under force, but while these oaths were in it, in which they were asked to accept the King of England as head of the Irish State and to accept the status of British subjects, they could not accept it ... It would be a complete spiritual surrender and would not bring peace but a bitter division to the country.[64]

Kathleen Clarke had been a Sinn Féin judge in the underground courts during the War of Independence. At the instruction of the Irish

Republican Brotherhood she had established the Republican Prisoners' Dependants' Fund to raise and distribute monies to the families of those imprisoned in the aftermath of the 1916 Rising. What is apparent from Clarke's own account and the reminiscences of others was that she was an independent thinker. In her early years, her single-minded approach was demonstrated when she set up her own dressmaking business in her native Limerick rather than joining the successful and expanding family bakery. An astute young woman, she built her business to be the second largest in the city until she closed it in 1901 to move to New York to marry Tom Clarke. Her steadfast commitment to marrying him (in opposition to her family's wishes) showed that she was not afraid to go against others when it came to her beliefs. In her contributions to the arguments for and against the ratification of the Treaty she was direct and uncompromising, as demonstrated during a public session on 22 December: 'It is to me the simple question of right and wrong. To my mind it is a surrender of all our national ideals.'[65]

The tragedies that Clarke had suffered, the death of her father and then the loss of her husband, brother and baby in 1916, marked her. There is a complexity to her story. This analysis has been made possible in recent times with private papers coming into the public domain. One of her personal political activism decisions, as demonstrated in a letter to Tom, was not to attend the inaugural meeting of Inghinidhe na hÉireann although, at the time, she was staying with Annie Egan, who became one of the vice-presidents of the organisation. She never joined the organisation despite the fact that her sisters were key members of the Limerick branch. Her sons did not take an active part in the War of Independence despite their father's express wish in his prison cell before his execution that they would follow his path. What role their mother had in this decision not to take part in conflicts that followed is unknown but serves to widen the discussion on her and, by extension, others involved in the conflict. By her decision to oppose the Treaty, she upheld her family tradition of separatism by force, saying at the public session on 22 December 1921:

> Arthur Griffith said he had brought back peace with England, and freedom of Ireland. I can only say it is not the kind of freedom I have looked forward to, and, if this Treaty is ratified the result will

be a divided people; the same old division will go on; those who will
enter the British Empire and those who will not, and so England's old
game of divide and conquer goes on.[66]

Did the Female TDs Ultimately Fulfil the Objectives of their Political Actions?

Margaret Pearse, the 65-year-old widow, matron and housekeeper of
St Enda's School, stated in the Treaty debates that she knew 'very little
of politics' in contrast to her eldest son P.H. Pearse's knowledge of all
things political. In her Dáil contributions, Pearse remained, as she would
until her death, the promoter of her sons' legacy. Patrick and his younger
brother William (Willie) were executed in 1916. Her contributions to the
Treaty debates are predictable. In the public session on 4 January 1922,
she stated: 'But even the Black-and-Tans alone would not frighten me as
much as if I accepted that Treaty; because I feel in my heart – and I would
not say it only I feel it– that the ghosts of my sons would haunt me.'[67]
Pearse's eldest son's writings had shaped her legacy. His poetry, written
from his prison cell, gave her a fictitious voice, as unreal as Cathleen ni
Houlihan in the play by W.B. Yeats and Lady Gregory. Henceforth, Pearse
was to be 'the mother'. She was not really of the 'peasant' stock that her
son's writing suggested. Born Margaret Brady in Dublin on 12 February
1857, she lived in Ballybough in Dublin city, although the family was
originally from County Meath. Her father was a dairyman and cab-driver
who was born and lived in Dublin. One of the few glimpses we get of
Pearse is an account recorded in James Pearse's love letters to her: 'a grand
looking young woman with dark hair and eyes, no nonsense about her
… she seems homely yet bright and full of life'.[68] Pearse took over the
running of her husband's business after his death in 1900 and maintained
a number of rented properties. In later years, she worked at St Enda's
School, which P.H. Pearse had established in 1900.

After she rejected the Treaty and left the Dáil, Margaret Pearse
did not remain in active politics but continued to remain in the public
eye. Placing her sons into a sanctified position is something she did
exceedingly well. Kathleen Clarke would rally less successfully until her
death about her husband's position. She had always maintained that Tom
was the president of the Republic proclaimed in 1916, as indicated by the

place of his name on the proclamation. When the prisoners returned in 1917, Clarke asked: 'who the hell made Pearse President?'[69]After 1921, TDs' roles were dictated by their stance. Mary MacSwiney and Kate O'Callaghan were elected as Cumann na Poblachta (anti-Treaty Sinn Féin, 'Republican Association') members to the Third Dáil, following the so called 'pact election', which was a bid to avert a civil war. This Dáil dissolved when hostilities began on 30 June 1922. MacSwiney and Countess Markievicz were elected to the Fourth Dáil in August 1923 but followed the anti-Treatyites' abstentionist policy and did not take their seats.

Éamon de Valera's political solution to describe the oath as 'an empty formality' allowed Fianna Fáil TDs to re-enter the Dáil in 1927. Markievicz broke with Sinn Féin, joined Fianna Fáil and chaired its first meeting. She died in July 1927 before she re-entered the Dáil. Who knows what her full legacy would have been had she lived? Something of her speech on the oath in the public session on 3 January 1922 seemed prophetic:

> Now, with regard to the oath, I say to anyone – go truthfully and take this oath, take it. If they take it under duress, there may be some excuse for them, but let them remember that nobody here took their Republican Oath under duress. They took it knowing it might mean death; and they took it meaning that. And when they took that oath to the Irish Republic they meant, I hope, every honest man and every woman – I know the women – they took it meaning to keep it to death.[70]

Ada English never re-entered the Dáil, nor was she arrested during the Civil War, although she continued to assist the anti-Treatyites and committed to the republican stance taken by Mary MacSwiney; she also attended the meeting of the TDs of the Second Dáil in Easter 1928. She remained working as a psychiatrist in Ballinasloe District Lunatic Asylum. After her death, English's influence was acknowledged by Senator Helen Concannon when the Mental Treatment Act of 1945 was passed. Concannon described English as 'brilliant and beautiful' and said that she 'worked for the principles embodied in this Bill' and that 'the things that make (the Act) … worthwhile are the things which she tirelessly pleaded'.[71]

Sinn Féin split when Éamon de Valera left and set up Fianna Fáil but Mary MacSwiney remained as vice-president of Sinn Féin. In 1929, when she reconvened the Second Dáil, it was referred to as 'Mary MacSwiney's Dáil'. She would remain outside the workings of the Irish Free State. One can only speculate, but had she been selected for the Irish delegation in 1921, could she have brought about a different outcome? Or indeed as Margaret MacCurtain argues: 'had they been more constitutionally agile in the Treaty Debates they might well have held the balance of power between both sides'.[72] In 1938, MacSwiney was among the members of the Second Dáil that gave governmental powers to the IRA and was attributed as the main advocate of that decision.

Kate O'Callaghan also continued to attend meetings of the Second Dáil, including in Easter 1928 (see illustration). One of O'Callaghan's surviving correspondences is a letter she wrote to de Valera following the publication of the draft Constitution in 1937:

> You indicated in your introduction to the Draft Constitution that you would welcome criticism from those who read it with care. I have read it and I read too your speech on the Second Reading and I want to lay before you the reasons why I could not vote for its acceptance ... The articles relating to the status of women were a great disappointment to me, as they must have been to the many who hoped for the 'equal rights and equal opportunities' which the Proclamation of the Republic in 1916 guaranteed to all its citizens.

She explained that

> Article 45.4.2 is the most objectionable ... as it charges the Creator with afflicting half the race with 'inadequate strength' ... I would ask you to delete these clauses, because they are a betrayal of what was regarded by all loyal Irishwomen as the charter of their freedom. In the period of the war with England, 1916–1923, the Irish nation rose to the test as never before in its history, men and women serving alike. There was no talk then of the inadequate strength of women, their differences of capacity, physical and moral and of social function and I am surprised that you, who lived through the

period in intimate contact with the ordinary people of the nation and valued, I think, the splendid service of the women of the people, now include in this Draft Constitution, clauses which, however well-intentioned, will militate against women in a state based on their work and sacrifice.

O'Callaghan's contribution, thus, was not in the Dáil chamber but in a letter sent to her former colleague.

Tragedy Defined Them and Those That Came After?

The discourse on women in Irish politics for the first half of the twentieth century had an added complication, where it existed; women's political roles were linked with their personal tragedies. The majority took their seats after the sudden and premature deaths of their spouses, including Cáitlín Brugha, Bridget Redmond, Mary Reynolds, Bridget Rice, Sheila Galvin, Honor Crowley, Eileen Desmond and Celia Lynch. Kathleen O'Connor replaced her father (Clann na Poblachta TD Johnny Connor) in the Dáil after his death. Bridget Hogan O'Higgins is often described as 'taking her father's seat'; yet the fact that he died when she was four years old and that she was not elected until twenty years later is not highlighted. This practice of being put on the party ticket after a tragedy is often linked back to those women and the Second Dáil. Margaret Pearse was followed into politics by her daughter, also called Margaret.

Maureen O'Carroll came into politics having come into the labour movement working on the establishment of the Lower Prices Council. Motivated by a cause, she was the successor to Countess Markievicz, not alone in her being a TD for Labour but in her motivation to help the poor and to fight for better conditions. Ironically, it is in the form of caricature that she is being brought to a wider public today, as the inspiration of 'Mrs Brown' and 'the Mammy' by her son Brendan O'Carroll. Yet, there is no biographical study of Maureen O'Carroll, as indeed there are no biographical studies of so many of the other female TDs due to a lack of personal papers outlining their contributions. The question must be raised, why do we have so little documentation surviving on the political women who served in the Dáil?

A Reassessment Overdue?

In preparation for this chapter, it was noted that on the University College Dublin Decade of Centenaries website, Mary MacSwiney was described as giving the 'the longest speech of the treaty debates, which was described as "a tirade against comprise".'[73] Across almost nine decades, the same negative language has been used about the female TDs of the revolutionary Dáil Éireann. Mary Beard, professor of Classics at the University of Cambridge, has examined women with a 'public voice'. She has suggested that 'to understand the way women were heard it was necessary to understand how attitudes were hardwired through culture over more than two millennia from Homer ... to [T]witter'.[74] Beard states: 'when we are thinking about underrepresentation of women in national politics, their relative muteness in the public sphere ... we have to think beyond issues of family-friendly hours, childcare provision or all women shortlists (important as those are) ... the fact remains women who put their head above the parapet have a much harder time than men. We have to think about that in a calm, historical, analytical way'.[75] A new generation of historians must reassess the material pertaining to the first women politicians in the state (twenty-two TDs between 1916 and 1966). Hopefully this chapter will assist in this new appraisal of the women of the Second Dáil and their contributions to the Treaty debates.

Notes

1   Piaras Béaslaí, *Michael Collins and the making of a new Ireland* (2 vols, Dublin, 1926), ii, p. 342.
2   There are no recordings of Mary MacSwiney's criticisms of the government. In December 1938, MacSwiney was one of a group of seven TDs of the Second Dáil which met with the IRA army council and handed over authority to it until a new Dáil could be democratically elected by the people in all of the thirty-two counties.
3   Margaret Ward, *Unmanageable revolutionaries* (Dingle, 1983), p. viii.
4   F.S.L. Lyons, *Ireland since the Famine* (London, 1973), p. 535.
5   Ibid., p. 286.
6   My own work formed a part of an examination of the women's narrative, which took place in Kilmainham Gaol in the 1990s with research undertaken for the eightieth anniversary of the Rising. *Guns and Chiffon*, the first designated exhibition on the women's role was held in Kilmainham Gaol in 1997. The evidence for this mass arrest was built up from a fragmentary archive that was put together from

surviving autograph books and supplemented by material from family archives and unpublished accounts. Oral accounts from survivors and their families emerged, giving a more complex and nuanced picture of the anti-Treaty women of this period. These accounts can now be read in conjunction with the Bureau of Military History witness statements and enhanced by material already released by the Military Archives from its pension records. The donations gathered at that time now form the largest single collection of women's material in the country.

7   Charlotte Fallon, 'Republican hunger strikes during the Irish Civil War and its immediate aftermath (M.A. thesis, University College Dublin, 1980).

8   Sinéad McCoole, *Hazel: a life of Lady Lavery* (Dublin, 1996), p. 105.

9   *Dáil Éireann deb.*, T, no. 8, 118 (21 Dec. 1921).

10   Ibid., no. 11, 250 (4 Jan. 1922).

11   Helga Woggon, *Silent radical – Winifred Carney, 1887–1943: a reconstruction of her biography* (Dublin, 2000), p. 19.

12   Ibid., p. 20.

13   Helen Litton (ed.), Kathleen Clarke, *Revolutionary woman* (Dublin, 1991), p. 170.

14   *Dáil Éireann deb.*, S2, no. 3, 206 (2 Mar. 1922).

15   Dorothy Macardle, *The Irish Republic* (Dublin, 1951), p. 29.

16   Countess Markievicz's book with personalised bookmark (Mayo County Council, Jackie Clarke Collection, 57/1).

17   Minute book of the Committee of the Women Delegates to the All-Ireland Conference, 19 Apr. 1917 (NLI (National Library of Ireland), Department of Ephemera, MS 21,194/47).

18   Ibid.

19   Margaret Ward, 'The League of Women Delegates & Sinn Féin' in *History Ireland*, iv, no. 3 (Autumn 1996), pp. 37–41.

20   Ibid.

21   Geraldine Plunkett Dillon, *All in the blood: a memoir of the Plunkett family, the 1916 Rising and the War of Independence*, ed. Honor O Brolchain (Dublin, 2006), p. 259.

22   Ward, 'League of Women Delegates & Sinn Féin', pp. 37–41.

23   Minute book of the Committee of Women Delegates to the All-Ireland Conference, 19 Apr. 1917.

24   Ward, 'League of Women Delegates & Sinn Féin', pp. 37–41.

25   Brian M. Walker (ed.), *Parliamentary election results in Ireland, 1918–92* (Dublin, 1992), p. 156.

26   Margaret Ward, *Hanna Sheehy Skeffington: a life* (Cork, 1997), p. 154.

27   *Dáil Éireann deb.*, S2, no. 3, 206 (2 Mar. 1922).

28   Senia Pašeta, *Irish nationalist women 1900-1918* (Cambridge, 2013), p. 13.

29   Jason Knirck, *Women of the Dáil: gender, republicanism and the Anglo-Irish Treaty* (Dublin, 2006), p. 62.

30   Mary MacSwiney to Éamon de Valera, 20 July 1921 (University College Dublin Archives (UCDA), Mary MacSwiney Papers, P48A/115).

31   Ibid.

32   Ibid.

33   Uinseann MacEoin, *Survivors* (Dublin, 1987), p. 352.

34   Éamon de Valera to Joseph McGarrity, 27 Dec. 1921 (NLI, Joseph McGarrity Papers, MS 17,440).

35   P.S. O'Hegarty, *The victory of Sinn Féin* (Dublin, 1924), p. 107.

36   *Dáil Éireann deb.*, T, no. 8, 118 (21 Dec. 1921), p. 118.

37   Jennie Wyse Power to unknown recipient, nd (UCDA, Sighle Humphreys Papers, P106/744).

38   Ibid.

39   *Dáil Éireann deb.*, T, no. 8, 118 (21 Dec. 1921).

40   Ibid., no. 10, 184 (3 Jan. 1922).

41   Ibid.

42   Brian P. Murphy, lecture on Kate O'Callaghan, Limerick City Library, 14 Jan. 2003.

43   Sr Loreto O'Connor, *Passing on the torch: a history of Mary Immaculate College, 1898–1998.* (Limerick, 1998), p. 20.

44   Madge Daly, 'Gallant Cumann na mBan of Limerick' in *The Kerryman* (ed.), *Limerick's fighting story, 1916–21* (Tralee, 1948), p. 204.

45   Kate O'Callaghan, matriculation record, 2 May 1904 (National University of Ireland).

46   O'Connor, *Passing on the torch*, p. 20.

47   Daly, 'Gallant Cumann na mBan of Limerick', p. 204; Walker (ed.), *Parliamentary election results in Ireland, 1918–92*, p. 103.

48   Kate O'Callaghan, *The Limerick curfew murders of March 7th 1921: the case of Michael O'Callaghan, councillor and ex-mayor, presented by his widow* (Limerick, 1921).

49   Eadem, 'A curfew night in Limerick' in William G. FitzGerald (ed.), *The voice of Ireland* (Dublin, 1925), p. 149.

50   *Dáil Éireann deb.*, T, no. 7, 59 (20 Dec. 1921).

51   Ibid., 60.

52   Ibid., 59.

53   Daly, 'Gallant Cumann na mBan of Limerick', p. 204.

54   *Dáil Éireann deb.*, T, no. 7, 59 (20 Dec. 1921).

55   Ibid.

56   Ibid.

57   Ibid.

58   Brendan Kelly, *Ada English: patriot & psychiatrist* (Dublin, 2014), p. 10.

59   File on Dr Ada English, nd (The National Archives, Kew (TNA), Register of Civilians Tried by Court Martial 1920/1922, War Office (WO) 35/208).

60   Ibid.

61   File on Dr Ada English, nd (TNA, Register of Civilians Tried by Court Martial 1920/1922, WO 35/206/75).

62   Kelly, *Ada English*, p. 31.

Éamon de Valera at a rally, c.1920 (Alamy).

Michael Collins addressing an election meeting, c.1922 (National Library of Ireland).

Michael Collins arriving at Earlsfort Terrace, Dublin, December 1921 (National Library of Ireland).

Pro-Treaty handbill, 1922 (National Library of Ireland).

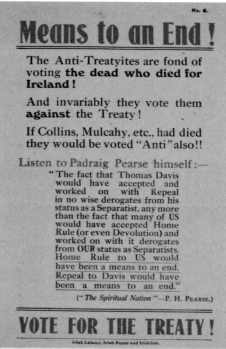

No. 6.

Means to an End!

The Anti-Treatyites are fond of voting **the dead who died for Ireland!**

And invariably they vote them **against** the Treaty!

If Collins, Mulcahy, etc., had died they would be voted "Anti"also!!

Listen to Padraig Pearse himself :—

"The fact that Thomas Davis would have accepted and worked on with Repeal in no wise derogates from his status as a Separatist, any more than the fact that many of US would have accepted Home Rule (or even Devolution) and worked on with it derogates from OUR status as Separatists. Home Rule to US would have been a means to an end. Repeal to Davis would have been a means to an end."

("*The Spiritual Nation*"—P. H. Pearse.)

VOTE FOR THE TREATY!

Irish Labour, Irish Paper and Irish Ink.

MORE PLATITUDES!

Platitudes are "empty remarks made as if they were important."

Here are a few more—with the answers:—

"If only it had been imposed on us like a Home Rule Bill we could have accepted it and fought for more."

Answer: If Parnell had obtained the Home Rule Bill of 1883 would he have continued his tactics of obstruction, or would he have consolidated his gains, and . . . .

      ◙   ◙   ◙

"If we accept this Treaty never again can we aspire to absolute independence."

Answer: "No man has the right to set a boundary to the march of a Nation. No man shall say: 'Thus far and no farther'!"

      ◙   ◙   ◙   ◙

"England never kept a Treaty, and she will never keep the present Treaty."

Answer: But she'd keep Document No. 2 all right!!

      ◙   ◙   ◙   ◙

"Never, never would we agree to the Partition of our country."

Answer: Document No. 2 conceded " to the people of the six counties, in the interests of peace, and out of a desire not to use force upon unwilling citizens, privileges and safeguards not less substantial than those provided for in the Treaty."

VOTE FOR THE TREATY

Irish Labour, Irish Paper and Irish Ink

Charles Stewart Parnell and the Home Rule Bill of 1886 channelled in support of the Treaty in a Labour Party election poster in 1922 (National Library of Ireland).

Anti-Treaty IRA convention at the Mansion House in Dublin in April 1922 (West Cork Regional Museum, Clonakilty, County Cork).

Meeting in Dublin being addressed by James Larkin on the occasion of a one-day strike held by the ITGWU on the anniversary of the death of Kevin Barry and to demand the release of anti-Treaty hunger-strikers, November 1923 (National Library of Ireland).

P.J. Moloney (Eunan O'Halpin).

Michael Staines, portrait painted at Frongoch internment camp by Nicholas T. Murray and photographed by Seán Malone (Garda Síochána Museum and Archives).

A Cumann na Saoirse 'points for canvassers' leaflet from 1922 outlining its pro-Treaty stance in advance of the general election (Alan Kinsella, Irish Election Literature).

Cumann na Saoirse

POINTS FOR CANVASSERS

The Treaty rids us of—

(1) The British Army, the instrument of British power in Ireland.

(2) A police force trained for political espionage.

(3) British control of education, which was killing the Irish language and destroying the soul of the nation.

(4) British legislation.

(5) British officialdom which ran the Government of Ireland for the benefit of England.

(6) British control of our purse, and British taxation which left Ireland the one country in Europe with a decreasing population.

(7) The stranglehold of Britain on Irish trade and industry.

The Treaty gives us—

(1) An Irish Regular Army, with modern equipment, sworn to the service of Ireland.

(2) An Irish Police Force designed solely for the maintenance of law and order.

(3) Irish control of education, with power to restore the language and build up a national culture.

(4) An Irish Parliament with full power to make laws and subject to **NO** British veto.

(5) An Irish Executive subject only to the authority of the Irish Parliament.

(6) Power to develop the resources and industries of Ireland, and to stop the drain of emigration.

(7) The raising and spending of our own revenue.

MAHON'S PRINTING WORKS, DUBLIN.

First Row........Phil Shanahan · Professor Stockley · Mrs O'Callaghan · Art O'Connor ·

Centre Row.......Count O'Byrne · Eamonn Dee · Seamus Lennon · M.P. Colivet · Austin St

Back Row.......Thomas Maguire · Sean McSwiney · Sean O'Farrell · Brian M

The last legitimate Dáil? The post-Treaty 'Second Dáil' in 1928
(Lafayette Photography).

REANN

· 1928

copy
Lafayette

y · Miss McSwiney · Daithi Kent · Count Plunkett · Brian O'Higgins

Charles Murphy · Sean O'Mahony · Dr. Ada English · Thomas O'Donoghue · Dr. Crowley

· Mrs Cathal Brugha · Miss Tubbard · Councillor Joseph Clarke
            (Stenographer)   (Courier)

Accepting the Treaty but also rejecting the Treaty: anti-Treaty IRA volunteers patrol Grafton Street in Dublin in the lead-up to the Civil War (National Museum of Ireland).

Michael Collins in Newcastle West, County Limerick, in early August 1922, just before he was assassinated (National Museum of Ireland).

63   *Dáil Éireann deb.*, T, no. 11, 249-50 (4 Jan. 1922).
64   File on Ada English, nd (TNA, Register of Civilians Tried by Court Martial 1920/1922, WO 35/208).
65   *Dáil Éireann deb.*, T, no. 9, 141 (22 Dec. 1921).
66   Ibid., no. 8, 141 (21 Dec. 1921).
67   Ibid., no. 11, 222 (4 Jan. 1922).
68   James Pearse to Margaret Brady, nd (NLI, Pearse Papers, 1870–1932, MS 21,082/8).
69   Clarke, *Revolutionary woman*, p. 144.
70   *Dáil Éireann deb.*, T, no. 10, 182 (3 Jan. 1922).
71   Kelly, *Ada English*, p. 131.
72   Margaret MacCurtain, 'Women, the vote and revolution' in Margaret MacCurtain and Donncha Ó Corráin (eds), *Women in Irish society: the historical dimension* (Dublin, 1978), p. 55.
73   Brian Murphy, Biography of Mary MacSwiney University College Dublin decade of centenaries website (reproduced from *Dictionary of Irish Biography*) (http://dib.cambridge.org.centenaries.ucd.ie/wp-content/uploads/2015/04/MacSwiney-Mary.pdf) (31 Mar. 2018).
74   Caroline Davies, 'Mary Beard: vocal women treated as "freakish androgynes"' in *The Guardian*, 14 Feb. 2014.
75   Ibid.

CHAPTER 7

'An Idea Has Gone Abroad that All the Women Were Against the Treaty': Cumann na Saoirse and Pro-Treaty Women, 1922–3

Mary McAuliffe

The Anglo-Irish Treaty divided many republican organisations in Ireland, including Cumann na mBan. Set up in 1914, Cumann na mBan was the largest Irish women's militant, separatist, nationalist organisation. Almost 300 of its members saw active duty during the 1916 Rising and over sixty members were imprisoned in the aftermath. Subsequent to the Rising, Cumann na mBan expanded, reaching a membership of around 20,000. Many of these women participated in the War of Independence as a force allied to the Irish Republican Army (IRA), serving as message and arms carriers, intelligence gatherers, propagandists, running safe houses, field hospitals and arms dumps. Once the truce was declared, Cumann na mBan, like the IRA, awaited the outcome of negotiations. The Treaty, once signed however, proved very problematic for the organisation. During the Treaty Dáil debates, the six women TDs, all of whom were senior members of Cumann na mBan, spoke vehemently against its acceptance. While their contributions to the Treaty debates reflected their ideological opposition to the Treaty, it was mirrored in the opposition to the Treaty of a majority in Cumann na mBan.[1] Outside the Dáil, the executive of Cumann na mBan affirmed its anti-Treaty stance, stating publicly, by mid-January 1922, that, 'the executive of Cumann na mBan reaffirms their allegiance to the Irish Republic and therefore cannot support the Articles of Treaty signed in London.[2] As yet the broader membership had not had a chance to consider the Treaty but the executive was making its opposition clear. As Brighid O'Mullane, a member of that 1922 executive, later wrote, 'as soon as the Articles of Agreement for a Treaty were published, the Executive of Cumann na mBan ... discussed the matter, and we were all with three exceptions opposed to accepting them. The exceptions were Mrs. Wyse-Power, her daughter Nancy and Mrs. Dick Mulcahy.[3] Not only were the executive and the female TDs anti-Treaty, younger members of the Dublin branches were already postering the city with anti-Treaty bills, much to the annoyance of Jennie Wyse Power. Power was one of the most senior and long-time female political activists in Ireland. She had been a member of the Ladies' Land League, the Gaelic League, Inghinidhe na hÉireann and the Irish Women's Franchise League, as well as a founder member of Cumann na mBan, and was, in 1922, a vice-president of Sinn Féin. In disgust at its opposition to the Treaty, she resigned from the Cumann na mBan executive.

A convention of the wider membership was held on 5 February 1922, in the Mansion House in Dublin, to consider the Treaty. Delegates attended from all parts of the country, with each branch being allowed two delegates. About 600 women were at the convention, although a rail strike prevented many delegates attending from counties Cork and Kerry. Historians have estimated that about 300 branches, of the estimated 800–900 branches of Cumann na mBan, did not send delegates.[4] This meant that the 600 women gathered at the convention represented just over half the membership. The atmosphere at the meeting was heated, as Lily Curran described in her witness statement, but 'it was clear from the trend of the debate that the majority of the meeting were opposed to accepting the Treaty.[5] While Jennie Wyse Power and Min Mulcahy, wife of Richard Mulcahy, minister of defence in the Provisional Government, were in attendance, many pro-Treaty women simply did not turn up, as they felt the aim of the convention was to rubber-stamp the anti-Treaty stance of the executive. However, even with an overwhelming opposition to the Treaty evident in Cumann na mBan, Wyse Power did attempt to get the membership to reserve its judgement. How much she could influence that judgement was open to question. Already the female TDs had alluded to violence if the Treaty was accepted. Both Mary MacSwiney and Countess Markievicz had made explicit threats of violence in their Dáil contributions. MacSwiney said: 'I will be their first rebel under their so-called Free State ... they will have the pleasure or pain, as it pleases them, of imprisoning me as one of their first and most deliberate and irreconcilable rebels', while Markievicz also declared that 'while Ireland is not free I remain a rebel, unconverted and unconvertible ... I am pledged as a rebel, an unconvertible rebel, because I am pledged to the one thing – a free and independent Republic'.[6]

At the convention on 5 February, the membership considered a resolution put forward by MacSwiney, which reflected the stance she – and the other female TDs – had already taken in the Dáil: 'that the executive of Cumann na mBan reaffirm its allegiance to the Republic, and therefore cannot support the Articles of Agreement signed in London, Dec. 6. 1921'.[7] Acceptance of the Treaty, MacSwiney said in support of her resolution, meant the subversion of the Republic.[8] Wyse Power, who feared she was living to see another acrimonious split, this time in an organisation she had co-founded, proposed an amendment to this resolution.[9] Conscious of the fact that the majority of those gathered in the Mansion House on that day were anti-Treaty, her amendment was more of a compromise than overtly pro-Treaty. She was also aware that the IRA had not made its stance on the Treaty official, and Cumann na mBan, she said, 'would be in a very curious position if they decided on policy that would be different from the policy of the IRA', as they were, after all, comrades and allies with the IRA.[10] She suggested that Cumann na mBan

> reaffirm our allegiance to the Republic, but realising that the treaty signed in London, will, if accepted by the Irish people be a big step along the road to that end, we declare that we will not work obstructively against those who support the treaty (1) either in putting the treaty before the people or (2) in their subsequent working of it should the majority of the people accept the treaty at a general election.[11]

This amendment, as news reports of the meeting suggest, 'asked the convention not to take sides in opposition to the treaty, leaving it for the people to decide the issue'.[12] She also made the point that Cumann na mBan, if it rejected the Treaty, would be placing itself in opposition to the Irish Free State and to the people of Ireland if they voted to accept the Treaty. She said, perhaps in an allusion to the female TDs who spoke against the Treaty in the Dáil on behalf of the dead patriots they were related to, that she had 'nothing to put before them in the way of a heroic record except that her life had been spent in drudgery for the service of Ireland'; now, she did not want them to make a decision that would mean they went out 'in the open against Irishmen who had fought and nobly worked for the Republic'.[13]

Wyse Power had some support in the room. Min Mulcahy who was also pro-Treaty, seconded the amendment, saying that affirming the allegiance to the Republic was 'common ground on all sides, ... [and] ... if those who supported the Treaty were allowed to carry out their policy in the working of the Free State they would give all that was aimed for – namely the total independence of their country'.[14] However, speaker after speaker showed 'uncompromising hostility [to the Treaty] combined with passionate allusions to principle and to the Irish Republic'.[15] Some held firm to their allegiance to the Proclamation and the Republic, some picked apart the arguments put forward by Wyse Power and her supporters. The Belfast delegate countered Wyse Power's claim that she had seen British troops leaving Ireland, stating that the army had not left as 'it [was] being drafted into the Six Counties. We want a Republic. Nothing else'.[16] Margaret Skinnider, who had been wounded on active duty during the 1916 Rising, said it was 'not a question between the Republic and the Free State. It is a question between the Republic and the British Empire ... Mrs Wyse Power asks are we going to oppose an Irish Government? Once a man takes an Oath of Allegiance to England, he is no longer an Irishman in my opinion'.[17] The result was 419 delegates against Wyse Powers' resolution, with only sixty-three votes in favour. Another resolution proposed by Margaret Pearse, mother of Patrick and William Pearse, following on from the anti-Treaty stance now taken, stated that Cumann na mBan would 'organise the women of Ireland to support in the forthcoming election only those candidates who stand true to the existing Republic proclaimed in Easter Week, 1916 ... that no branch of Cumann na mBan and no member of Cumann na mBan can give any help to a candidate standing for the Free State'.[18] She added that she had no word to say against those men who supported the Treaty; they had fought for Ireland, too; however, even though 'they had done their best ... they had erred'.[19] Margaret Pearse's resolution was carried, which meant that Cumann na mBan had not only taken a strong anti-Treaty stance; it intended to actively campaign against the Treaty in the upcoming election. This left Wyse Power, Mulcahy and the other pro-Treaty women in an impossible position, as it was also made clear to them by Markievicz that no pro-Treaty women could remain in the organisation. Áine Ní Riain, who was at the convention, remembered later that 'there was awful bitterness; I remember them when they were going out passing bitter remarks'.[20]

Leading Pro-Treaty Women

With the anti-Treaty result in the vote, the spilt, which Wyse Power had so feared, was inevitable. She offered her resignation, which was accepted with regret. She was not the only senior member of Cumann na mBan to leave because of its anti-Treaty stance. Among those who left in the coming weeks were many of those who had been the most dedicated, key members of Cumann na mBan since its foundation. One of the most prominent was Min Mulcahy (née Ryan), who had been active in Cumann na mBan since 1914. She had been of the 'geography of radical Dublin', that rising generation in young activist circles in Dublin inspired by nationalism, socialism and feminism, as described by Roy Foster in *Vivid faces*.[21] Mary Josephine 'Min' Ryan, though originally from Tomcoole in County Wexford, and her sisters, Mary Kate 'Kit' and Phyllis, were all living and working in Dublin prior to 1916. The Ryans were a large (twelve siblings) well-known Wexford family, many of whom were to play a prominent role in revolutionary and Free State politics. As well as Min, Kit and Phyllis (both of whom married Seán T. O'Kelly, firstly Kit and, after her death in 1934, Phyllis, in 1936), their sister Nell and brother Jim were involved in the Rising and the War of Independence. Unlike their sister Min, both were subsequently anti-Treaty and both were involved in Fianna Fáil. Nell became a Fianna Fáil county councillor in Wexford, while Jim was a founder member and, later on, a Fianna Fáil government minister who served in several ministries. In Dublin, the Ryan sisters were part of a network of radicals which included men like Seán Mac Diarmada, with whom Min Ryan had had an 'understanding'.[22]

She was involved in Cumann na mBan activism prior to 1916, organising a fundraising concert for the Irish Volunteers at the Foresters' Hall on Palm Sunday (a week before the Rising).[23] She participated in the Rising in 1916, carrying dispatches from Dublin to Wexford and back, and then joined the General Post Office garrison. She was the last person to see Mac Diarmada, visiting him in Kilmainham Gaol the night before he was executed. In July 1916, she was sent by Cumann na mBan to the United States to give John Devoy 'authentic news of the Rising'.[24] She remained active during the War of Independence, and, in 1919, married Richard Mulcahy.

She was not the only long-time member, the only founder member or, indeed, the only member who had been involved in 1916, to leave Cumann na mBan over its anti-Treaty stance. Founder members Elizabeth Bloxham and Louise Gavan Duffy also left. Bloxham was a journalist and a teacher, a member of the Gaelic League, a contributor to Arthur Griffith's newspaper, the *United Irishman*, a suffragette and a supporter of the Irish Women's Franchise League. She was one of the founder members of Cumann na mBan in 1914, spending her summer holidays in the following years travelling the country helping to establish branches. She was working as a teacher in Newtownards, County Down, when the Rising broke out so could not participate; however, her nationalist politics meant she was dismissed from her post. She subsequently secured teaching work in Wexford and continued her involvement in Cumann na mBan through the War of Independence. With Jennie Wyse Power she was one of the most senior members of Cumann na mBan to support the Treaty and resign her position because of that support. Another well-known pro-Treaty member was Louise Gavan Duffy. Born in 1884, she was the only daughter of Sir Charles Gavan Duffy, nationalist politician and journalist. Her brother George Gavan Duffy had unsuccessfully defended Sir Roger Casement at his trial for treason in 1916 and, in 1918, was elected Sinn Féin MP for Dublin County South. He was one of the plenipotentiaries sent to London to negotiate with the British in 1921, and as such, was a signatory of the Anglo-Irish Treaty. Louise Gavan Duffy was a secretary to the executive of Cumann na mBan from its formation in 1914 and participated in the Rising in 1916. Re-elected to the executive in 1917, she and several influential nationalist women, including Wyse Power and Bloxham, signed a petition demanding self-determination for Ireland, which was submitted to President Woodrow Wilson of the United States by Hanna Sheehy Skeffington on 1 March 1918. A teacher, she opened an Irish-speaking school on St Stephen's Green, Scoil Bhríde, with Annie McHugh (later married to pro-Treaty politician Ernest Blythe). The school was used by the IRA leadership for meetings throughout the War of Independence and was often raided by the Crown forces. In 1922, both Duffy and McHugh were pro-Treaty. Another 1916 woman who was pro-Treaty was Kathleen Browne. Browne was a long-time supporter of the nationalist movement and was a friend and supporter of Arthur Griffith and Sinn Féin. She was arrested in 1916 when she hoisted a tricolour over her home at Rathronan, south Wexford, on hearing the Rising had broken out. She worked for Sinn Féin in the 1918 election, and her house was a safe house through the War of Independence. She knew the Ryan sisters well and was very good friends with Nell, who had been arrested with her in 1916. Like Min Ryan, Browne was pro-Treaty, which caused a life-long falling out with her friend, Nell, who was vehemently anti-Treaty.

Other well-known women, supporters of nationalist politics, also voiced pro-Treaty stances. Among these was the well-known and well-connected Alice Stopford Green. Born in Kells, County Meath, in 1847, she moved to London in 1874 and, in 1877, she met and married the historian John Richard Green. She collaborated with him on his historical works and, after his death in 1883, she established herself as an historian in her own right. By the 1890s, she had become interested in Irish history and Irish nationalism, influenced by her close friendship with barrister and author John Francis Taylor. Her publication of *The making of Ireland and its undoing* in 1908 caused controversy within the establishment which regarded it as a deliberately provocative nationalist polemic. As Angus Mitchell noted, 'in the subsequent wave of controversy, she made reference to a tradition of conspiracy in the writing of Irish history that had deliberately sought to distort the past and misrepresent the Irish as the barbaric "other".[25] Stopford Green, moreover, was becoming more separatist, joining Cumann na mBan in 1914. She was instrumental in raising money and organising the importation of arms for the Irish Volunteers at the Howth gun-running in 1914. Although shocked by the violence of the 1916 Rising, she used her contacts within the British establishment to lobby hard, if unsuccessfully, to have Roger Casement's death sentence commuted to life in prison. She chaired a committee of several women's organisations, including Cumann na mBan, which organised the enormously successful anti-conscription day, Lá na mBan (Women's Day), held on 9 June 1918. A women's pledge signed on that day committed the women of Ireland to resisting conscription. In 1918, she moved into a house on St Stephen's Green, and it was a meeting place for leading republicans during the War of Independence. She was assisted in her work during this period by her secretary, Cumann na mBan member Máire Comerford. When it came to the Treaty, Stopford Green was pro-Treaty, while Comerford was anti-Treaty. Another senior woman activist to declare for the Treaty was Eileen Costello (née Drury). Born in London, in 1870, of Irish ancestry, Costello was a member of the London Gaelic League. She was a keen folklorist, collecting songs from immigrants in London, then, on moving to Tuam, County Galway, in 1903, when she married Dr Thomas Bodkin Costello, a medical doctor, folklorist and Gaelic Leaguer, she continued collecting folksongs in counties Galway and Mayo. She was very involved with Sinn Féin, standing in the local elections for the party in Galway, becoming the first woman district councillor in north Galway. In 1921, she was elected the first female member of the Tuam Town Commissioners and was its first female chairman (1921–2). During the War of Independence, her home was a safe house and she was a judge on the Sinn Féin arbitration courts between 1921 and 1922. She was in favour of the Treaty in 1922. Other women who declared in favour of the Treaty included: Alice Spring Rice, whose brother Cecil was British ambassador to the United States and whose cousin Mary Spring Rice had been involved in the Howth gun-running; Maud Griffith, wife of Arthur Griffith; Margaret O'Shea Leamy, widow of Irish Parliamentary Party MP, Edmund Leamy (died 1904); and Agnes (Mór) MacNeill, wife of Eoin MacNeill, who had been leader of the Irish Volunteers.

The Emergence of Cumann na Saoirse

Not only were leading members making their pro-Treaty stance known and leaving the organisations, around the country branches of Cumann na mBan were having their own internal debates on the Treaty. In Cork, Cumann na mBan member Lil Conlon later wrote that the pro-Treaty supporters had the co-operation of most branches 'as far west as Goleen,

where 99% of the people were in favour of the Treaty'.[26] Conlon, a central
member of the Shandon Cumann na mBan branch in Cork city, wrote her
history of Cumann na mBan fifty years after the events, as most histories
of the period had, to her disappointment, 'little or no mention of the
women who did such gallant and heroic work for the cause of Ireland'.[27]
Her sister, May Conlon, who had been secretary both of the Shandon
branch and the Cork District Council of Cumann na mBan, was one of
the senior pro-Treaty women in Cork. When the Cork District Council
met to consider the anti-Treaty resolution passed by the Cumann na
mBan executive, the majority voted against it and in favour of the Treaty.[28]
Much to the annoyance of the executive in Dublin, the Cork District
Council planned a welcome address to Michael Collins, distributed
leaflets in favour of the Treaty and put notices in the newspapers that all
pro-Treaty women were to communicate with pro-Treaty headquarters in
Cork, rather than with the executive in Dublin.[29]

Despite an effort by the female TDs in the Dáil, no compromise
between the pro- and anti-Treaty women seemed possible. Kathleen
Clarke proposed to chair a committee with five members from each side
of the debate. The six anti-Treaty TDs wrote to the pro-Treaty women
asking them to rethink their decision, arguing that 'it would be better to
face Lloyd George together than face a war with each other'.[30] This attempt
failed, and with the convention and the TDs now all openly anti-Treaty,
unity in Cumann na mBan was lost. As an anti-Treaty woman, Máire
Comerford later recalled that Cumann na mBan lost 'some fine women
… foundation members, others executive members who had helped guide
[it] through the war years; all had proved themselves'.[31] However, it soon
became evident that these fine women were not going to stand back and
let the anti-Treaty women have free reign. Despite the sorrow at the split,
years of organisational experience was soon put to work. While branches
like those in Cork were pro-Treaty and remained active under the name
Cumann na mBan, in most other parts of the country, pro-Treaty women
left their branches. On 18 February 1922, Jennie Wyse Power wrote to the
Freeman's Journal telling pro-Treaty branches not to return funds to the
central executive as instructed, asking that those branches 'not represented
at the convention and who may feel as the minority did' should send her
their secretaries' names and addresses.[32] The impetus was towards the
formation of a new pro-Treaty organisation for women.

Even as the debate raged between the pro- and anti-Treaty women in the newspapers and in the branches, another issue of importance to the women was raising its head. The June 1922 election would secure (or not) the Treaty position, and in that election under existing laws, all men over the age of twenty-one but only women over the age of thirty could vote. During the Dáil debates, the anti-Treaty women TDs argued that all women over the age of twenty-one should be given the vote, on a par with men. Despite the assurance that equal suffrage for men and women would be in the new Free State constitution, in the Dáil, Arthur Griffith argued that the new register would not be ready in time for the upcoming June election. In Cork, Michael Collins, in a speech to the pro-Treaty women, defended this position, saying, 'we had recently in the Dáil, mock heroics about votes for women, and we were forced into a position where we were supposed to oppose the rights of women. We didn't oppose it, and we don't oppose it, and we know better than our opponents what the women during the past few years have endured.'[33] Collins was reassuring the women in Cork that the Free State would keep its promise to women to introduce equal suffrage but it would not be ready in time for the June election. There was unease among pro-Treatyites that young women would be more inclined to vote against the Treaty, so there was no political will to add this potential anti-Treaty section to the voting register. Wyse Power, who had long campaigned for full suffrage for women, refused to join a delegation from Cumann na mBan and the Irish Women's Franchise League to Griffith and de Valera on the matter. She pointed out that as Cumann na mBan was opposed to the Treaty, its request, for legislation to be brought forward to lower the age at which women could vote, was inconsistent with its position.[34] The demand that the voting age be extended in time for the June election failed and only women over the age of thirty could vote.

Fearful of continuing splits and the growing activism of the anti-Treatyites, pro-Treaty supporters began to come together into organisations from March 1922. Wyse Power was an experienced organiser, as were several of the women who would join her on the pro-Treaty platform, so the women were among the first to come together in a group. Just over a month after the Cumann na mBan convention, a newspaper advertisement appeared announcing the inaugural meeting of a new women's group, one which would be supportive of the Treaty. This meeting, on 12 March 1922 in the

Mansion House, was attended by over 700 women. Wyse Power addressed the gathering and emphasised the necessity of having an organisation which would give a platform to those women who supported the Treaty:

> In the present critical crisis it is right and proper that Irish women should publicly declare their allegiance to the Free State. It is also important that they should have an organisation to represent their interests at the coming elections. An idea had gone abroad that all women were against the Treaty. Their presence there showed that in the City of Dublin there were women who saw that the course they proposed to adopt was the right one, from the national point of view. When the constitution of the new organisation was proposed they would see that women of Irish nationality need not be ashamed or afraid to go to them in that organisation. They believed that through the Treaty and through the Parliament of the nation that would be set up, they would get to freedom quicker than through any other means. The Women of Ireland, not a noisy faction of them, stood where they always stood on the bedrock of Irish Nationality.[35]

The arguments she put before the meeting were much of the manifesto the new organisation would adopt. The Treaty, was, Wyse Power argued, a stepping stone towards full independence. Women who supported that idea should not be ashamed to openly support the Treaty, and indeed, be proud of their position as the 'bedrock of the Irish nation'.[36] She still held to the idea which she outlined in her speech to the earlier Cumann na mBan convention in February, that 'it was easier to get the Republic from a Government worked in Ireland by Irishmen than from an Ireland under British rule'.[37] The fact that the 'idea had gone abroad that all women were against the Treaty' also concerned Wyse Power and other senior pro-Treaty women.[38] They were afraid that the women of Cumann na mBan, 'the noisy faction', would be blamed for any violence that might break out. This was not an unfounded fear as the anti-Treaty female TDs were accused by pro-Treatyites of 'rattling the bones of the dead heroes' in their incendiary speeches in the Dáil debates.[39]

As the Cumann na mBan name was now more associated with the anti-Treaty position, the new organisation named itself Cumann na Saoirse (Society of Freedom). Joining Wyse Power on the platform was Alice

Stopford Green, whose proposal for its platform was adopted. This read: 'Cumann na Saoirse is an independent body of Irish women, pledged to work for the securing and maintaining of Ireland's right as an autonomous and sovereign State to determine freely her form of Government.'[40] One of the first important activities of Cumann na Saoirse, it was agreed, was also to 'assist in the return at the following elections of the candidates who accept the treaty, as a step towards the complete independence of Ireland'.[41] That its acceptance of the Treaty was not an end in it itself, but a first step towards complete independence, was emphasised over and over again. These women acknowledged how bitterly the Treaty had been denounced, and that it had not been voluntarily offered by Ireland, but they accepted the expert opinion that, with the Treaty, Ireland had secured national rights.[42] Mrs Seán Connolly repudiated the idea that the women of Ireland, as a whole, were against the Treaty, and stated that it was the duty 'of every Irishwoman to do the utmost to carry the Treaty triumphant at the polls'.[43] Min Mulcahy recommended that Cumann na Saoirse work to get pro-Treaty candidates elected but 'not imitate the methods adopted by their opponents'; this was seconded by Kathleen Browne.[44] Sarah McGilligan from Ulster said that they 'were against obstructionist tactics and believed in the right of free speech'.[45] After all the speeches, an executive was proposed and accepted. This executive had many senior ex-Cumann na mBan members as well as senior nationalist and feminist activists. It included Jennie Wyse Power, Alice Stopford Green, Min Mulcahy, Kathleen Browne, Eileen Costello, Annie Blythe, Louise Gavan Duffy, Margaret O'Shea Leamy, Alice Spring Rice, Agnes MacNeill, Maud Griffith and Alice Mullan. Margaret Ward writes that members of Cumann na Saoirse were almost all 'related to the members of the new government, it would seem that most wives rallied round their husband's side'.[46] The new executive included the wives of Arthur Griffith, Ernest Blythe, Richard Mulcahy and Eoin MacNeill. Others such as Kathleen Browne, Alice Stopford Green, Margaret O'Shea Leamy and Louise Gavan Duffy were close to leading political men such as W.T. Cosgrove. This meant that Cumann na Saoirse would work closely with the pro-Treaty campaign from the beginning. However, the divisions between Cumann na Saoirse and Cumann na mBan, which were to become so bitter during the Civil War, were also evident on that day. The *Irish Times* reported that while the meeting was going on, a group of

Cumann na mBan members opposed to the Treaty gathered outside, and in attempting to rush the meeting, broke some windows.[47]

By early April 1922, the broader pro-Treaty campaign was getting organised and had set up offices at 3 and 4 St Stephen's Green. One of its most important activities was to show that the Treaty was not a betrayal of those who had fought for the Republic, the charge most often levelled against it. The months leading up to the June election were vital, as Lauren Arrington observed, and the struggle between the pro- and anti-Treaty factions was 'a war for public opinion'.[48] The women of Cumann na mBan had been central to republican propaganda campaigns after the 1916 Rising, while through the War of Independence they were, according to Máire Comerford, responsible for writing much of the material in the propagandist *Irish Bulletin* newsletter.[49] With the majority of Cumann na mBan now either anti-Treaty or neutral, and the anti-Treaty women also using propaganda to support their stance, it was up to the Cumann na Saoirse women to help with pro-Treaty propaganda. On 24 March 1922, an advertisement appeared in newspapers which indicated the work Cumann na Saoirse women had set themselves to do. It stated that its 'immediate policy' was to 'assist in the return in the forthcoming election of candidates who accept the Treaty as a step towards the complete independence of Ireland'.[50] In order to facilitate this work, it asked women all over Ireland to contact the secretary of the society and sent out an urgent appeal for funds.[51]

Cumann na Saoirse now began to organise countrywide and to distribute pro-Treaty propaganda produced by the propaganda subcommittees of the General and Election Committee. It is difficult to estimate how many branches of Cumann na Saoirse were established countrywide and certainly it never had the organisational footing of Cumann na mBan. However, branches were set up in several parts of Dublin, in Kilkenny, Waterford, Wexford, Bray, Cork and Sligo, while individuals were supportive of its work in many other parts of the country. As mentioned also, some Cumann na mBan branches, in Cork and elsewhere, were pro-Treaty, although retaining the Cumann na mBan name. However, the executive was Dublin-centred with 'sixteen of its twenty members resident' in the capital. The executive was also given a lot of power; it could alter the rules of the organisation without calling a convention, provided the alterations conformed to 'the principles on which the organisation was found.[52] Once it was on a firm standing after the inaugural meeting, as well as distributing pro-Treaty propaganda, it produced its own and also produced guidelines for its members to sell the Treaty to the Irish people. In 'Points for Canvassers', it had seven points on 'what the Treaty rids us of' and seven points on what 'the Treaty gives us':

The Treaty rids us of – (1) The British Army, the instrument of British power in Ireland. (2) A police force trained for political espionage. (3) British control of education, which was killing the Irish language and destroying the soul of the nation. (4) British legislation. (5) British officialdom which ran the Government of Ireland for the benefit of England. (6) British control of our purse, and British taxation which left Ireland the one country in Europe with a decreasing population. (7) The stranglehold of Britain on Irish trade and industry.

The Treaty gives us – (1) An Irish Regular Army, with modern equipment, sworn to the service of Ireland. (2) An Irish Police Force designed solely for the maintenance of law and order. (3) Irish control of education, with power to restore the language and build up a national culture. (4) An Irish parliament with full power to make laws and subject to NO British veto. (5) An Irish Executive subject only to the authority of the Irish Parliament. (6) Power to develop the resources and industries of Ireland, and to stop the drain of emigration. (7) The raising and spending of our own revenue.[53]

The ideas reproduced in the 'Points for Canvassers' by Cumann na Saoirse echoed the pro-Treaty handbills and propaganda produced by other pro-Treaty groups. One emphasis was on the departure of the British officials, military and police; the other was on the gains for Ireland. The Treaty would give Ireland, according to pro-Treaty supporters, its own parliament, control of its own land, laws, legislation and taxation, its own army and police force, a national flag, its own constitution, and a 'recognised place as a Separate State among the Nations'.[54] How much of a role Cumann na Saoirse propaganda played in the June 1922 election, which was effectively a de facto referendum on the Treaty, is open to question. In order to prevent violence, Collins and de Valera negotiated a controversial pact in mid-May 1922, for which the pro- and anti-Treaty sides agreed to fight the election jointly and form a coalition government afterwards. This meant the main activity of the organisation, to support pro-Treaty candidates, was moot, so it was decided that Cumann na Saoirse women could 'go on working for the return of pro-Treaty candidates but were not debarred from working for other panel candidates'.[55] In the June election, fifty-eight pro-Treaty Sinn Féin candidates were returned, as opposed to thirty-six anti-Treatyites. The remaining thirty-four seats were filled by pro-Treaty candidates from other parties. This was a success for the pro-Treaty side but also deepened the split in Sinn Féin and the IRA. Within weeks, violence had broken out and the country had descended into civil war.

Cumann na Saoirse had, no doubt, played some part in the success of the pro-Treaty candidates. But if it thought its work was over, the unstable political situation in the country meant it was still needed. On 28 June 1922, pro-Treaty troops opened fire on the anti-Treaty forces holed up in the Four Courts and civil war became an unfortunate reality. Many members of Cumann na mBan joined the garrison at the Four Courts and hundreds of women were on the anti-Treaty side during the Civil War. Cumann na Saoirse became the main women's organisation for those women who supported the national government and the Irish National Army. This war, often written as a tragic conflict between male comrades who had fought together, was also a war between women who had fought together during the War of Independence. The women of Cumann na Saoirse did not escape the bitter propaganda of the anti-Treaty side. In July, when Jennie Wyse Power, as a vice-president of Sinn Féin, closed its office on Harcourt Street, she was attacked in the republican news-sheet *The Fenian*, which referred to her as a leading light 'in the anaemic women's organisation known as Cumann na Saoirse'.[56]

Cumann na Saoirse and the Civil War

During the Civil War, women played different but important roles on both sides. Cumann na mBan anti-Treaty women resumed their activities as allies to the anti-Treaty IRA. They ran safe houses and protected arms dumps; they collected intelligence and transported arms to ambushes and other sites of military activity. So important was Cumann na mBan support to the anti-Treaty side that the Free State authorities arrested and imprisoned over 600 of them during the war. Cumann na Saoirse, which was not as active in the field, was also important as a support for the pro-Treaty side. There is, as Cal McCarthy writes, evidence of a sustained Civil War campaign by the organisation.[57] It continued its propaganda campaign, often directly in response to Cumann na mBan propaganda. It was much in evidence at the funerals of pro-Treaty politicians, such as Arthur Griffith (died 12 August 1922) and chairman of the Provisional Government and commander-in-chief of the National Army, Michael Collins (assassinated 22 August 1922). During the war it also engaged in support and fundraising for the National Army. It organised céilís, carnival dances, parties and ran appeals for subscriptions, all for the brave men 'who have gone into battle and have sustained their injuries in order that the rights and liberty of the unarmed people of Ireland might be secured and safeguarded'.[58]

At its second convention in February 1923, held in Dublin, Jennie Wyse Power was delighted to report that the return of a majority of pro-Treaty candidates in the 1922 election demonstrated that 'there was no justification, in fact, for the claim made that the great bulk of the women of Ireland were opposed to the acceptance of the treaty'.[59] She also stated that when the Civil War broke out, 'Cumann na Saoirse accommodating itself to the necessities of the new position, devoted its energies to assisting the Army and the Government. During the fighting in Dublin and elsewhere, [it] acted as a distributing agent for Government propaganda, and, by the activity of its members, even the remotest parts of the country were kept informed of the true state of affairs'.[60] Cumann na Saoirse, she said, 'would continue to exist for the duration of the present armed conflict against the Government of Ireland … it will have no purely political activities but all members of Cumann na Saoirse are advised to join Cumann na nGaedheal'.[61] Cumann na nGaedheal had been set up the previous December, and Wyse Power and Alice Stopford Green had represented Cumann na Saoirse at the conference.

Propaganda work and fundraising for injured National Army soldiers were not the only activities of Cumann na Saoirse during the Civil War. Many of the members had been active in Cumann na mBan during the War of Independence and were able to provide the same aid to the National Army that they had provided previously to the IRA. Many of its

members looked 'with horror and distaste on the wild women of Cumann
na mBan' and were determined to stop them supporting the anti-Treaty
IRA.[62] As well as providing intelligence-gathering services where it could,
Cumann na Saoirse collaborated with the National Army in controlling
the activities of anti-Treaty women. This was a very bitter feature of
the Civil War for women, with those who worked together during the
War of Independence policing and threatening each other. The IRA
and its Cumann na mBan allies watched Cumann na Saoirse with great
suspicion. It was thought that Cumann na Saoirse women were passing
information on the IRA to the National Army via 'call houses'; this was a
network of houses where information on IRA activity and personnel was
collected from 'callers' to the house.[63] This 'call house' network worried
the IRA so much that its general headquarters warned its membership
of its existence. The IRA was, however, occasionally able to use the cover
of Cumann na Saoirse to gather information. Cork Cumann na mBan
woman and anti-Treatyite Madge Barnes (née Coghlan) was staying
with a 'well known Free State family in Dublin' during the Civil War.[64]
The secretary of Cumann na Saoirse also lived there. Barnes, using her
contacts and, sometimes, posing as a member of Cumann na Saoirse,
collected intelligence for the IRA. She was the 'chief source of intelligence'
for anti-Treaty activities in Dublin.[65]

Cumann na Saoirse also helped the Free State government and the
National Army deal with other problems with anti-Treaty women. To
lessen the effectiveness of Cumann na mBan as intelligence gatherers
and message carriers for the IRA, Cumann na Saoirse co-operated with
army forces in stopping and searching suspected anti-Treaty women,
earning itself the bitter nickname of 'Cumann na Searchers'. It also helped
deal with the anti-Treaty women who were imprisoned in Kilmainham
Gaol. Dr Brigid Lyons Thornton, 1916 rebel, ex-Cumann na mBan,
now a member of Cumann na Saoirse, was given responsibility for the
welfare of the female prisoners, ironically in the jail she had been in
herself as a prisoner in 1916. Thornton, the only woman in the Army
Medical Corps of the National Army, referred to her Civil War service as
a 'highly trying time'.[66] While their imprisonment and hunger-strikes in
Kilmainham Gaol were fraught for the anti-Treaty women, one incident
was remembered with particular bitterness. On 30 April 1923, eighty of
the women prisoners were to be moved from Kilmainham Gaol to the

North Dublin Union. Mary MacSwiney and Kate O'Callaghan were still on hunger-strike, so the prisoners refused to be moved. According to the pro-Treaty reports, during the attempt to move them, the women attacked the warders but, according to the anti-Treaty side, the prisoners were attacked by CID men, warders and Cumann na Saoirse women, with one Cumann na mBan member, Sorcha McDermott, 'knocked on the floor, stripped, held on the floor and beaten with her own shoes by five Cumann na Saoirse women'.[67]

The violence was on both sides, however. Homes and businesses of those attached to Cumann na Saoirse were watched and sometimes attacked. On Tuesday 12 December 1922, the Irish Farm Produce Stores at 21 Camden Street in Dublin, which belonged to Jennie Wyse Power, was attacked with incendiary devices.[68] The headquarters of the organisation at 5 Parnell Street in Dublin was attacked several times, including on Saturday, 17 February 1923, when 'heavy rifle fire was directed at the building for half an hour'.[69] Individual members were also attacked. In County Kerry, two sisters were savagely attacked by republican men, who, after beating them up, said: 'now will you be a Free Stater?'[70] In Tipperary town, Celia Shaw, an organiser for Cumann na Saoirse, down from Dublin, was recognised by Cumann na mBan women. She was interrogated and her attaché case, which was found to contain 'notes and literature in connection with Cumann na Saoirse', was 'captured'.[71] The Cumann na mBan women communicated to Dublin that all branches of Cumann na Saoirse were banned in their 'area' and they would use 'every means in [their] power to make them ineffective'.[72]

The Civil War ended in May 1923, when the anti-Treaty forces dumped their arms and returned home on the orders of Éamon de Valera. Cumann na Saoirse, which came into existence to support pro-Treaty Sinn Féin politicians during the 1922 election and then extended its remit to supporting the Free State government and National Army during the Civil War, had no real reason to continue. The divisions between both women's organisations remained, with some Cumann na mBan women remaining imprisoned until December 1923. Cumann na Saoirse women continued to lend their support to the Cumann na nGaedheal government, with three, Jennie Wyse Power, Alice Stopford Green and Eileen Costello, appointed to the Free State Seanad.[73] The nominations of senior Cumann na Saoirse women to the Seanad demonstrates the connection between senior members of the organisation and the upper echelons of political power in the Free State. Certainly, as Margaret Ward pointed out, the central executive 'represented the aspirations of the emerging elite', while in the broader membership, women came from wider class backgrounds, certainly in places like Cork.[74] Despite this, Cumann na Saoirse represented more the middle and lower middle class, the class from which many of the power brokers in the new Free State came.

Cumann na Saoirse: The *Raison d'Être*

What was most important for Cumann na Saoirse was to demonstrate that not all Irishwomen rejected the Treaty, and subsequently to demonstrate that Irishwomen were not at fault for the bloodshed of the Civil War. Wyse Power and the executive of Cumann na Saoirse were determined to show that the 'noisy faction' of anti-Treaty women was not representative of Irishwomen broadly. Their efforts during the 1922 election and during the Civil War were certainly of benefit to the Free State government and National Army, even if it did bring bitterness and division among women who had fought together during the previous years.[75] The activities of Cumann na Saoirse showed that not all Irishwomen were among the 'fanatics and doctrinaires and pseudo-intellectuals who knew they were menacing the life of the nation by setting it an impossible task'.[76] However, their activities had little success in persuading the new ruling elite that Irishwomen could be trusted. Pro-Treatyites such as Batt O'Connor had already condemned their erstwhile female comrades, regretting that he had to say that 'our own brave good women and girls [who] gave so much help in our dark trying days of terror ... completely lost their heads when the president came out and condemned the treaty'.[77] In 1924, pro-Treaty historian P.S. O'Hegarty, in a chapter entitled 'the Furies', described the anti-Treaty women, whom he and other pro-Treaty men blamed for the Civil War, as 'unlovely, destructive-minded, arid begetters of violence, both physical violence and mental violence'.[78] This was the image the pro-Treaty women had wished to avoid but they were largely unsuccessful in achieving this.

Cumann na Saoirse no longer had a *raison d'être* as 1923 came to an end. By October 1923, it had vacated its headquarters at 5 Parnell

Street and, by December 1923, a notice appeared in the *Irish Times*, from Cumann na Saoirse secretary Annie Blythe, stating that any contributions that people intended to give the organisation to help 'provide Christmas festivities for wounded soldiers' should be given directly to the military hospitals as 'Cumann na Saoirse is no longer in existence'.[79] It had lasted just under two years, with many of its leading members now joining Cumann na nGaedheal. However, despite its short lifespan, it is important to recognise and remember the contribution of these pro-Treaty women to political life in these vital months as the Irish Free State was coming into existence. Revolutionary historiography has often been remiss in including the contributions of Cumann na mBan, and in those histories on Cumann na mBan, Cumann na Saoirse is often overlooked.[80] Acknowledging that the response of political and activist women to the Treaty was as nuanced and complex as the response of political men is important. The dismissive idea that the pro-Treaty women were simply adjuncts of their pro-Treaty spouses undermines the very real ideological positions these women, at great personal risk, took. Once the Civil War was over, many of the women in Cumann na Saoirse continued their activism, campaigning for the rights of women in the new Irish Free State. Interestingly, as the bitterness of the war faded, they often collaborated with Cumann na mBan women against the new threat to women's position in Irish society, the extreme conservatism and anti-women's equality ideologies of the new political masters, in both Cumann na nGaedheal and Fianna Fáil, in the Irish Free State.

Notes

1   See Chapter 6: Sinéad McCoole, 'Debating not negotiating: the female TDs of the Second Dáil' for a discussion on the contribution of these six TDs to the Treaty debates.
2   Cal McCarthy, *Cumann na mBan and the Irish Revolution* (Cork, 2007), p. 185. At a meeting on 11 January 1922, the executive of Cumann na mBan voted twenty-four to two against acceptance of the Treaty. The two executive members who supported the Treaty were Jennie Wyse Power and a Miss Mullan from County Monaghan.
3   Witness statement of Brighid O'Mullane, 13 Nov. 1950 (Bureau of Military History (BMH), 485), p. 2.
4   McCarthy, *Cumann na mBan*, p. 190.

5   Witness statement of Lily Curran, 17 Feb. 1953 (BMH, 805), p. 32.

6   Cited in Jason Knirck, '"Ghosts and realities": female TDs and the Treaty debate' in *Éire-Ireland*, xxxii & xxxiii, no. 4 (Geimhreadh/Winter 1997), p. 191.

7   *Irish Independent*, 6 Feb. 1922.

8   Ibid.

9   Marie O'Neill, *From Parnell to de Valera: a biography of Jennie Wyse Power, 1858–1941* (Dublin, 1991), p. 133. As a young woman, Wyse Power was politically active in the Ladies' Land League and was a supporter of Charles Stewart Parnell; she always remembered, with great sadness, the Parnellite split.

10   *Irish Independent*, 6 Feb. 1922.

11   Minutes of the Cumann na mBan special convention, 5 Feb. 1922 (National Library of Ireland (NLI), MS 49851/10).

12   *Irish Independent*, 6 Feb. 1922.

13   Ibid.

14   Minutes of the Cumann na mBan special convention, 5 Feb. 1922.

15   *Irish Independent*, 6 Feb. 1922.

16   Minutes of the Cumann na mBan special convention, 5 Feb. 1922.

17   Ibid.

18   *Irish Independent*, 6 Feb. 1922.

19   Ibid.

20   Witness statement of Áine Ní Riain, 18 Sept. 1953 (BMH, 887), p. 16.

21   Roy Foster, *Vivid faces: the revolutionary generation in Ireland, 1890–1923* (London, 2014).

22   Seán Mac Diarmada writing to his family before his execution stated that had he lived, Min Ryan would, in all probability, have been his wife (https://www.nli.ie/pdfs/mss%20lists/178_Se%C3%A1nT%C3%93CeallaighRyansOfTomcoole.pdf) (20 Feb. 2018).

23   Foster, *Vivid faces*, p. 222.

24   File of Mary Josephine Mulcahy, 31 Jan. 1965–1 Nov. 1977 (Military Archives of Ireland (MAI), Military Service Pensions Collection (MSPC), MSP34REF1692).

25   Angus Mitchell, 'Ireland, South America and the forgotten history of rubber' in *History Ireland*, xvi, no. 4 (July/Aug. 2008), pp. 41–5.

26   Lil Conlon, *Cumann na mBan and the women of Ireland, 1913–25* (Cork, 1969), pp. 260–1.

27   Ann-Marie Gallagher, Cathy Lubelska, Louise Ryan (eds), *Re-presenting the past: women and history* (London, 2001), p. 35.

28   Conlon, *Cumann na mBan*, p. 260.

29   Ibid.

30   Kathleen Clarke, *Revolutionary woman, 1878–1972: an autobiography*, ed. Helen Litton (Dublin, 1991), p. 265.

31   Senia Pašeta, *Irish nationalist women, 1900–1918* (Cambridge, 2014), p. 268.

32   *Freeman's Journal*, 18 Feb. 1922.

33   Conlon, *Cumann na mBan*, pp. 263–4.

34   O'Neill, *From Parnell to de Valera*, p. 138.
35   Conlon, *Cumann na mBan*, pp. 267–8.
36   *Irish Independent*, 6 Feb. 1922.
37   Ibid.
38   Ann Matthews, *Renegades: Irish republican women 1900-1922* (Cork, 2010), p. 322.
39   *Dáil Éireann deb.*, T, no. 7, 59 (20 Dec. 1921).
40   Conlon, *Cumann na mBan*, p. 268.
41   McCarthy, *Cumann na mBan*, p. 197.
42   *Irish Times*, 14 Mar. 1922.
43   Ibid.
44   Ibid.
45   Ibid.
46   Margaret Ward, *Unmanageable revolutionaries: women and Irish nationalism* (Dublin, 1981), p. 173.
47   *Irish Times*, 14 Mar. 1922.
48   Lauren Arrington, *Revolutionary lives: Constance and Casimir Markievicz* (Princeton, NJ, 2016), p. 216.
49   Chapter 17 of a draft of an unpublished autobiography by Máire Comerford entitled *The dangerous ground*, 1956 (University College Dublin Archives, Máire Comerford Papers, LA18/17). Comerford said that 'the British dreaded their pens as much as they dreaded an IRA column in the field'.
50   *Irish Times*, 25 Mar. 1922.
51   Ibid.
52   McCarthy, *Cumann na mBan*, p. 197.
53   'Cumann na Saoirse: Points for Canvassers', 1922 (NLI, Ephemera Collection, EPH B9).
54   'What the Peace Treaty Gives Ireland', 1922 (ibid., EPH B14).
55   McCarthy, *Cumann na mBan*, p. 197.
56   O'Neill, *From Parnell to de Valera*, p. 142.
57   McCarthy, *Cumann na mBan*, p. 198.
58   *Freeman's Journal*, 1 Aug. 1922.
59   *Irish Times*, 12 Feb. 1923.
60   Ibid.
61   Ibid.
62   Ward, *Unmanageable revolutionaries*, p. 173.
63   McCarthy, *Cumann na mBan*, p. 199.
64   File of Madge Barnes, 27 June 1945–3 Mar. 1976 (MAI, MSPC, MSP34REF60487).
65   Ibid.
66   Commandant Brigid Lyons Thornton (Retired), 'Women and the army' in *An Cosantóir: The Irish Defence Journal*, xxxv, no. 11 (Nov. 1975) (http://www.dfmagazine. ie/site-assets/uploads/Vol._35_No._11_-_Nov_1975-low.pdf) (3 Mar. 2018), p. 363.
67   *An Phoblacht*, 9 May 1923 (NLI, MS 15443).
68   *Irish Examiner*, 12 Dec. 1922.

69   Ibid., 19 Feb. 1923.

70   McCarthy, *Cumann na mBan*, p. 200.

71   Ibid., pp. 200–1.

72   Ibid.

73   Another former member of Cumann na Saoirse, Kathleen Browne, would be elected to the Seanad in 1929. Of the six women who served in the Free State Seanad between 1922 and 1936 (when it was abolished), four, Wyse Power, Green, Costello and Browne, were pro-Treaty Cumann na Saoirse women; one, the Countess of Desart was a unionist; and one, Kathleen Clarke, elected to the Seanad in 1928, had been anti-Treaty. However, as the bitterness of the Civil War receded, Wyse Power, Costello, Browne and Clarke did co-operate, particularly in resisting the anti-women measures introduced by both the Cumann na nGaedheal and Fianna Fáil governments during these years. All four also campaigned against the articles dealing with women in the 1937 constitution.

74   Ward, *Unmanageable revolutionaries*, p. 92.

75   Bryan Fanning, *Histories of the Irish future* (London, 2015), p. 162.

76   From the eulogy by Kevin O'Higgins at the graveside of Michael Collins, 28 Aug. 1922, quoted in ibid.

77   Kieron Curtis, *P.S. O'Hegarty (1879-1955): Sinn Féin Fenian* (London, 2010), p. 113.

78   P.S. O'Hegarty, *The victory of Sinn Féin* (Dublin, 1924), pp. 104–5.

79   *Irish Times*, 17 Dec. 1923.

80   Works which do include sections on Cumann na Saoirse are McCarthy, *Cumann na mBan*, pp. 193–203; Matthews, *Renegades*, pp. 322–9.

CHAPTER 8

Leaders or Followers? Sinn Féin, the Split and Representing the Farmers in the Treaty Debates

Tony Varley

Some years ago, W.E. Vaughan observed how the Land War (1879–82) created 'an alliance between nationalists and tenants that endured for decades and went a long way to securing self-government for Ireland'.[1] Fundamental to this alliance – more akin to a tacit understanding than to any formal pact – was a normative expectation that nationalists and tenant-farmers should support each other in pursuing their respective political and class interests. Depending on how it was seen and negotiated, this informal alliance (such as it was) could take on different guises at different junctures. David Fitzpatrick has detected a sense in which farmers – almost two-thirds of whom had become owners of their holdings by 1916 – came to lead, and nationalists to follow, during the revolutionary years.[2] He sees the farmers, in spite of their 'organisational weaknesses', managing 'by sheer weight of numbers, wealth and social status' to direct 'the course of revolution as though by right'.[3] Farmer conservatism thus proved powerful enough to keep the lid on whatever impulses towards radical 'social change' the Irish Revolution unleashed.[4]

Whether, under the strain of the Treaty split, farmers continued to 'lead' and Sinn Féin nationalists to 'follow' during the Treaty debates is explored in this chapter. Its concern is not with farmer deputies per se but with those on opposing sides of Sinn Féin's parliamentary party who – regardless of their occupations – saw themselves as representing farmers' political and economic interests.[5] As the split in Sinn Féin's parliamentary party was so recent and still developing, the rival factions had yet to decide how they should represent the farmers and their interests collectively. The emerging pro- and anti-Treaty positions will, therefore, have to be inferred from the speeches of individual deputies.

This chapter begins with a review of how well organised, and capable of exerting political influence, Irish farmers were by the end of 1921. Where farmers featured in pro- and anti-Treaty conceptions of 'the will of the people' during the Treaty debates is then examined. Following this, we discuss how pro- and anti-Treaty deputies perceived the economic, social and political consequences of either accepting or rejecting the Treaty settlement. An answer to the question of whether the divided Sinn Féin deputies were following or leading the farmers in the Treaty debates is then offered. Finally, we consider how relations between organised Irish farmers and pro- and anti-Treaty nationalists progressed in the years immediately following the Treaty.

Farmers as a Rising Political Force

Modelling itself on the English National Farmers' Union (NFU), established in 1908, the Irish Farmers' Union (IFU) began to emerge as a would-be national federation of county-based farmers' associations in 1911–12.[6] Recognising that Irish farmers – numbering some 383,167 in 1911 – were destined to stay relatively powerless as a class as long as they remained unorganised, the IFU leadership saw organisation as contributing vitally to farmers' material well-being and to their class formation.[7] The hope was that, with the deeper class-consciousness and solidarity that organisation would bring, the farmers might rise above the various internal divisions that historically had kept them apart.[8]

An organisational drive launched in 1917 left the IFU with 60,000 members in twenty-five counties by 1920.[9] Two years later a 'little short of 100,000' members were on the books.[10] On the strength of its expanding membership and its widening spatial reach, the IFU national executive's confidence in its authority to speak for the farmer class as a whole grew apace.[11] Registering itself formally as a trade union in 1920, the IFU 'had become a fairly powerful lobby in Irish politics' by 1921.[12]

At first, the IFU, following the NFU's practice, was determined to steer clear of direct participation in party politics. The attractiveness of such an approach was that it left the IFU better able 'to apply pressure to all political factions, whatever their colour'.[13] By the close of 1921, however, the IFU's national executive decided to form a political wing which, in 1922, materialised as the Farmers' Party. One suggestion is that the signing of the Anglo-Irish Treaty on 6 December 1921 cleared the way for this tactical shift.[14] Behind the scenes a number of threatening forces also appear to have been at work.

One notable threat was the perceived rise of a menacingly *dirigiste* state, a central plank of which was the 1917 Selborne Report's proposal to continue the wartime command economy in agriculture, thereby compromising private property rights in land.[15] The organised farmers were also fearful – especially in those counties heavily reliant on paid farm workers – of the rising militancy of rural labour, now being radicalised by syndicalist trade unionism, the Bolshevik revolution and the wartime compulsory tillage scheme (and accompanying wage regulation) introduced in 1917.[16] Another palpable fear was that the proposed lifting of the ban on importing Canadian store cattle into the United Kingdom (acted on in 1923) would undermine Ireland's vital cattle economy.[17]

Adding to these threatening forces was the political instability that followed the weakening and eventual collapse of the Irish Parliamentary Party in late 1918, the political hegemony of Sinn Féin, and the outbreak of the Anglo-Irish War in early 1919. In response to the perceived crisis of representation brought on by all this economic and political turbulence, some of the IFU's top leadership began to think seriously about competing with nationalists for the farmer vote.

Reading 'the Will of the People'

It was only after the Christmas recess in 1921 that the issue of how farmers viewed the Treaty become a topic of sustained discussion during the Treaty debates. Before then, what it was presumed farmers thought on the Treaty question was subsumed within general discussions of the 'will of the people'.[18] Across the Treaty divide there was considerable acceptance that public opinion as a measure of popular consent, the people's will, and especially the will of the majority, was indeed relevant to the Dáil's deliberations on the Treaty issue. Where the Sinn Féin deputies disagreed sharply was in relation to the main question to be put to public opinion, the means by which public opinion was best gauged and the direction it was seen to be taking.

For the anti-Treaty side, the central question was the opinion the public had of 'the Republic' or the fully independent state proclaimed in the 1916 Rising, and whose authority subsequently came to rest democratically on popular sovereignty derived from the ballot box. Leading anti-Treaty republicans regarded the elections of 1918 and 1921 as the only valid basis for gauging the people's will on the question of the Republic. 'We were elected by the Irish people', Éamon De Valera once again pointed out on 19 December 1921, 'and did the Irish people think we were liars when we said that we meant to uphold the Republic, which was ratified by the vote of the people three years ago, and was further ratified – expressly ratified – by the vote of the people at the elections last May?'[19]

Further confirming the reality of the Republic proclaimed in 1916 were the institutional arrangements Sinn Féin's counter-state had created after 21 January 1919 and the policies it had adopted and pursued.[20] Safeguarding this republic against those prepared to betray it became the paramount anti-Treatyite concern.[21] Believers in the Republic's existence were, therefore, always likely to reject Michael Collins's stepping-stone argument that the Treaty should be adopted as offering the 'freedom' to achieve 'the ultimate freedom that all nations desire and develop to'.[22]

At least three responses to 'the Republic' can be distinguished on the pro-Treaty side. Eoin MacNeill (the ceann comhairle or speaker), Alec McCabe (Sligo-Mayo East) and Commandant Eoin O'Duffy (Monaghan) insisted – in the Dáil's pre-Christmas private sessions – on still explicitly identifying themselves as 'Republicans' and defied anyone to say otherwise.[23] Michael Collins professed himself on his part completely in favour of Ireland eventually becoming a fully sovereign state. 'Let no man here', he said on 14 December, 'put me into the position to argue for anything less than full freedom for Ireland'.[24]

A very different pro-Treatyite response – voiced by the likes of Joseph McGrath (Dublin North-West), Patrick Hogan (Galway), Lorcán Robbins

(Longford-Westmeath) and J.J. Walsh (Cork Borough) – claimed that the Republic of the anti-Treatyites was more imagined than real.[25] Dismissing any suggestion that an Irish republic was already up and running, J.J. Walsh berated his opponents: 'you call yourself a Free Republic. You have an ideal, and an ideal only, and anything provided in this Act does not rob you of that ideal'.[26] Earlier Michael Collins had commented: 'It has not been a struggle for the ideal of freedom for 750 years symbolised in the name Republic'.[27]

The main question for pro-Treaty deputies, in attempting to read the 'will of the people', was not how the public viewed the Republic but how it judged the Treaty now that it had been signed. Several pro-Treatyite deputies, sensing that the great majority of the public (and of the farmers) favoured the Treaty's ratification, were keen to estimate the actual size of pro-Treaty popular support. At the very outset, Patrick Brennan (Clare) claimed that: 'The army in Clare have not said a word about the Treaty. They look upon themselves as soldiers. The civil population are out for the Treaty.'[28]

Over the Christmas recess, J.J. Walsh's soundings had led him to conclude that the public mood overwhelmingly backed ratification. In his highly optimistic appraisal, '95 per cent of the people of this country who have had an opportunity of expressing themselves', and 90 per cent of 'the people of Cork', favoured the Treaty.[29] Just prior to the vote on 7 January 1922, Arthur Griffith's still more upbeat estimation was that 'The people of Ireland are, you know – every one of you – ninety-eight per cent. for this Treaty ("No! no!" and "Yes! yes!"). Now, everyone of you knows that; they have told you to vote for it.'[30]

There were some less sanguine pro-Treatyites ready to accept that their anti-Treatyite opponents were indeed speaking for a dissenting minority, at once sizeable and intense. Before Christmas, Pádraic Ó Máille (Galway) presciently predicted that: 'If the Treaty is passed tomorrow there will be a large minority in the country against it and that party will be the nucleus of a Republican Party.'[31] Another clear-eyed sceptic was George Gavan Duffy (Dublin County) who observed, on 21 December, that: 'You may have a plebiscite in this country, which no serious man can wish to have, because after what you have seen here it is obvious that it will rend the country from one end to the other, and leave memories of bitterness and acrimony that will last a generation.'[32] Ó Máille and

Duffy, however, were exceptions to the general pro-Treatyite tendency
to dismiss their anti-Treatyite rivals as wildly out of kilter with public
opinion.

Some leading pro-Treatyites, possibly reflecting in part their reading
of the public mood, insisted that however much opposed individual
deputies might personally be to the Treaty they had no choice as public
representatives but to vote with the wishes of the majority of their
constituents. On the day of the vote (7 January 1922) Arthur Griffith
(Cavan) thus stated that: 'If representative government is going to
remain on the earth, then a representative must voice the opinion of his
constituents; if his conscience will not let him do that he has only one
way out and that is to resign and refuse to misrepresent them.'[33] Not to
accept the Treaty, Alec McCabe and Arthur Griffith further emphasised,
would leave Dáil deputies at risk of paying dearly for it at the polls. On
4 January, McCabe, in pondering how farmers might respond to the
Treaty's rejection, asked his anti-Treaty opponents did they: 'think the
farmers, the backbone of national Ireland, broken and disheartened by
the crash in prices, will stand idly by while we run the country to ruin?
For this is what rejection really means – not war ... It is not war we are
faced with but disunion, internal strife, chaos, and a retreat, perhaps, to
the position we held when this war began.'[34] 'I tell you', Arthur Griffith
likewise declared on 7 January:

> what is going to happen to you if you reject this Treaty. The Irish
> people are going to sweep you out as incompetent. We have got to
> deal with the people; we have got to believe that we are not superiors;
> we have got to remember that they are our flesh and blood ... As John
> Mitchell [sic] said: 'One Irish peasant's life is as dear and as sacred to
> us as any other man's life in the country is, be he who he may.'[35]

On the other side, some anti-Treatyites were keen to debunk the highly
optimistic pro-Treaty estimates of popular support for the Treaty and
dismissals of the Republic's real existence. On 21 December, Mary
MacSwiney (Cork Borough) rebuked the pro-Treatyites for taking 'it for
granted that the Irish people are going to jump at their own dishonour.
With a definite Republican Manifesto in your pockets, how dare you say
your constituents have changed until you have gone and asked them?'[36]

on the roadsides. They are the people who have combined together against the workers of Ireland, who have used the English soldiers, the English police, and every institution in the country to ruin the farmer, and more especially the small farmer, and to send the people of Ireland to drift in the emigrant ships and to die of horrible disease or to sink to the bottom of the Atlantic.[51]

O'Connor's and Markievicz's remarks relating to southern unionism clearly rankled with some pro-Treaty deputies. Lorcán Robbins was eager to defend the right of the southern unionists to have their say on the Treaty issue:

We want the Southern Unionists and we want every Irishman (hear, hear). I never believed more in Mr. Arthur Griffith and never believed him to be more of a statesman than when he sent his message to the Southern Unionists (hear, hear). The Southern Unionists are Irishmen, and, as Parnell once said, we need every Irishman ... I resent the remarks made by the Minister of Agriculture that the opinion behind this Treaty in the country is manufactured.[52]

A little earlier J.J. Walsh had pointed out how:

It is not the Southern Unionists who have asked you to support the Treaty. The Comhairlí Ceanntair are not Southern Unionists, the Sinn Féin Clubs are not Southern Unionists, the County Councils of the country are not Southern Unionists. The whole nation and all the public bodies of this country are not Southern Unionists; but they are as good Republicans as you are, and you know it.[53]

Nor could the vast bulk of the farmer class ever be described as unionist in their politics. Patrick Brennan, Michael Collins, William Sears (Mayo South-Roscommon South) and J.J. Walsh were all quick to point to the many instances of farmers (or farmers' sons) actively – and frequently at considerable cost to themselves and their families – supporting the military campaign of the Irish Republican Army (IRA). Were not the farmers, J.J. Walsh asked on 3 January, 'the back-bone of the fight through which we have gone – notwithstanding that they have enjoyed a prosperity which they didn't anticipate? Indeed, the well-to-do farmers were the great backers of our fight.'[54]

On the following day, William Sears, in replying to those who questioned 'the patriotism and the courage of the Irish race' – qualities he believed would be indispensable if the Treaty's transformative potential was ever to be realised – alluded to the parallel case of the farmers in recent Irish history: 'All that was said about the Irish people here reminds me, as it must remind others, of what was said about the Irish farmers. It was said that if the Irish farmer got the land he would betray the country. Yet we know that the sons of the Irish farmers and the Irish labourers were the back-bone of the I.R.A. (cheers).'[55]

After Sears ceased speaking, Art O'Connor rose to retract, and to apologise for, some of his remarks of the previous day. 'There is no man in this assembly', he now declared,

has a greater admiration for the work that the farmers have done for the Republic. It is an ill bird that fouls its own nest. I am a farmer's son. I come from farming people, and I hope and trust that the farmers of Ireland and the farming members of this Dáil will not think that I was attempting to throw dirty water on the farmers of the country. There is an old proverb which says that there are three things that cannot be recalled: the spoken word, the hunter's arrow, and the missed opportunity. The 'spoken word' was yesterday, perhaps the 'arrow' that might have hurt the feelings of some of the people of this country.[56]

O'Connor went on to acknowledge that: 'The members of the Farmers' Unions have helped me in my work as Minister of Agriculture. So now I take this opportunity of making this *amende honourable*, and apologising to the farmers for any of the things that might be misconstrued in anything I may have said.'[57]

Of course, that O'Connor was now willing to row back on his earlier remarks did not signify any change of heart towards the Treaty in response to the numerous pro-Treaty resolutions emanating from IFU branches up and down the country. Nor did O'Connor's statement of 4 January put an end to a discussion of the weight to be given to farmer opinion in deciding the Treaty question. On 7 January, Patrick Brennan rose to counter again the view that 'the farmers have no right to express their opinion on the matters before the House'.[58] While not claiming to speak 'for any particular class', Brennan stated that 'the farmers of Ireland, of Clare, anyway, were never asked in vain by the army or the civil organisation of Sinn Féin for any assistance, which they did not give, in money and in men to the fight – they were never backward; these people have every right to express their opinions'.[59]

Shortly after Brennan had finished speaking, Con Collins, an anti-Treaty deputy representing Kerry-Limerick West, repeated Art O'Connor's original contention that republicans could never accept the IFU's legitimacy as a representative body as long as some of its leaders had unionist sympathies. Collins related how he too had received a resolution 'subscribed to by a few individuals' who 'call themselves members of the Farmers' Union' during the Christmas recess. These people, he continued,

> have been known to us, and they have been, in reality, members of this body about which we have heard a good deal recently – the Southern Irish Unionists. These are the people who are calling on me to ratify the Treaty; these are the people who have been working against us in every step that we have taken, and in all the different phases of our activity in this Republic of ours.[60]

Later, on 7 January, Arthur Griffith referred to Constance Markievicz's remarks about the southern unionists and to her being

> perturbed over the letter I wrote about the Southern Unionists; she drew from that letter the idea that I was going to treat them as a privileged class; she wanted to know why I met these men. I met them because they are my countrymen (applause); and because, if we are to have an Irish nation, we want to start with fair play for all sections and with understandings between all sections (applause). I would meet to-morrow on that basis the Ulster Unionists, to seek to get them to join in the Irish nation (hear, hear).[61]

Better or Worse Times Ahead?

Predictably, what the Sinn Féin deputies believed the Treaty would mean economically and socially for Irish farmers, and for Irish society more generally, became another bone of contention. As the debates petered out, Joseph McGrath castigated his anti-Treaty colleagues for their utter refusal to see anything positive in the Treaty settlement. The Treaty's potentially transformative power, in McGrath's view, gave the 'southern' Irish the opportunity to create an infinitely better future. 'Under this Treaty', he suggested, 'every single thing in [the] Democratic Programme can be put into force, and the democrats in this assembly know that well. Not one of those on the other side have [*sic*] referred to this matter.'[62]

McGrath was not the first pro-Treatyite to refer to the Treaty's potentially transformative power. On 20 December 1921, Seán Milroy (Cavan) had also contrasted the deeply pessimistic anti-Treaty outlook with the numerous possibilities he saw the Treaty opening up for the Irish people. Milroy commented on how: 'President de Valera said that in this Treaty we were presuming to set boundaries to the march of the Irish Nation. So far from that being true, we are smashing down the barriers that obstruct the march of the Irish Nation … The Act of Union took away from the Irish people their right, such as they had, to direct, mould and control their own land. This Treaty brings back to Ireland these powers (hear, hear).'[63] To bolster his analysis, Milroy invoked the authority of Professor Alfred O'Rahilly of University College Cork who had affirmed that the Treaty bestowed on the 'southern' Irish

> all the really important powers required for our normal, political, social and economic life. We have unfettered freedom in forming our political constitution, in social legislation, in education, in developing our national resources, in fostering our agriculture and industries, in framing our tariff policy, in regulating our taxes, our currency laws, our finances, in appointing consular agents abroad, in concluding commercial treaties with other countries.[64]

After Christmas, Piaras Béaslaí (Kerry-Limerick West) gave something of an anti-capitalist twist to Milroy's and O'Rahilly's views of the Treaty containing the foundations of a developmental state capable of propelling Irish social and economic progress. 'I tell you', he maintained on 3 January:

> when the British have evacuated our country the Free State will be just what we make it; and we can make it a great and glorious land,

the home of a fine Gaelic culture, of a highly developed agricultural system that will rival Denmark; with industries developed perhaps as some people advocate, on co-operative, non-capitalistic lines; of brave and beautiful ideas worked into practice.[65]

Not alone was there in prospect 'a development under state protection of that system of co-operative agricultural development that has already done so much good', but other rural dwellers stood to benefit significantly as well.[66] 'We can', Béaslaí was convinced: 'have our fisheries organised on a national basis so that the poor fishermen of Ireland, in most cases the chief representatives of our historic Gaelic Ireland, will be able to compete on fair terms with the wealthy, state-aided foreigner. We can have our marshes and waste lands turned into plantations and our hillsides covered with trees.'[67]

The state powers the Treaty conferred, in Michael Collins's view, could be used to buffer Ireland against the 'economic penetration' of large-scale, British capitalist interests. 'Every day', he claimed,

our Banks become incorporated or allied to British interests, every day our Steamship Companies go into English hands, every day some other business concern in this city is taken over by an English concern and becomes a little oasis of English customs and manners. Nobody notices, but that is the thing that has destroyed our Gaelic civilisation. That is a thing that we are able to stop, not perhaps if we lose the opportunity of stopping it now.[68]

If some pro-Treaty speakers viewed ratification as opening the door to an economic future brimming with positive possibility, others dwelled on the sharp consequences they were sure would follow the Treaty being voted down. To reject the Treaty, these argued, could only worsen economic conditions already hugely stressed by the post-war price slump and the lingering labour and agrarian unrest of the revolutionary years. A clearly exasperated Arthur Griffith remarked, on 7 January, how some of the debate had proceeded eerily:

as if there were no Irish people outside of these doors as if there were no economic questions; as if there were not tens of thousands of unemployed; as if there were not tens of thousands of struggling farmers and of labouring people through the country; as if we could go on indefinitely making this kind of fight against England.[69]

Alec McCabe had earlier advised that it would be infinitely better to take what the Treaty offered rather 'than run the risk of war or chaos and all that it means to our people and the prosperity of the country'.[70] What further had to be borne in mind, McCabe reminded his audience, was that:

> We are in a very backward condition, socially and economically speaking. We have, in fact, as far as the other countries of Europe are concerned, been practically standing still for nine or ten years; the land question is still as far as ever from settlement; a number of our industries are leading a precarious existence; labour is restless and aggressive.[71]

Given such circumstances, the negative economic and social fall-out of the Dáil's failure to accept the Treaty, and of a resumption of war, could only be catastrophic. McCabe predicted that 'the moral effect of a prolonged state of war on the population' would create 'Mexican conditions in the country' in which 'murder, robbery [and] arson' would become daily events.[72] 'Men', in the dystopian civil strife he imagined would follow the Treaty being struck down: 'will settle their quarrels with Webleys instead of their fists. The striker will abandon the peaceful method of picketing for the bomb and the torch. The landless workers will have recourse to more deadly weapons than hazel sticks in attacking the ranches.'[73]

Among anti-Treatyites, by contrast, the tendency was to view the Treaty as wholly incapable of delivering a promising political or economic future to the Irish people. Before Christmas, President de Valera was ready to concede that:

> A war-weary people will take things which are not in accordance with their aspirations. You may have a snatch election now, and you may get a vote of the people, but I will tell you that Treaty will renew the contest that is going to begin the same history that the Union began, and Lloyd George is going to have the same fruit for his labours as Pitt had.[74]

Far from the Treaty bestowing economic independence on the country, a number of anti-Treaty deputies were convinced that Britain's capacity to oppress Ireland economically would carry on unabated. Ratification for de Valera was thus 'to set bounds to the onward march of a nation (applause)'.[75] Post-Treaty Ireland, in Mary MacSwiney's view, would still depend economically on, and be controlled by, Britain. She reminded her listeners how: 'Mr. Churchill, whom we all know is the *enfant terrible* of the British Government because he is always giving away what they mean but don't choose to say, has declared that the grant of fiscal autonomy did not matter, because Great Britain held Irish prosperity in the hollow of her hand.'[76] Convinced that the Treaty 'won't help our commerce', Constance Markievicz's belief was that it was: 'the capitalists' interests in England and Ireland that are pushing this Treaty to block the march of the working people in England and Ireland'.[77]

Traces of a class analysis are more detectable among the anti-Treatyites.[78] As well as taking the farmer class as highly differentiated economically and politically, this class analysis resonated with the soon-to-be evident tendency for big and small farmers to support political parties on opposite sides of the Treaty split.[79] We thus find Art O'Connor insinuating, on 3 January, that the real agrarian winners in post-Treaty Ireland would be those with unionist sympathies leading the IFU who were really gentlemen farmers and ex-landlords 'masquerading as farmers'.[80] Constance Markievicz shared O'Connor's original assertion that the southern unionists, responsible historically for the 'ruin' of 'the farmer, and more especially the small farmer', stood to do well economically under any regime based on the Treaty.[81]

A conviction that politics had to be regarded as superior to economics, in the event of a clash between them, further informed the anti-Treatyite discussion of the consequences of ratification. 'I am as anxious as anyone for the material prosperity of Ireland and the Irish people', de Valera declared on 19 December:

> but I cannot do anything that would make the Irish people hang their heads. I would rather see the same thing over again than that Irishmen should have to hang their heads in shame for having signed and put their hands to a document handing over their authority to

a foreign country. The Irish people would not want me to save them materially at the expense of their national honour.[82]

Other anti-Treatyites were even more adamant that economic well-being could be sacrificed if that was to be the cost of the Treaty's rejection. 'We would', as Liam Mellows put it, 'rather have the people of Ireland eking out a poor existence on the soil; as long as they possessed their souls, their minds, and their honour'.[83] 'You could not', Mary MacSwiney had earlier maintained, 'for the sake of a material advantage accept a spiritual surrender'.[84] 'I fear dishonour', Constance Markievicz made it known on 3 January: 'I don't fear death, and I feel at all events that death is preferable to dishonour; and sooner than see the people of Ireland take that oath meaning to build up your Republic on a lie, I would sooner say to the people of Ireland: "Stand by me and fight to the death".'[85]

Leaders or Followers?

Did then the pro- and anti-Treaty Sinn Féin deputies see themselves leading or following the farmers in their conceptions of the 'will of the people', and in their views of the consequences likely to follow acceptance or rejection of the Treaty? The direction public opinion was taking, as has been shown, was sharply contested between the opposing sides. The prevailing pro-Treatyite conviction – one many anti-Treatyites profoundly disagreed with – was that the farmers, no less than the people in general, overwhelmingly favoured ratification. With deputies of the opposing sides believing themselves to be reading the direction of public opinion correctly, they could equally claim to be following rather than leading the people (and the farmers) in their stances on the issues of the Treaty and the Republic.

Two diverging views of Ireland's economic and social future stand out when we consider how the opposing sides saw the consequences of accepting or rejecting the Treaty. One view saw the Treaty's acceptance as blighting the future, the other as securing it. Far from changing Ireland for the better, those on the anti-Treaty side could see the Treaty settlement delivering only a vassal state, in which the nightmare of colonial and neo-colonial political and economic domination would persist indefinitely.

The Treaty, in the optimistic eyes of its supporters, could give rise to a new dispensation in which the many material injuries inflicted by centuries of colonial rule could be healed. Failure to ratify would likewise mean that the long-term potential benefits of acceptance could never be realised. And, in the nearer term, ratification was viewed as helping to mitigate some of the worst effects of the post-war price slump. Pro-Treatyites like McCabe were clear – given post-partition Ireland's overwhelming economic dependence on agriculture, and the damage wrought by war and by the deepening post-war depression – they had to be actively guided by farmers' material interests. Only at their own peril could nationalists put their own political interests before the farmers' economic interests. For practical purposes, the farming interest and the national interest were to be regarded as one and the same.[86] This is not to say that pro-Treatyites were swayed purely by economic considerations. What proved crucial for many was the way the Treaty provided for the withdrawal – leaving the Treaty ports aside – of British armed forces.[87]

Several anti-Treatyites, in parallel to their pro-Treatyite rivals, presented themselves as speaking for (and thus following) the people (and the farmers) in proposing that the economic and political consequences of ratifying the Treaty would be largely or wholly negative for Ireland (even if good for well-to-do southern unionists). We further find among leading anti-Treaty deputies a strong conviction that, regardless of any likely economic costs for farmers and others, the political imperative of defending the Republic had to take precedence over economic considerations in deciding the Treaty question. Class and sectional interests had, therefore, to be subordinated when 'national honour' and the saving of the Republic from its pro-Treaty enemies were at stake. Many anti-Treaty deputies believed they would be failing shamefully in their duty to the Irish nation if, as public representatives, they did not lead the way in defending the embattled Republic from those would-be traitors ready to betray it.

Aftermath

The narrow result over the Treaty's ratification on 7 January 1922 illustrates not just the depth of the split in Sinn Féin's parliamentary party but how the Treaty, instead of being the symbol of bright possibility its advocates hoped for, was destined to become a bitterly contested symbol for years to come. Even before the split in Sinn Féin's parliamentary party had become general in the country, the IFU had moved, in December 1921, to establish its own Farmers' Party. Broad acceptance of the Treaty greatly influenced both the IFU's and the Farmers' Party's response to the emerging Free State. Not alone did Farmers' Party elected deputies (seven in 1922 and fifteen in the 153-seat Fourth Dáil of 1923–7) take their seats in the Third and later Dáils, but they were broadly sympathetic to the Cumann na nGaedheal ruling party's austerity and agricultural policies.[88] Competition for votes did not prevent co-operation between the IFU/ Farmers' Party and the ruling pro-Treatyites as the 1920s advanced.[89]

Closeness to the ruling party tended nevertheless to deprive the Farmers' Party of the oppositional identity required to be successful in competitive politics. It also had the effect of discrediting the argument that it took a farmer to represent a farmer adequately in the party-political sphere. Later in the 1920s, once it became apparent that the anti-Treaty Fianna Fáil party was well on its way to becoming a ruling party, the Farmers' Party tended to become closer to the Cosgrave party, even to the point of being progressively cannibalised by it from 1927 onwards.

A lesson many leading IFU figures learned from the Treaty split, anti-Treatyite abstentionism and the Civil War was that they could not trust anti-Treaty nationalists to represent their interests. Anti-Treaty nationalists, in turn, tended to view the IFU and Farmers' Party with deep suspicion.[90] Before long, Fianna Fáil activists were seizing on the manner in which the Farmers' Party was tending to win seats in constituencies where bigger farmers were more numerous.[91] In particular, Fianna Fáil highlighted the gentry backgrounds of some prominent IFU leaders (such as Colonel George O'Callaghan-Westropp and Sir John Keane) as proof positive that the Farmers' Party was, in reality, 'a party of landlords and ranchers' that had nothing to offer small farmers.[92]

Closeness to Cumann na nGaedheal and the enmity of Fianna Fáil were not the only challenges facing the IFU/Farmers' Party as the 1920s wore on. Factional infighting – stemming partly from the gentry origins of a section of its leadership – had long been a source of debilitation and bore continuing witness to how much internal divisions were still frustrating the IFU/Farmers' Party's desire to re-shape Irish farmers into a single united class.[93] Of course, what the IFU/Farmers' Party had to contend with after the Treaty split and the Civil War was not just a deeply divided farmer class economically but one deeply divided politically as well, thus rendering the IFU's early ideal of making the divisions between big and small farmers largely obsolete even more elusive.

Notes

1   W.E. Vaughan, *Landlords and tenants in Ireland 1848–1904* (Dublin, 1984), p. 36.
2   David Fitzpatrick, *Politics and Irish life 1913–21: provincial experience of war and revolution* (2nd ed., Cork, 1998), p. 229; E.R. Hooker, *Readjustments of agricultural tenure in Ireland* (Chapel Hill, NC, 1938), p. 222.
3   Fitzpatrick, *Politics and Irish life*, p. 229.
4   Ibid.
5   Among the sixteen farmer deputies voting on 7 January, nine were for and seven against the Treaty (Erhard Rumpf and A.C. Hepburn, *Nationalism and socialism in twentieth-century Ireland* (Liverpool, 1977), p. 35). On these figures, farmers, amounting to 21 per cent of the occupied workforce in 1911, found themselves as a class – and as a group of sixteen (13 per cent) among the 121 voting deputies – under-represented at the time of the Treaty vote (ibid., p. 35; *Census of Ireland, 1911: general report with tables and appendix*, Cd 6663, pp. 10, 17, 104). Brian Hanley's on-going study of the social composition of the members of the Second Dáil indicates that twenty (32 per cent) of sixty-three pro-Treaty deputies and eight (14 per cent) of fifty-six anti-Treaty deputies for whom he has reliable information were the sons (in the case of one anti-Treatyite, Kate O'Callaghan, the daughter) of farmers (personal correspondence with Brian Hanley (14 Nov. 2016)). See also Tom Garvin, *Nationalist revolutionaries in Ireland 1858–1928* (Oxford, 1987), pp. 49–53.
6   Tony Varley, 'On the road to extinction: agrarian parties in twentieth-century Ireland' in *Irish Political Studies*, xxv, no. 4 (2010), p. 584.
7   'Farmers', in this 32-county figure that includes 54,694 women, are aggregated with 'graziers' (*Census of Ireland, 1911*, pp. 10, 17).
8   See Tony Varley, '"The class that goes to the wall": Colonel George O'Callaghan-Westropp, class politics and identity in Cumann na nGaedheal Ireland' in John Cunningham and Niall Ó Ciosáin (eds), *Culture and society in Ireland since 1750: essays in honour of Gearóid Ó Tuathaigh* (Dublin, 2015), pp. 224–5. Organised farmers may have liked to look back on the Land War (1879–82) as a golden age of class unity among the tenant-farmers, but certain academic studies have stressed the divisions and conflicts that complicated and weakened the tenant-farmer challenge to landlord power in Ireland (see Paul Bew, *Land and the national question in Ireland 1858–1882* (Dublin, 1978), p. 223; Donald Jordan, 'Merchants, "strong farmers" and Fenians: the post-Famine political élite and the Irish land war'

in C.H.E. Philpin (ed.), *Nationalism and popular protest in Ireland* (Cambridge, 1987), p. 347).

9   Emmet O'Connor, *Syndicalism in Ireland* (Cork, 1988), p. 74.

10   Varley, "'The class that goes to the wall'", p. 224.

11   Efforts, however, to persuade the Ulster and Mid-Ulster farmers' unions to join with the southern organised farmers never came to anything (Fitzpatrick, *Politics and Irish life*, p. 225).

12   Ibid., pp. 224, 229.

13   Ibid., p. 225.

14   Ibid., p. 226.

15   Varley, "'The class that goes to the wall'", pp. 223–4.

16   Compulsory tillage orders, together with the regulation of farm-workers' wages, were dropped in 1921 (O'Connor, *Syndicalism in Ireland*, pp. 115, 33–44, 114–31).

17   John O'Donovan, *The economic history of livestock in Ireland* (Cork, 1940), pp. 227–9.

18   There was no mention of 'agriculture' in the articles of agreement that made up the Anglo-Irish Treaty of 6 December 1921.

19   *Dáil Éireann deb.*, T, no. 6, 24 (19 Dec. 1921). De Valera had earlier made this same point in his public letter conveying his rejection of the Treaty (Lord Longford (Frank Pakenham), *Peace by ordeal* (3rd ed., London, 1972), p. 265).

20   'Irish independence existed since 21st January 1919', observed Liam Mellows on 17 December, 'and it is not to-day that we ask for the Republic. We are defending it' (*Dáil Éireann deb.*, T, no. 5, 243 (17 Dec. 1921)).

21   Not all anti-Treatyites were in agreement about how the Irish Republic might best be preserved. It seems Seán Etchingham, Séamus Robinson and Liam Mellows were intent on rejecting 'Document No. 2', de Valera's alternative to the Treaty that proposed a republican state externally associated with the British Commonwealth (Earl of Longford (Frank Pakenham) and Thomas P. O'Neill, *Eamon de Valera* (London, 1974), pp. 173–7).

22   *Dáil Éireann deb.*, T, no. 6, 32 (19 Dec. 1921).

23   Ibid., no. 3, 158 (15 Dec. 1921); ibid., no. 4, 195, 205 (16 Dec. 1921); ibid., no. 5, 242 (17 Dec. 1921).

24   Ibid., no. 2, 139 (14 Dec. 1921).

25   Ibid., no. 15, 305–06 (7 Jan. 1922); ibid., no. 5, 236 (17 Dec. 1921); ibid., no. 10, 207, 188 (3 Jan. 1922).

26   Ibid., no. 10, 188 (3 Jan. 1922).

27   Ibid., no. 6, 32 (19 Dec. 1921).

28   Ibid., no. 2, 129 (14 Dec. 1921).

29   Ibid., no. 10, 187 (3 Jan. 1922). Alec McCabe believed there was a 'ten to one' majority for the Treaty in the country (ibid., no. 4, 207–08 (16 Dec. 1921)).

30   Ibid., no. 15, 341 (7 Jan. 1922).

31   Ibid., no. 4, 197 (16 Dec. 1921).

32   Ibid., no. 8, 88 (21 Dec. 1921).

33 Ibid., no. 15, 340 (7 Jan. 1922). For similar sentiments uttered earlier by Patrick Hogan, George Gavan Duffy and J.J. Walsh, see ibid., no. 7, 61 (20 Dec. 1921); ibid., no. 8, 88 (21 Dec. 1921); ibid., no. 10, 186–7 (3 Jan. 1922).
34 Ibid., no. 11, 221 (4 Jan. 1922).
35 Ibid., no. 15, 343 (7 Jan. 1922).
36 Ibid., no. 8, 119 (21 Dec. 1921).
37 Ibid., no. 10, 175 (3 Jan. 1922).
38 Ibid., no. 15, 309 (7 Jan. 1922).
39 Ibid., no. 2, 137 (14 Dec. 1921).
40 Ibid., no. 6, 25 (19 Dec. 1921).
41 Ibid., no. 15, 310 (7 Jan. 1922). See also Tom Garvin, *1922: the birth of Irish democracy* (Dublin, 1996), pp. 42–4.
42 *Dáil Éireann deb.*, T, no. 10, 173 (3 Jan. 1922).
43 Ibid., 174.
44 Ibid., 175.
45 Ibid.
46 Ibid.
47 Ibid.
48 Ibid., 174.
49 Ibid.
50 Ibid., 182.
51 Ibid., 181.
52 Ibid., 206–07.
53 Ibid., 187.
54 Ibid., 187. Before Christmas, Patrick Brennan had observed that for 'every one eye the enemy had [we had] a couple of thousand; that was the way we beat them not with a few rifles and ammunition but with the Intelligence Department, the farmers and labourers, the men of the country' (ibid., no. 5, 264 (17 Dec. 1921)).
55 Ibid., no. 11, 253–4 (4 Jan. 1922).
56 Ibid., 255.
57 Ibid.
58 Ibid., no. 15, 309 (7 Jan. 1922).
59 Ibid.
60 Ibid., 317.
61 Ibid., 338.
62 Ibid., 306.
63 Ibid., no. 7, 71 (20 Dec. 1921).
64 Ibid.
65 Ibid., no. 10, 177 (3 Jan. 1922).
66 Ibid., 179.
67 Ibid.
68 Ibid., no. 6, 34 (19 Dec. 1921).
69 Ibid., no. 15, 342–3 (7 Jan. 1922).

70   Ibid., no. 11, 214 (4 Jan. 1922).

71   Ibid., 221.

72   Ibid.

73   Ibid.

74   Ibid., no. 6, 24 (19 Dec. 1921).

75   Ibid., 27.

76   Ibid., no. 8, 109 (21 Dec. 1921).

77   Ibid., no. 10, 185–6 (3 Jan. 1922).

78   It is true, of course, that the pro-Treatyite J.J. Walsh did remark, on 3 January, that 'the well-to-do farmers were the great backers of our fight' (ibid., 187). For Piaras Béaslaí the 'true idealists' were not the uncompromising republicans but the pro-Treatyites who 'have the vision and the imagination to sense the nation that is trying to be born – the poor, crushed, struggling people who never got a fair chance, the men and women of all Ireland, the Orangemen of Portadown, the fishermen of Aran, the worker of the slum and the labourer in the fields' (ibid., 180).

79   See Warner Moss, *Political parties in the Irish Free State* (New York, 1933), pp. 18–19; Rumpf and Hepburn, *Nationalism and socialism*, p. 36; Gavin Foster, 'The social basis of the Civil-War divide' in John Crowley, Donal Ó Drisceoil, Michael Murphy and John Borgonovo (eds), *Atlas of the Irish Revolution* (Cork, 2017), p. 667.

80   *Dáil Éireann deb.*, T, no. 10, 175 (3 Jan. 1922).

81   Ibid., 181–2.

82   Ibid., no. 6, 25 (19 Dec. 1921).

83   Ibid., no. 11, 231 (4 Jan. 1922).

84   Ibid., no. 5, 254 (17 Dec. 1921).

85   Ibid., no. 10, 185 (3 Jan. 1922).

86   See O'Connor, *Syndicalism in Ireland*, p. 118.

87   See, for instance, the speeches by Piaras Béaslaí (*Dáil Éireann deb.*, T, no. 10, 177 (3 Jan. 1922)) and Arthur Griffith (ibid., no. 15, 342 (7 Jan. 1922)).

88   For a recent discussion, see Jason Knirck, '"A regime of squandermania": the Irish Farmers' Party, agriculture and democracy 1922–27' in idem, Mel Farrell and Ciara Meehan (eds), *A formative decade: Ireland in the 1920s* (Dublin, 2015), pp. 177–96.

89   Michael Heffernan, TD and future leader of the Farmers' Party, may have complained in March 1923 of the Provisional Government having left the farmers 'hopelessly in the hands of the Red Flag men', but it would soon become apparent that the Free State's coercive intervention would tilt the balance of class warfare decisively in the farmers' favour in the most strike-torn counties of Munster and Leinster (Varley, 'On the road to extinction', p. 585; O'Connor, *Syndicalism in Ireland*, pp. 114–31).

90   This suspicion of organised farmers was set to last for decades (see Peter Moser and Tony Varley, 'Corporatism, agricultural modernisation and war in Ireland and Switzerland, 1935–1955' in Paul Brassley, Yves Segers and Leen Van Molle

(eds), *War, agriculture, and food: rural Europe from the 1930s to the 1950s* (London, 2012), pp. 137–55).

91   The Farmers' Party, despite having contested each of the province's constituencies, failed to win a single seat in Connacht in 1923 (Michael Gallagher, *Irish elections 1922–44: results and analysis*: i (Limerick, 1993), pp. 34–40).

92   *Connacht Tribune*, 1 Oct. 1927. Neither did the ruling Cumann na nGaedheal party escape criticism for its alleged pro-rancher sympathies (M.A.G. Ó Tuathaigh, 'The land question, politics and Irish society, 1922–1960' in P.J. Drudy (ed.), *Ireland: land, politics and people* (Cambridge, 1982), p. 182; Emmet O'Connor, *A labour history of Ireland 1824–2000* (Dublin, 2011), pp. 128–9).

93   See Varley, '"The class that goes to the wall"', pp. 225–38.

CHAPTER 9

'More Than Words': A Quantitative Text Analysis of the Treaty Debates

Liam Weeks, Mícheál Ó Fathartaigh,
Slava Jankin Mikhaylov and Alexander Herzog

While most of the other chapters in this book have primarily examined the historical context of the Treaty debates, this chapter focuses on their political legacy and, in particular, their impact on the Irish party system. It is often claimed that the Irish party system is exceptional because it is not the product of social conflict, but rather stems from a civil conflict. This is because the circumstances from which it emerged were different. In an oft-quoted phrase, John Whyte noted that 'Irish party politics should be sui generis: the context from which they spring is sui generis also'.[1] The context is the split in 1922 in the then dominant party, Sinn Féin, and the Dáil, over the Anglo-Irish Treaty of 1921. The two main parties in the contemporary party system are the inheritors of this divide, with the once-dominant Fianna Fáil originating from the anti-Treaty element in Sinn Féin, and Fine Gael from the pro-Treaty side. In spite of this split, the two parties have remained very similar and what divides Fianna Fáil and Fine Gael has long been a puzzle of Irish politics. This chapter attempts to solve this riddle by examining the debates over the Treaty and what they reveal about the divisions within Sinn Féin. The aim is to assess if there was an underlying dimension to the split, using the parliamentary debates as the source of data. Almost all TDs contributed and this is an example of a parliamentary debate that had a real and tangible effect on political competition, something quite rare in a parliamentary democracy. It is, therefore, perhaps surprising that there has not been a great deal of analysis of these debates before, both in terms of their context and in terms of their contribution to the formation of the party system.

The primary methodology employed is an innovative quantitative analysis of the text spoken in parliament, using a statistical software program that codes words in terms of the frequency of their usage and allows us to determine individuals' policy positions. Our findings are that most TDs cluster around each other, with there being very little difference in their positions. This implies that there was very little difference between the pro- and anti-Treaty sides, and that they were not divided. Consequently, any searches for such divisions are likely to be fruitless. The Treaty, and in particular the manner in which some elites opposed it, generated the split, but it was artificial, generated from a necessity to take a stance on the document. Consequently, the party system that emerged from the split was not a typical European one modelled on social conflict. It rather reflected an artificial division and explains why there has historically been little difference between Fianna Fáil and Fine Gael, a pattern that persists to the present day.

The structure of the chapter is as follows. Firstly, it discusses the nature of the Irish party system and its origins. It then discusses the data and methodology, in particular the quantitative text analysis that is used to analyse the Treaty debates. The final section constructs an analysis based on this method to assess the nature of the debates and, more significantly, to position parliamentarians' policy preferences based on their contributions in the chamber.

The Irish Party System

The debate over the exceptionalism of the Irish case is the main source of attention for its party system, with one set of authors describing it as 'one of the most intriguing mysteries of Irish politics'.[2] Most party systems in Europe are structured, or founded, on cleavages stemming from social conflict, whether between owner and worker, church and state, urban and rural areas, or between centre and periphery interests.[3] In contrast, the Irish party system lacks a social basis, as the two main parties stem from a civil war fought within a nationalist power bloc. This endurance of parties from a civil conflict is why commentators often speak of 'civil war politics' to explain the nature of political competition in Ireland, even though memories of the conflict have long since faded. For this reason, the traditional argument regarding the formation of the Irish party system remains that 'in the beginning was the treaty'.[4]

To summarise, in the beginning was a monolithic organisation that initially faced little competition. It may well have split in the future over a different issue but it did so in 1922 over a treaty that granted Ireland a qualified form of independence. This split resulted in two parties (plus a small splinter third, on-going Sinn Féin), Fianna Fáil and Fine Gael, which, in different forms, have dominated the political landscape of the Irish state since. Between 1932 and 2016, Fianna Fáil won an average 43 per cent of the first preference vote and Fine Gael 30 per cent. In addition, these two parties provided every Taoiseach in this period and have shaped the nature of political competition.

Unlike the Finnish case, where a party system also evolved from a civil war, there was little in the way of a class dimension to the internal Irish conflict.[5] It initially appeared that the sole source of division between the two main protagonists, Fianna Fáil and Fine Gael, was attitudes to the country's external relationship with Britain. However, as memories of the civil conflict faded, it became especially difficult to define the policy differences between these two parties. While the extent of these differences varied at times, in particular in the early decades of the party system, when Fianna Fáil claimed to represent the 'men of no property' and Fine Gael was more readily associated with the merchant and middle classes, these divisions did not translate into voters, among whom there was little evidence of a class conflict.[6] Both parties have remained relatively centrist, sometimes switching sides between the left and right of the ideological spectrum, resulting in their promoting policies with flavours of conservatism, Christian democracy and social democracy, but not to the extent that either has ever fitted clearly into any of these categories. The best description of the parties is that they are 'catch-all', appealing above class and ideological divisions before the term 'catch-all' was even devised.[7]

Even among party members, who we might expect to be more radical than either voters or TDs, a survey of Fine Gael members in 1999 found that a plurality see no real difference between the parties.[8] The same generally holds true for both voters and candidates of the two parties.[9] Consequently, Ken Carty's description of party competition between Fianna Fáil and Fine Gael as a 'symbolic, ritualised conflict' remains valid.[10] It also explains why former Fianna Fáil leader (and co-founder), Seán Lemass, when asked to explain the difference between his party and Fine Gael, stated: 'That is easy, we are in and they are out!'[11]

There are a number of arguments that the foundation of the party system goes back a lot further, some contend to the nineteenth century, and another interesting perspective that it is based on population migrations from the twelfth century.[12] It is possible that there is an element of truth in both these theories but it cannot be disputed that the Anglo-Irish Treaty became the polarising issue that split Sinn Féin and led to the formation of the modern Irish party system. Given the importance of the Treaty split, it is somewhat surprising that few have examined it in more detail, both in terms of why Sinn Féin divided and in terms of the background of the TDs. The common line of thinking is that the division between the two sides stemmed from attitudes to Ireland's 'affinity' with Britain.[13] This, in part, explains why some see the differences between Fianna Fáil and Fine Gael to do with attitudes over nationalism, with anti-Treaty Fianna Fáil seen as more nationalist than pro-Treaty Fine Gael.[14] It also explains why, historically, Fine Gael has been seen as more pro-European and softer on neutrality.[15]

Whatever the nature of the division, the split over the Treaty was undoubtedly the key moment that shaped the pattern of future party competition in the fledgling Irish state and continues to do so. Rather than examine more contemporary policy divisions, it is arguably of more importance to consider the original division and why it occurred. While some have considered the background of the TDs present in the Dáil that approved the Treaty and patterns of electoral support for them, few have delved deep into the crucial parliamentary debates that precipitated this split.[16] What was said in the Dáil can be taken as a proxy measure of policy preferences and it is perhaps naïve to assume that the division was simply between pragmatic and principled nationalists. After all, there was a range of other consequences arising from the Treaty, both social and economic. It is this chapter's contention that since most TDs contributed to the Treaty debates, which lasted over two weeks, an analysis of the text should reveal the underlying dimension(s) to the party split.

Analysing political texts to test theories of political behaviour is a growing area of research that has been facilitated by the development of new approaches in computerised content analysis. Statistical techniques, such as Wordscore, now enable researchers to systematically compare documents with each other and to extract relevant information from them.[17] Applied to party manifestos, for which most of these techniques have been developed, these methods can be used to evaluate the similarity or dissimilarity between manifestos, which can then be used to derive estimates of parties' policy preferences and their distance to each other.

One area of research that increasingly makes use of quantitative text methods are studies of legislative behaviour.[18] Only a few parliaments in the world use roll-call votes (the recording of each legislator's decision in a floor vote) that facilitate the monitoring of individual members' behaviour. In all other cases, contributions to debates are the only outcome that can be observed from individual members. Using such debates for social science research, however, is often limited by data availability. Although most parliaments keep written records of parliamentary debates and often make such records electronically available, they are never published in formats that facilitate social science research. A significant amount of labour is usually required to collect, clean and organise parliamentary records before they can be used for statistical purposes, often requiring technical skills that many social scientists lack. This analysis overcomes this hurdle thanks to a database compiled by Alexander Herzog and Slava Mikhaylov, which contains all debates as well as questions and answers from the Second to the Thirtieth Dáil Éireann (1921–2009), covering almost a century of political discourse.[19] These debates are organised in a way that allows users to search them by date, topic or speaker. More importantly, and lacking in the official records of parliamentary debates, they identify all speakers and link their debate contributions to the information on party affiliation and constituencies from the official members database. This enables researchers to retrieve member-specific speeches on particular topics or within a particular time frame, which is necessary for applying computerised content analysis software.

Data and Methodology

This chapter's data comprises the Dáil parliamentary debates on the Treaty, held over fifteen days in December 1921 and January 1922. For the purposes of analysis, the full text of the debates was downloaded from the website of the Irish parliament, the Houses of the Oireachtas (www.oireachtas.ie/debates), which is a complete transcript of everything that was said in the chamber. To estimate speakers' positions the chapter uses Wordscore, a computer algorithm developed by Michael Laver, Ken Benoit and John Garry.[20] In a similar application, these authors have already demonstrated that Wordscore can be effectively used to derive estimates of TDs' policy positions. Documents were pre-processed by removing all numbers and stop words (the most commonly used words in English that are normally filtered out before natural language processing analysis), lower-casing all text and performing stemming (reducing words to their root form). The methodology also involved weighting the resulting document-feature matrix using the tf-idf schema that helps to adjust for the fact that some words appear generally more frequently.[21] Wordscore uses two documents with well-known positions as reference texts. The positions of all other documents are then estimated by comparing them to these reference documents. The underlying idea is that a document which, in terms of word frequencies, is similar to a reference document, will have been produced by an author with similar preferences. The selection of reference documents furthermore determines the (assumed) underlying dimension for which documents' positions are estimated. For example, using two opposing documents on immigration would scale documents on the underlying dimension 'immigration politics'.

The chapter assumes that contributions in the debates on the Treaty have the underlying dimension of being either pro or contra the Treaty. The interpretation from reading the speeches is that all contributions, to a large extent, either attack or defend the acceptance of the Treaty. The analysis, therefore, can use contributions during the debates as an indicator of how much a speaker is supporting or opposing the Treaty. The chosen reference texts were the speeches by Éamon de Valera and Michael Collins, the two main figures within Sinn Féin. De Valera was the leader of the party but was fervently against accepting the Treaty and became the leader of the anti-Treaty opposition. Collins had participated in the negotiations with the British government that resulted in the Treaty and was the chief supporter within Sinn Féin in favour of accepting the agreement as a stepping-stone to complete independence. He later became head of the Provisional Government, acknowledging his de facto leadership of the pro-Treaty side. This Wordscore analysis calculates a position for every speaker along a single dimension and uses this method to determine what the debates reveal about the underlying policy preferences of the TDs. There are no *a priori* assumptions, but while previous analyses of Irish parliamentary debates have found clear government vs opposition cleavages, it should be noted that the Dáil being examined here comprised one party and there was no party whip, with TDs free to vote according to their conscience.[22] In addition, the chapter analyses the two sides before the split had actually occurred, so it would be partly erroneous to speak of a pro- and anti-Treaty division, as it was a future event.

The Debates

The Dáil had rarely met during the revolutionary period of 1919–21 (just eight times), whereas the cabinet had met 108 times, so the Dáil was not very well informed on issues and many TDs were not really aware of what was going on when it assembled on 14 December 1921 to discuss the Treaty. This is one controversial area concerning the Dáil debates because the lack of an electoral contest for the Second Dáil meant that many of the TDs were simply party nominees who were excluded from much of the political process. Some TDs complained of being treated like sheep and this affected some of the quality of the debates. In spite of this, and what is highly unusual and makes this a very significant source, is that almost every TD spoke during the debates, amounting to over 258,000 words. Aside from conjunctions and prepositions such as 'the', 'and', 'of', the most commonly used word was, not surprisingly, 'treaty' (1,704); next came 'people' (1,404), 'Ireland' (1,247), 'Irish' (1,112), 'country' (634), 'republic' (604) and 'British' (593). Perhaps surprisingly, given what was at stake for the Irish economy with the proposal to leave the United Kingdom, 'economic'/'economical'/'economies' were mentioned just fifty-two times. Nationalism seemed to take precedence over fiscal interests.

At the same time, there was little discussion of a key consequence of the Treaty – its confirmation of the partition of the island, as established by the Government of Ireland Act, 1920. Just nine of the 338 pages of public debates discussed partition. There was even less discussion of this in the private debates (three of 183 pages). Related to this, Ulster was a major non-issue. The northern province (with six counties of its nine to comprise Northern Ireland but with the border to be reviewed by a boundary commission) was mentioned just seventy-nine times, with unionists referred to even less, just thirty-five times. Overall, the tone of the debates was, at times, quite bitter, with the pro-Treaty side, including Michael Collins, questioning the class, nationality and religion of its opponents. For their part, those on the anti-Treaty side perceived those supporting the Treaty to be traitors, with accusations that Collins had been won over by high society in London during the Treaty negotiations.

The nature of what was discussed can be analysed in a more quantitative fashion. The quantitative analysis of text is primarily based on the proposition that preference profiles of speakers can be constructed from their word frequencies.[23] This makes word frequencies the most important data input for almost all existing methods of text analysis. Word frequencies can be easily visualised as word clouds. These word clouds show the most frequently used words in a text with font size being proportional to frequency of appearance. This method is popular with political pundits and has been popularised in recent presidential elections in the United States, where it has been used to 'visualize some of the most pressing issues that the presidential candidates would like to imprint upon voters' minds'.[24] In terms of the Treaty debates, in Figure 10.1, word clouds are deployed to indicate the most pressing issues for each day of the public debates, leading up to the vote on 7 January. All

14 December

15 December (Private)

16 December (Private)

17 December (Private)

19 December

20 December

21 December

22 December

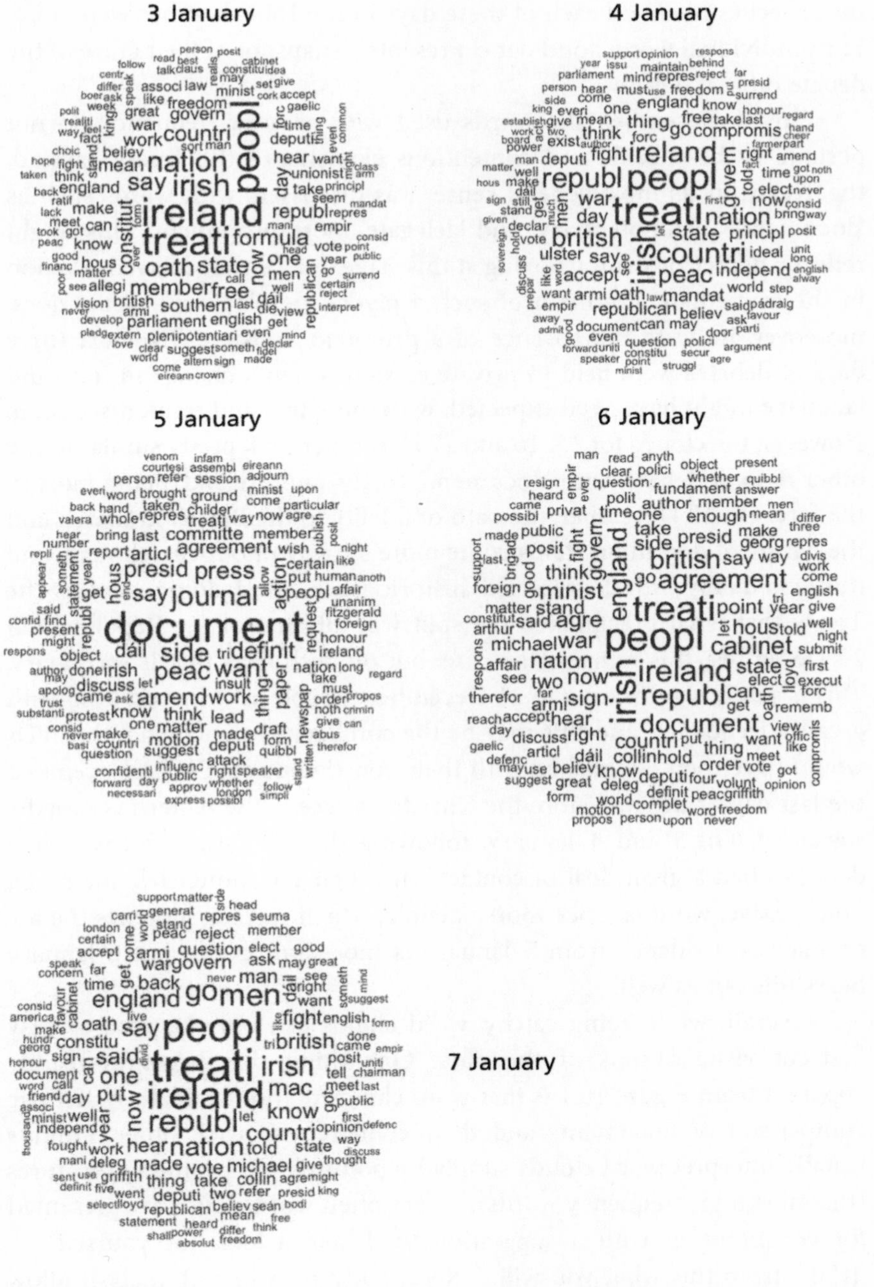

FIGURE 10.1. Daily Word Clouds of Dáil Debates on 1921 Anglo-Irish Treaty

the speeches made on each of these days in the Dáil chamber were used. Each individual word cloud panel presents a snapshot of the nature of the debate on that day.

On 14 December, the words used with greatest frequency do not pertain to the specific and contentious elements of the Treaty. Instead, the Treaty, in its most general sense, was discussed, with words such as 'document', 'plenipotentiary' and 'delegate' more prominent. This might reflect a degree of shadowboxing at this stage or a certain delayed reaction in the immediate aftermath of such a pivotal development. Yet it does, moreover, indicate the absence of a profound division. The next three days of debates were held in private session, when a change in tone and language might have been expected, with more free and frank discussion. However, the clouds for 15, 16 and 17 December look pretty similar to the other days of debate, with 'document', 'treaty' and 'Ireland' being most to the fore. On 19 December, the oath of fidelity to the British monarch and the nature of dominion status come more sharply into focus, though; and this would tally with the received, historiographical wisdom regarding the Treaty that what precipitated the split was dilution of the Republic. On 20 December, this remains the case, but on both days that is secondary. This is surely significant. On 21 December, 'people' is the word used with greatest frequency, and this may be the corollary of the contact that TDs would have then established with their constituencies. On 22 December, the last day of debate before the Christmas recess, the pattern is broadly sustained. On 3 and 4 January, following that Christmas break, when deputies had a great deal of contact with their constituencies, the main, non-passive, word is, once more, 'people', which further supports the arc of analysis. Evidence from 5 January is more ambiguous but 6 January bears this out as well.

Overall, while being catchy, word clouds can only be used as easy first-cut visualisations of the data. One thing that becomes readily apparent from Figure 10.1 is that word clouds do not facilitate systematic comparison of documents and their content with each other. Pundits usually interpret word clouds simply by pointing out prominent features (the most high-frequency words).[25] Very often word clouds are presented for consumption with a suggestion to '[t]ake a look for yourself' or '[t]ake from this what you will'.[26] Recent advances in text analysis allow for further analysis than simple punditry, however. In the next section, the chapter demonstrates how the data facilitates the application of text analysis techniques to answer more complex empirical questions without the ambiguity in interpretation that is inherent in word clouds.

Before such analysis, how the tone of the debates changed over the two weeks can be assessed. In particular, it is possible to determine if the debates became more complex, as more arcane and technical issues concerning sovereignty were introduced into them. A standard approach in computational linguistics to measure complexity of spoken language is lexical diversity. However, measures of lexical diversity are notoriously dependent on document length.[27] Here, the chapter presents Dugast's Uber Index, which takes into account text length and has been shown to perform reasonably well in short text linguistic richness studies.[28] A high index indicates a large amount of lexical variation and a low measure indicates relatively little lexical richness. Figure 10.2 shows the Uber Index for each of the days of the debates, both private and public. The main pattern of observation is the considerable level of variation in the diversity of the text spoken, with three particular dips over the three weeks of debate. The first decline in the lexical diversity came on 17 December following the introduction of 'Document No. 2' by de Valera, his alternative to the Treaty, in the private sessions. This document was

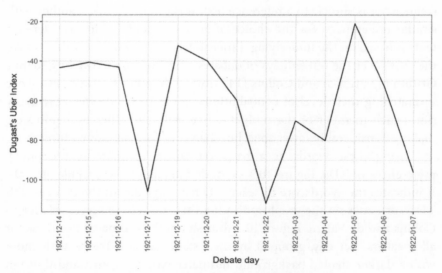

Figure 10.2. Lexical Diversity Measure of Treaty Debates

not released to the public until after the Treaty vote and differed little from the original document, except in de Valera's complex definition of external association. To outline his understanding of this concept, de Valera drew a number of mathematical graphs for deputies, which probably contributed to a lower level of debate, perhaps owing to a confusion on the part of the rest of the Dáil to de Valera's proposal. The diversity index dipped again in the last session before the Christmas break and on the day of the vote on 7 January. This may well reflect an increasingly bitter and simplistic tone as TDs resorted to more basic language to outline their views as the day of reckoning drew closer and constitutional questions became less and less abstract.

The Speakers

In this section, the chapter uses Wordscore to estimate speakers' positions. Based on what TDs said in their parliamentary contributions, it is possible to estimate their preferences concerning the Treaty. To do this, the speeches made by de Valera (-1) and Collins (+1) are used as the reference texts for each day of the debates. The positions of all other speakers are then estimated by comparing them to these reference texts. The underlying assumption is that a text which, in terms of word frequencies is similar to a reference text, was produced by an author with similar preferences. So, the choice of de Valera and Collins as reference texts is based on the underlying dimension of the Treaty. De Valera spoke the most over the fifteen days of debates (254 times), followed by Arthur Griffith (154 times) and Collins (143 times). No other speaker came close to matching their level of contributions. Table 10.1 indicates how many times each member of the cabinet spoke, with the other four ministers making considerably fewer speeches than the aforementioned three.

Using these words as a basis on which to examine the policy preferences of TDs, Figure 10.3 expands the analysis to include all TDs. It indicates the Wordscore for each TD for every day of the debate, with TDs' surnames on the graph indicating their respective scores relative to Collins and de Valera. Figure 10.3 thus shows the estimated positions for all speakers, per day, grouped by their stance on the Treaty, with those with a darker-shaded background ultimately voting against and those in the lighter-shaded background ultimately voting in favour.

Table 10.1. Contributions of Cabinet Ministers in the Treaty Debates

Minister	Total Words	Unique Words	Sentences	Speeches
De Valera	40,140	17,349	1,955	256
Griffith	21,937	9,885	986	155
Collins	20,041	9,486	1,025	144
Brugha	13,111	6,077	480	56
Cosgrave	6,631	3,052	283	30
Stack	3,233	1,537	157	18
Barton	1,703	845	99	4

It is quite apparent that on the first few days of the debates, the TDs were furthest apart than at any stage in the debates, perhaps reflective of the general element of confusion, bewilderment and ignorance about the details of the Treaty. Following the private sessions of 15–17 December, the TDs came closer together but, they had now, en masse, moved closer towards de Valera, perhaps because of his introduction of Document No. 2. For the remainder of the debates the striking feature is the clustering of the TDs, particularly in a centrist position, implying they were caught between the poles of de Valera and Collins. In the run-up to the vote on 7 January the TDs swung towards Collins, but on the day of the vote itself there is a clear swing back towards de Valera. This may reflect the general sense of the party pleading with de Valera not to generate a split and for a sense of unity, and also a sense of loyalty to the leader of the party, commonly known as 'chief'.

Aside from these generally marginal movements, the most glaring pattern from the debates is the congruence of TDs. There is no clear divide between pro- and anti-Treatyites. This suggests that there was no division between the TDs but that it was manufactured by the Treaty. The notion that there was a division between pragmatism and principles is over-exaggerated. Based on this analysis of the debates, there is little difference in the policy positions of all TDs, with the exception of the two leaders, de Valera and Collins.

The overall impression from the data is that there were no obvious differences in the policy preferences of most of the members of the

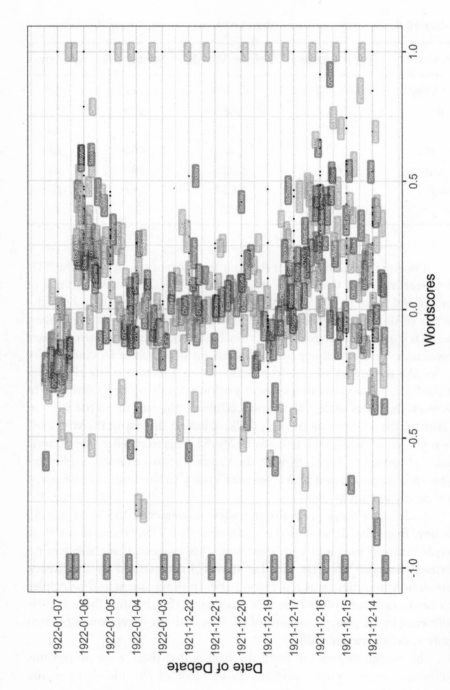

Figure 10.3. Wordscore Analysis of Treaty Debates (De Valera vs Collins)

Second Dáil. This is because they were not actually divided, but the binary nature of the option facing them over the Treaty constructed an artificial split. The TDs had to choose one side; there was no other option. As Ken Carty has noted, the division did not correlate with any economic or social divisions – 'it was a purely partisan cleavage'.[29] Consequently, the reason why commentators and academics alike have struggled to define the differences between Fianna Fáil and Fine Gael, the inheritors of this split, is precisely because there are no differences. So, when in 2016, it was suggested by a Sinn Féin TD that there was barely the width of a cigarette paper between the two parties on most policies, he may well have been talking about 1921.[30] There never were any differences between the pro- and anti-Treaty TDs. It was simply the Treaty, and the resultant Civil War, which split them. This explains why it is still valid to speak of civil war politics. It was the only issue that divided what seemed quite a monolithic Sinn Féin in 1921. The party system that emerged then and remains in place today was an artificial construct, engineered by a vote over a treaty that granted Ireland a qualified form of independence.

Conclusion: Tweedledum and Tweedledee

Party competition in most European democracies is centred on social conflicts that date from the nineteenth century. This did not happen in the Irish case, but what is remarkable is not necessarily that the party system that emerged was structured around a civil conflict but that there was little division in the first place. In this chapter it has been shown that the nationalist movement was pretty homogenous and that the two parties that resulted from it were just wings of the same movement. There were no differences between pro-Treaty and anti-Treaty TDs and this is why Fianna Fáil and Fine Gael have remained remarkably similar in the decades of party competition that have followed. Both sides of the so-called divide demonstrated few differences in policy preferences and it was only the vote on the Treaty that forced the Sinn Féin parliamentarians to pick a side. Without this issue, it is entirely possible that the Sinn Féin party may not have split. The party system might have evolved into a dominant party system, with Sinn Féin permanently in government, akin to the Party of the Revolution in Mexico, the African National Congress in South Africa, the Christian Social Union in Bavaria or perhaps the

Liberal Democrats in Japan. It is not as if a dominant party system would have been unusual in the Irish context, given the dominant status of the Home Rule Party from 1874 to 1918 and Daniel O'Connell's Repeal Association in the 1830s.

So, the Treaty really was the defining issue in shaping the political system in the newly independent Irish state. In the absence of other divisions, it proved the fulcrum around which political competition evolved. To this day, commentators still speak of the 'civil war parties' with reference to Fianna Fáil and Fine Gael, but really we should call them the 'Treaty parties'. They are the Tweedledum and Tweedledee who agreed to have a battle, but unlike Lewis Carroll's fictional characters, they did not forget their quarrel and ultimately went to war over the Treaty.

Notes

1   John H. Whyte, 'Ireland: politics without social bases' in Richard Rose (ed.), *Electoral behavior: a comparative handbook* (New York, 1974), p. 648.

2   Michael Gallagher and Michael Marsh, *Days of blue loyalty: the politics of membership of the Fine Gael party* (Dublin, 2002), p. 180.

3   S.M. Lipset and Stein Rokkan, 'Cleavage structures, party systems, and voter alignments: an introduction' in idem (eds), *Party systems and voter alignments* (New York, 1967), pp. 1–64.

4   Liam Weeks, 'Parties and the party system' in John Coakley and Michael Gallagher (eds), *Politics in the Republic of Ireland* (6th ed., London, 2018), p. 112.

5   John Coakley, 'Political succession during the transition to independence: evidence from Europe' in Peter Calvert (ed.), *The process of political succession* (London, 1987), pp. 59–79.

6   J.J. Lee, *Ireland 1912–1985: politics and society* (Cambridge, 1989), p. 160; Richard Sinnott, *Irish voters decide: voting behaviour in elections and referendums since 1918* (Manchester, 1995), pp. 114–34.

7   Michael Gallagher, *Political parties in the Republic of Ireland* (Manchester, 1985).

8   Gallagher and Marsh, *Days of blue loyalty*, pp. 180–8.

9   Ken Benoit and Michael Laver, 'Estimating Irish party positions using computer Wordscoring: the 2002 elections' in *Irish Political Studies*, xvii, no. 2 (2003), pp. 97–107; Karin Gilland Lutz, 'Irish party competition in the new millennium: change or *plus ça change*?' in ibid., xviii, no. 2 (2003), pp. 40–59.

10   R.K. Carty, *Party and parish pump: electoral politics in Ireland* (Waterloo, ON, 1981), p. 108.

11   Seán McGraw, 'Ideological flexibility and electoral success: an analysis of Irish party competition' in *Irish Political Studies*, xxxi, no. 4 (2016), pp. 461–2.

12   Tom Garvin, *The evolution of Irish nationalist politics* (Dublin, 1981), p. 137; Kevin
     Byrne and Eoin O'Malley, 'Politics with hidden bases: unearthing the deep roots
     of party systems' in *British Journal of Politics and International Relations*, xiv, no. 4
     (2012), pp. 613–29.
13   Garvin, *Irish nationalist politics*, p. 135.
14   Peter Mair, *The changing Irish party system: organisation, ideology and electoral
     competition* (London, 1987), pp. 142–4.
15   Katy Hayward and Jonathan Fallon, 'Fianna Fáil: tenacious localism, tenuous
     Europeanism' in *Irish Political Studies*, xxiv, no. 4 (2009), pp. 491–510; Theresa
     Reidy, 'Blissful union? Fine Gael and the European Union' in ibid., pp. 511–26;
     Karen Devine, 'Irish political parties' attitudes towards neutrality and the evolution
     of the EU's foreign, security and defence policies' in ibid., pp. 467–90.
16   Carty, *Party and parish pump*; Sinnott, *Irish voters decide*.
17   Benoit and Laver, 'Irish party positions'; Michael Laver, Ken Benoit and John
     Garry, 'Extracting policy positions from political texts using words as data' in
     American Political Science Review, xcvii, no. 2 (2003), pp. 311–31; J.B. Slapin and
     S.O. Proksch, 'A scaling model for estimating time-series party positions from
     texts' in ibid., lii, no. 3 (2008), pp. 705–22.
18   Daniela Giannetti and Michael Laver, 'Policy positions and jobs in the government'
     in *European Journal of Political Research*, xliv, no. 1 (2005), pp. 91–120; Michael
     Laver and Kenneth Benoit, 'Locating TDs in policy spaces: Wordscoring Dáil
     speeches' in *Irish Political Studies*, xvii, no. 1 (2002), pp. 59–73; Burt L. Monroe,
     Michael P. Colaresi and Kevin M. Quinn, 'Fightin' words: lexical feature selection
     and evaluation for identifying the content of political conflict' in *Political Analysis*,
     xvi, no. 4 (2008), pp. 372–403; Sven-Oliver Proksch and J.B. Slapin, 'Position
     taking in European Parliament speeches' in *British Journal of Political Science*, xl,
     no. 3 (July 2010), pp. 587–611; Bei Yu, Stefan Kaufmann and Daniel Diermeier,
     'Classifying party affiliation from political speech' in *Journal of Information
     Technology & Politics*, v, no. 1 (2008), pp. 33–48; Etienne Charbonneau, 'Talking
     like a tax collector or a social guardian? The use of administrative discourse by US
     state lottery agencies' in Louis Imbeau (ed.), *Do they walk like they talk?: speech
     and action in policy processes* (London, 2009), pp. 223–41; Emma Galli, Veronica
     Grembi and Fabio Padovano, 'Would you trust an Italian politician? Evidence
     from Italian regional politics' in ibid., pp. 109–31; Louis Imbeau, 'Dissonance in
     fiscal policy: a power approach in ibid., pp. 167–85; Daniel Hopkins and Gary
     King, 'A method of automated nonparametric content analysis for social science'
     in *American Journal of Political Science*, liv, no. 1 (2010), pp. 229–47; K.M. Quinn,
     B.L. Monroe, Michael Colaresi, Michael Crespin and D.R. Radev, 'How to analyze
     political attention with minimal assumptions and costs' in ibid., pp. 209–28; Justin
     Grimmer, 'A Bayesian hierarchical topic model for political texts: measuring
     expressed agendas in Senate press releases' in *Political Analysis*, xviii, no. 1 (2010),
     pp. 1–35.

19   Alexander Herzog and Slava Mikhaylov, 'Database of parliamentary speeches in Ireland, 1919-2013' in IEEE: Proceedings of the 2017 International Conference on the Frontiers and Advances in Data Science (FADS) (23–5 Oct. 2017), pp. 29–34.

20   Laver, Benoit and Garry, 'Extracting policy positions'.

21   All pre-processing and text analysis was performed using R package *quanteda* (Kenneth Benoit, *quanteda: quantitative analysis of textual data* (doi: 10.5281/zenodo.1004683, R package version 1.3.0, http://quanteda.io) (23 Apr. 2018).

22   Laver and Benoit, 'Locating TDs in policy spaces'.

23   R.H. Baayen, 'Word frequency distributions' in *Text, Speech and Language Technology*, xviii (2001), pp. 1–38.; J.L. Bybee, *Phonology and language use* (Cambridge, 2001).

24   Laura Yao, 'We've looked at clouds from both sides now' in *Washington Post*, 3 Aug. 2008.

25   For example, Stephanie Condon, 'Word cloud of Obama and Cheney speeches', *CBS News*, 21 May 2009.

26   Patrick Gavin, 'Word cloud: Obama's speech' (*Politico.com*) (9 Sept. 2009); Yao, 'Clouds from both sides'.

27   Fiona J. Tweedie and R. Harald Baayen, 'How variable may a constant be? Measures of lexical richness in perspective' in *Computers and the Humanities*, xxxii, no. 5 (1998), pp. 323–52.

28   Daniel Dugast, 'Sur quoi se fonde la notion d'etendue theoretique du vocabulaire?' in *Le francais moderne*, xlvi, no. 1 (1978), pp. 25–32; Scott Jarvis, 'Short texts, best fitting curves, and new measures of lexical diversity' in *Language Testing*, xix (2002), pp. 57–84.

29   Carty, 'Party and parish pump', p. 90.

30   Joe Brennan and Donal Griffin, 'Biggest Irish parties signal ready for first grand coalition', 27 Feb. 2016 (http://www.bloomberg.com/news/articles/2016-02-26/irish-government-falls-well-short-of-majority-exit-poll-signals-il4b1vr1) (27 Feb. 2016).

Conclusion:
Judging the Treaty

Mícheál Ó Fathartaigh and Liam Weeks

In the cathedral on the monastic site at Clonmacnoise in County Offaly is buried Ruaidrí Ua Conchobair, or Rory O'Connor. He rests beside the altar where he was interred in 1198. A lot of Irish people know that Ruaidrí was the last high king of Ireland. What a lot of Irish people do not tend to know, though, is why he was the last of a titular line that stretched back over 3,000 years. Ruaidrí was the last high king as a consequence of the Treaty of Windsor. In 1175, the Treaty of Windsor, signed in Windsor Castle, transferred the overlordship of Ireland from Ruaidrí to the Plantagenet king of England, Henry II. The Treaty of Windsor paved the way for seven centuries during which Ireland would be socially and politically absorbed into the English sphere of influence and control. Only the Anglo-Irish Treaty of 1921 would bring to an end the era of colonisation set in train by the Treaty of Windsor in 1175. Therefore, in the long narrative of Irish history, the Anglo-Irish Treaty is of almost peerless significance. Furthermore, for most Irish people, the restoration of the Irish polity that it delivered is a source of pride. Yet the Anglo-Irish Treaty is not celebrated in Ireland. It is remembered more for its concessions on Irish sovereignty than for the achievement of substantive independence. It is also seen as having engendered, or having propagated, a distractive divisiveness both in the new Irish state and on the island of Ireland generally. The 121 Sinn Féin TDs who, between December 1921 and January 1922, debated the Anglo-Irish Treaty, voted on it and either accepted it or rejected it in Dáil Éireann undoubtedly shaped these opinions on the Anglo-Irish Treaty. Since then, however, opinions on the Treaty, both academic and popular, have contorted and have crystallised. On the occasion of the approaching centenary of the debates, of the vote and of the split, this book's reassessment of what the Sinn Féin TDs said and did in December 1921 and January 1922 will hopefully promote a reassessment of opinions on the Anglo-Irish Treaty.

On the subject of the split in Sinn Féin over the Anglo-Irish Treaty, the split that led to the Civil War, this book makes its biggest point. Countless commentators on the Irish Revolution have argued that the Treaty split brought to the fore fundamental but hitherto latent divisions within Sinn Féin. These divisions were based on political principle or socio-economic considerations. It has been consistently argued, for instance, that those who supported the Anglo-Irish Treaty from January 1922 were the political pragmatists and that those who opposed it were the doctrinaire ideologues. It has consistently been argued, too, that those who supported the Anglo-Irish Treaty had a vested interest in maintaining the on-going ascendancy of the Catholic bourgeoisie and that those who opposed it had a vested interest in preferring the rural peasantry and the urban proletariat. The corollary of these arguments is that when the Sinn Féin party was projected at the Anglo-Irish Treaty in December 1921 and January 1922, the Treaty acted like a prism and it diffracted the party along the lines of the baser imperatives of its membership. The implication of this is that Sinn Féin was not, and had never been, a true political party: one that had a widely concerted agenda and a real organisational coherence. Instead, Sinn Féin had been a movement that had simply captured the zeitgeist of the revolutionary generation. This study has shown otherwise. It has shown that the Sinn Féin parliamentary party shared, almost universally, a deep-rooted commitment to the political principle of Irish republicanism and that socio-economic considerations did not cleave the Sinn Féin parliamentary party. Right up until the vote on the Anglo-Irish Treaty, the Sinn Féin party was a monolith. The Anglo-Irish Treaty was not a prism, it was a battering ram, and it shattered the Sinn Féin party.

The concessions made in the Treaty on Sinn Féin's Irish republican agenda, as set out by Liam Weeks, Mícheál Ó Fathartaigh, Slava Mikhaylov and Alexander Herzog – specifically, the oath of fidelity to the British monarch and the dominion status of the state – ruptured the Sinn Féin party in a very arbitrary way. The fault line of the split, in terms of who voted for the Treaty and who voted against it, could not have been predicted and, considered retrospectively, does not follow either. As Eunan O'Halpin and Mary Staines highlight, no simplistic consensus can be imposed on the Treaty split; and, certainly, perceptions such as the six female TDs voting against the Treaty because they were inherently extreme are, as Sinéad McCoole and Mary McAuliffe stress, anachronistic. The fault line of the split did not reflect any fundamental, latent divisions within Sinn Féin on the political principle of Irish republicanism. Nor, as Brian Hanley asserts, did the fault line reflect any fundamental, latent divisions within Sinn Féin over socio-economic considerations. Most of the members of the Sinn Féin parliamentary party were of a similar class cohort; they came from a relatively privileged background, which had seen most of them educated up to secondary level at least. Those sixty-four Sinn Féin TDs who voted for the Treaty did not, by and large, see it as an ideal settlement any more than those fifty-seven Sinn Féin TDs who voted against the Treaty. For that reason, the Anglo-Irish Treaty has been as unloved by the pro-Treaty tradition in Irish politics as much as by the anti-Treaty tradition in Irish politics. As a consequence of this, the concessions made in the Anglo-Irish Treaty on Irish republicanism have eclipsed the broader significance of the Treaty. Moreover, they have eclipsed the achievement of substantive independence for Ireland that the Anglo-Irish Treaty brought about. A century later this remains the case.

The foremost social and political divisions in the Irish state and on the island of Ireland generally were not engendered, or even propagated, by the creation of the Irish state or by the split over the Anglo-Irish Treaty. Socially speaking, the Irish state has been characterised by a division between a relatively advantaged elite – an Irish establishment – and a relatively disadvantaged common class. The broad dynamic of this social division is characteristic of most capitalist societies to a greater or a lesser extent but, in the Irish instance, it is of more recent provenance. Thus, the opinion has grown that the social division in the Irish state began with the state and, moreover, that it began with the split over the Anglo-Irish Treaty. It is a presumption that only a self-governing Irish dispensation could produce an indigenous elite and only the adversarial split over the Anglo-Irish Treaty could account for its perpetuation. In reality, the roots of the social division in the Irish state lie in the decades and centuries that precede the creation of the state and the split over the Anglo-Irish Treaty. They can be traced to when the Catholic middle-class started to emerge following the Penal Laws and to when it started to take the place of the Protestant aristocracy following the land-ownership reform of the late nineteenth century. By the time of the probationary new state and the split over the Anglo-Irish Treaty in 1922 there was already a profound social division between an Irish Catholic establishment and an Irish Catholic underclass.

The new state and the split over the Anglo-Irish Treaty did not strictly propagate this social division either. As well as being a coherent political party with a concerted political agenda before the split over the Anglo-Irish Treaty, Sinn Féin was neither torn by the social division in Catholic nationalist Ireland nor located conspicuously on one side of the division or the other. Therefore, the pro-Treaty faction of Sinn Féin only became associated with the Irish Catholic establishment subsequently. Furthermore, it only became associated with it after the Irish Catholic establishment began gravitating towards it and towards its political successors Cumann na nGaedheal and Fine Gael. For example, as set out by Martin O'Donoghue, supporters of the Home Rule Party, the old party of the Irish Catholic establishment, made their way to the pro-Treaty faction following its demise rather than it being the case that the pro-Treaty faction reached out to them. In due course, additional social, and political, tendencies were absorbed into the pro-Treaty faction, which became more multi-layered and which cumulated into the pro-Treaty tradition. Equally, additional, countervailing, social and political tendencies were absorbed into the anti-Treaty faction, which also became more multi-layered and which cumulated into the anti-Treaty tradition. The propagation of social and political division in the Irish state was a consequence of this process rather than a consequence of the split over the Anglo-Irish Treaty.

The political division on the island of Ireland, the division between the unionist population in the northeast and the nationalist population there and throughout the rest of the island also preceded the state and the split over the Anglo-Irish Treaty. The sporadic solidarity of the 1790s aside – when the Society of United Irishmen exhorted Gael and Planter to make common cause – from the Plantation of Ulster in the seventeenth century, the Protestant and the Catholic populations of Ireland identified with different political trajectories. By the late nineteenth century, this political division had cauterised around Ulster unionism and Irish nationalism. Moreover, by 1920, it had prompted the provisional partition of the island of Ireland and the establishment of Northern Ireland. The Anglo-Irish Treaty and the creation of the Irish state, and the split over the Anglo-Irish Treaty, did not engender this already institutionalised political division. Ulster unionists and the British government had already guaranteed that partition. The Anglo-Irish Treaty and the split over it did not propagate the institutionalised political division on the island of Ireland either. The Anglo-Irish Treaty had made the provision for the Boundary Commission to re-examine the position of the northeast. In addition, in the course of the debates on the Treaty, only four speakers stated that their position and, therefore, the imminent rupture in the Dáil, was related to partition (with only Seán MacEntee citing partition exclusively). At whatever point a *rapprochement* between Ulster unionism and Irish nationalism became impossible, it was before the Anglo-Irish Treaty and before the split over the Anglo-Irish Treaty.

On the subject of partition, though, it is, in one sense, curious nonetheless that it was not a primary reason for the split over the Anglo-Irish Treaty and, indeed, that it was not the main reason for the split over the Treaty. If somebody largely unfamiliar with Irish history were to be asked what caused the split over the Treaty and the resultant Civil War they would, presumably, assume, and very reasonably, that it was the effective exclusion of the six northeastern counties from the territory of the independent Irish state. In another sense, though, the non-issue of partition is easily explicable. As discussed, the political division of the island of Ireland had become entrenched before, and long before, the split over the Anglo-Irish Treaty. A proposal to partition the entire province of Ulster from the rest of Ireland had first been mooted in 1892 in the context of the debates surrounding the first two home rule bills. In addition, from then, as momentum had gathered behind the suggestion, the Home Rule Party had failed consistently to head off the notion. Consequently, between the 1890s and the 1910s, a partitionist mentality had gestated, even in nationalist Ireland. Indicative of how widespread the mentality became was the position of the Royal Dublin Society. Since the eighteenth century, it had been a significant all-island organisation, which had, moreover, been led by the aristocratic and latterly unionist caste. Yet from the late nineteenth century, the geographical ambit of its operations became increasingly coterminous with the geographical area that would become the jurisdiction of the new Irish state. Not unsurprisingly, therefore, even the 121 Sinn Féin TDs who voted on the Anglo-Irish Treaty were not immune from the partitionist mentality. Even if they held to the republican credo that there were not two nations on the island of Ireland, rather 'differences carefully fostered by an alien government', there was a recognition that these differences between unionists and nationalists would have to be carefully unfostered and that was a job for another day. Furthermore, the vague provision of the Boundary Commission allowed them to indulge a fallacy that partition could be addressed in due course.

So apparent was the tacit acceptance of temporary partition that of the six Sinn Féin TDs in the Second Dáil who were originally from the North – Ernest Blythe, Patrick McCartan, Joseph O'Doherty, Seán MacEntee, Francis Ferran and Séamus Robinson – it was only Seán MacEntee who cited partition as the reason for his vote on the Anglo-Irish Treaty, and Ernest Blythe and Patrick McCartan actually voted for the Treaty. Moreover, Seán O'Mahony, the only TD in the Second Dáil to represent a Northern constituency exclusively, Fermanagh and Tyrone, while he did not vote for the Treaty did not cite partition as his reason for not doing so. In addition, in 1922, there were five border constituencies and, of the twenty-one Sinn Féin TDs who represented them, only one cited partition before voting. Furthermore, that, again, was Seán MacEntee (who although he was originally from Belfast represented Monaghan). Finally, only five of the twenty-one border TDs voted against the Treaty. That over three-quarters of the border TDs voted for the Anglo-Irish Treaty, whereas just over half of Sinn Féin TDs generally voted for it, underscores the impression that partition was seen as a separate issue which could be dealt with later. The Sinn Féin TDs' perception that the vote on the Anglo-Irish Treaty was not a vote on partition means that the support for it should not be interpreted as an artifice through which pro-Treaty TDs intended to abandon the North. Indeed, it was subsequently Michael Collins, the leader of the pro-Treaty faction, who would continue to supply arms to the Northern Command of the Irish Republican Army

(IRA) following the Treaty split and not Éamon de Valera, the leader of the anti-Treaty faction (Collins's seniority in the militant movement notwithstanding).

That partition was not a major reason for the split over the Anglo-Irish Treaty is all the more unremarkable when it is considered that the oath of fidelity to the British monarch and the dominion status of the new state did not, strictly speaking, cause the Treaty split either. More than anything else, it was the Irish people who were responsible for the split over the Anglo-Irish Treaty. It was the prevailing wish of the Irish people, or at least the majority of them, who were the constituents of the Sinn Féin TDs, that the Sinn Féin TDs ratify the Anglo-Irish Treaty. Duly, therefore, a majority of the Sinn Féin TDs did ratify it. In giving their reasons for voting for the Anglo-Irish Treaty, only fourteen of the sixty-four pro-Treaty TDs cited support for the Treaty in their constituencies explicitly. However, as set out by Weeks, Ó Fathartaigh, Mikhaylov and Herzog, after the Dáil had reconvened following the Christmas recess there had been a definite swing in favour of the Treaty. Many of those TDs who would ultimately vote for it – but not exclusively those TDs – began articulating categorically their support for Michael Collins's position on the Treaty. Between 4 and 6 January 1922, roughly half of the Sinn Féin TDs who would vote for the Anglo-Irish Treaty on 7 January voiced their support for his position. Perhaps even more tellingly, twenty of the fifty-seven Sinn Féin TDs who would vote against the Anglo-Irish Treaty also voiced their support for his position.

Over the eleven-day Christmas break, a majority of the constituents of the Sinn Féin TDs made it clear to them that they wanted the Anglo-Irish Treaty to be ratified. As set out by Mel Farrell, there were a slew of Christmas conversions to Collins's position on the Treaty and there was no more of the vacillation that had characterised the positions of individual TDs during the debates that had taken place in December. There was a dramatic swing back to de Valera's position on the Treaty immediately before the vote by a smaller number of TDs – from both sides – but this did not change the outcome. Then, as now, in Irish democracy, the politicians took the course that the people wanted them to take, and in the final analysis, political principles were not the decisive factor. As Eunan O'Halpin and Mary Staines find, responsibility to constituents was the decisive factor. If there was a divide between political pragmatists and doctrinaire ideologues reflected in the split over the Anglo-Irish Treaty, it was a divide that was not so much within the Dáil itself but more so between a pragmatic electorate and the ideological members of Sinn Féin. Conspicuously, when the Anglo-Irish Treaty was, effectively, put to the Irish electorate in the June 1922 election, 38.5 per cent of Irish voters gave their support to pro-Treaty candidates and 21.8 per cent of Irish voters gave their support to anti-Treaty candidates.

If the Irish people influenced the split over the Anglo-Irish Treaty to such an extent, though, how can the Civil War that followed on from it be explained, especially when the main protagonists in the Civil War were not the Irish people? What, of course, accounts for this principally is that it was not the pro-Treaty faction seeking to assert the Irish Free State which started the Civil War; it was, instead, the anti-Treaty faction seeking to defend the Irish Republic. Furthermore, in moving against the anti-Treaty forces, Michael Collins used his status as head of the Irish Republican Brotherhood (IRB) to mobilise a significant proportion of the IRA as the Free State army (just as he had a significant proportion of Sinn Féin TDs, one-third of whom were members of the IRB, in advance of the Treaty vote). All of this is discussed by John Dorney in his chapter. Collins claimed to fight in the name of the Irish people; in the cause of Irish democracy, but he and the shadowy, undemocratic IRB provided the impetus. The parallels with the 1916 Easter Rising, when the IRB also acted in the name of the Irish people, are striking.

In claiming to defend the Irish Republic, and starting the Civil War, the anti-Treaty forces were indubitably anti-democratic. Éamon de Valera in particular, because he was the leader of anti-Treaty Sinn Féin and president of the Irish Republic, has been censured for repudiating both the Anglo-Irish Treaty and, moreover, the vote in favour of it. He has been accused of behaving autocratically and is widely blamed for the ruinous Civil War. Much of the popular opprobrium against him has stemmed from the portrayal of this period in the 1996 film *Michael Collins*. However, the case against de Valera himself should be reconsidered. In rejecting the Anglo-Irish Treaty, de Valera was not actually dogmatic and divisive. Instead he was pragmatic and conciliatory. His reason for opposing the Treaty was his belief that it would not end the conflict between Britain and Ireland because nationalist Ireland would not ultimately be satisfied with the settlement.

He believed that only articles of agreement that accommodated Britain's interests and Ireland's interests to the greatest possible extent would ensure peace. Furthermore, he set forth what he thought could be the basis for a completely mutually satisfactory compromise in his famous Document No. 2, through which he proposed that Ireland could be fully sovereign but could be associated externally (internationally) with Britain. Thus, in rejecting the vote in favour of the Anglo-Irish Treaty, de Valera was protesting at what he saw as the really dictatorial line: the implacability of the pro-Treaty position. From January 1922 to the outbreak of the Civil War in June, attitudes to the Anglo-Irish Treaty hardened, as Mel Farrell and Mary McAuliffe explain. In March, de Valera made a notorious speech in Thurles where he stated that the IRA would have to wade through, perhaps, the blood of some members of the Provisional Government in order to get Irish freedom.[1] Yet these visceral and ultimately ill-judged words were born of de Valera's frustration with the implacability of the pro-Treaty position, not of a blood lust. When anti-Treaty forces occupied the Four Courts in June, de Valera would not be amongst them, nor did he feature in the anti-Treaty legion of the rearguard between then and the end of the Civil War in May 1923. De Valera was not, as John Dorney highlights, an obdurate militant republican. He was, in fact, quite the opposite.

Given what was at stake, almost all of the contributions to the debates over the Anglo-Irish Treaty were remarkable for their moderation. They were predominantly devoid of that animus, hubris and vitriol that could surely have been expected and for which a certain allowance could surely have been made. Most notably, the debates over the Anglo-Irish Treaty were unsullied by consistent Anglophobia. The same maturity and parliamentary decorum was not, however, the order of the day when the Anglo-Irish Treaty was debated at the Palace of Westminster on 16 December 1921. The debates over the Treaty in the British House of Commons and the British House of Lords have been overlooked but a comparison between them and the debates in the Dáil is hugely instructive. The tenor of the debates in 'The mother of parliaments' reflects as well on Sinn Féin as it reflects poorly on the British political establishment. As discussed above, the compromise represented by the Anglo-Irish Treaty favoured the British side more so than the Irish side. It was a compromise that had been instigated by British Prime Minister

David Lloyd George and his government's deputation and not by the
Irish delegation. As a consequence, it is unsurprising that the House of
Commons ratified it by a very large majority, 401 votes to 58, and that the
House of Lords also ratified it by a substantial, if much smaller, majority
of 166 votes to 47. What is perhaps surprising is the size of the majorities,
especially in the House of Commons, but Lloyd George's government was
a coalition government, comprising both the Conservative and the Liberal
parties, and the opposition Labour Party was generally supportive of Irish
nationalism. Yet, in the course of the short debates over the Anglo-Irish
Treaty in the British houses of parliament, several of the MPs and peers
who rose to speak still made the most risible of comments.

In the House of Commons, John Rawlinson, a Conservative MP
for Cambridge University, was outraged at the lack of deference shown
to the British government by Sinn Féin and, moreover, by Ireland itself:
'Have the people in Ireland for one moment thanked the Government
for what they have done? We have had pre-paid telegrams galore from
the Dominions to the Prime Minister, but have we had one telegram
from Sinn Feiners thanking us for our generosity?'[2] He went on to liken
Ireland to South Africa and argued against reaching an agreement with
the Irish because when agreements had been reached with the Boers this
had been a mistake: 'when people believe they are at the top, it does not
bring gratitude from them, but only adds to their conceit'.[3] This brings
home the bigger concerns that the British had about their empire, but
the language was nonetheless unreconstructed in its prejudice (and
confirms, ironically, why the British Empire was in decline). Rawlinson's
contribution to the House of Commons debate on the Treaty would also
be echoed by other voices in the chamber.[4] While the republican dead
were invoked constantly in the Dáil debates over the Anglo-Irish Treaty,
their summoning was not accompanied by intemperate language about
the British. In recalling the death of a British officer – whom he did not
know – during the War of Independence, though, the Conservative MP
Sir Frederick Banbury declaimed: 'That makes my blood boil'.[5] Pointedly,
he did not recall the deaths of any Irish nationalist figures or of any
Irish civilians. The backlash against the Anglo-Irish Treaty in the House
of Commons did not go unchallenged but it was a socialist MP, Jack
Jones, who challenged it most conspicuously and with an erudition that
suggested that he had a handle on Irish affairs.[6] However, although Jack

Jones represented West Ham, he was originally from Nenagh in County Tipperary.

If the tone in the House of Commons was often ungracious, the tone in the House of Lords was often deceitful, ignorant and racist. George Clarke, Baron Sydenham, described the Anglo-Irish Treaty as a 'stupendous surrender' and questioned the validity of the Irish general election in 1921 and whether the Irish people really wanted independence: 'If His Majesty's Government had been able to negotiate with the freely-elected representatives of the Irish people we might know where we stand, but we have not the least idea what the real public opinion of Ireland wants.'[7] There was nothing to say that the 1921 election in 'Southern Ireland' (corresponding to the Irish Free State), in which Sinn Féin won 124 seats out of a possible 128, was not legitimate simply because the Sinn Féin candidates were returned unopposed. In the 1918 general election, Sinn Féin had contested and won the sole seat in all but three of the constituencies in the same area. Furthermore, considering that Sinn Féin was an Irish republican party and only recognised the Irish Republic as proclaimed in 1916, it could not have been clearer that the people of 'Southern Ireland', along with those 104,917 people who voted for Sinn Féin in Northern Ireland in 1921, wanted Irish independence and had done since 1918. As in the House of Commons, the effect of the Anglo-Irish Treaty on the British Empire was a salient concern; however, for Sydenham this was not simply a political concern, it was a racial concern. He prophesised that the fall of the 'white' British Empire would be inescapable if the Anglo-Irish Treaty were to be ratified and he called for the memory of Jefferson Davis and the American Confederacy to be channelled.[8]

Also during the House of Lords debate on the Anglo-Irish Treaty, John Hamilton, Viscount Sumner, posited that he was a keen student of Irish nationalism but 'that the task of satisfying Irish aspirations, of appeasing Irish animosities, and of reducing Irishmen to humdrum paths of peace and order and contentment … is one that has always passed man's understanding and, I think, exceeds human hopes.'[9] This snide, not to mention irresponsible, reduction was compounded by the offhand observation that in signing the Anglo-Irish Treaty, the Irish 'signatories attached their signatures to it in a language which none of us understands'.[10] Then, in reaching his peroration, Sumner opined of the

Irish in general: 'They are a strange people.'[11] The debates in the British houses of parliament over the ratification of the Anglo-Irish Treaty were far more incommensurate with what was supposed to be a whole new political narrative on the islands of Britain and Ireland than were the debates in Dáil Éireann.

The Irish election in June 1922, in which pro-Treaty Sinn Féin defeated anti-Treaty Sinn Féin, was distinguished, too, by the emergence of a new electoral constituency. Since Irish Catholics had begun to be enfranchised from the late eighteenth century, and since the emergence of Daniel O'Connell in the early nineteenth century, Catholic Ireland had given its political support exclusively to Irish nationalist candidates. Initially, these were candidates in favour of repealing the Act of Union and subsequently, and until the emergence of Sinn Féin, they were candidates in favour of home rule. Therefore, for three centuries, Catholic Ireland had been interested only in achieving Irish self-government in some way, shape or form. Yet in the June 1922 election, 40 per cent of the votes cast were not cast for Sinn Féin candidates. This is not to say that the thirty-four non-Sinn Féin TDs elected were not nationalist, or even republican – as the vast majority of them were, at least ostensibly. Rather, what it indicates is that for a lot of Irish people, the Anglo-Irish Treaty had substantively resolved the national question and now a significant minority of them wanted to move onto vocational, class-based politics. Indeed, most of the non-Sinn Féin TDs elected, twenty-four, were members of the Labour Party or the Farmers' Party.

As discussed above, Sinn Féin TDs had not favoured one socio-economic grouping over another. For instance, the radical left-wing agenda put forward in the Democratic Programme of the First Dáil in 1919, which declared that Ireland's assets were essentially public property, was alluded to by only one Sinn Féin TD, Countess Markievicz, as part of her reasoning for voting on the Treaty. Thus, the vocal socialist-republican in the Treaty debate in the 2006 film *The wind that shakes the barley*, Dan, who quotes from the Democratic Programme, was not representative of a Sinn Féin tendency during the Treaty debates. However, he was representative of a political position in Ireland more widely, as evinced by the support for the Labour Party, whose leader, Thomas Johnson, had helped to draft the Democratic Programme. Equally, as Tony Varley shows, the farmers' lobby also saw the time as opportune to de-hitch from nationalist politics and it was even encouraged in this by various members of pro-Treaty Sinn Féin who wanted to see agricultural interests prioritised in the new state.

What the June 1922 election indicates as well is that a conclusive majority of the Irish people did not then favour the anti-Treaty position and definitely did not want a civil war to be fought to defend the Irish Republic. In fact, the Labour Party received almost as many votes as anti-Treaty Sinn Féin in June 1922, with 21.3 per cent of the first-preference vote to anti-Treaty Sinn Féin's 21.8 per cent.

Interestingly, the Irish Republic, as proclaimed in 1916, was supposed to be a socialist dispensation and on that basis, it could have been expected that Irish voters with socialist proclivities would have supported anti-Treaty Sinn Féin. Republicanism, as James Connolly had recognised when he had backed the republican cause in 1916, is an ideology centred on the precept that the people are sovereign. Yet historically, Irish republicanism had been pared back to mean simply a commitment to the full independence of Ireland. In keeping with this pattern, it had also diminished from 1916. The economic agenda that Sinn Féin had held with was protectionism, believing that Ireland would become a universally prosperous society if Irish indigenous production were to be protected from the competition of imports. It would only be when anti-Treaty Sinn Féin largely evolved into Fianna Fáil in 1926 that it too reconnected with something of a socialist economic agenda.

As far as the majority of Irish people were concerned, the Anglo-Irish Treaty of 1921 realised substantive independence for the area of the Irish Free State and they readily endorsed that. This is confirmed by their much greater support for pro-Treaty Sinn Féin than for anti-Treaty Sinn Féin in the general election of June 1922 and, moreover, by the pressure that constituents brought to bear on Sinn Féin TDs during the 1921 Christmas recess of the Dáil. It is also confirmed by the significant support that the Irish electorate transferred to non-Sinn Féin, effectively to post-nationalist, candidates in the June 1922 election. The 121 Sinn Féin TDs who actually voted on the Anglo-Irish Treaty were not as convinced that it offered – as it did – substantive independence. The eight days of debate in the Dáil before the Christmas recess convey a definite sense of increasing uncertainty on their part. Furthermore, following the Christmas recess, of the sixty-four Sinn Féin TDs who voted for the Treaty, only eleven cited their satisfaction with it as a *fait accompli*. It should not be surprising that there was this inconsistency between the views of the Sinn Féin TDs and the Irish people. Up until the 1916 Easter Rising or, more specifically, up until its aftermath, the majority of Irish people had supported the campaign for home rule and now the Treaty was offering substantive independence. For most of them, therefore, the Treaty represented dramatic headway. In contrast, the Sinn Féin TDs were pledged to the Irish Republic and for many of them, however insubstantial the concessions on the Irish Republic might have been, the Treaty represented an unconscionable compromise. The anti-Treaty Sinn Féin TDs were not fanatical fantasists. For example, their leader, Éamon de Valera, simply wanted an equitable compromise. Moreover, the main future leaders of the anti-Treaty IRA who fought the Civil War, men like Rory O'Connor, Liam Lynch, Ernie O'Malley and Frank Aiken, were not to be found in their ranks. Michael Collins's famous assertion on the substance of the Treaty: 'it gives us freedom, not the ultimate freedom … but the freedom to achieve it' would, within four years, be accepted by most within anti-Treaty Sinn Féin.[12] As Fianna Fáil, they would, on coming to power in 1932, go about validating the veracity of Collins's words by successfully reconstituting the Irish Free State as a republic.

Owing to the fact that the Irish people, pro-Treaty Sinn Féin and, ultimately, most of anti-Treaty Sinn Féin recognised or came to recognise that the Anglo-Irish Treaty gave Ireland substantive independence it is now time for the Treaty's achievement to be observed. What will probably continue to prevent this, though, is the one on-going concession on the Irish Republic, namely Northern Ireland. It is not just that Northern Ireland represents a monumental qualification of Irish independence, particularly as the hard border of a hard Brexit looms on the horizon, it is also that the peculiar circumstances of the North were, however myopically, sidestepped by both the Anglo-Irish Treaty and by the debates in the Dáil on the Anglo-Irish Treaty.

Notes

1   *Irish Independent*, 18 Mar. 1922.
2   *Hansard 5 (Commons)*, cxlix, 327 (16 Dec. 1921).

3   Ibid., 329.
4   Ibid., 333.
5   Ibid., 349.
6   Ibid., 335.
7   *Hansard 5 (Lords)*, xlviii, 145 (16 Dec. 1921).
8   Ibid., 147.
9   Ibid., 163.
10   Ibid.
11   Ibid., 167.
12   *Dáil Éireann deb.*, T, no. 6, 32 (19 Dec. 1921).

The Treaty: An Historical and Legal Interpretation

Laura Cahillane and Paul Murray

> *Article 1, Anglo-Irish Treaty:*
> *Ireland shall have the same constitutional status in the Community of Nations known as the British Empire as the Dominion of Canada, the Commonwealth of Australia, the Dominion of New Zealand, and the Union of South Africa, with a Parliament having powers to make laws for the peace, order and good government of Ireland, and an Executive responsible to that Parliament, and shall be styled and known as the Irish Free State.*

The constitutional status granted by the Treaty went far beyond the arrangement which had been provided for in the Government of Ireland Act, 1920, which was essentially a home rule arrangement. However, it was less than the status of a republic, which the Irish side had originally sought. It was also somewhat less than the idea of 'external association', which was formulated subsequently by Éamon de Valera, who believed the new Irish state could be sovereign and separate from the Commonwealth while still 'associated' with it. Although external association would have provided the appearance of a more separate state (and therefore the hope was a more sovereign state), essentially the major difference between this position and the position of the Free State was, in reality, symbolic.

Dominion status itself was a vague concept in 1921. In practice, this effectively meant internal autonomy, despite the relics and symbols of colonial subordination which persisted. There was confusion over the exact powers of the governor general, in particular the question as to whether the United Kingdom government could exercise any control through this position in relation to the assent to legislation. While the dominions had virtually full control over domestic matters, their external powers were unclear. They did not have the power to legislate with extra-territorial effect and they had only begun to establish a power to make treaties (something which the Irish Free State already had a head start on). The key here was that the Treaty recognised dominion 'usage' and 'practice' and not just the (often obsolete) law. That division between what is practised and what is 'law' is still a feature of the British system today and can be seen, in particular, in relation to powers which are theoretically held and exercisable by the monarch but are, in fact, exercised by the prime minister or the government. It was well recognised at the time that dominion 'practice' went beyond the limits of the law and it was a big step to grant to Ireland the same usage and, therefore, the same level of autonomy that the dominions had secured for themselves in practice.[1] Also, as the dominions went on to carve out new areas of autonomy for themselves these would apply to the fledgling dominion as well.

Leo Kohn has aptly described the constitutional status of the new state as follows:

> In substance this implied full internal self-government, unrestricted fiscal autonomy, the right to maintain an Irish Police Force and an Irish Army subject only to the control of the Irish Parliament. In the sphere of external relations, it involved the concession of the new international status of the British Dominions, the right to enter into agreements with foreign States, freedom from obligations arising from treaties not specifically approved by the Irish Parliament, full discretion in the matter of Irish participation in British wars, and, lastly, membership of the League of Nations. In form it connoted the conclusive recognition of Irish internal sovereignty.[2]

The words 'Community of Nations known as the British Empire' are used here, whereas the words 'group of nations forming the British Commonwealth of Nations' is used in Article 4. There is no difference between the two and it is unclear why two different formulae would be used in the same document but the word 'Commonwealth' had only just begun to be used to describe the dominions.

The name *Saorstát Éireann*, which was translated as 'Irish Free State', is an assertion of the sovereignty of the state. The appellation was the official title which was given to the state at the first session of Dáil Éireann in 1919 and then also in the Treaty. While literally translated it means 'free state of Ireland', its broader meaning is that of an Irish republic. There was no established direct translation into Irish of the word republic besides the word *saorstát* but the word *poblacht* had been created as a Gaelicisation of the word. Rather than base the name of the state on a foreign loan word, it was evidently decided, in 1919, to use a 'truer' Irish term. The word *poblacht* was used in the 1916 proclamation but the Declaration of Independence and the other documents from 1919 had all favoured *saorstát*. The word *saorstát*, the 'alternative neologism based on purer Gaelic roots', was also used on official headed paper, including that which was used by de Valera in 1921 in order to provide credentials for the plenipotentiaries who negotiated the Treaty.[3]

In *Peace by ordeal*, Frank Pakenham refers to a 'fragment of dialogue' between Arthur Griffith and Max Aitken, Lord Birkenhead, during the Treaty negotiations, where Griffith commented: 'You may prefer to translate "Saorstát Éireann" by "Free State" (instead of republic). We shall not quarrel with your translation.'[4] Birkenhead answered: 'The title, Free State, can go into the Treaty.'[5] It is unclear whether the British truly understood the connotations of the Irish word. This may have felt like a secret coup to the Irish but, particularly with the passage of time, it seems the true connotations of the title have been forgotten in Ireland. Indeed, the name 'Free State' or 'Free Stater' later became a derogatory term directed towards 'partitionists'.

The name of the state is something which caused confusion for a number of decades following this and still many Irish people are confused about the official name of the state. In 1937, when the new Constitution was promulgated, the Irish Free State was still legally in existence and, because of the External Relations Act of 1936, Ireland was still within the Commonwealth. A decision was taken to rename the state: Éire, or Ireland (but not Republic of Ireland). There are a number of probable reasons for the avoidance of the word republic at this time: firstly, Ireland was still partitioned and it may have been felt in some quarters that the declaration of a republic without having achieved a united Ireland would be a betrayal of the Easter Rising of 1916; the use of the word might also have angered unionists in the North and the state, supporters of dominion status in Ireland, and the British. Also, at the time, declaring a republic would have meant leaving the Commonwealth and it suited Ireland, for economic reasons, to remain within this entity. However, de facto independence had already been achieved with the passing by the British parliament of the Statute of Westminster in 1931, which gave autonomy to the dominions, and in 1945, in response to a question in the Dáil about the status of the state, Taoiseach Éamon de Valera replied, with what became known as his 'Dictionary Republic' speech, that Ireland was a republic in everything but name. In fact, it was not until 1949 that Ireland officially became a republic with the passing of The Republic of Ireland Act, 1948, which provided a legislative basis for the description of the state as a republic. However, the Constitution remains unchanged and the name of the state remains Éire or Ireland.[6]

Article 2:
Subject to the provisions hereinafter set out the position of the Irish Free State in relation to the Imperial Parliament and Government and otherwise shall be that of the Dominion of Canada, and the law, practice and constitutional usage governing the relationship of the Crown or the representative of the Crown and of the Imperial Parliament to the Dominion of Canada shall govern their relationship to the Irish Free State.

During the Treaty negotiations, Lord Birkenhead suggested Canada as a model for the Irish Free State but this was not the first time Canada had been mentioned as a model for Ireland. In 1886, when framing his home rule bill, Prime Minister W.E. Gladstone took inspiration from the colonies and decided that his bill was 'strictly and substantially analogous' to the Canadian constitution.[7] Erskine Childers, in *Framework for home rule*, also argued for a development along Canadian lines.[8] At the time of the negotiations, the Irish were unsure whether they would obtain the same level of autonomy which the dominions had secured for themselves in practice and, presumably, the insertion of the guarantee that the relationship between the Irish Free State and Britain would be identical to that of Canada and Britain was designed to reassure the Irish.[9] As noted above, the specification of dominion usage and practice in the Treaty was crucial. For example, in Canada this meant unrestricted legislative autonomy since the royal legislative power had not been used for such a long period in Canada that it had generally been agreed to be extinct.[10] In writing about the choice of linking the Irish Free State to Canada in particular, Hugh Kennedy, who was the Irish state's first attorney general, explained that:

> The reason was that during the period of more than fifty years which had elapsed since Canada as a group of British Colonies had received her constitution by the enactment of the British North America Act, 1867, Canada had outgrown her colonial status as well as her constitution, and in the gradual evolution of law practice and constitutional usage had reached national stature and exhibited marks of national sovereignty. Canada is, in fact, the great example to-day of the truth of the statement that no man can set bounds to the onward march of a nation, even by a written constitution.[11]

On the Irish side, there was a feeling that because constitutional usage had been secured, this would allow the new Irish state to avoid the strict dominion forms and law. On the British side, it was felt that linking the Irish Free State to Canada would mean that dominion forms would have to be followed to a certain extent. For example, there seems to have been a presumption that the royal prerogatives of appointing ministers, summoning and dissolving parliament etc would be maintained in the Irish Free State. However, the subsequent Irish Free State Constitution completely ignored the royal prerogatives and thus the Irish hope that the use of Canada would enable Ireland to gain further autonomy was gradually borne out.

As far as Kennedy was concerned, the link with Canada was crucial to securing autonomy within the agreed framework: 'The fact thus appears that Canada provided the key to the problem for solution by the parties to the negotiations, the problem, namely, how the association of Ireland with the Community of Nations known as the British Empire might best be reconciled with Irish National aspirations.'[12] Two things, in particular, impressed Kennedy about Canadian practice – the right to separate diplomatic representation which had been asserted by Canada for some years and the right which had been asserted by Canada to have a controlling voice in the selection of the representative of the Crown.

One issue which Kennedy questioned, however, was whether an issue would later arise through case-law on whether Canadian usage would have to be ascertained to decide points of Irish law: 'This may possibly give rise to legal questions in the future throwing upon our Courts the burden of ascertaining from authoritative Canadian sources Canadian law practice or constitutional usage for the purpose of deciding such questions.'[13] But it seems this never happened.

Article 3:
The representative of the Crown in Ireland shall be appointed in like manner as the Governor-General of Canada and in accordance with the practice observed in the making of such appointments.

Interestingly, the title of governor general is not insisted upon in the Treaty. During the negotiations, the Irish successfully argued for the absence of a title in the Treaty itself and it was agreed that this would be settled later when the Constitution was drafted.

Drafts A and B of the 1922 Irish Free State Constitution both contain a short identical section containing one article on external relations. This article provides, among other things, that the representative of George V will 'be styled Commissioner of the British Commonwealth, and shall be appointed only with the previous assent of the Aireacht [Executive Council] of Saorstát Éireann'.[14] It was specified that he would sign acts which have been passed by the Oireachtas 'to signify the assent of His Majesty the King'.[15] Historically, high commissioners were envoys of the Imperial government appointed to manage protectorates or groups of territories not fully under the sovereignty of the British Crown, for example Cyprus. Evidently, the Irish wished to distance themselves further from the Crown colonies, which were administered by a governor general, in order to show that the Irish Free State was a sovereign state in itself. Presumably, the name 'commissioner' rather than governor general was supposed to play down the possible significance of this figure. However, when the Constitution was brought to London in May 1922, the British refused to agree to this and the title governor general went into the constitution.

This article of the Treaty states that the Irish figure should be
appointed in the same manner as the governor general of Canada. This
meant that the appointment would be made by consultation between
both governments. However, the practices which developed around the
governor general in the Irish Free State differed considerably from that of
Canada and many of the formalities were dispensed with. For example,
the governor general of the Irish Free State was never greeted with a gun
salute; secondly, after a couple of half-hearted efforts, the practice of
the opening of parliament adhered to in the dominions was suspended;
thirdly, the Cabinet was not regarded as responsible if the governor general
spoke out on a public issue as it would be in Canada; finally, even the
practice in relation to the sending of despatches to London differed.[16] As
one writer has put it: 'One is therefore led to the conclusion that the office
of the Governor-General of the Irish Free State, due essentially to the fact
that the Free State was an entity *sui generis* in the Commonwealth, was in
practice rather a ceremonial Presidency of a Republic than a Governor-
General of a real Dominion.'[17]

> *Article 4:*
> *The oath to be taken by Members of the Parliament of the Irish Free*
> *State shall be in the following form:—*
>
> *I _____ do solemnly swear true faith and allegiance to the*
> *Constitution of the Irish Free State as by law established and that I*
> *will be faithful to H.M. King George V., his heirs and successors by law,*
> *in virtue of the common citizenship of Ireland with Great Britain and*
> *her adherence to and membership of the group of nations forming the*
> *British Commonwealth of Nations.*

This is the controversial oath, which provided that Irish members of
parliament swore true faith and allegiance to the Constitution of the
Irish Free State and fidelity to the king. As was later continuously
repeated by members of the Irish government both during the Treaty
discussions and the Constitution debates, this was not the 'full-blooded'
oath which members in other dominions had to swear. The general
Commonwealth oath was: 'I AB do swear that I will be faithful and
bear true allegiance to His Majesty King X', with the words 'So help me

God' sometimes added on at the end. The Irish oath had to be sworn to the Irish Constitution and faithfulness is all that was required for the king. In comparison, the dominion oath provided that members of parliament would swear true allegiance to the Crown. It seems that allegiance to the Crown was a much more serious matter than simply swearing to be faithful.[18]

Ironically, de Valera's alternative to the Treaty, 'Document No. 2' (which set out his 'external association' proposition), originally contained a surprisingly similar oath: 'I do swear to bear true faith and allegiance to the Constitution of Ireland and to the Treaty of Association of Ireland with the British Commonwealth of Nations, and to recognise the King of Great Britain as head of the Associated States'.[19] However, recognition of the king was not as significant as swearing faithfulness.

In the end, this was the article of the Treaty which was most problematic. It was not until de Valera broke with Sinn Féin and founded a new republican party (Fianna Fáil) that most anti-Treaty republicans reluctantly subscribed to the oath and took their seats in the Free State Dáil in 1927.

Article 5:
The Irish Free State shall assume liability for the service of the Public Debt of the United Kingdom as existing at the date hereof and towards the payment of war pensions as existing at that date in such proportion as may be fair and equitable, having regard to any just claims on the part of Ireland by way of set off or counter-claim, the amount of such sums being determined in default of agreement by the arbitration of one or more independent persons being citizens of the British Empire.

This rather vague article required the Irish Free State to pay a 'fair and equitable' share of the UK's public debt and war pensions. However, a major difficulty later arose in relation to the lack of precision in this provision and the failure to define what exactly constituted the 'Public Debt'. It is another provision which also originally formed part of de Valera's alternative to the Treaty. His slightly different version provides, rather sensibly, that if the sums are not agreed then they would be subject to independent arbitration:

That Ireland shall assume liability for such share of the present public debt of Great Britain and Ireland and of the payment of war pensions as existing at this date as may be fair and equitable, having regard to any just claims on the part of Ireland by way of set off or counter claim, the amount of such sums being determined, in default of agreement, by the arbitration of one or more independent persons being citizens of Ireland or of the British Commonwealth.[20]

During the negotiations on the Treaty, it seems the Irish side was content not to settle the detail of the financial liability but it is clear that the Irish delegation wished for an independent tribunal to be set up to decide on the sum owed.[21]

Once the dust had settled after the Civil War in Ireland, the arguments began about the state's liability under this provision. The Irish argued that they should be compensated by the British for over-taxation in the past, as well as for destroyed industries and the millions of emigrants lost to the state over the years. A memorandum written by the secretary of the Irish Department of Finance, Joseph Brennan, in 1925 on this issue contains various arguments for the reduction of the figures sought by the British and comes to the conclusion that due to the amount of over-taxation in the past, nothing now should be owed.[22]

An interim arrangement was reached in February 1923, referred to as the Hills/Cosgrave pact.[23] It included British funding of and guarantees for land purchase (from the Anglo-Irish landlord class) and the Irish Free State agreed to pay the land annuities (the monies loaned by the British government to the tenant farmer class to purchase the land, which amounted to about £3 million per annum at the time). The deal was done in secret, however, and was never ratified by the Dáil. The question of the liability for the land annuities was a difficult one as it was not specifically mentioned in the Treaty and it was unclear if it should be regarded as 'Public Debt' under Article 5 or whether it was simply a separate legal debt.

A more favourable financial settlement was eventually negotiated in 1926 after the Boundary Commission report. In December 1925, as part of an agreement signed in London, the Irish Free State was released from its obligations under Article 5 but, in return, assumed liability for malicious damage done since 1919. A final settlement was then reached in 1926, which determined the remaining financial issues. However, the question of the land annuities remained unsettled and while the Irish agreed in 1926 that these would be paid in full, further agitation on the issue meant that, by 1932, de Valera refused to pay, thus sparking the Economic War (1932–1938) between Ireland and Britain. This eventually came to an end with the Anglo-Irish Agreement which provided for a one-off payment of £10 million for the remaining annuities and also saw the return of the Treaty ports (see below).[24]

> *Article 6:*
>
> *Until an arrangement has been made between the British and Irish Governments whereby the Irish Free State undertakes her own coastal defence, the defence by sea of Great Britain and Ireland shall be undertaken by His Majesty's Imperial Forces. But this shall not prevent the construction or maintenance by the Government of the Irish Free State of such vessels as are necessary for the protection of the Revenue or the Fisheries.*
>
> *The foregoing provisions of this Article shall be reviewed at a Conference of Representatives of the British and Irish Governments to be held at the expiration of five years from the date hereof with a view to the undertaking by Ireland of a share in her own coastal defence.*

This article can be read in conjunction with the following article, the effect of which was to protect Britain from any threats which might occur due to a sudden withdrawal of coastal defences. While the Irish side resisted this provision, arguing that an invasion of Ireland was unlikely and that no naval defence was required, British fears prevailed.

Notwithstanding limitations imposed on the Free State's ability to engage in coastal defence activities, Britain supplied twelve armed trawlers to the Free State's coastal patrol service; as Eunan O'Halpin notes, to 'prevent gun-running' and to make sea transport available for army units.[25] O'Halpin further comments that while this development represented 'a clear contravention of article 6 of the Treaty', the limitations attaching thereto were circumvented by the British.[26] This was achieved by classifying the vessels given by the British as 'revenue vessels', which were permissible under Article 6 of the Treaty.[27] However, the quid pro quo, in this regard, was that such vessels 'should not be used against foreign ships outside British or Irish territorial waters'. [28]

The article was removed along with Article 7 in 1938 during the Anglo-Irish negotiations in London.

Article 7:
The Government of the Irish Free State shall afford to His Majesty's Imperial Forces:—

(a) *In time of peace such harbour and other facilities as are indicated in the Annex hereto, or such other facilities as may from time to time be agreed between the British Government and the Government of the Irish Free State; and*

(b) *In time of war or of strained relations with a Foreign Power such harbour and other facilities as the British Government may require for the purpose of such defence as aforesaid.*

This article was designed to address a vital British national interest as well as a significant, and understandable, British fear: that Irish independence would pose a threat to British security. The effect of the article was to ensure that an independent Ireland would not be free to conduct an entirely independent Irish defence policy. The background to this article was the traditional Irish revolutionary practice of entering into alliances with the enemies of Britain: Spain under Philip II, Napoleonic France, or Germany under the Kaiser. The effect of Article 7 was to ensure Britain's security against the danger that hostile foreign powers might attempt to use Ireland as a base from which to launch an attack on her. The military clause in Article 7 attracted little attention during the debates on the Treaty. This might seem surprising, in view of the demands imposed on the Free State by the article in general and by the second part of the article in particular. The first part provided for the retention by Britain of three bases at Berehaven and Queenstown (Cobh), County Cork, and Lough Swilly, County Donegal, but the second part had a far wider potential significance for the future of the Free State and its population: 'The Government of the Free State shall afford to His Majesty's Imperial Forces in time of war or of strained relations with a foreign power such harbour and other facilities as the British Government may require for the purposes of such defence.' If this clause were to take effect, it would make it impossible for the Free

State to avoid becoming involved in Britain's wars, irrespective of the wishes of the population. There was no limit to the facilities the British government might demand, not merely in wartime, but even at a time of 'strained relations' unilaterally defined by Britain. The British would decide, while the Free State would have no say in how its territory would be used, as the clause makes clear: 'The Government of the Free State *shall* [our emphasis] afford to his Majesty's Imperial Forces ...'

One explanation of the fact that this menacing clause in Article 7 attracted little or no hostile attention when the Treaty was being discussed in the Dáil is that it was difficult, if not impossible, for deputies to imagine Britain becoming involved in an international crisis or strained relations with a foreign power, given the circumstances prevailing in December 1921 and January 1922 when Britain had recently emerged triumphant from a world war and an economic slump had overtaken Europe.

The abolition of Articles 6 and 7 was brought about during the Anglo-Irish negotiations in London in 1938. The most significant outcome of these negotiations was the British agreement to evacuate the three naval bases retained by Britain under the terms of the Anglo-Irish Treaty. Taoiseach Éamon de Valera, who led the Irish delegation, was then free to put into practice his policy of neutrality during the Second World War. As Ronan Fanning points out, the key element of this policy was that 'Ireland would be free to pursue an independent foreign policy ... insofar as that policy did not represent a threat to Britain's vital strategic interests.'[29] A benevolent neutrality involving considerable logistical assistance to Britain was as far as de Valera was prepared to put into practice his theory of Anglo-Irish interdependence. Having induced the British side to abandon Article 7 of the Treaty, he ensured that the Irish state would not be involved involuntarily in Britain's wars.

Article 8:
With a view to securing the observance of the principle of international limitation of armaments, if the Government of the Irish Free State establishes and maintains a military defence force, the establishments thereof shall not exceed in size such proportion of the military establishments maintained in Great Britain as that which the population of Ireland bears to the population of Great Britain.

John P. Duggan comments that the ability of the new state 'to raise its own defence force was conceded as a necessary condition of the signing of the Treaty itself' and further observes that this right was not conceded in the home rule acts of 1914 or 1920.[30] O'Halpin emphasises that in the aftermath of the signing of the Treaty, Britain's initial concern 'was not to restrict the size of the provisional government's army but to strengthen it', owing to concerns that the anti-Treaty IRA would be able to defeat Provisional Government forces in the event of armed confrontation.[31] To prevent this, Britain was content to make available all weapons and supplies which the Provisional Government requested to engage in its campaign against the anti-Treaty IRA.[32] At the start of hostilities in June 1922, with the outbreak of the Civil War, Provisional Government forces comprised 'about 10,000 men under arms'. [33]

Notwithstanding the reality that observance by the Provisional Government of the terms of Article 8 were not zealously enforced by the British, the economic cost and related financial burdens of the Civil War forced the Free State government to undertake a drastic reduction in army numbers following the Civil War. These numbers had quadrupled to 60,000 'between the autumn of 1922 and April 1923', which J.J. Lee refers to as 'a major administrative feat'.[34] However, when the process of demobilisation commenced, the category referred to as 'other ranks' was reduced to 32,821 by 17 November 1923 and this figure was further reduced to 13,306 by 31 March 1924.[35] The officer class was cut by 1,000 in December 1923 and a further 1,000 in March 1924, with others having their rank reduced.[36] By November 1925, the number of army personnel in all ranks was 17,439.[37]

Article 9:
The ports of Great Britain and the Irish Free State shall be freely open to the ships of the other country on payment of the customary port and other dues.

This article was also included in de Valera's alternative to the Treaty and it places on a legal footing the presumption in international law that ships may enter ports of foreign jurisdictions on certain conditions. The Irish side recognised the need for coastal harmony between the two countries and there was no opposition to this article.

It appears the concern was mainly to prevent any restriction on trade as an earlier version of the provision read as follows: 'Neither Great Britain nor the Irish Free State shall impose restrictions for protective purposes upon the flow of transport, trade and commerce between Great Britain and Ireland.'[38]

Article 10:

The Government of the Irish Free State agrees to pay fair compensation on terms not less favourable than those accorded by the Act of 1920 to judges, officials, members of Police Forces and other Public Servants who are discharged by it or who retire in consequence of the change of government effected in pursuance hereof.

Provided that this agreement shall not apply to members of the Auxiliary Police Force or to persons recruited in Great Britain for the Royal Irish Constabulary during the two years next preceding the date hereof. The British Government will assume responsibility for such compensation or pensions as may be payable to any of these excepted persons.

This seemingly innocuous provision was the subject of considerable litigation in the years following the acceptance of the Treaty. The provision was elaborated on in the Irish Free State Constitution in Article 78 which provided that: 'Every such existing officer who was transferred from the British Government by virtue of any transfer of services to the Provisional Government shall be entitled to the benefit of Article 10 of the Scheduled Treaty'. Article 76 also included judges within the remit of the Treaty provision.

The cases which arose were all concerned with the amount of compensation payable to the British civil servants who had transferred back to Britain from Ireland or who had retired upon the creation of the new state, but they became important in relation to the bigger questions around the state's relationship with the appeal to the Judicial Committee of the Privy Council. The appeal was not something which had been included in the Treaty and during the negotiations on the Constitution, it was vehemently resisted by the Irish side, which expressed fears in relation to the possibility of former Ulster unionist leader Sir Edward Carson

and his allies sitting in judgment on Irish cases.[39] In particular, Griffith
pointed to the fact that the Judicial Committee comprised persons who
had used their positions for 'party political purposes hostile to the Irish
people'.[40] This, he noted, had 'aroused keen indignation and antipathy
to the Tribunal of which they are members'.[41] In addition, he observed
that the great volume of Irish litigation was concerned with 'very small
money interests' and thus the appeal would be 'a rich man's appeal which
may be used to the destruction of a man not well off'.[42] He stated that
he did not think the insertion of the appeal to the Privy Council in the
Constitution was a necessary incident of the Treaty position. However,
the British insisted that the appeal would have to apply to the Irish Free
State as it did in the other dominions but reassured the Irish that the
practice would be akin to that in South Africa, where a limited appeal
was in place, and also by encouraging Irish hopes that the appeal would
soon be abolished.[43] Thus the appeal was inserted into Article 66 of the
Irish Free State Constitution, providing that 'nothing in this Constitution
shall impair the right of any person to petition His Majesty for special
leave to appeal from the Supreme Court to His Majesty in Council or the
right of His Majesty to grant such leave'.

There were a series of cases on the issue of compensation but the
most significant case was that of *Wigg and Cochrane v Attorney-General*
in 1927.[44] The case involved an interpretation by the Supreme Court of
Article 10 of the Treaty, on the issue of the amount of compensation
payable to the British civil servants who had transferred back to Britain
from Ireland or who had retired upon the creation of the new state and
also on Article 78 of the Constitution. Two questions had to be considered:
whether these provisions guaranteed a personal right or whether this was
non-justiciable as a treaty obligation between international actors; and
also, was this a personal right to a minimum amount of remuneration, or
was it simply a guarantee to have remuneration calculated in the manner
guaranteed under the Government of Ireland Act? In both the High Court
and the Supreme Court, it was decided that Article 78 of the Constitution
guaranteed a personal right but the courts differed on the nature of the
right. Mr Justice James Meredith's decision in the High Court essentially
meant that since a constitutional right was at issue, the pensions were not
a gift of the minister for finance but rather were enforceable and would be
determined in the courts. The government appealed this to the Supreme

Court, where the judgment was more nuanced. While Mr Justice Charles O'Connor confirmed the right in Article 78, he also clarified that it was 'not a right to any particular sum or sums of money, or to have these moneys calculated in any particular way, but a right to the benefit of an agreement by the Irish Free State on terms not less favourable than those accorded by the Act of 1920'.[45] He held that the right was 'to be treated in a like manner as a Civil Servant under the British scheme of Government'.[46] In his view, 'it was not intended by the Treaty to give Civil Servants rights of action for the recovery of compensation. The creation of such rights would completely alter their status as servants of the Crown.'[47] This effectively reversed the High Court's decision and meant that the minister for finance had the authority to determine the pension amounts. However, there was strong dissent from Mr Justice William Johnston who felt that the case was broadly about the constitutionally guaranteed rights flowing from Article 10 of the Treaty and, in his view, if the government was to be allowed to disregard this aspect of the Treaty then it undermined the whole agreement. The case was appealed to the Privy Council where the decision of the Supreme Court was reversed.

Martin Maguire explains the effect of the judgment well:

This judgement sent shock waves through the governments in Dublin and in London. Under the British administration civil servants were by law employed 'at the pleasure of His Majesty' and status and pensions were by gift rather than by right. It was also the British view that the Irish Free State was not the creation of revolution but was a devolved government, created by Westminster legislation, continuous with the former administration. The Privy Council decision implied that the Irish Free State was in fact a break with the former British administration. Far more seriously, from a financial point of view, the decision also meant there was now a group of civil servants within the British and Irish system whose status and security were far superior to their colleagues' and were in fact under-pinned by constitutional guarantees.[48]

However, following the controversial result, it emerged that a mistake of fact had occurred and the Judicial Committee was forced to rehear the case. The mistake was the actual date upon which the civil servants had been transferred. Nevertheless, the committee upheld its original decision but the Irish government refused to accept this decision. Moreover, even members of the House of Lords (in its legislative capacity) spoke out against the decision of the Privy Council.[49] In the eyes of the Irish government, this was a betrayal of the position which had been originally promised to it since it was led to believe that the appeal would not be of great consequence and that judges who were seen as partisan, such as George, Lord Cave, who gave the judgment, would not sit on Irish appeals. The case had become much more than a dispute over pensions. The result on the narrow issue of compensation was unfavourable to both the British and Irish governments and so they decided to come to an agreement on the matter of compensation to be paid and essentially to by-pass the judgment of the Privy Council. Both parliaments passed acts which, in effect, revised Article 10 of the Treaty – the Civil Servants (Transferred Officers) Compensation Act, 1929 (Ireland) and the Irish Free State (Confirmation of Agreement) Act, 1929 (Britain), which granted the more favourable terms to civil servants with the British government agreeing to pay the difference.[50]

The case also had much wider consequences in terms of increasing the calls for the abolition of the appeal to the Privy Council. The Irish argued that the case had demonstrated an anti-Irish bias on the part of the court and the matter was repeatedly raised during the Imperial conferences. In 1931, the Statute of Westminster was passed which, in repealing the Colonial Laws Validity Act of 1865, gave full legislative autonomy to the dominions, and so in 1933 the appeal was unilaterally abolished by the Irish government as part of de Valera's campaign to dismantle the Treaty.[51]

Article 11:
Until the expiration of one month from the passing of the Act of Parliament for the ratification of this instrument, the powers of the Parliament and the government of the Irish Free State shall not be exercisable as respects Northern Ireland and the provisions of the Government of Ireland Act, 1920, shall, so far as they relate to Northern Ireland, remain of full force and effect, and no election shall be held for the return of members to serve in the Parliament of the Irish Free State for constituencies in Northern Ireland, unless a resolution is passed by

both Houses of the Parliament of Northern Ireland in favour of the
holding of such elections before the end of the said month.

Under this article, the terms of the Treaty were deemed to apply to the
entire island, notwithstanding the provisions of the Government of Ireland
Act, 1920. In this regard, a scheme of home rule within the Free State
was being proposed, but David Fitzpatrick observes that 'loyalist interests
were protected by the opt-out clause' which provided that in the event of
the Northern parliament addressing the monarch 'within a month of the
Treaty's ratification, its powers were to be perpetuated', with the limitation
that such powers could be circumscribed by either the convening of the
Council of Ireland or the establishment of a boundary commission, both
captured by Article 12.[52] When an address before the Northern Ireland
parliament in December 1922 petitioned King George V to allow it to opt
out of the jurisdiction of the Free State, Article 12, which was represented
as a penalty clause upon Northern Ireland, was triggered.[53] Article 12 was
abrogated by the 1925 Tripartite Agreement (see below), which made the
1920 partition permanent.

Article 12:
If before the expiration of the said month an address is presented to His
Majesty by both Houses of the Parliament of Northern Ireland to that
effect, the powers of the Parliament and Government of the Irish Free
State shall no longer extend to Northern Ireland, and the provisions
of the Government of Ireland Act, 1920, (including those relating to
the Council of Ireland) shall, so far as they relate to Northern Ireland,
continue to be of full force and effect, and this instrument shall have
effect subject to the necessary modifications.

Provided that if such an address is so presented a Commission
consisting of three persons, one to be appointed by the Government
of the Irish Free State, one to be appointed by the Government of
Northern Ireland and one, who shall be Chairman, to be appointed by
the British Government shall determine in accordance with the wishes
of the inhabitants, so far as may be compatible with economic and
geographic conditions, the boundaries between Northern Ireland and
the rest of Ireland, and for the purposes of the Government of Ireland

> *Act, 1920, and of this instrument, the boundary of Northern Ireland*
> *shall be such as may be determined by such Commission.*

The idea of a boundary commission to adjust the frontier between
Northern Ireland and the Free State originated in a proposal put forward
by Prime Minister David Lloyd George and Thomas Jones, principal
assistant secretary to the British Cabinet, to Arthur Griffith, the leader
of the Irish delegation, on 9 November 1921. At this point, the chances
of concluding a Treaty appeared remote. The proposal was put to Griffith
in the absence of the other Irish negotiators and was outlined in a
document drawn up by Lloyd George and Jones. The document made
provision for what would happen if Northern Ireland refused to accept
the principle of a parliament for all-Ireland. In that case, it would be
necessary to revise the boundary, and a commission set up to do this
'would be directed to adjust the line both by inclusion and exclusion so
as to make the boundary conform as closely as possible to the wishes
of the population'.[54] Griffith assented to this proposal because he was
led to believe that the commission outlined in the document would be
likely to settle the Ulster Question permanently in favour of the Free
State. He told de Valera that the commission arrangement would give
'most of Tyrone and Fermanagh, and part of Armagh, Derry and Down,
etc' to the Free State.[55] When the British side presented a draft treaty to
the Irish negotiators on 16 November 1921, the boundary commission
envisaged in this would 'determine in accordance with the wishes of the
inhabitants the boundaries between Northern Ireland and the rest of
Ireland'. This benign version of the role of the boundary commission,
from a Free State point of view, was part of a clever strategy devised by
Lloyd George and Jones to entice Griffith and the other Irish negotiators
to sign the Treaty.

However, the terms of the boundary commission clause in Article
12 of the Treaty which Griffith and the other negotiators signed on 6
December 1921 differed radically from those envisaged in the versions
Griffith had been shown. The chairman of the three-person commission
provided for in the Treaty was to be appointed by the British government,
and the boundary was to be determined in accordance with the
wishes of the inhabitants, but such wishes had to be 'compatible with
economic and geographic conditions'. Thus, a process which originally

seemed straightforward was now open to an unpredictable variety of interpretations and made to depend in the final analysis on the character and outlook of a chairman appointed by one of the two contesting parties. As de Valera remarked in a letter to Frank Pakenham in 1963, the trap in the Treaty version of the boundary clause – the qualifying phrase 'so far as may be compatible with economic and geographic conditions' – was used ultimately to nullify, as a whole, the provision 'in accordance with the wishes of the inhabitants'.[56]

On his return to Dublin on 3 December 1921 for the final meeting between the Treaty delegates and the Dáil cabinet, John O'Byrne, the legal adviser to the Irish delegation, warned Griffith that the boundary clause did not mean what Griffith thought it did (a major reduction of the territory of Northern Ireland), and that it was too vague to admit of a single unequivocal interpretation. O'Byrne suggested an alteration of the clause which would at least delimit the territorial units to be considered in applying it. Pádraic Colum, who recorded this episode as a biographer of Griffith, was puzzled that Griffith did not argue for the kind of alteration suggested by O'Byrne during the meeting with the Dáil cabinet on 3 December. The only explanation that Colum could think of was that the meeting was so preoccupied with the oath, the Crown and the empire that nobody adverted to the unsatisfactory formulation of the boundary clause.[57]

No representative of the Provisional or Free State administration publicly interpreted Article 12 as promising anything less than a radical reduction of the area governed by the Northern parliament. Michael Collins, for example, assured Bishop Edward Mulhern of Dromore that the boundary would be adjusted 'on the basis of fairness' and that the boundary commission would be obliged to proceed on the basis of self-determination principles, and that no doctrine of the Northern government could take south and east Down, including Newry, 'away from the Irish Government'.[58] The reality of what was going to happen when the boundary commission got to work was hinted at by Lloyd George ten days following the signature of the Anglo-Irish Treaty. During a House of Commons debate on the Treaty on 16 December 1921, Lloyd George emphasised that the economic and geographic qualifications contained within Article 12 of the Treaty would curtail the boundary commission's latitude in relation to any substantial transfer of territory from Northern Ireland to the Free State.[59] This interpretation should be understood in the light of the fact that, in 1920, when a parliament was established in Belfast, the British government gave guarantees to the unionist leadership that the six-county area would remain inviolable. Unionist support for the Government of Ireland Act of 1920 was given 'on the clear understanding, unanimously sanctioned by Lloyd George's Cabinet, that the Six Counties, as settled after the negotiations [on the 1920 Act] should be theirs for good and all, and there should be no interference with the boundaries'.[60] One of Lloyd George's peculiar talents was to deceive both parties to a dispute by encouraging each to believe that measures he was introducing to resolve this dispute would benefit each of them to the detriment of the other.

Free State leaders who were involved in the Treaty negotiations, for example Collins and Griffith, and Ernest Blythe, who was not, persisted in maintaining that the boundary clause was weighted in favour of the Free State, and that the British government had taken a definite political decision to give them two of the six counties, or the greater part of three. Blythe foresaw a truncated Northern Ireland consisting of Belfast and the rest of County Antrim, the greater part of counties Down, Derry and Armagh, and possibly a portion of Tyrone.[61] It is difficult to reconcile these public stances with the contrary views expressed in the British parliament by Lloyd George at the same time. There is evidence of a wide gap between the public discourse of Free State ministers and their actual views on what a boundary commission would involve. A telling example of this can be discerned from the firm assertion by W.T. Cosgrave in the Dáil on 20 July 1923, following his appointment of Eoin MacNeill as the Free State Boundary Commissioner. Cosgrave declared that the Free State government 'cannot possibly ignore the discontent and dissatisfaction of those supporters of the Free State in the North who are kept against their will and wish out of the jurisdiction of the state to which they do not belong'.[62] Here, Cosgrave had in mind the entire nationalist majorities of counties Tyrone and Fermanagh as well as parts of counties Armagh and Down.[63] This contrasts with his talks with Northern Prime Minister Sir James Craig on 17 July, only three days prior to making his Dáil commitment to border nationalists and to uphold their rights as enshrined in Article 12 of the Treaty. On 30 July, Craig informed his cabinet that 'during his interview with Mr. Cosgrave the latter referred personally to the Boundary Commission and stated that in view of the coming [Free State] elections it was necessary for him [Cosgrave] to have a political cry etc'.[64]

The boundary clause in Article 12 is the most significant component of the Anglo-Irish Treaty for the reason that the Irish delegates would not have subscribed to the Treaty unless they had been persuaded by their British counterparts that major adjustments to the boundary to the benefit of the Free State would follow from the implementation of Article 12. This point was emphasised by Cosgrave in 1924, at a time when some of those who had been signatories to the Treaty on the British side were openly proclaiming that the implementation of Article 12 by a boundary commission could result in merely minor adjustments to the boundary. Cosgrave observed that had the same British signatories amplified such opinions during the Treaty negotiations, the Irish plenipotentiaries would not have signed the Treaty. Cosgrave was suggesting that the revisionist British interpretation of Article 12 was deliberately concealed from the Irish side during the negotiations, which implied that the boundary-commission component of Article 12 was a dishonest device on the part of Lloyd George to get the Treaty over the line.[65]

The Tripartite Agreement of December 1925

The leak by the conservative London newspaper, the *Morning Post*, of 7 November 1925, of the Boundary Commission's recommendations, caused outrage in the Free State and the nationalist North.[66] Impelled by this, W.T. Cosgrave sought to limit the damage to his government's position which was threatened by the debacle, particularly by the recommendation that parts of east Donegal be ceded to Northern Ireland. This contrasted with the expectation that large tracts of the North would be ceded to the Free State. Cosgrave persuaded British Prime Minister Stanley Baldwin, British Chancellor of the Exchequer Winston Churchill, commission chairman Judge Richard Feetham and Northern Ireland boundary commission representative J.R. Fisher to agree to the suppression of the Boundary Commission's report, and the abrogation of Article 12 of the Treaty which provided for the establishment of a Council of Ireland. This made permanent the partition of the island of Ireland as defined by the Government of Ireland Act, 1920. This arrangement had the effect of rendering nugatory Articles 13, 14 and 15 of the Treaty. In accepting the status quo, Cosgrave pledged 'neighbourly comradeship with Craig's Government'.[67] The terms of the Tripartite Agreement concluded between the governments of the Free State, Great Britain and Northern Ireland on 3 December 1925 were unanimously approved by the British houses of parliament and, following a vote, in the Dáil and the Seanad.[68]

> Article 13:
> For the purpose of the last foregoing article, the powers of the Parliament of Southern Ireland under the Government of Ireland Act, 1920, to elect members of the Council of Ireland shall after the Parliament of the Irish Free State is constituted be exercised by that Parliament.

The provisions of this article were contingent upon the provisions of Article 12. The Council of Ireland as captured by Article 12 was never convened. This was due to the Tripartite Agreement of 1925 (see above), which set aside the provision of Article 12 which mandated the convening of a Council of Ireland.

> Article 14:
> After the expiration of the said month, if no such address as is mentioned in Article 12 hereof is presented, the Parliament and Government of Northern Ireland shall continue to exercise as respects Northern Ireland the powers conferred on them by the Government of Ireland Act, 1920, but the Parliament and Government of the Irish Free State shall in Northern Ireland have in relation to matters in respect of which the Parliament of Northern Ireland has not power to make laws under that Act (including matters which under the said Act are within the jurisdiction of the Council of Ireland) the same powers as in the rest of Ireland subject to such other provisions as may be agreed in manner hereinafter appearing.

As an address was presented to King George V by both houses of the Northern Ireland parliament, the link between Northern Ireland and the Free State as provided for in Article 12 was nullified.[69] The Council of Ireland provision was nullified by the Tripartite Agreement of 1925 (see above), which maintained the scope of the existing border, as defined in the Government of Ireland Act, 1920.

> *Article 15:*
> *At any time after the date hereof the Government of Northern Ireland and the provisional Government of Southern Ireland hereinafter constituted may meet for the purpose of discussing the provisions subject to which the last foregoing article is to operate in the event of no such address as is therein mentioned being presented, and those provisions may include:—*
> *(a) Safeguards with regard to patronage in Northern Ireland;*
> *(b) Safeguards with regard to the collection of revenue in Northern Ireland;*
> *(c) Safeguards with regard to import and export duties affecting the trade or industry of Northern Ireland;*
> *(d) Safeguards for minorities in Northern Ireland;*
> *(e) The settlement of the financial relations between Northern Ireland and the Irish Free State.*
> *(f) The establishment and powers of a local militia in Northern Ireland and the relation of the Defence Forces of the Irish Free State and of Northern Ireland respectively;*
>
> *and if at any such meeting provisions are agreed to, the same shall have effect as if they were included amongst the provisions subject to which the Powers of the Parliament and Government of the Irish Free State are to be exercisable in Northern Ireland under Article 14 hereof.*

Due to the address to King George V and the Tripartite Agreement of 1925 (see above), the provisions of Article 15 were never implemented.

> *Article 16:*
> *Neither the Parliament of the Irish Free State nor the Parliament of Northern Ireland shall make any law so as either directly or indirectly to endow any religion or prohibit or restrict the free exercise thereof or give any preference or impose any disability on account of religious belief or religious status or affect prejudicially the right of any child to attend a school receiving public money without attending the*

religious instruction at the school or make any discrimination as
respects state aid between schools under the management of different
religious denominations or divert from any religious denomination or
any educational institution any of its property except for public utility
purposes and on payment of compensation.

This provision is very similar to earlier provisions which had been contained in the various home rule bills and the Government of Ireland Act, 1920. However, those earlier enactments had contained a prohibition on the 'establishment' of any religion whereas this clause simply prohibits its 'endowment'. Furthermore, the earlier enactments had also placed a prohibition on making any religious belief or ceremony a condition of a valid marriage but this is not dealt with here. This omission led to controversy in the House of Commons during debates on the issue. Earlier provisions had also prevented an Irish parliament from interfering with the constitution of a religious body without the approval of its governing body. Another important distinction between this provision and earlier versions is that this article adds the important prohibition of discrimination in respect of educational bodies and grants to schools.

The prohibition on the diversion of religious property except for public utility purposes and the requirement of compensation had been included in the earlier legislation and was significant given that the Irish Free State Constitution drawn up later did not contain a right to private property. This article was followed up by Article 8 in the Irish Free State Constitution which provided:

Freedom of conscience and the free profession and practice of religion are, subject to public order and morality, guaranteed to every citizen, and no law may be made either directly or indirectly to endow any religion, or prohibit or restrict the free exercise thereof or give any preference, or impose any disability on account of religious belief or religious status, or affect prejudicially the right of any child to attend a school receiving public money without attending the religious instruction at the school, or make any discrimination as respects State aid between schools under the management of different religious denominations, or divert from any religious denomination or any educational institution any of its property except for the purpose of roads, railways, lighting, water or drainage works or other works of public utility, and on payment of compensation.

Article 17:
By way of provisional arrangement for the administration of Southern Ireland during the interval which must elapse between the date hereof and the constitution of a Parliament and Government of the Irish Free State in accordance therewith, steps shall be taken forthwith for summoning a meeting of members of Parliament elected for constituencies in Southern Ireland since the passing of the Government of Ireland Act, 1920, and for constituting a provisional Government, and the British Government shall take the steps necessary to transfer to such provisional Government the powers and machinery requisite for the discharge of its duties, provided that every member of such provisional Government shall have signified in writing his or her acceptance of this instrument. But this arrangement shall not continue in force beyond the expiration of twelve months from the date hereof.

On 14 January 1922, a meeting of the members elected to the House of Commons of Southern Ireland (largely correspondent with the Second Dáil) took place at the Mansion House, Dublin, in order to approve the Treaty and a Provisional Government was elected under the chairmanship of Michael Collins. The Provisional Government took up office two days later on 16 January 1922 and became the de facto government as Dublin Castle, the centre of British administration in Ireland, was handed over. The Westminster parliament had not yet formally appointed the new Irish ministers or conferred the government with any powers. Thus, it was still a 'provisional' government, from the British perspective at least. This power was conferred following the Irish Free State (Agreement) Act, 1922, which was passed on 31 March 1922.[70] This Act gave the force of law to certain provisions of the Treaty and, in relation to Article 17 in particular, it provided that the British government could, by orders in council, transfer powers to the Provisional Government of Southern Ireland, that the Parliament of Southern Ireland would be dissolved within four months from the passing of the Act, and that elections would be held for 'the House of the Parliament' to which the Provisional Government would be responsible.

On 1 April 1922, an order in council was then passed, entitled the Provisional Government (Transfer of Functions) Order, 1922, which in pursuance to this article of the Treaty, transferred the administration of public services in Southern Ireland from existing government departments and officers to the departments and officers of the Provisional Government. This order transferred the full authority of the state within Southern Ireland to the Provisional Government, including all the laws that applied to Southern Ireland when under British rule. The ministerial appointments became official and were announced in *Iris Oifigiúil*, the new gazetteer of the Irish government, on 4 April 1922.

Article 18:
This instrument shall be submitted forthwith by His Majesty's Government for the approval of Parliament and by the Irish signatories to a meeting summoned for the purpose of the members elected to sit in the House of Commons of Southern Ireland, and if approved shall be ratified by the necessary legislation.

The ratification of the Treaty is something which has caused quite a bit of confusion. In international law, ratification may take different forms but because this instrument specified the particular method of its ratification, then this was the only method by which it could be validly ratified. However, when writing about the debates in the Dáil of January 1922, during which the Treaty was approved, some commentators refer to the approval as formal ratification.[71] Similarly, the approval of the British parliament in December 1921 has been mistaken for ratification.

In late January 1922, a question was put to Michael Collins by one of the members of the Constitution Committee as to whether the Treaty would be ratified before the Constitution was finished.[72] D.H. Akenson and F.P. Fallin have written that this question of ratification 'so disturbed Collins that he and Hugh Kennedy soon left for London to press for the Treaty's immediate ratification'.[73] The writers maintain that Lloyd George eventually agreed to Collins's demand, on the understanding that the draft Constitution would be shown to the British cabinet before being published. They claim that Lloyd George kept his bargain and that the Treaty was ratified by the Irish Free State (Agreement) Act on 31 March 1922.[74]

However, another confusion seems to have arisen here in that section 1(5) of that Act specified that it was not the act for ratification of the Treaty. This was due, for the most part, to the fact that the 'Ulster month' (the period during which Northern Ireland could opt out of Irish independence as provided for in the Treaty) would begin on formal ratification, so instead it was decided that formal ratification would occur when the Constitution was being promulgated and the month could run from then. Instead, the purpose of this Act was to fulfil the Treaty obligations in relation to the formal handing over of power to the Provisional Government under Article 17. Formal ratification was thus completed by the British in December in the Irish Free State (Constitution) Act, 1922, to which the Constitution forms a schedule.[75] On the Irish side, the Treaty was ratified by the Irish Free State Constitution Act in the same month.[76] By this Act, the Treaty was also made part of Irish law because of the incorporation of the Treaty into the constitution.[77]

In summary, therefore, the Treaty essentially provided for the following points:

1. Ireland was to become a self-governing dominion, like Canada.
2. The British Crown would be head of state and would be represented by a governor general figure.
3. Members of the Irish parliament would have to swear an oath of allegiance (to the Constitution – and faithfulness to the king).
4. The Irish Free State would assume some responsibility for the payment of the Imperial debt.
5. For its own security, Britain would retain the Treaty ports and the size of the Irish army would be limited.
6. Northern Ireland would have the option of remaining within or separating from the Irish Free State and arrangements were made for both possibilities.

In reality, the document seems too pithy and lacks the detail one would imagine would be required for an agreement which sets out the new status of a country. It is evident, therefore, that the provisions were simply the main points of an otherwise oral understanding.[78] For example, it is never actually provided for in the Treaty that the Irish Free State would draft its own Constitution, which would govern and set out the actual constitutional position of the state. But, of course, it was understood by both sides that this would happen. The only place the Constitution is mentioned in the Treaty is, in fact, in the oath. Neither is it expounded in the Treaty that any Constitution would be inferior to the Treaty itself or that were any conflict to arise, the Treaty would be held to be supreme. However, it was evidently always understood by both sides that the Treaty would, in fact, be superior to the Constitution and that the Constitution would set out the law along the lines of what had been agreed in the Treaty.[79]

Imperial Conferences (1923 and 1930) and Their Implications for the Stability of the Anglo-Irish Treaty

Two Imperial conferences, one in October and November 1926, the other in 1930, had particular significance for the status of the Irish Free State as a distinct dominion comparable to Australia, New Zealand, Canada and South Africa.

The Imperial Conference of 1926 brought together the South Africans and Irish in a joint endeavour to define the future of the Commonwealth and 'in so doing to place beyond argument the freedom and equality of the dominions'.[80] There was strong pressure from both delegations to devise a formula adequately descriptive of the Commonwealth as it was in 1926. What emerged was, as F.S.L. Lyons puts it, 'one of the great landmarks in the Constitutional history of the empire', as Great Britain and the dominions were defined as: 'autonomous Communities within the British Empire, equal in status, in no way subordinate to one another in any aspect of their domestic or external affairs, though united in a common allegiance to the Crown, and freely associated as members of the British Commonwealth of Nations'. [81]

The 1930 Imperial Conference, in which the Irish delegation led by Minister for External Affairs Patrick McGilligan played a leading part, reached its climax in the Statute of Westminster, which received the royal assent on 11 December 1931. The statute implemented a resolution taken in 1930 at the Imperial Conference. The Statute of Westminster laid down that the British parliament could no longer legislate for any of the dominions, and that dominions could repeal or amend any Act of the British parliament that affected them. The statute also provided that no law made by the parliament of a dominion should be void and inoperative on the grounds that it was repugnant to the law of England. The parliament of a dominion was granted the full power to make laws having extra-territorial operation. Significantly for the Free State, the statute provided that no future Act of the British parliament should extend to a dominion unless it was expressly declared in that Act that the dominion had requested it and consented to its enactment. This was interpreted by Winston Churchill, who was, at this stage, a Conservative backbencher, as meaning that it would allow the Free State to repudiate the terms of the Anglo-Irish Treaty. Churchill argued that the Irish Free State should be excluded from any provision of the Statute of Westminster that might allow it to evade or repudiate the terms of the Treaty. W.T. Cosgrave believed firmly that the statute was subordinate to the Anglo-Irish Treaty, that the Treaty could be altered only by consent and that the Irish government viewed it with 'solemnity'.[82] However, shortly after the Statute of Westminster took effect, Cosgrave's administration was replaced by a Fianna Fáil one led by de Valera, who welcomed the outcomes of the 1926 and 1930 Imperial conferences as facilitating his scheme for dismantling the Anglo-Irish Treaty.

De Valera was barely in office when he began his campaign to dismantle the Treaty. His first move was to remove the oath to be taken by members of the Free State parliament. This was the oath prescribed in Article 4 of the Treaty. A second component of de Valera's campaign was to suspend land annuity payments to the British exchequer. In May 1933, the Removal of Oath Bill became law.

A further major attack on the Treaty involved taking the Crown out of the Constitution by diminishing the powers of the governor general, the Crown's representative. In 1932, the holder of that office, James McNeill, was dismissed or allowed to resign. His successor, Domhnall Ua Buachalla, a country shopkeeper, was installed, not in the Viceregal Lodge but in a suburban house, his main responsibility being to sign acts of parliament. The British government, in common with W.T. Cosgrave, challenged de Valera's right to dismantle the terms of the Treaty without British agreement. However, in 1935, the British Privy Council, in its judgment in *Moore v Attorney General*, settled the issue, making it clear that before 1931 the Irish Free State parliament had not been competent to abrogate the Treaty but as a consequence of the Statute of Westminster, it had acquired the necessary power to do so. The substance of the decision of the Privy Council was summarised: 'The simplest way of stating the situation is to say that the Statute of Westminster gave to the Irish Free State a power under which they could abrogate the Treaty, and that, as a matter of law, they have availed themselves of that power.'[83] In this way, the Privy Council confirmed its own abolition with respect to the Irish Free State with respect to all other constitutional amendments aimed at dismantling the settlement imposed by the Anglo-Irish Treaty. The process of dismantling the Treaty culminated in the passage of a new Constitution in 1937. The Constitution of Ireland/Bunreacht na hÉireann made the articles of the Anglo-Irish Treaty irrelevant.

Notes

1   See Thomas Towey, 'Hugh Kennedy and the constitutional development of the Irish Free State, 1922–1923' in *Irish Jurist*, xii (1977), p. 354.

2   Leo Kohn, *The Constitution of the Irish Free State* (London, 1932), p. 50.

3   John Coakley, '"Irish Republic", "Eire" or "Ireland"? The contested name of John Bull's other island' in *Political Quarterly*, lxxx, no. 1 (Jan.–Mar. 2009), pp. 49–50.

4   Frank Pakenham (Lord Longford), *Peace by ordeal: an account from first-hand sources of the negotiation and signature of the Anglo-Irish Treaty 1921* (3rd ed., London, 1962), p. 244.

5   Ibid.

6   See Laura Cahillane, 'Éire, Ireland or the Republic of Ireland – what's in a name?' in *Irish Law Times*, xxiii (2005), p. 303.

7   See A.J. Ward, *The Irish constitutional tradition: responsible government and modern Ireland, 1782–1992* (Dublin, 1994), p. 62.

8   See Erskine Childers, *Framework for home rule* (London, 1911).

9   Hugh Kennedy wrote: 'Canada was chosen because of the great advance that has been made by that Dominion on the road to liberty in association.' (Select working papers, 1922 (University College Dublin Archives (UCDA), Hugh Kennedy Papers, P4/308)).

10   A.B. Keith, letter to *The Times*, 16 June 1922, as quoted in Alexander Brady, 'The new dominion' in *Canadian Historical Review*, iv, no. 3 (Sept. 1923), p. 204.

11   Hugh Kennedy, 'The association of Canada with the Constitution of the Irish Free State' in *Canadian Bar Review*, vi (1928), p. 750.

12   Ibid., p. 749.

13   Ibid., p. 752.

14   Article 79 in Draft B and Article 78 in Draft A.

15 Ibid.
16 See Brendan Sexton, *Ireland and the Crown, 1922–1936: the governor-generalship of the Irish Free State* (Dublin, 1989), p. 178.
17 Ibid., pp. 178–9.
18 During the Dáil debates on the Treaty, Ernest Blythe argued that faithfulness was not identical with fealty (*Dáil Éireann deb.*, T, no. 10, 194 (3 Jan. 1922)).
19 See Michael Collins, *The path to freedom* (3rd ed., Cardiff, 1996), p. 42.
20 'Proposed Treaty of Association between Ireland and the British Commonwealth presented by Éamon de Valera to Dail Eireann' (Document No. 2), Jan. 1922 (http://www.difp.ie/docs/Volume1/1921/218.htm) (3 Apr. 2018).
21 See 'Memorandum by the Irish Representatives', 22 Nov. 1921 (http://www.difp.ie/docs/Volume1/1921/199.htm) (3 Apr. 2018).
22 '£117 millions in respect of public debt and £12 millions in respect of war pensions. They proposed to add a further amount of £27 millions as compound interest on these amounts at 5 per cent. during the four years following the Treaty. Thus the actual total of the British claim is £157 millions' ('Memorandum by Joseph Brennan on Article 5 of the Anglo-Irish Treaty', 30 Nov. 1925 (http://www.difp.ie/docs/1925/Financial-concessions-on-Article-5-of-the-1921-Treaty/694.htm) (3 Apr. 2018)).
23 'Text of financial agreements between the Irish Free State government and the British government', 12 Feb. 1923 (http://www.difp.ie/docs/Volume2/1923/372.htm) (3 Apr. 2018). Major John Walter Hills was financial secretary to the British Treasury from 1922 to 1923.
24 See Nicholas Mansergh, *The Irish Free State – its government and politics* (London, 1934), ch. xiv and Donal P. Corcoran, *Freedom to achieve freedom: the Irish Free State 1922–1932* (Dublin, 2013), ch. 10.
25 Eunan O'Halpin, *Defending Ireland: the Irish state and its enemies since 1922* (Oxford, 2000), p. 15.
26 Ibid.
27 Ibid.
28 Ibid., pp. 15–16.
29 Ronan Fanning, 'The evolution of Irish foreign policy' in Michael Kennedy and J.M. Skelly (eds), *Irish foreign policy 1919–66: from independence to internationalism* (Dublin, 2000), p. 311.
30 John P. Duggan, *A history of the Irish army* (Dublin, 1991), p. 121.
31 O'Halpin, *Defending Ireland*, p. 15.
32 Ibid.
33 Ibid., p. 16.
34 J.J. Lee, *Ireland 1912–1985: politics and society* (Cambridge, 1990), p. 99.
35 Ibid.
36 Ibid.
37 Duggan, *Irish army*, pp. 150, 155. Over five years, the total numbers of army personnel as constituted on 31 March each year was: 1923, 48,176; 1924, 16,382; 1925, 15,838; 1926, 15,522; and 1927, 11,572.

38   *Dáil Éireann deb.*, T, no. 4, 183 (16 Dec. 1921).

39   Record of negotiations on Irish Constitution entitled 'Conference on Ireland', May
      1922 (The National Archives, London (TNA), Cabinet Office Files (CAB) 43/7, pp.
      93–8).

40   Letter from Arthur Griffith to the prime minister, 2 June 1922 (TNA, CAB 24/137,
      p. 74). Presumably, he means Carson and John, Lord Atkinson, who were also
      criticised by Thomas Jones (principal assistant secretary to Lloyd George) for being
      involved in politics as judges (see Thomas Jones, *Whitehall diary*, iii: *Ireland, 1918–
      1925*, ed. Keith Middlemas (London, 1971), p. 204).

41   Griffith to the prime minister, 2 June 1922.

42   Ibid.

43   Barra Ó Briain has given the following explanation of the South African position
      in relation to the Privy Council appeal: 'The general rule is that no leave is given
      where the question is one that can best be determined in South Africa, or if it
      is essentially a South African question, no matter how important it may be' (see
      Barra Ó Briain, *The Irish Constitution* (Dublin, 1929), p. 120). It has also been
      described in a South African legal textbook as follows: 'The privy council will not
      readily grant leave to appeal. It will not do so in cases raising questions of a local
      nature; it may do so in cases raising serious constitutional questions. Very few
      appeals indeed are heard from the appellate division of the supreme court by the
      privy council' (see W.P.M. Kennedy and H.J. Schlosberg, *The law and custom of the
      South African constitution* (London, 1935), p. 376).

44   *Cahill v Attorney General* [1925] IR 70; *Londsdale and Others v Attorney General*
      [1928] IR 35; *Fitzgibbon and Others v Attorney General* [1930] IR 49; *Cassidy and
      Others v Attorney General* [1930] IR 65; (1924) 58 ILTR 131 (HC); [1925] 1 IR 149
      (SC); [1929] AC 242 (PC). A more complete version of Meredith's judgment at
      first instance may be found as an appendix to the first appeal to the Privy Council;
      [1927] 1 IR 285 at 293.

45   [1925] 1 IR 149, at 161–2.

46   Ibid.

47   Ibid.

48   See Martin Maguire, *The civil service and the revolution in Ireland, 1912–38: shaking
      the blood-stained hand of Mr Collins* (Manchester, 2008), p. 190.

49   The dominions secretary stated in the House of Commons 'that the interpretation
      placed in Art. 10 by the Judicial Committee was not in conformity with the intentions
      of those who had framed the Settlement'. In addition, Lord Birkenhead stated that
      Lord Cave, who had presided over the court, had admitted that the conclusion he had
      drawn was 'probably wrong in law'. He also stated that 'this being so, the Irish Free
      State in his opinion had a constitutional right to amend the error by Irish legislation
      agreed with the British Parliament' (*Hansard 5* (*Lords*), lxxi, 808-56 (25 Apr. 1928)).

50   20 Geo. 5, c. 4.

51   The Colonial Laws Validity Act, 1865, had previously prevented colonies from
      enacting any legislation which would contradict legislation emanating from

Westminster. The Irish had argued the Act did not apply to Ireland in any case as Ireland was not a colony. The legality of the action was confirmed by the Privy Council in the case of *Moore v Attorney General* [1935] IR 472 and [1935] AC 484. The judgment was somewhat contradictory from an Irish perspective because while it declared that the legal origin of the Irish Constitution was the British Act rather than the Irish one – an argument which was never accepted in Ireland – it also held that, consequently, the Statute of Westminster meant the Irish Free State now had full legislative autonomy and could, therefore, abolish the appeal.

52   David Fitzpatrick, *The two Irelands: 1912–1939* (Oxford, 1998), p. 107.
53   *Belfast News-Letter*, 7 Dec. 1922.
54   Pakenham, *Peace by ordeal*, pp. 177–8; Jones, *Whitehall diary*, p. 164.
55   Arthur Griffith to Éamon de Valera, 9 Nov. 1921 (National Archives of Ireland (NAI), Dáil Éireann series files (DE) 2/304/8).
56   Éamon de Valera to Lord Longford, 25, 27 Feb. 1963 (National Library of Ireland, Erskine Childers Papers, MS 7848/302/2-10).
57   Pádraic Colum, *Arthur Griffith* (Dublin, 1959), pp. 295–8.
58   Michael Collins to Bishop Edward Mulhern, 28 Jan. 1922 (NAI, Department of An Taoiseach (DT) S 1801/2), cited in Paul Murray, *The Irish Boundary Commission and its origins 1886–1925* (Dublin, 2011), p. 106.
59   *Hansard 5 (Commons)*, cxlix, 314-15 (16 Dec. 1921).
60   John Kendle, *Walter Long: Ireland and the Union, 1905–20* (Dublin, 1992), pp. 191–8.
61   Notes on Blythe's election address, 1923, (UCDA, Ernest Blythe Papers, P24/621(a)). Blythe's views regarding the desirability of a boundary commission subsequently changed. He came to view the establishment of the commission as an act of folly and expressed his regret that the government to which he belonged had participated in the commission's proceedings. Significantly, Blythe believed that any award of territory to the Free State would serve to consolidate partition and would give rise to further partition due to the division of counties.
62   *Dáil Éireann deb.*, iv, 1226 (20 July 1923).
63   Ibid.
64   Northern Ireland cabinet conclusions, 30 July 1923 (Public Record Office of Northern Ireland, CAB 4/84/9).
65   *Dáil Éireann deb.*, xii, 2502 (15 Oct. 1924).
66   Murray, *Boundary Commission*, pp. 192–3.
67   David Harkness, *Northern Ireland since 1920* (Dublin, 1983), p. 40.
68   The agreement was approved by way of the Ireland (Confirmation of Agreement) Act, 1925 (*Hansard 5 (Commons)*, clxxxix, 309-63 (8 Dec. 1925); *Hansard 5 (Lords)*, lxii, 1229-71 (9 Dec. 1925)). The Treaty (Confirmation of Amending Agreement) Act, 1925, gave effect to the Tripartite Agreement in the Free State. It was passed in the Dáil by 71 votes to 25 (*Dáil Éireann deb.*, xiii, 1653-769 (10 Dec. 1925)). The Seanad passed the legislation by 35 votes to 7 (*Seanad Éireann deb.*, vi, no. 4, 123-242 (16 Dec. 1925)).

69   *Belfast-Newsletter*, 8 Dec. 1922.

70   12 & 13 Geo. V, c. 4.

71   For example, Nicholas Mansergh has written that the Treaty was formally ratified on 14 January 1922 (Mansergh, *Irish Free State*, p. 39).

72   It is evident that this confusion did not exist at the time and that all sides knew that approval had not meant ratification.

73   D.H. Akenson and F.P. Fallin, 'The Irish Civil War and the drafting of the Irish Constitution' in *Éire-Ireland*, v, no. 1 (1970), p. 20.

74   12 & 13 Geo. V, c. 4.

75   13 Geo. V, c. 1, session 2.

76   No. 1 of 1922.

77   The Constitution also specifies in the preliminary that any laws or provisions which are inconsistent with the Treaty are invalid.

78   Unwritten conventions are a feature of the British tradition (see A.V. Dicey, *General characteristics of English constitutionalism: six unpublished lectures*, ed. Peter Raina (Oxford, 2009), p. 67).

79   'The procedure was that the Provisional Government should decide on the draft of its Constitution and then there should be a meeting with the British government at which it should be agreed that this draft did not conflict with the Treaty' (Record of negotiations on Irish Constitution (TNA, CAB 43/7, p. 61)).

80   F.S.L. Lyons, *Ireland since the Famine* (London, 1973), p. 508.

81   Ibid.

82   Michael Laffan, *Judging W.T. Cosgrave* (Dublin, 2014), p. 266.

83   Per Sankley, L.C. [1935] I.R. 472 at 486-7 and [1935] A.C. 484 at 499, cited in Thomas Mohr, 'The Privy Council appeal as a minority safeguard for the Protestant community of the Irish Free State, 1922–1935' in *Northern Ireland Legal Quarterly*, lxiii, no. 3 (Oct. 2012), p. 392. The Privy Council's verdict permitted the Free State parliament to amend the Constitution based on the provisions of the Statute of Westminster 1931, which did not prevent this course of action.

APPENDIX 1

The Anglo-Irish Treaty, 6 December 1921

TREATY.

between

GREAT BRITAIN & IRELAND.

signed

6th December, 1921.

at LONDON.

SECRET.

PROPOSED ARTICLES OF AGREEMENT.
———

1. Ireland shall have the same constitutional status in the
Community of Nations known as the British Empire as the Dominion
of Canada, the Commonwealth of Australia, the Dominion of New
Zealand, and the Union of South Africa, with a Parliament having
powers to make laws for the peace order and good government of
Ireland and an Executive responsible to that Parliament, and
shall be styled and known as the Irish Free State.

2. Subject to the provisions hereinafter set out the position
of the Irish Free State in relation to the Imperial Parliament and
Government and otherwise shall be that of the Dominion of Canada,
and the law, practice and constitutional usage governing the relationship of the Crown or the representative of the Crown and of the
Imperial Parliament to the Dominion of Canada shall govern their
relationship to the Irish Free State.

3. The representative of the Crown in Ireland shall be appointed
in like manner as the Governor-General of Canada and in accordance
with the practice observed in the making of such appointments.

4. The oath to be taken by Members of the Parliament of the
Irish Free State shall be in the following form:-

> I.......do solemnly swear true faith and allegiance to
> the Constitution of the Irish Free State as by law
> established and that I will be faithful to H.M.King
> George V., his heirs and successors by law, in virtue
> of the common citizenship of Ireland with Great Britain
> and her adherence to and membership of the group of na-
> tions forming the British Commonwealth of Nations.

1.

5.   The Irish Free State shall assume liability for the service of the Public Debt of the United Kingdom as existing at the
date hereof and towards the payment of war pensions as existing
at that date in such proportion as may be fair and equitable, having regard to any just claims on the part of Ireland by way of
set off or counter-claim, the amount of such sums being determined in default of agreement by the arbitration of one or more
independent persons being citizens of the British Empire.

6.   Until an arrangement has been made between the British and
Irish Governments whereby the Irish Free State undertakes her
own coastal defence, the defence by sea of Great Britain and Ireland shall be undertaken by His Majesty's Imperial Forces. But
this shall not prevent the construction or maintenance by the Government of the Irish Free State of such vessels as are necessary
for the protection of the Revenue or the Fisheries.

The foregoing provisions of this Article shall be reviewed
at a Conference of Representatives of the British and Irish
Governments to be held at the expiration of five years from the
date hereof with a view to the undertaking by Ireland of a share
in her own coastal defence.

7.   The Government of the Irish Free State shall afford to His
Majesty's Imperial Forces:-

(a) In time of peace such harbour and other facilities as
    are indicated in the Annex   hereto, or such other
    facilities as may from time to time be agreed between
    the British Government and the Government of the Irish
    Free State; and

2.

(b)   In time of war or of strained relations with a Foreign
      Power such harbour and other facilities as the British
      Government may require for the purposes of such defence
      as aforesaid.

8.   With a view to securing the observance of the principle of
international limitation of armaments, if the Government of the
Irish Free State establishes and maintains a military defence
force, the establishments thereof shall not exceed in size
such proportion of the military establishments maintained in
Great Britain as that which the population of Ireland bears to
the population of Great Britain.

9.   The ports of Great Britain and the Irish Free State shall
be freely open to the ships of the other country on payment of
the customary port and other dues.

10.   The Government of the Irish Free State agrees to pay fair
compensation on terms not less favourable than those accorded
by the Act of 1920 to judges, officials, members of Police Forces and other Public Servants who are discharged by it or who
retire in consequence of the change of government effected in
pursuance hereof.

      Provided that this agreement shall not apply to members
of the Auxiliary Police Force or to persons recruited in Great
Britain for the Royal Irish Constabulary during the two years
next preceding the date hereof. The British Government will
assume responsibility for such compensation or pensions as may
be payable to any of these excepted persons.

11. Until the expiration of one month from the passing of the
Act of Parliament for the ratification of this instrument, the
powers of the Parliament and the government of the Irish Free
State shall not be exercisable as respects Northern Ireland and
the provisions of the Government of Ireland Act, 1920, shall,
so far as they relate to Northern Ireland remain of full force
and effect, and no election shall be held for the return of
members to serve in the Parliament of the Irish Free State for
constituencies in Northern Ireland, unless a resolution is
passed by both Houses of the Parliament of Northern Ireland in
favour of the holding of such election before the end of the said
month.

12.   If before the expiration of the said month, an address
is presented to His Majesty by both Houses of the Parliament
of Northern Ireland to that effect, the powers of the Parliament and Government of the Irish Free State shall no longer
extend to Northern Ireland, and the provisions of the Government
of Ireland Act, 1920, (including those relating to the Council
of Ireland) shall so far as they relate to Northern Ireland, continue to be of full force and effect, and this instrument shall
have effect subject to the necessary modifications.

        Provided that if such an address is so presented a Com-
mission consisting of three persons, one to be appointed by
the Government of the Irish Free State, one to be appointed by
the Government of Northern Ireland and one who shall be Chairman to be appointed by the British Government shall determine
in accordance with the wishes of the inhabitants, so far as may
be compatible with economic and geographic conditions, the boundaries between Northern Ireland and the rest of Ireland, and for
the purposes of the Government of Ireland Act, 1920, and of this
instrument, the boundary of Northern Ireland shall be such as
may be determined by such Commission.

13. For the purpose of the last foregoing article, the powers of the Parliament of Southern Ireland under the Government of Ireland Act, 1920, to elect members of the Council of Ireland shall after the Parliament of the Irish Free State is constituted be exercised by that Parliament.

14. After the expiration of the said month, if no such address as is mentioned in Article 12 hereof is presented, the Parliament and Government of Northern Ireland shall continue to exercise as respects Northern Ireland the powers conferred on them by the Government of Ireland Act, 1920, but the Parliament and Government of the Irish Free State shall in Northern Ireland have in relation to matters in respect of which the Parliament of Northern Ireland has not power to make laws under that Act (including matters which under the said Act are within the jurisdiction of the Council of Ireland) the same powers as in the rest of Ireland, subject to such other provisions as may be agreed in manner hereinafter appearing.

15. At any time after the date hereof the Government of Northern Ireland and the provisional Government of Southern Ireland hereinafter constituted may meet for the purpose of discussing the provisions subject to which the last foregoing article is to operate in the event of no such address as is therein mentioned being presented and those provisions may include:

(a) Safeguards with regard to patronage in Northern Ireland:
(b) Safeguards with regard to the collection of revenue
    in Northern Ireland:
(c) Safeguards with regard to import and export duties affecting the trade or industry of Northern Ireland:
(d) Safeguards for minorities in Northern Ireland:

(e)   The settlement of the financial relations between
      Northern Ireland and the Irish Free State.

(f)   The establishment and powers of a local militia in
      Northern Ireland and the relation of the Defence Forces
      of the Irish Free State and of Northern Ireland res-
      pectively:

and if at any such meeting provisions are agreed to, the same
shall have effect as if they were included amongst the provisions subject to which the Powers of the Parliament and
Government of the Irish Free State are to be exercisable in
Northern Ireland under Article 14 hereof.

16.   Neither the Parliament of the Irish Free State nor the
Parliament of Northern Ireland shall make any law so as
either directly or indirectly to endow any religion or prohibit or restrict the free exercise thereof or give any preference or impose any disability on account of religious belief or religious status or affect prejudicially the right
of any child to attend a school receiving public money without attending the religious instruction at the school or
make any discrimination as respects state aid between schools
under the management of different religious denominations or
divert from any religious denomination or any educational
institution any of its property except for public utility
purposes and on payment of compensation.

17.   By way of provisional arrangement for the administration of Southern Ireland during the interval which must
elapse between the date hereof and the constitution of a
Parliament and Government of the Irish Free State in accord-
ancetherewith, steps shall be taken forthwith for summoning
a meeting of members of Parliament elected for constituencies

in Southern Ireland since the passing of the Government of
Ireland Act, 1920, and for constituting a provisional Government, and the British Government shall take the steps necessary to transfer to such provisional Government the powers
and machinery requisite for the discharge of its duties, provided that every member of such provisional Government shall
have signified in writing his or her acceptance of this instrument. But this arrangement shall not continue in force
beyond the expiration of twelve months from the date hereof.

18. This instrument shall be submitted forthwith by His
Majesty's Government for the approval of Parliament and by
the Irish signatories to a meeting summoned for the purpose
of the members elected to sit in the House of Commons of
Southern Ireland, and if approved shall be ratified by the
necessary legislation.

On behalf of the Irish
Delegation

Art Ó Gríobhtha / Arthur Griffith

Mícheál Ó Coileáin

Riobárd Barton

Eudmonn S. Ó Dugáin

Seóirse Gabhán uí Dhubhthaigh

On behalf of the British Delegation

D Lloyd George

Austen Chamberlain

Birkenhead.

Winston S. Churchill

December 6, 1921.

7.

<u>ANNEX</u> .

1.   The following are the specific facilities required.

Dockyard port at Berehaven.

(a) Admiralty property and rights to be retained as at the date
    hereof. Harbour defences to remain in charge of British
    care and maintenance parties.

Queenstown.

(b) Harbour defences to remain in charge of British care and main-
    tenance parties. Certain mooring buoys to be retained for
    use of His Majesty's ships.

Belfast Lough.

(c) Harbour defences to remain in charge of British care and
    maintenance parties.

Lough Swilly.

(d) Harbour defences to remain in charge of British care and
    maintenance parties.

Aviation.

(e) Facilities in the neighbourhood of the above Ports for coastal
    defence by air.

Oil Fuel Storage.

(f) Haulbowline) To be offered for sale to commercial companies
) under guarantee that purchasers shall maintain
    Rathmullen) a certain minimum stock for Admiralty purposes.
)

2.   A Convention shall be made between the British Government and the

Government of the Irish Free State to give effect to the following

conditions:-

(a) That submarine cables shall not be landed or wireless sta-
    tions for communication with places outside Ireland be estab-
    lished except by agreement with the British Government; that
    the existing cable landing rights and wireless concessions
    shall not be withdrawn except by agreement with the British
    Government; and that the British Government shall be entitled
    to land additional submarine cables or establish additional
    wireless stations for communication with places outside Ireland.

(b) That lighthouses, buoys, beacons, and any navigational marks
    or navigational aids shall be maintained by the Government
    of the Irish Free State as at the date hereof and shall not
    be removed or added to except by agreement with the British
    Government.

(c) That war signal stations shall be closed down and left in
    charge of care and maintenance parties, the Government of the
    Irish Free State being offered the option of taking them over
    and working them for commercial purposes subject to Admiralty
    inspection, and guaranteeing the upkeep of existing telegraphic
    communication therewith.

3.   A Convention shall be made between the same Governments for the

regulation of Civil Communication by Air.

8.

L. Worthington Evans

Hamar Greenwood

Gordon Hewart.

The Sinn Féin TDs of the Second Dáil Éireann (August 1921–June 1922)

PRO-TREATY

Robert Barton*

Constituency:	Kildare-Wicklow
Year and Place of Birth:	b. 1881, Annamoe, County Wicklow
Occupation:	Agriculturalist
Education (primary and secondary level):	Educated to secondary level (Rugby School, Warwickshire)

Piaras Béaslaí*
Kerry-Limerick West
b. 1881, Liverpool, England
Journalist
Educated to secondary level (St Xavier's College, Liverpool)
1916 Easter Rising participant (Four Courts)

Ernest Blythe (Earnán de Blaghd)*
Monaghan
b. 1889, Lisburn, County Antrim
Journalist
Educated to primary level

Patrick Brennan
Clare
b. 1892, Meelick, County Clare
Farmer
Educated to primary level
1916 Easter Rising participant (Banna Strand)

Francis Bulfin
Leix-Offaly
b. 1874, Birr, County Offaly
Farmer
Educated to primary level

James Burke (Séamus de Búrca)*
Tipperary Mid, North and South
b. 1893, Roscrea, County Tipperary
Barrister
Educated to secondary level (Fordham College, New York; Clongowes
Wood College)

Christopher Byrne*
Kildare-Wicklow
b. 1886, Dublin City
Farmer
Educated to primary level

Thomas Carter
Leitrim-Roscommon North
b. 1876, Carrigallen, County Leitrim
Shopkeeper
Educated to primary level

Michael Collins*
Cork Mid, North, South, South East and West
b. 1890, Clonakilty, County Cork
Accountant
Educated to primary level

1916 Easter Rising participant (General Post Office: aide-de-camp to Joseph Plunkett)

Richard Corish*
Wexford
b. 1889, Wexford, County Wexford
Machine Fitter
Educated to secondary level (Wexford Christian Brothers' School)

Philip Cosgrave*
Dublin North-West
b. 1884, Dublin City
Publican; Grocer
Educated to secondary level (Francis Street Christian Brothers' School)
1916 Easter Rising participant (Marrowbone Lane)

W.T. Cosgrave*
Carlow-Kilkenny
b. 1880, Dublin City
Publican; Grocer
Educated to secondary level (Francis Street Christian Brothers' School)
1916 Easter Rising participant (South Dublin Union)

James Crowley
Kerry-Limerick West
b. 1880, Listowel, County Kerry
Veterinarian
Educated to secondary level (St Michael's College, Listowel)

Michael Derham
Dublin County
b. 1896, Balbriggan, County Dublin
Publican
Educated to primary level
1916 Easter Rising participant (Four Courts)

Liam de Róiste*
Cork Borough
b. 1882, Fountainstown, County Cork
Organiser for Sinn Féin
Educated to primary level

James Dolan*
Leitrim-Roscommon North
b. 1884, Manorhamilton, County Leitrim
Merchant
Educated to primary level

George Gavan Duffy*
Dublin County
b. 1882, Birkenhead, England
Barrister
Educated to secondary level (Stonyhurst College, Lancashire, England)

Éamonn Duggan*
Louth-Meath
b. 1874, Longwood, County Meath
Solicitor
Educated to primary level
1916 Easter Rising participant (Four Courts)

Séamus Dwyer (O'Dwyer)
Dublin County
b. 1886, Dublin City
Merchant
Educated to secondary level (Blackrock College)

Desmond FitzGerald*
Dublin County
b. 1888, London, England
Clerk; Journalist
Educated to secondary level (West Ham Grammar School, London)
1916 Easter Rising participant (General Post Office)

Paul Peter Galligan
Cavan
b. 1888, Cahersiveen, County Leitrim
Draper
Educated to secondary level (St Patrick's College, Cavan)
1916 Easter Rising participant (General Post Office; Enniscorthy)

Arthur Griffith*
Cavan
b. 1871, Dublin City
Journalist
Educated to primary level

Seán Hales*
Cork Mid, North, South, South East and West
b. 1880, Ballinadee, County Cork
Farmer
Educated to secondary level (Warner's Lane School, Bandon)

Michael Hayes*
National University of Ireland
b. 1889, Dublin City
Academic
Educated to secondary level (Synge Street Christian Brothers' School)
1916 Easter Rising participant (Jacob's Factory)

Richard Hayes*
Limerick City-Limerick East
b. 1882, Bruree, County Limerick
Doctor
Educated to secondary level (Scoil Bhanríon na hEagna, Rathkeale)
1916 Easter Rising participant (Ashbourne)

Seán Hayes
Cork Mid, North, South, South East and West
b. 1890, Glandore, County Cork
Journalist

Educated to primary level
1916 Easter Rising participant (General Post Office)

William Hayes
Limerick City-Limerick East
b. 1893, Kilteely, County Limerick
Farmer
Educated to primary level

Patrick Hogan*
Galway
b. 1891, Kilrickle, County Galway
Farmer; Solicitor
Educated to secondary level (St Joseph's College, Garbally)

Peter Hughes*
Louth-Meath
b. 1878, Dundalk, County Louth
Merchant
Educated to primary level

Andrew Lavin
Leitrim-Roscommon North
b. 1886, Ballyfarnon, County Roscommon
Teacher
Educated to secondary level (St Nathy's College, Ballaghaderreen)

Frank Lawless
Dublin County
b. 1870, Swords, County Dublin
Farmer
Educated to primary level
1916 Easter Rising participant (Ashbourne)

Seán Liddy
Clare
b. 1890, Cooraclare, County Clare

Farmer
Educated to primary level

Fionán Lynch*
Kerry-Limerick West
b. 1889, Cahersiveen, County Kerry
Teacher
Educated to secondary level (St Brendan's College, Killarney; Rockwell College; Blackrock College)
1916 Easter Rising participant (Four Courts)

Joseph Lynch
Leix-Offaly
b. 1874, Mountmellick, County Laois
Grocer
Educated to primary level

Joseph MacBride
Mayo North and West
b. 1861, Westport, County Mayo
Harbour Official
Educated to secondary level (Westport Christian Brothers' School; St Malachy's College, Belfast)

Seán Mac Eoin*
Longford-Westmeath
b. 1893, Ballinalee, County Longford
Blacksmith
Educated to primary level

Alexander McCabe (Alasdair Mac Cába)*
Sligo-Mayo East
b. 1886, Keash, County Sligo
Teacher
Educated to secondary level (Summerhill College, Sligo)

Patrick McCartan*
Leix-Offaly
b. 1878, Carrickmore, County Tyrone
Doctor
Educated to secondary level (St Patrick's College, Armagh; St Macartan's College, Monaghan; St Malachy's College, Belfast)

Daniel McCarthy*
Dublin South
b. 1883, Dublin City
Gaelic Athletic Association Organiser
Educated to primary level
1916 Easter Rising participant (South Dublin Union)

Seán McGarry*
Dublin Mid
b. 1886, Dundrum, County Dublin
Electrician
Educated to primary level
1916 Easter Rising participant (General Post Office: aide-de-camp to Thomas Clarke)

Joseph McGinley
Donegal
b. 1892, Glenswilly, County Donegal
Doctor
Educated to secondary level (St Eunan's College, Letterkenny)

Patrick McGoldrick
Donegal
b. 1865, Buncrana, County Donegal
Travelling Salesman
Educated to primary level

Joseph McGrath*
Dublin North-West
b. 1888, Dublin City

Accountant
Educated to secondary level (James's Street Christian Brothers' School)
1916 Easter Rising participant (Marrowbone Lane)

Joseph McGuinness*
Longford-Westmeath
b. 1875, Tarmonbarry, County Roscommon
Draper
Educated to primary level
1916 Easter Rising participant (Four Courts)

Justin McKenna
Louth-Meath
b. 1896, Mullagh, County Cavan
Solicitor
Educated to secondary level (Kells Christian Brothers' School;
Castleknock College)

Seán Milroy*
Cavan
b. 1877, Maryport, Cumbria, England
Journalist
Educated to primary level
1916 Easter Rising participant (General Post Office)

Richard Mulcahy*
Dublin North-West
b. 1886, Waterford City
Clerk; Engineer
Educated to secondary level (Mount Sion Christian Brothers' School;
Thurles Christian Brothers' School)
1916 Easter Rising participant (Ashbourne)

James (Séamus) Murphy
Louth-Meath
b. 1887, Dunshaughlin, County Meath
Draper

Educated to primary level
1916 Easter Rising participant (Marrowbone Lane)

George Nicolls
Galway
b. 1886, Dublin City
Solicitor
Educated to secondary level (Newbridge College)
1916 Easter Rising participant (Galway)

Thomas O'Donnell
Sligo-Mayo East
b. 1877, Gurteen, County Sligo
Teacher
Educated to secondary level (St Nathy's College, Ballaghadereen)

Eoin O'Duffy*
Monaghan
b. 1890, Castleblayney, County Monaghan
Clerk
Educated to primary level

Kevin O'Higgins*
Leix-Offaly
b. 1892, Stradbally, County Laois
Barrister
Educated to secondary level (Portlaoise Christian Brothers' School;
Clongowes Wood College; Knockbeg College, County Carlow)

Patrick O'Keeffe (Pádraig Ó Caoimh)*
Cork Mid, North, South, South East and West
b. 1881, Cullen, County Cork
Clerk
Educated to primary level
1916 Easter Rising participant (General Post Office)

Pádraic Ó Máille*
Galway
b. 1878, Maum, County Galway
Farmer
Educated to secondary level (Home-Schooled)
1916 Easter Rising participant (Galway)

Daniel O'Rourke
Mayo South-Roscommon South
b. 1888, Manorhamilton, County Leitrim
Teacher
Educated to secondary level (St Nathy's College, Ballaghaderreen)

Gearóid O'Sullivan*
Carlow-Kilkenny
b. 1891, Skibbereen, County Cork
Teacher
Educated to secondary level (St Fachtna's – De La Salle College, Skibbereen)
1916 Easter Rising participant (General Post Office: aide-de-camp to
Seán Mac Diarmada)

Lorcán Robbins
Longford-Westmeath
b. 1884, Moate, County Westmeath
Bank Clerk
Educated to primary level

William Sears*
Mayo South-Roscommon South
b. 1869, The Neale, County Mayo
Journalist
Educated to primary level

Michael Staines*
Dublin North-West
b. 1885, Dublin City

Ironmonger
Educated to primary level
1916 Easter Rising participant (General Post Office)

Joseph Sweeney*
Donegal
b. 1897, Burtonport, County Donegal
Accountant
Educated to secondary level (St Eunan's College, Letterkenny; St Enda's
School, Rathfarnham)
1916 Easter Rising participant (General Post Office)

James J. Walsh
Cork Borough
b. 1880, Bandon, County Cork
Clerk; Businessman
Educated to primary level
1916 Easter Rising participant (General Post Office)

Peter Ward
Donegal
b. 1891, Killybegs, County Donegal
Solicitor
Educated to secondary level (St Eunan's College, Letterkenny)

Joseph Whelehan
Galway
b. 1882, Tyrellspass, County Westmeath
Teacher
Educated to secondary level (St Finian's College, Mullingar)

Vincent White
Waterford-Tipperary East
b. 1885, Waterford City
Doctor
Educated to secondary level (Clongowes Wood College)

ANTI-TREATY

Edward Aylward
Carlow-Kilkenny
b. 1895, Callan, County Kilkenny
Businessman
Educated to secondary level (Callan Christian Brothers' School; St Kieran's College, Kilkenny)

Harry Boland*
Mayo South-Roscommon South
b. 1887, Dublin City
Tailor; Shopkeeper
Educated to secondary level (De La Salle College, County Laois)
1916 Easter Rising participant (General Post Office)

Cathal Brugha*
Waterford-Tipperary East
b. 1874, Dublin City
Salesman; Businessman
Educated to secondary level (Belvedere College)
1916 Easter Rising participant (South Dublin Union: vice-commandant)

Patrick Cahill*
Kerry-Limerick West
b. 1885, Tralee, County Kerry
Cinema Owner
Educated to secondary level (Blackrock College)
1916 Easter Rising participant (Banna Strand: involved in *Aud* landing plan)

Frank Carty*
Sligo-Mayo East
b. 1897, Ballymote, County Sligo
Farmer
Educated to primary level

Robert Erskine Childers*
Kildare-Wicklow
b. 1870, London, England
Civil Servant
Educated to secondary level (Haileybury and Imperial Service College, Hertfordshire, England)

Kathleen Clarke (Caitlín Bean Uí Chléirigh)*
Dublin Mid
b. 1878, Limerick City
Dressmaker; Shopkeeper
Educated to primary level
1916 Easter Rising participant (Confidant of Leadership)

Michael Colivet*
Limerick City-Limerick East
b. 1884, Limerick City
Foundry Manager
Educated to secondary level (St Joseph's College, Galway)

Con Collins
Kerry-Limerick West
b. 1881, Newcastle West, County Limerick
Post Office Clerk
Educated to primary level
1916 Easter Rising participant (Banna Strand)

Daniel Corkery*
Cork Mid, North, South, South East and West
b. 1883, Clondrohid, County Cork
Shopkeeper
Educated to primary level

John Crowley
Mayo North and West
b. 1870, Waterfall, County Cork

Doctor
Educated to secondary level (Presentation Brothers' College, Cork)

Bryan Cusack
Galway
b. 1882, Granard, County Longford
Doctor
Educated to secondary level (St Mel's College, Longford)

Éamon Dee
Waterford-Tipperary East
b. 1875, Dungarvan, County Waterford
Farmer
Educated to primary level

Thomas Derrig (Tomás Ó Deirig)*
Mayo North and West
b. 1897, Westport, County Mayo
Headmaster
Educated to secondary level (Westport Christian Brothers' School)

Éamon de Valera*
Clare
b. 1882, New York
Teacher
Educated to secondary level (Charleville Christian Brothers' School;
Blackrock College)
1916 Easter Rising participant (Boland's Mills: commandant)

James (Séamus) Devins
Sligo-Mayo East
b. 1885, Grange, County Sligo
Farmer
Educated to primary level

Séamus Doyle
Wexford

b. 1885, Craanford, County Wexford
Teacher
Educated to secondary level (Gorey Christian Brothers' School)
1916 Easter Rising participant (Enniscorthy)

Ada English*
National University of Ireland
b. 1875, Cahersiveen, County Kerry
Psychiatrist
Educated to secondary level (Loreto College, Mullingar)
1916 Easter Rising participant (Galway)

Seán Etchingham*
Wexford
b. 1870, Courtown, County Wexford
Jockey; Journalist; Singer; Humourist
Educated to primary level
1916 Easter Rising participant (Enniscorthy)

Frank Fahy*
Galway
b. 1879, Kilcreest, County Galway
Teacher
Educated to secondary level (Mungret College, Limerick)
1916 Easter Rising participant (Four Courts)

Francis Ferran
Sligo-Mayo East
b. 1887, Magherafelt, County Derry
Doctor
Educated to secondary level (St Patrick's Grammar School, Armagh)

Séamus Fitzgerald
Cork East and North-East
b. 1896, Cobh, County Cork
Engineer
Educated to secondary level (Presentation Brothers' College, Cork)

Thomas Hunter
Cork East and North-East
b. 1883, Castletownroche, County Cork
Draper; Tailor
Educated to primary level
1916 Easter Rising participant (Jacob's Factory: vice-commandant)

David Kent (Dáithí Ceannt)*
Cork East and North-East
b. 1867, Fermoy, County Cork
Farmer
Educated to primary level
1916 Easter Rising participant (Cork)

James Lennon*
Carlow-Kilkenny
b. 1880, Borris, County Carlow
Farmer
Educated to secondary level (Knockbeg College, County Carlow)

Joseph MacDonagh
Tipperary Mid, North and South
b. 1883, Cloughjordan, County Tipperary
Income Tax Recovery Expert; Insurance Broker
Educated to secondary level (Rockwell College)
1916 Easter Rising participant (General Post Office)

Seán MacEntee*
Monaghan
b. 1889, Belfast, County Antrim
Electrical Engineer; Writer
Educated to secondary level (St Malachy's College, Belfast)
1916 Easter Rising participant (Louth; General Post Office)

Mary MacSwiney*
Cork Borough
b. 1872, London, England

Headmistress
Educated to secondary level (St Angela's College, Cork)

Seán MacSwiney
Cork Mid, North, South, South East and West
b. 1889, Cork City
Clerk
Educated to secondary level (North Monastery Christian Brothers'
School, Cork)

Tom Maguire*
Mayo South-Roscommon South
b. 1892, Cross, County Mayo
Coach Builder; Businessman
Educated to primary level

Constance Markievicz*
Dublin South
b. 1868, London, England
Artist; Activist
Educated to secondary level (Home-Schooled)
1916 Easter Rising participant (St Stephen's Green: vice-commandant)

Liam Mellows*
Galway
b. 1892, Ashton-Under-Lyne, Manchester, England
Shop Clerk
Educated to secondary level (Royal Hibernian Military School, Dublin)
1916 Easter Rising participant (Galway)

P.J. Moloney
Tipperary Mid, North and South
b. 1871, Tipperary, County Tipperary
Pharmacist
Educated to secondary level (Rockwell College)

Seán Moylan*
Cork Mid, North, South, South East and West

b. 1889. Kilmallock, County Limerick
Carpenter; Building Contractor
Educated to primary level

Seán Nolan
Cork Mid, North, South, South East and West
b. 1899, Cork City
Auctioneer
Educated to primary level

Patrick O'Byrne
Tipperary Mid, North and South
b. 1870, Roscrea, County Tipperary
Barrister
Educated to secondary level (Beaumont College, Berkshire, England)

Daniel O'Callaghan (Dónal Ó Ceallacháin)
Cork Borough
b. 1892, Cork City
Accountant
Educated to secondary level (North Monastery Christian Brothers' School, Cork)

Kate O'Callaghan*
Limerick City-Limerick East
b. 1885, Lissarda, County Cork
Lecturer
Educated to secondary level (St Mary's College, Dublin)

Art O'Connor*
Kildare-Wicklow
b. 1888, Celbridge, County Kildare
Engineer
Educated to secondary level (Blackrock College)

Joseph O'Doherty*
Donegal

b. 1891, Derry City
Teacher; Activist
Educated to secondary level (St Columb's College, Derry)

Thomas O'Donoghue (Tomás Ó Donnchadha)
Kerry-West Limerick
b. 1890, Cahersiveen, County Kerry
Farmer
Educated to primary level

Samuel O'Flaherty
Donegal
b. 1895, Castlefin, County Donegal
Civil Servant
Educated to secondary level (St Columb's College, Derry)

Brian O'Higgins*
Clare
b. 1882, Kilskyre, County Meath
Irish Language Teacher; Poet; Writer; Editor
Educated to primary level
1916 Easter Rising participant (General Post Office)

J.J. O'Kelly (Seán Ua Ceallaigh/Sceilg)*
Louth-Meath
b. 1872, Valentia Island, County Kerry
Editor *Catholic Bulletin*; Irish Language Teacher
Educated to primary level

Seán T. O'Kelly (Seán T. Ó Ceallaigh)*
Dublin Mid
b. 1882, Dublin City
Press Business Manager
Educated to secondary level (O'Connell Christian Brothers' School)
1916 Easter Rising participant (General Post Office)

Seán O'Mahony
Fermanagh and Tyrone

b. 1864, Thomastown, County Kilkenny
Hotel Proprietor
Educated to primary level
1916 Easter Rising participant (General Post Office)

Cathal Ó Murchadha
Dublin South
b. 1880, Dublin City
Law Clerk
Educated to secondary level (Westland Row Christian Brothers' School)
1916 Easter Rising participant (Boland's Mills)

Margaret Pearse*
Dublin County
b. 1857, Dublin City
Housewife
Educated to primary level

George Noble Plunkett*
Leitrim-Roscommon North
b. 1851, Dublin City
Lawyer; Academic; Writer
Educated to secondary level (Clongowes Wood College)

Séamus Robinson*
Waterford-Tipperary East
b. 1890, Belfast, County Antrim
Engineering Worker; Farm Hand
Educated to secondary level (St Mary's Christian Brothers' Grammar
School, Belfast; De La Salle College, Belfast; Marist College,
Dumfries, Scotland; St Michael's College, Dumfries)
1916 Easter Rising participant (O'Connell Street)

Edmund (Éamonn) Roche
Kerry-Limerick West
b. 1884, Bansha, County Tipperary
Business Manager
Educated to primary level

P.J. Ruttledge*
Mayo North and West
b. 1892, Ballina, County Mayo
Solicitor
Educated to secondary level (St Muredach's College, Ballina)

James Ryan*
Wexford
b. 1891, Taghmon, County Wexford
Doctor
Educated to secondary level (St Peter's College, Wexford)
1916 Easter Rising participant (General Post Office)

Philip Shanahan
Dublin Mid
b. 1878, Upperchurch, County Tipperary
Publican
Educated to primary level
1916 Easter Rising participant (Jacob's Factory)

Austin Stack*
Kerry-Limerick West
b. 1879, Tralee, County Kerry
Income Tax Inspector
Educated to secondary level (Tralee Christian Brothers' School)
1916 Easter Rising participant (Banna Strand)

William Stockley*
National University of Ireland
b. 1859, Templeogue, County Dublin
Professor of English
Educated to secondary level (Rathmines School)

Domhnall Ua Buachalla (Dónal Ó Buachalla/Buckley)*
Kildare-Wicklow
b. 1866, Maynooth, County Kildare
Shopkeeper

Educated to secondary level (Belvedere College; Catholic University School, Dublin)
1916 Easter Rising participant (General Post Office)

CEANN COMHAIRLE (SPEAKER)

Eoin MacNeill*
National University of Ireland
b. 1867, Glenarm, County Antrim
Professor of History
Educated to secondary level (St Malachy's College, Belfast)

ABSENT

Frank Drohan
Waterford-Tipperary East
b. 1879, Carrick-on-Suir, County Tipperary
Coach Builder
Educated to secondary level (Clonmel Christian Brothers' High School)

Laurence Ginnell*
Longford-Westmeath
b. 1852, Delvin, County Westmeath
Clerk; Barrister; Journalist
Educated to primary level

Thomas Kelly*
Dublin South
b. 1868, Dublin City
Book and Picture Dealer
Educated to secondary level (Synge Street Christian Brothers' School)

* Denotes entry in *Dictionary of Irish Biography* (Cambridge)

Notes on Contributors

Laura Cahillane is a lecturer in the School of Law, University of Limerick. She holds a PhD from University College Cork, for which she was awarded an IRCHSS Government of Ireland Scholarship. It considered the drafting of the 1922 Irish Free State Constitution, and was published as a book, *Drafting the Irish Free State Constitution* (Manchester, 2016). Her research interests lie in the areas of Constitutional Law, Legal History, Judicial Politics and Comparative Law and she has published nationally and internationally in these areas.

John Dorney is an independent historian, specialising in the Irish Revolution, 1912–24, especially the Civil War of 1922–3. He is the author of two books on the topic, *'Peace after the final battle': the story of the Irish Revolution 1912–1924* (Dublin, 2014) and *The Civil War in Dublin: the fight for the Irish capital, 1922–1924* (Dublin, 2017). He is also the editor of The Irish Story website.

Mel Farrell is Director of the Irish Humanities Alliance. He also works as an occasional lecturer with the School of History, University College Dublin, where he teaches Irish and southern African history. He holds a PhD from NUI Maynooth, for which he was awarded an IRCHSS Scholarship. His new book, *Party politics in a new democracy: the Irish Free State, 1922–37* (London, 2017) is a significant expansion of his doctoral research. He has published a number of peer-review articles, the most recent of which examined the Irish Party's campaign in the South Longford by-election *(New Hibernia Review*, 2017). He was also a co-editor of *A formative decade: Ireland in the 1920s* (Dublin, 2015).

Brian Hanley is an AHRC Research Fellow in Irish History at the University of Edinburgh. He is the author of several books on Irish republicanism, including *The IRA, 1926–36* (Dublin, 2002) and (with Scott Millar) *The lost revolution: the story of the Official IRA and the Workers' Party* (Dublin, 2009). He has recently completed a study of the impact of the Northern Ireland conflict on the Republic of Ireland and is currently writing a global history of the Irish Revolution.

Alexander Herzog is a lecturer in the School of Computing at Clemson University, South Carolina. Before joining the School of Computing, he was awarded his PhD in political science from New York University, and taught at the London School of Economics. His research is in computational social science, with a focus on text analysis and big data analytics.

Mary McAuliffe is an assistant professor in gender studies at University College Dublin and holds a PhD from the School of History and Humanities, Trinity College Dublin. Her latest publications are *'We were there': 77 women of the Easter Rising* (co-written with Liz Gillis) (Dublin, 2016), and *Kerry 1916: histories and legacies of the Easter Rising* (Dublin, 2016), for which she was a co-editor. Her latest research includes a forthcoming biography of Margaret Skinnider (Dublin, 2018), and a major research project on gendered and sexual violence during the Irish revolutionary period, 1919–23.

Sinéad McCoole is an historian and curator in the Commemorations Unit of the Department of Culture, Heritage and the Gaeltacht. She was curatorial and historical adviser on the 2016 project team that co-ordinated the National Commemoration and is a member of the government's expert advisory group on the Decade of Commemorations 2012–22. She has written extensively on the role of women in modern Irish history, including *Hazel: a life of Lady Lavery* (Dublin, 1996), *Guns and chiffon* (Dublin, 1997), *No ordinary women* (Dublin, 2003) and *Easter widows* (Dublin, 2014).

Slava Jankin Mikhaylov is a professor of public policy and data science at the University of Essex, holding a joint appointment in the Department of Government and School of Computer Science and the Electronic Engineering Institute for Analytics and Data Science (IADS). He is a Chief Scientific Adviser to Essex County Council focusing on embedding AI across the public sector in Essex. His research and teaching are primarily in the field of machine learning and natural language processing.

Paul Murray is an author and barrister. He holds a PhD in politics from the National University of Ireland Galway, where he was an IRCHSS scholar from 2000 to 2003. He also holds a PhD in law from Trinity College Dublin. His publications include *The Irish Boundary Commission and its origins 1886–1925* (Dublin, 2011).

Martin O'Donoghue is the recipient of the National Library of Ireland Research Studentship for 2017–18 held in conjunction with the Irish Committee for Historical Sciences. He has taught history at the National University of Ireland Galway for the past four years where he was formerly an Irish Research Council Government of Ireland Scholar. His first book will be *The legacy of the Irish Parliamentary Party in independent Ireland* (Liverpool). He is the Academic Director of the 2018 Parnell Summer School.

Mícheál Ó Fathartaigh is a college lecturer in the Department of Humanities & Social Science at Dublin Business School, a research officer with Teagasc and a member of the Social Sciences Research Centre at the National University of Ireland Galway. He holds a PhD in history from Trinity College Dublin. His first book was *Irish agriculture nationalised: the Dairy Disposal Company and the making of the modern Irish dairy industry* (Dublin, 2014). His third will be *Developing rural Ireland: a history of the Irish agricultural advisory services* (Dublin, 2019).

Eunan O'Halpin MRIA is Bank of Ireland Professor of Contemporary Irish History at Trinity College Dublin. Amongst his publications are *The decline of the Union: British government in Ireland, 1891–1920* (Dublin, 1987), and *Defending Ireland: the Irish state and its enemies since 1922* (Oxford, 1999).

Mary Staines completed her MPhil in modern Irish history at Trinity College Dublin in 2016 following her retirement as a clinical director/ consultant psychiatrist. The general theme of her PhD in history, which she commenced in 2017, is the exploration of the origins of the 1921 Anglo-Irish Treaty split from multidimensional perspectives.

Tony Varley is an adjunct lecturer in politics and sociology at the National University of Ireland Galway. His research interests include the study of rural societies and agrarian politics. He has written on the agrarian dimension of the 1916 Rising, a chapter entitled 'The eclipsing of a radical agrarian nationalist: Tom Kenny and the 1916 Rising in County Galway' in Marie Mannion (ed.), *Centenary reflections on the 1916 Rising: County Galway perspectives* (Galway, 2016). He has co-edited *A living countryside? The politics of sustainable development in rural Ireland* (Farnham, Surrey, 2009); *Integration through subordination: the politics of agricultural modernisation in industrial Europe* (Turnhout, Belgium, 2013); and *Land questions in modern Ireland* (Manchester, 2013).

Liam Weeks is a college lecturer in the Department of Government and Politics at University College Cork and an Honorary Senior Research Fellow at Macquarie University, Sydney. He is author of *Independents in Irish party democracy* (Manchester, 2017), co-editor (with Alistair Clark) of *Radical or redundant: minor parties in Irish politics* (London, 2012), and co-author (with Aodh Quinlivan) of *All politics is local: a guide to local elections in Ireland* (Cork, 2009). He is an associate editor with ECPR Press.

Index

Note: Page numbers in **bold** indicate tables.